YOUTH SOCIOLOGY

YOUTH SOCIOLOGY

ALAN FRANCE, JULIA COFFEY,
STEVEN ROBERTS AND
CATHERINE WAITE

First published 2020 by
RED GLOBE PRESS

Red Globe Press in the UK is an imprint of Macmillan Education Limited, registered in England, company number 01755588, of 4 Crinan Street, London, N1 9XW.

Red Globe Press® is a registered trademark in the United States, the United Kingdom, Europe and other countries.

ISBN 978-1-137-49040-7 hardback
ISBN 978-1-137-49041-4 paperback

This book is printed on paper suitable for recycling and made from fully managed and sustained forest sources. Logging, pulping and manufacturing processes are expected to conform to the environmental regulations of the country of origin.

A catalogue record for this book is available from the British Library.

A catalog record for this book is available from the Library of Congress.

BRIEF CONTENTS

TABLE OF CONTENTS

LIST OF FIGURES AND TABLE

Figures

Table

1 WHAT IS YOUTH?

In this chapter you will learn about:

- A sociological approach to understanding youth and how this is different from other approaches
- What is meant by youth as a 'social category' or 'social construct'
- The most significant social, cultural and historical changes affecting youth today
- The key debates in youth sociology, including transitions, cultures and the social generation perspective.

Defining youth sociologically

The aim of this book is to provide a broad yet in-depth exploration of youth sociology, and how it can be used to make sense of the struggles and issues facing the current generation of young people. In the chapters that follow, you will be introduced to a wide range of debates on what it means to be young, and how best to understand the world in which young people live. We will discuss:

- How recent changes to education systems worldwide have affected young people

- Whether young people and adults can be categorized into distinct 'generations'

- Young people's relationship with paid work

- How social media influences young people's social relationships

- How young people engage with and respond to popular culture

- What frameworks help us to best understand young people's lives in an era of rapid social change.

A wide range of disciplines, including psychology, social policy, cultural studies, social geography, urban studies and criminology, contribute to what is known as **youth studies**. A sociological approach, however, offers distinct tools and knowledge to help understand *all* areas of young people's lives, and to recognize the *interconnectedness* between areas. It acknowledges that we cannot make sense of young people's lives without locating our understandings (and analysis) beyond the individual, in their social, cultural, and historical context. Sociology has a long history of studying youth and has developed a wide range of tools and theories that can enable a holistic analysis of how large-scale social processes intersect with and shape young people's individual experiences. Before we explore further what a sociological approach looks

> **Youth studies:** A multidisciplinary field within the humanities and social sciences including sociology, education and politics, which seeks to understand the lives of young people.

like and how it helps us understand people's lives and the world they live in, it is worth reflecting on the dominant view of youth that tends to influence the 'common sense' and political perspectives of youth. Its weaknesses, we suggest, are addressed by youth sociology.

'Discovering' adolescence

🗯 Thinking points

- What impact do you think developmental stages have on young people's behaviour?
- What 'social markers' or characteristics makes someone an 'adult'?

Historically, psychology has had a major impact on defining what it means to be young. Across a wide range of influential settings and sites, the ideas of psychology continue to shape and form popular beliefs about what youth means. As a discipline, it is focussed on the individual mind and body, aiming to show causal linkages between psychological and physiological developments and behaviour. This view of human nature as a form of development is commonly accepted as a legitimate way of understanding child and youth development. In fact, psychology 'discovered' the adolescent as a scientific term. It was used for the first time in the 20th century by evolutionary psychologist G. Stanley Hall (1904). For him, adolescence was a period of 'great revolution' brought about by biological changes associated with puberty, when an individual underwent a tumultuous period of 'storm and stress' that subjected body, mind and morals to an intense process of reassessment and change. The logic and 'naturalness' of this developmental approach to youth as a 'life stage' has become common sense in everyday life: adolescents 'come of age' into adulthood; are 'at the threshold of', or 'transition into', adulthood (Lesko, 1996). The notion that youth has a number of developmental stages that are normal and possibly fixed by psychology or biology remains a legacy in psychology that defines what it means to do adolescent studies. Problems in the transition into adulthood are then explained by causal relationships in puberty that are seen to create 'storm and stresses' and erratic, 'problem' behaviour. In contrast, sociologists highlight that this view of youth is problematic in setting up boundaries between 'normative' and 'deviant' youth, which may actually exacerbate existing social inequalities (Lesko, 1996).

Brain science: involves cognitive psychologists, sometimes studying how the human brain works in how we think, remember and learn. They use psychological science to understand how we perceive events and make decisions.

More recently, we have seen the emergence of '**brain science**'. Understanding the brain and how it functions has always been a challenge to scientists, but with the emergence of new technology, new research is allowing psychologists to explore the relationship between the human brain, the mind and social action. This research has created an opportunity for scientists to get 'inside the heads' of teenagers. Magnetic resonance imaging (MRI) technology can now create images of the functioning brain. As a result, it is being claimed that the brain is not fully formed until at least the age of 30. This is said to explain why young people take risks and do not fully understand the consequences of their actions

(Johnson et al., 2010). Such approaches have been very influential in public policy, creating a view that the young cannot be trusted to make 'good' decisions (France, 2012).

These approaches are seen by sociologists as severely limited in terms of understanding the complex dynamics of culture and society, which shape young people's lives (France, 2007). Psychological perspectives tend to search for universals and 'cause and effect' relationships, while failing to understand difference. Much of psychology's ability to link psychological dysfunction to behaviour remains inconclusive and unproven, and in many cases, it fails to recognise that the social, cultural and economic context can greatly influence the choices and decisions young people make (France, 2007). Finally, while brain science is seen as providing new insights, it is still in its infancy (Choudhury, 2010). In fact, what we see is neuroscience over-claiming the knowledge gained (Bessant, 2008; Kelly, 2001; France, 2012), and as in other areas of developmental science, failing to recognise the cultural context of adolescence.

Defining youth sociologically

Psychology and developmental approaches have made important contributions to our understanding of youth. However, as we have suggested, such perspectives understand youth in specific ways that are limited to the individual. While the environment is seen as important, it only acts to change the impact of individual dysfunction and problems. Such approaches are unable to give a holistic picture of how youth is formed, constructed and understood as a social category. In addition, such views see young people as driven by internal forces and their bodies. As sociologists, we reject such a narrow view and propose that youth has to be understood in its historical, social, political and cultural contexts. For example, understanding youth means that we must also recognise that youth 'today' is itself a product of history. As we saw, G. Stanley Hall 'made up' the notion of adolescence; it did not exist as a field of study until the 20th century. It has been created. In addition, the issues facing young people today are vastly different from those in Hall's time. While psychology continues to have an influence, the meaning of youth today is also strongly shaped by changes in the economy (i.e. in work), in changing notions of the family, in the institutions (the ones that educate our young) and in the norms and values of society. We therefore need to understand that youth is a more fluid category which is shaped by a wide range of external forces. How we will define it in a hundred years will depend on the social, cultural, economic, institutional contexts of that time. As youth sociologists, we believe there is no universal (or essential) definition of youth: rather, we recognise that 'youth' is contingent on our time and place and the socio-cultural norms within it. A good starting place to understand this approach is in the work of C. Wright Mills.

The sociological imagination

Sociology is fundamentally concerned with exploring the relationship between individuals and their broader context, and how this interacts to influence their social practices and **social identities**. C. Wright Mills' (1959) idea of the sociological imagination can be used here in thinking about what a sociological approach to understanding youth means, and how it can be used practically to understand the key problems

Social identities: A sociological view of social identity is concerned with how human action and reflection influence the way people construct themselves. Our social identity is not something that is given or fixed but something that has to be routinely sustained and reflected upon, and can change.

affecting young people worldwide. The sociological imagination can be used as a template to apply to any issue of study. Sociological analysis uses four equally important dimensions to understand an issue: historical, structural, cultural and critical:

1. The *historical dimension* includes exploring how past events have influenced the present issue. This entails exploring historical conceptualizations of youth, as they have been influenced by different fields of study, including psychology. These ideas, as we have seen above, have created a dominant discourse of youth and adolescence, which sociology challenges.

2. The *cultural dimension* focusses on the importance of the current cultural context, including norms, speech and behaviours related to the issue. In relation to youth, this could, for example, include aspects of youth consumer culture in the West, such as music, media and popular culture; and all assumptions about what young people 'are like', since these ideas are culturally and historically specific.

3. The *structural dimension* investigates how forms of social organization, such as institutions, governments and the economy, affect people's lives and influence issues. These factors are highly influential in contextualizing, for example, what society expects from young people in relation to schooling and work. The decline of the full-time job market for young people in the West is generally seen as a defining structural feature of the contemporary experience of youth. As we will see in Chapters 3 and 4, young people must now stay in school for longer and gain post-school qualifications, rather than being able to find full-time work from the age of 15, as was the case in previous generations in Australia and many other countries.

4. Finally, *the critical dimension* or *gaze* is slightly different from the previous areas of focus, and involves thinking critically about issues of inequality, advantage and disadvantage. This prompts the questions 'Why are things the way they are? Who is privileged and powerful, and who is at the bottom of the pile? And, most crucially, how could things be different? In relation to young people today, this would mean asking why some groups of young people are arrested and incarcerated at higher rates than others (e.g. Indigenous youth in post-colonial societies such as Australia, New Zealand, Canada and the USA).

Sociological imagination: A template for doing sociological analysis derived from C. Wright Mills (1959), comprising four equally important dimensions: historical, structural, cultural and a critical gaze.

Why are young women's dress and behaviours, when they go out at night, policed more strictly than those of young men? The critical aspect of the **sociological imagination** has an inherent orientation to questions of social justice.

These four aspects of the sociological imagination are central to how we approach the study of youth within sociology. In the chapters that follow, this perspective will be central to the analysis.

'Youth' in social context

When sociologists say things like 'youth is a social construction', or 'there is no such thing as youth', what do they actually mean? What both of these statements imply is that what we currently understand as 'youth', especially in wealthy, Western countries such as Australia, New Zealand, the UK, the USA or a wide range of Northern European countries, is in fact mediated by a range of historical, social and cultural factors specific to these countries. While there are similarities among these countries, there is no one set way of defining youth, as what it means to be a young person will depend on the circumstances of the time and place. It is also important to recognise that the '**life courses**' available to youth in non-Western countries can be very different and there are questions as to whether Western concepts of 'youth' bear any relevance in these settings (Everatt, 2015). For example, in Western societies, engagement in education through to the age of 24 is 'the norm', yet in many non-Western parts of the world, large numbers of young people are engaged in paid employment in their early teens or straight after any form of schooling. In such circumstances, it is often also common for girls to marry in their teenage years and become mothers early, while girls in the Western world are unlikely to become mothers until their middle or late 20s. Therefore, what 'youth' means depends strongly on the circumstances of place and location.

Life course: This perspective elaborates the importance of time, context, process and meaning on human development, while life cycle is more concerned with seeing fixed categories and stages of development that people pass through – childhood, youth, middle age, old age.

The 'youth phase' is therefore one that is constructed by a series of processes, structures and representations that give meaning to the concept of youth. These processes can be economic, political, social and cultural, and they can exist in perceptions, narratives and representations across a wide range of media and discourses. It is important to remember that the social worlds young people inherit and inhabit are not of their making. What it means 'to be young' at a particular historical moment in time in a specific space or place is defined by others. The issue of location (historical and spatial) creates and shapes the possibilities and opportunities that are available; It frames the types of experiences young people will have as they 'grow up' and move towards adulthood. This is not to deny the role of young people as social actors and contributors to their own lives and trajectories, but it is important to recognise that the *social context* of young people's lives is one that they largely inherit from previous generations. This operates at multiple levels, across and through a range of ideas, structures and everyday social practices.

Thinking points

- What do you think are the most important social and cultural dimensions shaping young people's lives today?
- How are the major issues for young people today different from those in the past?

'Age' is of critical importance to how youth is defined and understood. Age has always been seen as vital in that it is strongly related to how others perceive what young people are capable of, what they should be protected from and what role they should have in choosing their own futures. In fact, what we see is that '... it is the political importance attached to age that in many respects shapes young people's lives.' (Mizen, 2004, p. 20). What Mizen means is that how the laws, policies and practices of institutions define and understand youth can be highly influential in shaping young people's experiences. Therefore, we should always recognize the political nature of these processes; the construction of youth does not happen in a vacuum separate from political ideologies, moral judgements, value-led motivations and economic developments. Youth therefore is political in its nature. So, what does that mean in practice? If we look at the age at which a young person can marry, we can start to see some of these processes at work.

Youth, 'social markers' and the institution of marriage

Marriage is a strong social marker of adulthood. 'Social markers' are those activities that are recognised by society as 'adult'. Issues that we might consider to be important markers in the Western world include living outside of the family home and especially having a mortgage; having children; and having an independent income and career. Being married or having a recognised de facto relationship often positions a person as an adult (and not a child or youth). It is generally assumed that a married person is responsible for themselves (and others); is financially independent; and, of course, lives outside of the family home in some form of independent living arrangement. Added together, being married has traditionally signified that one is an adult. For this reason, the meanings and structures that shape when and who can be married are critical in constructing the youth phase. Many societies value marriage as a 'natural' institution of adulthood, although as we shall see in the chapters that follow, some of these assumptions and claims do not always hold up when scrutinised. However, the point to acknowledge here is that the concept of marriage acts across many societies as a social marker of adulthood, and therefore how marriage is legally and morally defined also shapes what it means to be young (i.e. not married).

If we look at countries such as New Zealand, Australia and the UK, we would not be surprised to find that a number of similarities exist. For example, the age at which a young person can marry is 16 (with parental consent). But this has not always been the case, and different laws have applied in each country. In the UK, the 1929 Age of Marriage Act was passed, which set the age of consent in law. Prior to this, no age limit existed, although parental consent was needed for those under 21 to marry. This judgement was made on the view that they had reached the 'age of puberty'. Alternatively, we can consider Australia, where marriage was initially shaped by English Law, but which originally limited the rights of convicts; only those who exhibited 'good character' and were recognised as being 'sober' were permitted to marry. Between 1901 and 1961, marriage was governed by local territories, creating a situation where the age at which a person could marry varied between states. Restrictions also existed on the rights of Indigenous aboriginals to marry outside of their peoples. Within these three countries we also see the issue of parental consent varying significantly. In New Zealand, up until the 1960s, a young person could not marry until they reached the age of 21 unless they had the consent of *both* parents. This was changed to 18 in the 1970s, with those who wanted to be married at 16 and 17 requiring the permission of only one parent or guardian.

Of course, throughout history, marriage has predominantly been seen as a formal and legal relationship between opposite sexes. It operated to formalise a person's access to social benefits, inheritance and access to children. From the 1960s onwards, governments around the world started to give legal acknowledgement to 'de facto relationships'. For example, in Australia in 1975, the Family Law Act acknowledged a de facto relationship where there was evidence of some form of sexual relationship and cohabitation that could also include the care of children, public recognition of the relationship and sharing of property and finances. The establishment of this in law arose as a result of growing societal change, especially amongst the younger generation of the time, where marriage was becoming less popular and people were wanting to organize their lives in different ways.

More recently, we have also seen significant change to the presumed heterosexuality of marriage, as many countries have legalized same-sex marriage in recent years. While the movement towards laws that permit same-sex marriage is still not universal, the momentum towards the legalization of such relationships has grown. For example, the first state to legislate for this was The Netherlands (in 1979); since then, another 21 countries have made it legal, with New Zealand legislating in 2013, the UK in 2014 and Australia in 2017. There are also 18 other countries that have created some form of legal recognition other than marriage at a national level. Again, this change has come about as a result of public pressure for recognition of other types of relationships as legitimate.

The age and significance of marriage vary significantly across the globe. A good case in point is countries in the Middle East and North Africa (MENA) region. Not only do they have laws on the minimum age for marriage, ranging from 13 years of age in Iran to 20 in Tunisia for females, and from 15 years of age in Yemen to 21 in Algeria for males, but also they have so far resisted the inclusion of same-sex marriages. Such countries can also have high numbers of young people marrying before they are 20. Reducing the rate of child marriage is considered a crucial human rights issue; early marriage seriously harms the development and wellbeing of girls, as it correlates with limited education and employment opportunities, and higher rates of social isolation, domestic violence and rape (UNFPA, 2017). In Yemen, for example, one-third of women aged 20 to 24 were married by the age of 18. In many of these countries, religion plays a crucial role in guiding conventions and traditions on marriage. Many religions have clear guidelines regarding who can marry and when. While many of these rules will not be laws (as set by the state), they are strong moral codes that define who can marry whom, and when people can get married. For example, in some religions, clear restrictions exist that prevent people marrying someone from outside of the religion; in others, men can take more than one wife (polygamy); and of course, the age when a young person is allowed to marry can also vary significantly, with some countries seeing 'child brides' as young as 11 as acceptable and legitimate.

🗨 Thinking points

- How relevant do you think marriage is today for young people – do you think it remains a key 'social marker' of adulthood?
- What might be the most important social markers of adulthood for young people today?

What this overview shows is that the complexity of how marriage is defined, and how it works across time and space, highlight how ideas and perceptions operate to shape not only the institution but also the transition of relationships into formal adult-defined roles.

What is clear from the previous discussion is that historically, same-sex marriage was non-existent until the early 1980s. Societal values, ideas and beliefs about what constitutes 'natural behaviour' historically constructed heterosexuality as 'normal' and therefore defined same-sex relationships as 'unnatural'. Such perspectives of sexual identity and practice were also upheld and propagated by a wide range of religious faiths that rejected any form of relationship other than those between men and women as 'unnatural' or 'ungodly'. This idea was (and is) also strongly supported by 'science' claiming that a natural order, driven by the need to maintain and reproduce the species, defines what is normal. As these ideas have been challenged and found to be lacking in evidence, alternative ideas have gained ground and influence. As a result, the idea of what is a 'normal' relationship, especially in terms of marriage, has been reconfigured in legal and policy terms. This is not to say that the 'battle of ideas' has seen the total rejection of heterosexuality as the 'norm'. As we shall see, it not only continues to play a significant role in shaping the lives of the young but also remains a powerful discourse that is continually re-enforcing and embedding same-sex relationships as 'unnatural' across a range of institutional settings.

What is also clear from our discussion is that the fluidity and dynamic nature of what is 'legal' and 'illegal' for young people result in changes over time and different meanings in different contexts. Age has been important in this debate, but so have social morals, values and beliefs. If we broaden this analysis to recognise other social markers that have historically been important in defining the difference between 'childhood and youth' or 'youth and adulthood', we can see that youth is consistently being reconfigured and constructed in different ways. For example, leaving school has always been seen as a significant social marker for the movement from childhood to youth, and historically, paid employment and independent living away from the family home (not just through marriage) have been important social markers in the shift towards adulthood. As we will see over the coming chapters, major changes have been taking place in these processes, which shift the meaning and experience of being young.

Current debates in youth sociology

In this final section of this chapter, we will explore a range of contemporary debates in youth sociology. Traditionally, youth sociology has built its analysis around two main areas: that of transitions and youth culture. These frameworks explore a wide range of activities of the young and have developed a number of key areas of focus in order to understand the complex dynamics influencing young people's lives. More recently, a 'social generations' approach has been proposed to understand how young people's social identities and future trajectories are formed against the backdrop of large-scale social, cultural and economic changes that have occurred generationally. The historical background and theoretical underpinnings of these three perspectives will be explored in depth across the chapters that follow; however, the section below sketches their main areas of focus, setting the different approaches in their historical and social contexts.

Youth transitions

🗨 Thinking points

- What do we mean by adulthood, and how do young people become adults?
- What might be the key features of young people's 'transitions'? Have they changed?

'Transitions' has been a dominant theme in youth research. This perspective encapsulates a number of empirical interests in young people's transitions to adulthood. Throughout the chapters that follow this theme will be central. As we saw in the previous discussion, youth is continually constructed and perceived as a stage of transition that exists between childhood and adulthood, and how young people make this movement has dominated much of youth sociology. Historically, it has had a strong focus on highlighting the significant differences that existed between classes and genders. Much of this work concentrated on the 'school to work' transitions, but more recently it expanded its focus to include 'domestic transitions', 'housing transitions' and 'transitions into citizenship'. Furlong and Evans in their article 'Metaphors of Youth Transitions: Niches, Pathways, Trajectories or Navigations' (1997) discuss how youth researchers have drawn on a number of metaphors at different historical moments to theorise youth transitions. In the 1960s, they focussed on and were reflective of psychological models and the accomplishment of developmental processes, and the idea that transitions were about integrations. Alongside the rise of unemployment in the UK in the 1970s, youth researchers argued for seeing transitions as 'routes' and 'pathways' – reflecting thinking in sociology that wanted to emphasise 'opportunity structures'. In the 1980s, as transitions were apparently becoming more complex, the concept of 'trajectory' became fashionable. In the 1990s, with the rise of theoretical approaches where structural explanations fell out of favour, concepts such as 'navigation' and individual agency became new metaphors for explaining young people's transitions. These shifting metaphors broadly mirror conceptual shifts in mainstream sociology, from **functionalism** to **structuralism** to **postmodernism**. As we shall see across the chapters in this book, many who theorise young people's 'transitions' between education and work try to create 'hybrid models' to account for the specific context in question. At the heart of discussions of youth transitions tends to be the question of 'structure and agency' or the degree to which young people's transitions are shaped and how much they are in the control of young people themselves.

While the transitions approach remains influential in youth sociology, numerous scholars have been critical of it as an approach to understanding youth. It is seen as primarily interested in people's capacity to transition *out of* youth and can therefore ignore the specific experience or state of being young.

Functionalism: A sociological theory founded by Emile Durkheim that sees society as an organic whole with individual parts working to maintain others. It is a theory of how social order is maintained.

Structuralism: Refers to an approach in sociology that regards social structure as having priority in producing social action.

Postmodernism: A rejection of modernism and the force of structuralism, emphasizing fluidity and instability between social categories.

The dominance of the transitions model has also been argued to: (1) devalue the importance of youth in its own right as it categorises youth against an idealised notion of adulthood; (2) assume a simplistic linear model of development; and (3) depend on economistic models of youth, which view young people primarily in terms of their ability to contribute capital and labour through employment. For example, in terms of housing transitions, we now talk about 'nesters', who are living in the family home until they are 30, and the 'boomerang generation', who are moving in and out of independent living, using the family home as a springboard. These are seen as 'yo–yo' transitions, where the process of moving into adulthood is not linear or smooth.

Wyn and Woodman (2006) also argue that '... current approaches inevitably identify education, work and family patterns of young people's lives as evidence of their faulty, failed transitions, measured against the standard of the previous generation' (Wyn and Woodman, 2006, p. 495). They go on to suggest that a *social generations* approach can offer a more nuanced conceptualization of youth, which places biography, social context and the state at the centre of the analysis (see below). One of the central issues in 'transitions' debates relates to tensions between exploring macro social systems (such as the 'transition' patterns of large cohorts) and the micro dimensions, in which these patterns play out in young people's lives. Which framework youth sociologists prefer largely depends on whether they envisage their research as addressing micro or macro patterns. As we explore across a number of chapters, this debate over the relevance of transitions remains core to youth sociology.

Youth (sub)cultures

A second major debate in youth sociology, which will be explored in depth in Chapter 5, relates to the cultural context and practice of youth, or what is called 'youth culture'.

Thinking points

- What youth cultural practices can you think of?
- What is the difference between youth cultures and subcultures?

> In a wide sense, 'youth cultures' refer to the way in which young people's social experiences are expressed collectively through the construction of differentiating lifestyles, mainly in their leisure time, or in interstitial spaces in the institutional life. In a more restricted sense, the term defines the emergence of 'youth micro-societies', with significant degrees of independence from the 'adult institutions', that provide specific space and time. (Feixa and Nofre, 2012, p. 1)

As the above quote suggests, what we mean by youth culture is something that is distinctive to young people and is expressed collectively in leisure through active engagement in different spaces and places. One of the major influences on debates about culture in youth sociology is the Birmingham Contemporary Centre for Cultural Studies (CCCS). The work that emerged from the CCCS was foundational in the field of youth sociology. It focussed on how social inequalities were maintained within different groups of youth, especially inequalities of class, and on the role of culture in both maintaining and perpetuating social class inequalities. Historically, culture was seen as an important form of youth resistance. Young people, according to the Birmingham School, used subcultural activities as a means of managing the tensions inherent in a class-based society. For them, culture was the way in which groups 'handled' the raw material of their social and material 'experience' – and specifically their class experience. But these class cultural differences are further complicated by generational differences associated with geographical locations.

For example, Phil Cohen (1972a), writing about the impact of social change in the East End of London, argued that the breakdown of traditional culture and structure led to tensions existing for the young. With the loss of traditional labour opportunities and the fragmentation of family and neighbourhood, young people had to find new identities. It was also the case that production was being replaced by consumption as an important part of mainstream society and young boys were caught in the contradictions between the ideology of mass consumption and the traditional ideology of production (i.e. the work ethic). Finding a solution to these tensions was problematic for the young. The parent culture that had worked for previous generations was unable to offer them a realistic solution; therefore the young East End boys created subcultures as a means to 'express and resolve albeit "magically" the contradictions that remain hidden or unresolved in parent culture' (Cohen, 1972a). As a result, young people created new forms of cultural practice through subcultures such as the mods, teddy boys and skinheads as a means of managing the economic tensions being played out in their communities.

Others argued that social difference was far more complex than the previous CCCS theorists had argued. Punk, for example, was seen as a **'semiological guerrilla warfare'** (Hebdige, 1979) used by youth against the dominant culture. It took resistance to its extremes, taking aspects of previous youth cultures and 'cutting them up' to create completely new epochs and cultural forms, many of them anarchistic, including features such as safety pins, plastic clothes, bondage and an attraction to horror and anti-establishment approaches. Punk became a mix of many styles and was more challenging and threatening to the state. What is interesting in Hebdige's argument is the way he starts to show that, even when subcultures are so anarchistic, they can be codified and commodified by the mainstream. While Punk created new forms of cultural practice, these practices also became translated into new commodities, appropriated by producers and sold to whole generations as a 'new' form of youth style. The classic example is the use of plastic bags by punks as an anti-fashion statement, which, within months, were appropriated by the fashion industry as sales of plastic bags as fashion items emerged in the high streets.

> **Semiological guerrilla warfare:** A term created by Umberto Eco, an Italian literary critic and philosopher, who suggested that to make changes to the status quo there would need to be a form of warfare that operated through the use of communication media.

In the 1990s, youth subcultural studies were challenged by post-structural ideas. This '**cultural turn**', as it became known, led to the emergence of what has been called post-subcultural theory (Bennett, 2011). This approach challenged the

> **Cultural turn:** The shift towards making culture the focus of contemporary debates in the social sciences and humanities.

Taste cultures: A subculture that reflects the preference of a group for a particular cultural product or activity.

Neo-tribes: A term created by French sociologist Michel Maffesoli to refer to ways in which groups of people come together in a shared interest. He sees this as a move away from individualism, and more fluid than subcultural groups.

Scenes or music scenes: These are situated as spaces that allow individuals to come together, not constrained or shaped by class or community, but by musical tastes and aesthetic relationships.

class-based approach of the CCCS, which saw youth subculture as a form of resistance or a form of political expression. It focussed on 'youth identities' and the 'lifestyle projects that appropriate and combine resources from both local, social-cultural environments and from global cultural industries.' (Bennett, 2011, p. 28). This approach generated substantial new work that used a sociological lens to look at 'clubbing' and **'taste cultures'**. We also see the emergence of the new concepts of **'neo-tribes'** and **'scenes'**, which aimed to capture both the creative nature of youth and the everyday activities of youth cultural practice while also rejecting a class-based analysis.

The cultural turn was not just about music. A whole series of studies emerged showing that young people do not just passively accept mass culture or even use it as a form of resistance; they use it in creative ways that are often not intended, and in ways that allow them to actively construct their own cultures and identities in new and challenging ways. For example, early feminist youth scholars highlighted the ways shopping gave girls access to a public world in ways that had previously been denied (McRobbie, 1994). For young women, shopping was shown to be about more than girls' passive subordination to the market or the empty purchase of meaningless and often useless things (McRobbie, 1994).

Practices of consumption are a key dimension for youth scholars studying the relationship between youth cultures and identities. Some 'transitions' theorists are sceptical of the focus on youth consumption and identities, arguing that too much emphasis is given to young people's 'capacity to choose', rather than paying attention to the ways in which those choices are limited by structures such as class and gender. In recent years, youth scholars have explored the dynamics of 'critical consumption' and its connections with youth political action. Many young people engage their 'consumer power' politically by boycotting particular goods and products for ethical or environmental reasons.

Young people's contemporary engagements with youth culture occur through negotiations between global and local flows; and of course, online. Suggestions that youth are not politically engaged or active denies the diverse ways the young are expressing their concerns or practising resistance in a range of on- and off-line contexts. Environmental movements and 'Climate strikes', animal rights movements, and anti-capitalist movements such as 'Occupy' are all such examples. While the sites and places in which young people operate collectively may look different from previous generations', young people's political activism and engagement is alive and well.

'Bridging the gap'

More recently, a number of youth sociology scholars have set about the task of trying to 'bridge the gap' between transitions research and cultural studies research. This dualism or 'two track' approach that has structured the work of youth sociology is criticised for failing to understand both the complexity of youth and the holistic nature of their lives. Youth transitions is usually seen as about 'becoming', while youth (sub)culture tends to concentrate on the spectacular activities of certain groups of young people. What is missing is an understanding of the 'middle ground' and the interrelationship between transitions and youth culture. For example, it is proposed that transitions studies tend not to be 'culturally rich', while youth cultural studies need to be more aware of social and spatial divisions (Threadgold, 2017).

These critiques of the traditions of youth sociology have been met with mixed responses. On the one hand, it is argued that this focus on youth sociology around the notion of a 'dualism' is overstated and ignores a rich history within the discipline that explores the interplay between transitions and youth culture. For example, MacDonald argues that, although much of his own work has focussed on transitions, the importance of culture has also been present (MacDonald, 2011). Others have also started to show that transitions are embedded in cultural practice. For example:

- The emergence of the 'can-do girl' that is re-enforced through broader cultural representations of young women in Australia suggests that cultural representation has had a major impact on young women entering the education and labour market (Harris, 2004).

- Cultural practices embedded in the 'night-time economy' such as clubbing, drinking and taking drugs have a critical part to play in young people's transitions, highlighting both the importance of these practices and the way they affect different social classes (Chatterton and Holland, 2002).

- The emergence of 'DIY careers' where young people in Australia are opting out of the 'rat race' to concentrate on creative artistic activities such as playing in a band, making jewellery or doing screen printing, many of which draw upon their own youth subcultural identities as a way of 'getting by' (Threadgold, 2017).

- Social practices on the internet can also have a transitional role. For example, the 'community' on Tumblr uses selfies and blogs as a way of creating self-identified personal transitions. They become new markers that catalogue self-growth, and tools for tracking their transitioning in a new cultural context (Allaste and Tilidenberg, 2016).

💭 Thinking points

- What do you think youth culture means to a young person living in Tonga or India?
- How important might youth culture be to young people living in some of the world's poorer nations? Will it have the same significance?

Debates surrounding youth culture in youth sociology have been strongly influenced by core sociological theories that have been dominant in the Northern Hemisphere. Studies of youth cultural practices have focussed largely on the activities of young people living in countries such as the UK, USA, Australia and other Western environments. What this debate often lacks is an understanding of how youth culture might mean different things outside of this context. Where, in these debates, are the young people of the countries that make up Africa or South America? Likewise, what about youth in the Pacific islands, the Philippines, or India, Pakistan or Bangladesh? This relative absence raises questions about how youth cultural practices might be variable in different contexts and whether their meaning and significance to the lives of young people may also vary significantly as a result of young people's access to resources and opportunities. This is something we need to keep in mind when thinking about what is meant by youth culture.

Social generations

The third and final body of work that is influential in youth sociology is defined as a social generational approach. As mentioned above, in the mid-2000s, Australian-based researchers Wyn and Woodman (2006) advocated that youth sociologists (and youth researchers more generally) make use of 'social generation' as an analytical tool. In doing so, they revived a concept from an older strand of sociology, associated with the work of the sociologist Karl Mannheim. Rather than a wholesale theory per se, social generation is better understood as a concept or an approach to understanding young people's lives. Wyn and Woodman explain that social generation '…locates young people within specific sets of economic, social, cultural and political conditions [and therefore] offers a way beyond seeing generations as a series of birth cohorts because age is no longer the defining feature' (Wyn and Woodman, 2006, p. 499). The distinction made here is crucial. As a popular term, generation usually corresponds with familiar categories such as 'baby boomers' (referring to those born between roughly 1945 and 1964), 'Generation X' (those born between 1965 and 1984) or 'millennials' (those born in the mid-80s onwards and who were coming into adulthood in the first 15 years or so of the 21st century). While each person in these categories 'grew up' into adulthood during roughly the same era, year of birth is the most important way of categorizing who belongs to which group. However, the 'social generation' approach advocates more than this, prioritizing the social and economic conditions that one grows up in as being pivotal.

Thinking points

- What is distinctive about your generation's experience of youth compared with your parents' generation?
- What differences are there *within* your generation?
- Do you feel a part of a generation, and how important is that to you?

One of the central arguments for the approach centres on the rapid and radical structural changes to the economy and significant social changes that have occurred in many industrialised nations since the end of the 1970s. The distinctiveness of contemporary conditions underpins why these researchers think that youth should no longer be understood as a 'transition'. They argue that retaining the transition metaphor inappropriately compares the lives of contemporary young people with the experiences of young people growing up in the 1960s, when the journey from school to work, from living with one's parents to starting a family of one's own, was for older generations quicker, more predictable and more 'linear'. In contrast, the contemporary experience of youth is theorised as 'non-linear', involving steps forward, back and sideways in terms of education, work and housing arrangements. Rather than seeing this as 'extending' the transition to adulthood, social generational theorists instead suggest that these changes have given rise to a new youth, or indeed a 'new young adulthood'.

Some youth sociologists use this framework to discover how young people engage with and negotiate these new landscapes, and advocates of the approach are explicit that new concepts are needed to be able to grasp young people's changed experience. Alternatively, France and Roberts (2016) argue that some potential pitfalls of this approach include overgeneralizing the experience of all youth within a generation, and risk missing the importance of inequalities between different groups of young people, particularly those related to social class. They suggest that a generational framework implies a research aim of investigating *commonality*, with the *different* experiences *within* generations, and commonalities *between* generations, then potentially becoming overlooked. For example, the way social class resources (dis)advantage and differentiate young people's experience of youth, the ways that young lives are bound up with the lives of other generations (especially older family members) risk being overlooked in favour of comparisons of whole generations and a focus on change over continuity.

The 'generation wars'

Interest in 'generations' is not limited to youth sociologists. 'Generations' have become a popularised way of understanding differences between different age groups, and different categories such as 'millennials' are primarily used by market research and advertising companies as a way of studying consumer preferences and behaviour. 'Generation wars' has also become a key trope in the media, highlighting points of tension and divisions between different age groups: most commonly 'millennials' and 'baby boomers'. These 'wars' are exemplified in the issue of housing (un)affordability for the current generation of Australian youth. In what became the 'smashed avocado debate', a conservative columnist wrote in an Australian new publication that young people could afford to buy a house if only they stopped buying expensive brunches, and instead saved that money for a house deposit.

This commentary generated significant debate and attention, with the piece being run in news outlets throughout the English-speaking world, where similar issues of housing affordability are pervasive. Some eight months on, Australian property millionaire Tim Gurner used similar rhetoric in articulating that his success was at least in part due to his thriftiness and desire to go without his 'smashed avocado and four coffees' so that he might afford to buy his first home. The 'smashed avocado breakfast', then, came to symbolise millennials as irresponsible spenders, geared towards short-term pleasure and luxury rather than 'hard work' and responsibility. Many other commentators have since pointed out that even denying oneself an occasional smashed avocado breakfast would still mean that saving for a home deposit will likely take *several decades*; and that does not take into account the generous tax concessions in Australia, which benefit owners of more than one property (as many baby boomers do), or the fact that house prices are in many countries growing much faster than incomes.

The smashed avocado debate is symbolic of 'generation wars'. Crucial for sociologists is the recognition that, rather than being something new, the rhetoric of 'generational wars' is actually cyclical, too. From Aristotle's lamenting of young people's taste for luxury and contempt for authority in Ancient Greece, through to Shakespeare's portrayal of the recklessness of youth, and various media depictions of troublesome generations occurring in most decades of the 20th century, concerns about the young people of the time are significant, enduring features of many societies.

However, in their current format, these 'generational wars' draw attention away from the very real structural changes brought about by globalization and the rise of service economies that have occurred in the last 30 years, and which now form the contextual backdrop to young people's lives. Part-time, flexible, low-wage and precarious work is now more prominent than it has been for many decades, as too is the demand for higher levels of education. What this debate fails to recognise is the patterns of structural change which have fundamentally altered the 'path' of youth followed by previous generations. Leaving home and becoming financially independent is increasingly difficult. The current generation can no longer expect to simply follow a path to adulthood of completing education; finding ongoing, full-time work; and buying a house. While many young people today still hold on to these dreams, structural changes to the economy and exorbitant housing costs mean achieving these 'goals' of adulthood remain practically out of reach for many.

School strike for the climate

From 2018, school students across the globe have been mobilizing to strike with the aim of challenging the lack of action by adults on global warming. This is an international movement of pupils and students who, instead of attending classes, are taking part in demonstrations to demand action to prevent further global warming and climate change. It was started by Greta Thunberg, who staged an action outside the Swedish Riksdag (parliament), holding a sign that read 'Skolstrejk för klimatet' or 'School strike for climate' during August 2018. From that moment onward, strikes have taken place and increased across the globe. In August 2018, 270 cities in countries such as Australia, Austria, Belgium, Demark, Japan, Switzerland, the UK, the USA and New Zealand had school strikes. By May 2019, the number of schools involved had increased substantially, with schools from over 2000 cities taking part in strike action.

The importance of 'structure and agency' debates

Finally, it is important to recognise that across these key debates in youth sociology are questions over the relationship between structure and agency. These debates are not dissimilar to those that take place in mainstream sociology, and they relate to the dynamics that people are shaped by, and the power that people have to shape and control their own lives. As you will see in the chapters that follow, these discussions about structure and agency have become essential to some of the most significant conceptual debates currently driving the field of youth sociology. Historically, youth sociologists have introduced terms such as 'opportunity structures', 'bounded agency' and 'structured individualism' as ways of conceptualizing and trying to explain the way that structure and agency intersect (France, 2007).

In empirical work in this field, an emphasis on social structure is used to demonstrate instances of social reproduction, or examples in which young people are constrained by social conditions not of their making or choosing, while an emphasis on individual agency is mobilised to present examples of creative resistance or social change. There is often confusion about just what agency is: is it an individual property residing in all bodies that can be stifled by structures, or somehow 'unlocked' or let loose? Is agency therefore a necessary dimension of subjectivity or 'the human condition'? In relation to these debates, Coffey and Farrugia (2014) have argued that there are significant conceptual problems associated with discussions of structure and agency in youth studies and that agency needs to be more rigorously theorised. While social structures such as social class are undoubtedly powerful, young people are not simply or passively inscribed by social class, or other social categories. However, as we shall see in the chapters that follow, neither do young people simply have the 'power to choose' their life trajectories, as the numerous social and cultural forces they are born into, not of their choosing, have a large influence on what they can do and who they may become. Understanding these dynamics is at the core of youth sociology, and in negotiating 'structure and agency' debates.

 ## Summary

- Youth can only be understood in its social, cultural, and historical context.

- The sociological imagination can help us make sense of young people's experiences.

- Youth is a fluid social category that is shaped by social, economic, cultural and political processes.

- Key debates in youth sociology centre on youth transitions and cultures, social generations, and structure and agency.

Exercise: The sociological imagination

Ask an older member of your family (parent, guardian, aunt or uncle) what they were doing when they were your age. Compare their answer to your own life today. What are some of the broad social changes you can identify that shaped their lives, and yours today? You might find it useful to use the sociological imagination to help you to think about the historical, structural, cultural and critical elements that have shaped your life.

Key readings

Bennett, A. (2011) 'The post-subcultural turn: some reflections 10 years on', *Journal of Youth Studies*, vol. 14, no. 5, pp. 493–506.

Evans, K. & Furlong, A. (1997) 'Metaphors of youth transitions: Niches, pathways, trajectories or navigations' in Bynner, J., Chisholm, L. & Furlong, A. (eds.) *Youth, Citizenship and Social Change in a European Context* (Aldershot: Ashgate).

France, A. & Roberts, S. (2016) 'The problem of social generations: a critique of the new emerging orthodoxy in youth studies', *Journal of Youth Studies*, vol. 18, no. 2, pp. 215–230.

Lesko, N. (1996) 'Denaturalizing adolescence: the politics of contemporary representations', *Youth & Society*, vol. 28, no. 2, pp. 139–161.

Woodman, D. & Bennett, A. (2017) *Youth Cultures, Transitions and Generations* (London: Palgrave Macmillan).

Wright-Mills, C. (1959) *The Sociological Imagination* (Oxford: Oxford University Press).

Wyn, J. & Woodman, D. (2006) 'Generation, youth and social change in Australia', *Journal of Youth Studies*, vol. 9, no. 5, pp. 495–514.

2 DIMENSIONS OF DIFFERENCE

In this chapter you will learn about:

- Why youth sociology is interested in dimensions of difference
- The importance of using theory in exploring the lives of young people
- A history of how youth sociology has used theory
- The different theories of class, gender, sexuality and ethnicity and how they inform youth sociology
- How knowledge hierarchies between the Global North and Global South influence how we understand young people's lives.

Theorizing youth and inequalities

At the heart of sociology is an interest in understanding human societies, especially how they are organized and structured, and the outcomes that follow from such configurations. As sociologists, we are particularly concerned with what the famous French sociologist Émile Durkheim called 'social facts', and how the arrangements of a society, such as traditions, customs and cultures, produce and shape individual preferences and life outcomes. Sociologists also aim to 'debunk' the ways in which social arrangements of inequality, which seem 'natural', actually result from *social processes*. As a critical discipline, therefore, sociology seeks to expose these social processes, explain the basis of inequalities, and provide theories that will help develop the human condition and lead to a more socially just society.

Such a goal is clear in the work of significant sociological theorists. Karl Marx, a founding figure in sociology, suggested that the discipline should do more than describe the world; it should also use theory and research to change the world. C. Wright Mills (1959) also called for sociology to illuminate how seemingly private troubles are often public issues and proposed that we, as sociologists, have a responsibility to bring these to the attention of others. A similar argument was proposed by French academic Pierre Bourdieu (2000), who described sociology as a 'martial art'; a discipline that ought to be used as to defend the marginalized and the voiceless. More recently, we have also seen feminist, queer and post-colonial perspectives having more impact on sociological theorising. These perspectives challenge the traditional White, male, Eurocentric perspectives, and study the ways in which gender, sexuality, race/ethnicity and nationality are core features of difference and how they stratify social life. To this extent, sociology has always been concerned with illuminating injustice and producing theories and research that act as 'myth busters' (Elias, 1990). It seeks to ameliorate systematic injustices in socio-economic and cultural/symbolic domains.

A starting point for most youth sociologists has therefore always been to focus on how inequality across societies (and between societies) affects the lives of the young. The discipline has a long and rich history of researching and theorizing social inequality, especially in terms of social class, gender and ethnicity. More recently, the focus has expanded into other marginalized groups in society, such as young people with disabilities or those who are sexually diverse. As a result, theories and research are geared towards understanding how social processes 'continue to mean that some get a lot where others end up with very little' (MacDonald et al., 2001: para 5.8). In the broadest sense, our theorizing is therefore premised on an engagement with the question of domination and injustice. In the chapters that follow, the themes of difference, inequality and injustice will be paramount. As a result, we will explore a wide range of questions, including:

- Why do young people from poorer and particular ethnic minority backgrounds consistently do less well throughout the entire education system?

- Why, despite more women than men attending university, do young men still have better employment and earning outcomes than young women?

- How does 'where young people come from' influence their futures?

- Why are those from lower social classes more likely to get insecure, poorly paid jobs?

- Why do young Black and Indigenous youth disproportionately end up in the criminal justice system?

To be able to understand how such questions can be answered, youth sociology has engaged with a range of sociological theories that both identify the problem and aim to explain why such phenomena exist. Therefore, a good familiarity with how the discipline has used theory is required. This allows us to develop *assumptions*, which we combine to create *frameworks* for understanding a range of social issues. The rest of the chapter is thus dedicated to outlining some of the cornerstone theories used in youth sociology, which are useful for thinking through many of the themes that follow in the remainder of the book.

What is theory?

Thinking points

- How is theory connected to experience and context?
- What is the relationship between data, research and theory?

It is important firstly to clarify what we mean by theory.

> In a world where we don't know all about anyone (including ourselves), or anything, we have to have theories, whether we are aware of our 'theorising' or not. (Dawes, 1998, p. 329)

This quote from Milton Dawes captures a great deal about both the simplicity and the complexity of theory. We all have theories about a great many things, and in this way the quote speaks to those intuitions, those hunches we might have that help us fill gaps in what we know; that is, how we *make sense* of things. Theorizing at this everyday level tends to operate as a form of speculation. We might intuitively 'theorize', for example, why someone we know appears to be particularly grumpy on a given day, why a particular peer dresses differently from us, or as discussed in Chapter 1, why buying avocados might be bad for our dreams of buying a house. These may seem like slightly ridiculous examples, but they provide insight into how we understand the more complex bases of all scientific theory; in each case our intuition is usually not simply a random guess, but instead is built on a series of experiences and exposure to various bits of information. We might know, for example, that our grumpy friend has a lot of essay deadlines, and has also been working long hours, and that both of these have resulted in a lack of sleep. Our friend is grumpy, we theorize, as a result of being stressed and tired.

Sociological theory, like all scientific theory, is similarly predicated on a very important relationship with observable, empirical data. It is much more than an idea, belief or ideology. Indeed, the collection and/or observation of quantitative or qualitative data in sociological research is a systematic and ongoing process that facilitates the production of theory, which in essence works to describe, explain and predict, that is, to theorize social phenomena. It can operate at the level of explaining specific events (sometimes called the micro or idiographic level) or can be more generalizable in explaining a group of events or occurrences that applies to a wider context (sometimes called the macro or nomothetic level).

The relationship between theory and data is mutual, such that while theory is grounded in research evidence, new studies always build from, use and often test theories generated by previous thinking and research. Richard Swedberg (2016) articulates this by explaining how theory can be *established* in the *context of discovery*, through observation of data, or that theory can be *tested* or used *in the context of justification*. In the latter, we can think of theory as being a testable proposition that can be confirmed, denied, or even seen as partially accurate and in need of refinement.

Social theory, however, is to some extent necessarily abstract, and no theory will entirely explain the experiences of every individual in any given sub-population. This leads to different theories that sometimes offer competing explanations; in other words, despite resting on empirical evidence, theories are often contested. These contestations can lead to very different positions on a specific issue, or sometimes similar but not quite identical positions. Even within disciplines there are rival frameworks, as we illustrate below, where we set out some of the key concepts and theories that are or have been prominent in youth sociology. At a very basic level, the role of theory is to establish the what, how and why of any social phenomena.

Class studies in youth sociology

Thinking points

- How important is class in shaping young people's experience today?
- Do you see social class as important in your own life?

We start our discussion with an exploration of class theory. For youth sociology, class has always been an important question and has therefore had a significant impact on the thinking and research of the discipline. Of course, class theory has also always been central to sociological analysis, and from its inception, sociology drew on the works of Karl Marx, Emile Durkheim and Max Weber. While class has remained important to both mainstream sociology and youth sociology, its influence from the 1990s onwards waned, being seen as either 'dead' (Pakulski and Waters,1996) or as a 'zombie category' (Beck, 2002). It was thought to be of little value conceptually or analytically, as the world we lived in had changed dramatically and class seemed to have less influence on people's lives. More recently, we have seen a resurgence of class studies in youth sociology, especially with the impact of the work of Pierre Bourdieu, someone we will return to later. It is also important to note that the history of class theory as a core tool for analyzing the social life of the young emerged out of the Global North, especially the UK and America. Its ability to 'make sense' of social relations in other parts of the world, such as in Africa, Asia and Central America, has since led to debates over its relevance in understanding other non-Western societies. This is a point we shall return to towards the end of this chapter.

Youth as 'an institution'

Thinking points

- What do we mean when we say that youth is an institution?
- How might such an approach explain young people's transitions to adulthood?

Structural functionalism: Regards society as consisting of many complex and interdependent parts which ideally contribute to stability and consensus.

Much of the early work on youth and social class was developed in the USA by Durkheim scholars around the ideas of **structural functionalism**. This saw society as a 'biological structure' where each institution has an important role to play in keeping society functioning as a whole. Issues of class inequality, or 'stratification' as they called it, existed as a 'natural' way of ensuring that talented individuals were motivated to undertake training. This ensured that the most important social roles were filled by the most talented. In this sense inequality was a necessary part of society. When it came to youth, functionalists argued that some form of inequality, and especially the *age grading system*, was an important societal institution. It acted to distribute roles and responsibilities and to enhance socialization while also helping the young to make connections to other structural components of society, i.e. occupational and educational structures. Functionalists argued that all societies needed systems that helped move children into adult roles. Youth is therefore an institution that makes this happen, and social class within it was functional as it helped socialize different social groups into relevant forms of employment for their class. The interest in youth was taken up particularly by Parsons (1942) and Eisenstadt (1956), who argued that the emergence and expansion of industrial society created new sets of strains and tensions for the young working class. Parsons, for example, writing during the post-war boom, observed the emergence of the troubled teenager. He suggested that this was evidence that young people were finding it increasingly difficult to make the transition from childhood to adult social life. In particular, he pointed out that children who were brought up in working class families, a relic of the pre-industrial era, were struggling to make the transition and were looking more to their own peer groups as a way of easing the difficulties of coping with adult social life. In the UK, structural functionalism was used as way of thinking about youth transitions, seeing it as an institutional practice that aimed to help the young become adults.

In youth sociology this position was challenged by Allen (1968). She proposed that structural functionalism had little to offer in explaining or understanding the position of youth in capitalist societies. In particular, she pointed out that age relations were not a precondition of social stability but were the outcome of economic, ideological and political power. It was these that determined what it meant to be young. Structural functionalists also struggled to explain social change and how this led to new forms of practices emerging. Such a perspective was influential in early work on youth transitions, but as unemployment grew and family structures changed in shape and formation, functionalist theories were seen as unable to fully grapple with the impacts of these changes. Simple models of transition to adulthood became inadequate for understanding the complex interplay between new social arrangements and their impacts on young people's trajectories.

Marxist and Weberian responses

As mentioned above, the works of Karl Marx and Max Weber had a significant impact on class theorizing. Marx's work emphasized the importance of the '**ownership of production**', arguing that social classes were formed through the struggles over any '**surplus value**' and the creation of a '**division of labour**'. Weber on the other hand saw social classes defined not by a person's relationship to the means of production but by the sharing of a '**common market position**' that shaped life chances. While these differences are significant, debates over class in sociology in the 1980s and '90s were less about theory building or its testing and more about a shared collective interest in how to measure class in a changing society. Such an approach has been highly criticized for being almost 'theory free' and a distraction involving advanced statistical procedures. More importantly, it also constructed class as static and involved a limited assessment of the economic relationships, particularly in relation to the labour market, while having little to say about the lived experience of class. Its focus on trying to identify the boundaries between working class and middle class also meant that it had nothing to say about the elites or very wealthy.

Ownership of production: Karl Marx argued that those who owned the raw materials, facilities, machinery and tools used in the production of goods and services also had the greatest power and influence. This ownership was central to how classes were created.

Surplus value: The excess of value produced by the labour of workers over the wages they are paid.

This form of class analysis came to characterize transitions research, and a considerable evidence base was developed. For example, Ashton and Field (1976), researching youth transitions from school to work, were able to show the incongruence

Division of labour: The breaking down of tasks in the workplace to increase the profit levels of the production process. This can have significant impact on the structuring of class relations.

Common market value: A term used by the sociologist Max Weber. He proposes that a person's class situation is connected to their relationship to the market, i.e. their ownership of property or goods, and the availability (or lack of availability) of opportunities to obtain specific types of income in the market (e.g. lawyers, entertainers).

Post-structuralism: A set of ideas developed in France in the 1960s challenging the 'structuralist' theory of knowledge. Post-structuralist approaches argue that all knowledge is contingent; there are no 'absolute truths'. Instead, all knowledge is produced in context.

between working class young people's expectations and the realities of the labour market. In this, they claimed that class was clearly still relevant even though young people did not always see it this way. By the early 2000s the dominance of this approach was being challenged, not only by the emergence of **post-structuralist** ideas that class was 'dead', but also by the growing problems of being able to capture the lived experience of class. It was becoming increasingly difficult to attune the contradictions of how (or if) class operated in the everyday lives of the young, especially in a rapid period of social change. One approach that attempted to tackle the growing contradiction between what was seen as a growing individualism where young people denied the impact of class on their transitions, believing that they had control over their own trajectories was the idea of the epistemological fallacy. Furlong and Cartmel (1997) suggested that the growing expectation embedded in policy frameworks that emphasized choice and responsibility meant that, if they failed, they blamed themselves. As they state, '… Blind to the existence of powerful chains of interdependency, young people frequently attempt to resolve collective problems through individual action and hold themselves responsible for their inevitable failure' (p. 114).

The 'cultural tradition' of class analysis

A second strand of work in youth sociology of class theorizing emerged out of the Centre for Contemporary Culture Studies (CCCS) in the UK. In the previous chapter we gave a brief overview of this approach. One of the major developments in class theorizing was the theorizing of how class was being *socially reproduced* in ways that ensured young people from working class backgrounds got working class jobs. This approach has its roots in the research of Paul Willis (1977) who, in his book *Learning to Labour: How Working Class Kids Get Working Class Jobs*, tracked a group of young working class 'lads', who opposed school and its authority, showing how they ended up getting typical working class jobs. As a part of this process he showed how they created a counter-culture that included 'having a laff', 'skiving', 'being tough' and 'being racist and sexist'. These practices prepared them for coping with their future work in the factory. Willis argued that this counter-culture, while *resisting* conformity, was also a factor in preparing the young men for working class jobs. It instilled in them important values and understandings that existed in the manual environment where they were likely to work. In the 1990s, during a period of high unemployment, we saw the growth of what Phil Mizen (1995) called the 'training state', which replaced the traditional school-to-work transition. It was here that approaches using a social reproduction model were also able to show how class inequality was being reproduced (see the box on the next page).

Social reproduction in the training state

Inge Bates showed how a group of school leavers who entered a local college had their aspirations either 'warmed up' or 'cooled down'. Her first study (Bates, 1993), on young women who were being trained to be 'care-givers' in old people's homes, illustrated how vocational training provided them skills in dealing with incontinence and laying out the dead, but also operated to get them to adjust to this type of work and to seek out employment in an area that was gender-stereotyped and low paid. In her second study (Bates, 1993), on young women wanting to be fashion designers, she found that vocational training 'cooled out' their ambition and then saw them take low-level work in the garment industry doing low skilled and low paid jobs such as sewing and pattern cutting. In both cases young working class women ended up in traditional gendered and classed occupations.

The growing influence of Pierre Bourdieu

🗨 Thinking points

- How do concepts of 'capital' relate to contemporary expressions of social class?
- How do the most privileged or elite manage to maintain their class position?

More recently, class theory in sociology has been invigorated by the work of Pierre Bourdieu (see Savage, 2015). Bourdieu's concepts show that class is not just about economic circumstances such as income and wealth ownership, or about labour market positions or relations to the mode of production. It is about the social and cultural relationships and the struggles for power, influence and domination of one lifestyle over another. People are positioned in particular social spaces according to their possession of various types of capitals (social and cultural resources) and their habitus (their embodied identity and history). Cultural capital is concerned with language, the appreciation of art and ownership of cultural artefacts. It is also about the institutional recognition and accreditation of qualifications that symbolize success. Social capital is about the range of social networks that people accrue over time. These can usually be mobilized to gain information about opportunities and to give access to resources. Habitus is the '…system of durable and transposable dispositions… acquired through lasting exposure to particular social conditions and conditions' (Wacquant, 2006, p. 267). Bourdieu's work helps us to consider how habitus and capitals help to socially reproduce class inequality. For example, studies using Bourdieu's tools have been able to show how those from working class backgrounds are denied opportunities because of their lack of capital(s) and also how middle-class parents are able to use their economic resources and networks to advantage their children and ensure they get the best qualifications at school. This not only affects the experience of schooling but also the future trajectories of young people, ensuring that middle-class young people get access to the best universities and the best jobs (France and Roberts, 2017). Bourdieu's work has been most influential in educational and school studies, but as we shall see in Chapters 3 and 4, its influence has expanded within youth sociology to explore how class inequality is also happening in transitions from higher education into the workplace.

Gender and sexualities

Thinking points

- What is the difference between sex, gender and sexuality?
- How important do you think gender and sexuality are in shaping your life and the pathways available to you?

Until relatively recently, sociology has been dominated by men, and has centred on men and male perspectives in understanding society. Feminists argue that, without gender as a central analytic of social life, work, family, the economy, politics, education and religion cannot be adequately studied or understood (Winkler, 2010). Feminist approaches highlight the ways that socio-cultural norms of gender are learned and 'performed' by people, rather than being natural extensions of sexual differences in 'biology'. The phrase '…one is not born, but rather becomes, a woman' is one of the most widely recognized feminist statements, originating from French philosopher Simone de Beauvoir in 1972. This statement aims to disconnect notions of inequality from women's bodies, and to emphasize that gender is something one 'does', rather than 'is'. These points tend to be classified as 'second wave' forms of feminism that focus on the construction of femininity and the role of women, and also highlight the structural change to the dominant order of society that is needed to address the fundamental causes of gender inequality. Simone de Beauvoir highlighted that the body is the product of social inequalities, rather than the basis for it. This political move was important because the female body was for so long considered to be 'naturally' inferior to the male body, and this bodily difference was used to legitimate the exclusion of women from public life as the 'household' was rationalized as a woman's 'natural' place.

Biological determinism: A belief that individual characteristics are the inevitable result of biology.

Eighteenth-century **biological determinist** perspectives, which saw racial and class differences as inherent and 'natural' in the body, were used to position the White, upper-class European male body as the 'human' norm against which all others were judged to be lacking. This 'standard' was legitimated by the rise in modern 'science' through fields such as phrenology and **social Darwinism**, and formed the basis of some of the most heinous atrocities in human history, including genocide and slavery. The involvement of fields of science, medicine and technology in the naturalisation of inequality and discrimination is a continuing critique made by sociologists and other fields of social science.

Social Darwinism: The incorrect application of Darwin's evolutionary laws of natural selection to human society.

Defining sex and gender

- **Sex** relates to the physical body and to the biological differences that exist between 'male' and 'female' genital and reproductive organs.

- **Gender**, by contrast, relates to the socially and culturally specific meanings associated with sex and the division between categories of 'masculine' and 'feminine' which define norms, roles, and behaviour.

- **The gender binary** ascribes gendered characteristics to sex and bodily characteristics. This does not account for the vast variations between sexed categories (including 'intersex') and gendered performances. The gender binary has been strongly criticized by feminists on the grounds that it plays on an implicit cultural hierarchy in which women are assumed to be inferior to men.

- **Transgender**: A person whose personal or social identity and gender does not correspond with their assigned birth sex. The gender binary causes significant problems for the numerous people whose sexed bodies do not conform to their gendered identities.

- **Cisgendered** is the term to describe someone who is not transgender or gender diverse, and who identifies with the sex they were assigned at birth.

- **Non-binary** – Gender identities should not be tied to binary notions of sex. It is more useful to see both sex and gender as socially and culturally contingent, rather than the sexed body as 'natural' and gender as 'social'.

Beyond binaries of gender and sexuality

Judith Butler's (1990, 1993) theories of sex and gender have become central to contemporary sociological understandings of gendered norms and practices. Her concepts are used to deconstruct the gender binary, as they hold that gendered behaviour and norms are not the result of biology but are instead constructed, reinforced and maintained by continuous performance in society and culture and by us, ourselves. In this context, both gender and sexualities are produced through repeated practices rather than essentially determined by one's 'sex'. Within sexuality, all kinds of gender may be 'performed', not necessarily aligned with binary 'roles'. Butler's work helps to theorize and explain the increasingly visible variations in sexed and gendered identities as evidence of the 'performativity' of gender and sexuality. Butler's work goes on to also explore and challenge the way heterosexuality is constructed as normal, and the power relationships which keep this in place. Queer theory challenges the traditional divide between gay and heterosexual, suggesting that sexual identity is fluid across different stages of life and sex/gender. For example, in *Gender Trouble* (1990), Butler argues we should challenge and 'trouble' these traditional binary views on gender and sexuality because they do not reflect the diversity of people's contemporary sexed and gendered identities. Furthermore, adherence to these binaries often forms the basis for sexist, homophobic language and behaviour – and even legitimizes violence against women and non-binary persons. The binary categories of gender and sexuality norms are very limiting and potentially repressive for everyone – but particularly those who identify as lesbian, gay, bisexual, trans, intersex, queer (LGBTIQ+).

Landmark studies of gender and sexuality in youth sociology

The first feminist studies of youth emerged in the 1970s. Carol Smart (1976) was one of the most influential feminist scholars of youth. Writing in criminology, she pointed out that most studies of girls and delinquency made two core problematic assumptions:

- The constitution of 'good' women naturally disposes them towards motherhood, home-making, passivity and obedience. Women's biology therefore naturally positions them as chaste and pure.

- Deviations from this natural state are 'unnatural' and in some way intimately linked to sexual misconduct. That is, the causes and consequences of girls' delinquency are sexualized.

These two assumptions about gender have continued to influence both how the criminal justice system responds to girls and how girls are understood in the academic literature more generally. They are of particular significance in psycho-dynamic explanations, where biology and genes are seen as critical in 'driving' how girls behave.

As feminist youth scholars have pointed out, prior to the 1970s there had been an absence of focus on young women's lives. In a wide range of studies, girls and young women remained 'invisible', or were seen as a problem because of their biology. Feminist writers set about to challenge both the absence and the psycho-dynamic influence. A major starting point for this was criticism of male scholars in CCCS. This led to a new movement in youth sociology, which still reverberates today in 'girlhood studies'. Angela McRobbie's landmark study (1978) of young femininities was a 'reply to Willis's famous text '*Learning to Labour*'. Her analysis of girls' bedroom culture highlighted the broader contexts of gendered inequality, which meant young women had to seek out places of privacy indoors, afforded by bedrooms, as they were marginalized and excluded from enacting these modes of femininity in public or in street-based youth cultures typically dominated by young men. Research at this time by Griffin (1985) and Lees (1986) also highlighted the impacts of sexual double standards for young women, showing that, alongside the real threat of physical assault, girls' presence on the street could also be associated with sexual promiscuity and carried the ensuing risk of a damaged reputation. These early UK studies put girls and young women 'on the agenda' for sociological scholarship, and highlighted the 'subordinate status of young women' in relation to class and gender inequalities at the time in the UK.

From the 2000s onwards, youth sociological research recognized the importance of studying diverse sexualities in understanding youth inequalities. The study of 'queer youth' and their participation in youth cultures and subcultures is particularly relevant for understanding the growth of LGBTIQ rights (Halberstram, 2005). Susan Driver's edited collection *Queer Youth Cultures* (2008) draws together ground-breaking research exploring the practices and activities of 'queer youth' in defining and developing their own cultures and subcultures through DIY media projects, popular culture, local drag performances, anti-oppression activisms, online communities and music subcultures. As Driver (2008, p. 12) explains, 'queer' was often used by young people in the studies as a self-descriptor and heuristic device to evoke a 'transitional' process, or refusal of definition or simple categorisation. Gender and sexuality are now front-and-centre in the study of contemporary youth cultures and subcultures, countering historical studies of youth cultures originating from the Centre for Contemporary Cultural Studies, which focussed squarely on social class. It provides the groundwork for intersectional analyses (which we explore later in this chapter) in the field of youth cultural studies, enabling investigation of the ways young people negotiate sexual, racial, class and gender identities, and an understanding of young people's cultural practices within multiple relationships of power and privilege.

'Post-feminism' and 'new femininities'

Thinking points

- What impacts has feminism had on young people's lives?
- What does it mean to be 'feminine' today?

In a period of rapid social changes, we start to see the emergence of popular discourses around what is called '**post-feminism**'. This suggests that women have now 'achieved equality' or 'near equality' as a result of large-scale social changes. In this view, young women are seen as 'winners' and are no longer restricted by previous gender norms. For example, data from the Australian Bureau of Statistics shows a huge generational change in women's participation in the labour force from 1961

Post-feminism: The idea that feminist goals of gender equality have been achieved. Contemporary feminist authors strongly challenge this.

to 2011, rising from 34 per cent to 59 per cent (ABS, 2014). In popular discourse and advertising in the 1990s and beyond, young women are heralded as harbingers of social change and the promise for the future: as powerful, assertive and capable subjects of late modernity, unconstrained by gendered inequalities and ready to take on the world. It is suggested that young women have more choice, more control and can be who they want to be. In other words, we cannot think about being young and female as a fixed category but need to recognize there are many 'femininities'. Representations of women's equality are also encapsulated in youth culture. Images of the 'can-do' girl (Harris, 2004) or the 'top girl' (McRobbie, 2007), embodying young women's so-called equality and newfound capacity to succeed in education and work, were taken up in popular media and advertising. The images of the 'can-do girl' or 'top girl' were used by some commentators to herald the goals of feminism as 'achieved', but were also seen as having been achieved to the detriment of boys and men as part of a political backlash against feminism which arose in the 2000s.

Feminist scholars argue that the idea that feminism is 'past' and 'no longer relevant' in fact serves to *continue* existing inequalities on the pretence that equality has been achieved (McRobbie, 2015). The discourse that equality is achieved leaves women feeling they only have themselves to blame if they are structurally impeded from sustainable careers, do more unpaid work in the home, and feel unsafe in public spaces.

This discourse is seen in current educational debates around girls' and young women's achievements in education and employment and boys' supposed 'under-achievement'. Anita Harris's landmark work on 'can-do girls' (2004) who believe they can 'have it all' showed the tensions, contradictions and invisibilizations of gender, class and racial inequalities within this discourse. The idea that young women's educational success will lead to economic prosperity and stability on the basis of their enthusiasm for work and having a career obscures the numerous factors that continue to shape inequalities in the labour market for women. Further, ideals of choice and empowerment also function in particularly regulative ways for those young women who do not have the resources or capital required for success in education or employment.

Research and theorizing on 'young femininities' have received significant attention in youth sociology (Aapola et al., 2005). Contemporary studies of femininity are diverse, focussing on the dynamics of young women's lives in the context of the post-feminist and neoliberal discourses described above, and the conditions of possibility shaping subjectivities. The intersections of feminism, sexualisation and media culture are a primary focus. For example, how do young women negotiate and engage in feminist discourse online? How do they navigate sexualized media that invite them to 'be sexy', whilst other narratives of individual self-responsibility punish girls who are 'slutty'? Feminist studies in Australia, New Zealand and the UK have critiqued consumer society's demand for young women to embody hypersexualized modes of femininity. Images of girls' bodies proliferate in Western visual media, regulating 'what it is to be a sexual subject' and providing a 'technology of sexiness' (Gill, 2008, p. 53). Paradoxically, there is little information regarding positive sexual embodiment (Rice & Watson, 2016). Feminist youth sociologists seek to disrupt moral panics regarding young women's 'sexualization', which tend to individualize young women's experiences, and instead draw attention to the sexist ways young women are addressed in media culture (see Retallack et al., 2016; Renold and Ringrose, 2011). This 'post-feminist media culture' of sexiness through bodily display increasingly extends to young men's bodies too, particularly through new digital technologies and social networking. The gendered power dynamics of sexting and social media are explored further in Chapters 7 and 9.

Masculinities and power

Thinking points

- What is traditional masculinity, and how has it changed over time?
- What does it mean to be 'masculine' today?

The study of men and masculinities is an important theme in sociology, largely stemming from feminist attempts to denaturalize sex and gender categories. In other words, if we agree women and men are not simply 'born' with gender, but rather it is something we all learn and do, then it is important to also understand how men 'do' gender, and how more equal articulations of gender may become possible. Many social science studies prior to the 1990s tended to take male biology 'for granted', naturalising traditionally 'masculine' traits as the simple outcome of biological or sociological determinism rather than being socially learned. Men's social behaviour was explained either as biological destiny (in men's 'genes' or hormones) or sociological fate (men will always be socialized into being aggressive or dominating). Such biological determinist perspectives are now considered overly simplistic and reductionist. Masculinity can be studied as a negotiated process where there are opportunities for other, less oppressive identities to be lived.

A solution to reductionist understandings of men and masculinities has been developed by the Australian sociologist, Raewyn Connell (1995). Connell uses the concept of 'hegemony' to explain why ascendancy, or being at the top of a hierarchy, is not necessarily achieved through force or violence. Rather, when a set of practices or way of being is *hegemonic*, it is ascendant because it has achieved the status of common sense or an ideal. Connell argues that hegemonic masculinity is a 'culturally exalted' model of masculinity that subordinates softer masculinities and femininity. Some organising aspects of hegemonic masculinity include 'being White', 'being heterosexual', and 'being rational'. These are idealized characteristics possessed by those men deemed 'most powerful' in society. Hegemonic masculinity can perhaps be better thought of as a set of fantasies and ideas about what men 'should be', rather than 'actual', attainable characteristics of men, though you will no doubt recognize men's attempts or successes in embodying these ideals. Importantly, maintenance of these ideals sustains the power of men as a group, even while some men are disadvantaged by the narrowness of these ideas.

As a result of this work and increasing social change, youth sociology has seen a body of work emerge, similar to 'new femininities', which suggests there are many masculinities available to young men today. The study of young men and masculinities has been crucial in exploring the dynamics of privilege and inequality in contemporary gender relations in relation to school and work; and cultural and subcultural practices such as drinking and drug taking, and punk and music scenes (Driver, 2011; Farrugia, 2014; Nayak, 2006). For example, Mac An Ghaill (1994) shows how the hegemonic ideal of heterosexuality dominates the public lives of young men. Having to continually 'perform' and present themselves as sexually active and desiring is a requirement of being a young man.

Young men's relationship with heterosexuality is also raised as a part of this analysis. Frosh et al. (2001) suggest that masculinity is in many ways constructed in opposition to femininity and homosexuality. Being masculine and heterosexual requires young men to distance themselves from women, femininity and gay males because they have to maintain the superiority of heterosexuality to continue the process of control and domination. The public ideal of 'heterosexual man' is usually expressed within young men's own peer groups and amongst their 'mates'. Stepping outside of it by showing 'unmale desires' such as effeminate or homosexual traits opens them up to sanctions from other young men. This process can be enforced through physical violence and threats, but it can also work in other ways. Hollands (2002) suggests that this process can work in more subtle ways, in that it can also be constructed within young men's discourses of 'being male'. They suggest that an important aspect of sexual understanding is gained through sex talk, or what they call the sexual narrative. The sexual story telling of young men involves boasting about and exaggerating sexual conquests and male fantasies, in which women are reduced to passive subjects who are there to serve male urges, needs and desires. Such talk acts to set sexual parameters and boundaries, ensuring that 'heterosexuality', and certain forms of sexual practice such as vaginal penetration, are constructed as the 'norm'. This in effect not only informs others but also acts to police young men's behaviours. Mac An Ghaill (1994) and Hollands (2002) then go on to show that in reality this public notion of heterosexuality is both fragile and problematic for young men. Fragile in the sense that privately, most young men reject it and want to construct alternative ways of being; and problematic because it constrains and regulates their ability to do this.

The focus on masculinities in youth research has also responded to 'masculinity in crisis' public discourses, which hold that the broad-scale social changes which have given young women more opportunities in education and work have negatively affected young men (McLeod and Yates, 2006; Roberts, 2014). Youth scholars have highlighted a 'massive' amount of evidence that concerns about masculinity in crisis drastically oversimplify the issue as being between 'boys' and 'girls' rather than seeing the way gender intersects with ethnicity, rurality, class and poverty, which are much more meaningful for understanding the impact of social change on young people's lives (White and Wyn, 2013, p. 55).

Youth and ethnicity

💭 Thinking points

- How important is a young person's ethnicity in shaping their experience?
- How does ethnicity connect to issues of racism, Whiteness, and power?

The dual concepts of race and ethnicity are both slippery and difficult to categorically define. Both are socially constructed and contingent on a range of social structures. In spite of a lack of conceptual consensus, race and ethnicity are terms that emerge in strong ways for researchers and policy-makers, and more broadly in the community. Their influence in youth sociology has also been highly influential. Historically, much of the work on ethnicity has focussed on 'race' and was strongly influenced by biological definitions that conceptualize and problematize 'non-White groups' as either 'outsiders' or 'underdeveloped' compared with the dominant White groups in countries such as the USA or the UK.

In terms of youth sociology again, similar to studies of class and gender, we see the CCCS at the University of Birmingham making a significant early contribution to the issue of race and ethnicity. It was highly critical of the way race was being used both politically and academically. For example, the CCCS started to broaden the notion of resistance to include a racial dimension. It focussed on second-generation young Black Caribbeans, who were encountering high levels of racism, especially as there was a growing political tension over immigration. This was seen as a time when young people started to create a resistant culture that emphasized an oppositional lifestyle to mainstream White society. Hebdige (1979) for example, showed how Rastafarianism and the culture of the Jamaican 'rude boy' was used as a method of both moving away from White British society and offering new forms of resistance. Interestingly, Hebdige shows how British skinheads appropriated Black reggae music (an important symbol of resistance from Black youth) in creating their own culture. Other seminal work from CCCS included that of Hall et al. (1978) in their work, *Policing the Crisis*. In this they show how 'mugging' became a crime committed by Black youth, which then contributed to a wider moral panic in the UK about race.

'New' ethnicities

From this early work of the CCCS, we can see that writers such as Stuart Hall (1996) continued to write and theorize about the re-conceptualizing of 'ethnicity', especially about Black cultural politics in the UK. Such work identified two relevant phases, or 'moments', that spoke to what he called the emergence of 'new ethnicities'. The first phase refers to the initial development of the term 'Black' as a way to talk about the collective experience of marginalisation and racism in the UK. During the 1970s, this was a way to organize a novel form of resistance for people from diverse cultural, histories and minority ethnic backgrounds. As Hall explains, over time, a hegemony developed that ultimately served to subsume other ethnic or racial identities within the one dominant identifier. On the whole, however, this new way of conceptualizing raced identities emerged as a way to challenge what it is to be 'Black' as an 'invisible other' among White cultural discourse. The second 'moment' signalled the end of the 'essentialized Black subject' and a movement towards a more heterogeneous representation of ethnicity. This signified the introduction of multiple identity positions, such as class or sexuality, in the constitution of Black identities and an acknowledgement of 'unities within difference' (Back, 1996). In this 'moment', the notion of ethnicity was re-negotiated, while dominant discourses of race and ethnic relations, and nationalism were put aside. Instead, the context of global networks was taken into account when considering the 'Black cultural production' analyzed by Hall. This was shaped and created via local and global dynamics, which then saw 'new ethnicities' emerge from this milieu. The 'new ethnicities' paradigm is different from earlier approaches, which were more situational and relied on biological definitions of ethnicity. Instead, the local and non-local aspects of identity development could be recognized.

Anoop Nayak (2016) applied a 'new ethnicities' approach in his research on young people living in North-East England. Nayak situates his participants as part of a 'racialized world' even though they engage in 'post-race practices' and have opportunities for 'undoing race'. As Hall conceptualized, these young people move across race-based boundaries and 'create' ethnicities drawing on transnational shaping factors (Nayak, 2016, p. 58). Using an example from his own research to illustrate the new ethnicities framework, Nayak describes a group of young people in North-East England, a mostly White-Anglo area, who were keen basketballers. The young men appropriated several aspects of 'Black style' and were inspired by global cultures such as music and sport, as well as media representations of urban/Black 'street styles'. Some members of the group superficially identified with aspects of a transnational 'Black' set of identity resources. Others, however, were able to develop more 'post-race attitudes' and form relationships with others across race-based lines, based on shared practices and values (Nayak, 2016). Nayak's work demonstrates how 'cultural hybridity' plays a crucial role in the contemporary lived experience of ethnicity. The natural peer relationships that emerged from the basketball group '[gave] rise to new ethnicities and ways of being ...' (Nayak, 2016, p. 62). The concept of 'new ethnicities' represents a way to resolve the analytical problems that have plagued much of the theoretical work in this area, as it facilitates a move away from the more categorical identity positions linked to essentialized notions of race or ethnicity. Instead, it helps us to think about young people in the context of mobilities, the historical context of local places and critical approaches to diaspora communities (Back, 2016).

Multiculturalism and youth

💭 Thinking points

- What do we mean by multiculturalism, and do you think we live in a multicultural society?
- What are some of the challenges for researchers and politicians in defining and using the term multiculturalism?

Multiculturalism is a common term used by many in the academic, policy, legal and political arenas; however, its meaning can change because of different uses in different disciplines. Enzo Colombo offers a broad definition in which multiculturalism:

> refers to situations in which people who hold "different" habits, customs, traditions, languages and/or religions, live alongside each other in the same social space, willing to maintain relevant aspects of their own difference and to have it publicly recognised. (Colombo, 2015, p. 801)

Colombo's definition is situated within identity, and difference, and as is often the case, it is posed in a positive way. The importance of difference is enshrined at the core of this principle, and there is a political emphasis on people having a platform in the public arena, in particular those who have been marginalized (Colombo, 2015). Multiculturalism is not merely a descriptor for the contemporary global condition of cultural diversity in many countries. More than demographic change, it refers to an attempt to develop ways to deal with cultural difference that are accommodated in cultural, legal and political spheres (Colombo, 2015).

The rise of multiculturalism as a concept, and as a policy tool, developed throughout the 1970s and onwards. It was a response to assimilationist perspectives that saw the integrated melding of ethnic difference into a White, hegemonic whole as the endpoint of a successful society. Multiculturalism also represented a challenge to colonialist approaches that had tended to subjugate certain groups (Colombo, 2015). As a form of state policy, it has included, for instance, the dedication of government funding in support of ethnic-based organizations, enabling them to facilitate cultural activities that conserve traditions. In the late 1990s and 2000s, however, there has been a backlash against multiculturalism. Challenges have come from conservative political discourses. These represent a broader movement away from policies emphasizing cultural diversity and a turning back toward 'assimilationist' approaches. Multiculturalism was accused of being a failure in terms of its ability to support the forming of ethnically diverse, harmonious societies. Local, host cultures were seen to be weakened at the expense of an 'exaggerated support' of incomer and minority ethnic groups (Colombo, 2015, p. 806).

Multicultural policies have been criticized and accused of being ineffective, or not well developed (Harris, 2013). Much of this relates to the forms of representational politics and notions of cultural groupings related to the homogenous, discrete representation of ethnic and cultural groups living side-by-side in a 'receiving' or host country. The idea of an unchanging identity, and belonging to just one national context, are the assumed norm in many multiculturalism frameworks. However, while essentialized cultural and ethnic representations have been challenged and accused of 'freezing' group difference, such an approach can also serve as a political strategy to gain recognition and rights (Colombo, 2015).

In the sociology of youth, multiculturalism critique emerges out of a dissatisfaction with its ability to speak to everyday life in a culturally diverse society. Young people are uniquely positioned to speak to the disjuncture between policy frameworks and a more lived, grass-roots form of multiculturalism. This is because they have grown up during a time of backlash and witnessed the rise of the 'anti-diversity, pro-integration agenda' (Harris, 2013, p. 139). But young people are the subject of concern about diversity as well. In Western countries characterized by significant rates of cultural and ethnic diversity, young people have often been cast as the 'problem' for not being able to adequately 'adapt' to host societies. In response, educational and other forms of intervention often focus on young people and their 'attitudes' and 'identities' as something needing to be fixed or managed (Harris, 2013). A counter 'image' or narrative sees young people as uniquely positioned to resolve differences in diverse societies. Certain stories and experiences are held up as 'successful' when there is an 'appropriate acculturation' that is unthreatening and palatable to the dominant ethnic majority. While young people have been seen as caught between host and home cultures, they are still most likely to move easily and uncritically across difference.

Anita Harris posits a form of multiculturalism that resolves many of the criticisms outlined above, and which accounts for the messy, day-to-day experiences of young people living in diverse places. For Harris, multiculturalism is more a way of living, or a process, than an end-product to be successfully achieved (Harris, 2013). Young people are more likely to take cultural and ethnic diversity as the norm, and for them, local places tend to be the sites of belonging for a range of others. Young people '…can do this with enthusiasm, indifference, and sometimes hostility, but when it is underscored by an acknowledgement of the rights of all to participate this can be a predominantly productive, dynamic, everyday politics' (Harris, 2013, p. 143). Indeed, mundane, routine interactions across differences are more likely to be negotiated as a form of 'settlement' than of outright 'consensus'. There is an acknowledgement, or a form of respect, accorded based on the right of the other to be in collective neighbourhood spaces. Harris is careful to point out that young people are by no means perfect multicultural citizens. Indeed, they engage in exclusion and racism, and can contradict themselves in terms of their multicultural values and awareness. Young people partake in the 'integration' or collective 'values' narrative as a way to find stability and a sense of belonging in the broader national discourse in the same way many others do (Harris, 2013). Ultimately, young people do not need to be guided and directed to the right forms of behaviour and practice in a multicultural society. They are negotiating these things themselves and on their own terms in order to 'find ways to live productively together and create new kinds of solidarities and identities' (Harris, 2013, p. 143).

Intersectionality

💭 Thinking points

- How are our identities and trajectories shaped by intersecting categories of gender, sexuality, ethnicity and class?
- How does inetersectionality help us make sense of the relationship between these categories, and a young person's identity and position in society?

Intersectionality explores how different forms of inequality and oppression intersect and overlap, in areas such as race, class, sexuality and gender. This approach was an important remedy to suggestions that second-wave feminism was mainly preoccupied with the lives and struggles of White, middle-class women. While intersectionality has gained recent popularity in online circles, as a framework for understanding oppression it has a history that long predates the internet. Gender, race and class as mutually shaped attributes that structure life opportunities have been analyzed by feminists for some time, led in particular by Black feminist scholars in the USA. Kimberlé Crenshaw (1991), a critical legal scholar, developed the term to describe an approach that tries to understand how intra-group differences are productive of different experiences at particular *intersections*. She used intersectionality to critique the application of anti-discrimination law in the case of *Degraffenreid v General Motors*, brought by five Black women against their former employer. Though the plaintiffs in that case were clearly discriminated against, as Black women they were not considered to be representative of women, and not considered to be representative of Black people, either. Thus, the court found that they did not meet the tests of sex discrimination and race discrimination, and the law was interpreted in such a way as to deny the plaintiffs a legal remedy. Crenshaw argued that we need to be attentive to how dominant ways of understanding gender and race exclude certain populations, like Black women in this case. As such, intersectionality emerged from a legal and policy context in focussing on the intersections of gender, race and class, but is now used across disciplines.

More recently, intersectionality has been called a 'buzzword' (Davis, 2008) because of its frequent and often contradictory use. Intersectionality has also been critiqued because it has been used in an 'additive' way (Purdie-Vaughns and Einbach, 2008), contributing to the term 'Oppression Olympics' (Martinez, 1993). It is important to recognize that simply adding gender, race and class disadvantage together often does not produce a sophisticated understanding of how power operates in practice in specific contexts. Rather, we need to understand local contexts when using an intersectional framework. For example, although intersectionality can be a powerful lens for understanding the intra-action of gender, race and class, Aileen Moreton-Robinson (2008) argues that prevailing US-based scholarship often falls short in failing to consider the situation of Native Americans in race dynamics. In countries such as Australia and New Zealand, an intersectional framework needs to attend to the particular history of colonization, the continuing dispossession of Indigenous peoples, and the local management of multiculturalism and immigration, rather than presuming that US-based theory is straightforwardly applicable.

Youth scholars have drawn on intersectional approaches to explore how broadscale social changes in education and work participation influence young people's lives along the intersecting lines of gender, ethnicity, race, rurality, class and poverty (Nayak, 2006) and the dynamics of gender and sexuality in non-binary and transgender youth (Zeeman et al., 2017). Studies such as that of Allen (2014) in the UK illustrate how young working class women are often subjected to intensified scrutiny and usually portrayed as 'immoral' and not conveying the 'right' types of femininity. Similarly, in terms of race and class, Rollock et al. (2011) show that, to succeed in a White middle class society, 'speaking properly' and walking in certain ways signify middle-class status. 'Sounding Black', is rejected and using a 'middle class accent' helps individuals minimize discrimination on the basis of their race and class. In this case, young people and their parents actively engage in both 'exclusionary' and 'inclusionary' boundary work, making it clear what class they do and do not belong to. These examples show how an intersectional approach, which brings together class and race, for example, can be useful in better understanding the multiple ways in which inequalities shape the lives and opportunities available to young people.

Knowledge making and the dominance of the Global North

💭 Thinking points

- How is social and academic knowledge produced, and who controls it?
- How do you think this influences our understanding of the social world of young people in different parts of the world?

To finish our discussion on key influences in youth sociology, we want to raise the issue of the production of social knowledge. Historically in sociology and youth studies, the majority of research and literature produced in an effort to understand young people's lives and contexts has originated from the Western 'power centres' and wealthy post-industrial societies of the UK and USA (the Global North), and more recently, Australia and New Zealand. Where possible, we have throughout this text drawn on examples and case studies to illustrate the stark contrasts in young people's lives and opportunities globally.

Criticism by a wide range of international scholars, especially those working in the Global South or what is sometimes called the 'periphery', has rightly drawn to our attention the role social science has played in the colonial and domination practices of nation states. There have thus been calls to 'de-colonize' sociology. This critique originated in a growing Indigenous literature (Smith, 1999) and has also been raised by Raewyn Connell (2007), who argues for sociology to show how theories and knowledge from the Global South can provide new insights and understandings. Linda Tuhiwai Smith (1999), writing from New Zealand, argues that

The Enlightenment period: Also known as the Age of Reason, the Enlightenment was a philosophical movement that took place primarily in Europe and, later, in North America, during the late 17th and early 18th centuries. It claimed to be illuminating human intellect and culture after the 'dark' Middle Ages.

the **Enlightenment period** in England gave rise to Western science as a part of the modernizing project. It was seen as creating 'true knowledge' about the world. As a result, 'Indigenous peoples were ranked as, "nearly human", "half human" or "sub human"' (Smith, 1999, p. 60). This form of categorization became a way of legitimising various colonial practices. For example, anthropology set about studying the 'other' in places such as the Pacific, defining the social and cultural practices of such groups as a form of 'primitivism'. The 'ethnographic gaze' was seen as 'takers and users' creating a science of imperialism that reinforced the idea of the need to civilize the savage (Kuper, 1988). Scientific research became synonymous with colonialism, creating suspicion and criticism that reaffirmed the notion that Northern social science held the 'truth', and other belief systems were primitive; this speaks to the ongoing divide in anthropology and area studies on the one hand and sociology on the other. The former often focusses on so-called residual social realities, while the latter usually focusses on the so-called modern world (Phillips, 2018). In this process, many theories and 'world views' of the Global South have been marginalized or ignored and seen as 'second class theories'.

More recently, these imbalances in the research environment have been addressed. Linda Tuhiwai Smith (1999) and other Indigenous researchers (Walker, 1996) assert the need to give priority to other 'world views' and other forms of knowledge. Connell (2007) argues that 'colonised and peripheral societies produce social thought about the modern world which has as much intellectual power as metropolitan social thought, and more political relevance' (p. xii in Introduction) – this is now seen as knowledge that the North ought to learn from, not just about. Connell engages substantively with a range of Southern theorists, showcasing their diverse contributions to social theory, while arguing for their relevance, which is grounded in particular political, economic and cultural experiences, drawing from African, Latin American and South-West Asian concepts.

This line of thought also emerged in youth sociology through writers such as Pam Nilan (2011), who has been especially critical of the idea that we can simply apply Western concepts universally across other countries and cultures. For Nilan, the notion of an adulthood signalled as complete independence from one's parents simply does not make sense in many countries, where family and community relationships remain, overtly and constantly, pivotal social dynamics. Recognition of this is evidenced to some extent in a collection put together by Wyn and Cahill (2015), which deliberately sought to showcase ideas and evidence about young people's lives from both the Global North and South. Similarly, Cuervo and Miranda (2019) point to the theoretical and empirical work produced in youth and childhood sociology in the last two decades or so, as well as showcasing recent Global South scholarship that picks up the issues young people face and engage with in Nigeria, Mexico, Malaysia, Argentina, Brazil, Ecuador, Fiji and many other countries.

One example of the importance of locally developed concepts from the Global South is Kaupapa Māori in New Zealand (Walker, 1996). It is not a new concept, having its origins in history reaching back well over a thousand years. It gives meaning to the 'life of Māori' (Walker, 1996) and is developed through an oral tradition expressing the way Māori people think, understand, interact with and interpret a world that is different from the **Pākehā** version. It encapsulates a Māori theory, or world view, of how the world operates and is owned and controlled by Māori through te reo Māori (the Māori language). As Smith states '... there is more to Kaupapa Māori than our history under colonialism or our

> **Pākehā:** A term used for New Zealand first-generation White settlers and their descendants.

desires to restore rangatiratanga (self-determination). It has a different epistemological tradition that frames the way we see the world, the way we organize ourselves in it, the questions we ask, and the solutions we seek.' (L. Smith, 1999, p. 230). Although each *iwi* (local tribe) has its own historical experiences, dialects, customs and practices, they share common cultural and genealogical connections to knowledge creation and transmission. It is very much about Māori philosophy, customs, ways of living and doing things (its culture) and beliefs. By recognizing and understanding the Kaupapa Māori worldview, social researchers gain greater insights into the life worlds of young Māori. It helps us understand why and how they make decisions in their lives. It can explain the key influences on their thinking and how this shapes their everyday practices in ways that Northern theory fails to grasp (Smith, 1999).

One of the major issues for youth sociology is to recognize that knowledge itself is not neutral and value free: there is no 'view from nowhere'. All knowledge is context specific. What is sometimes taken for granted in the theorizing of young people's lives in the Northern Hemisphere is determined by a particular set of values and beliefs about the world. The growth of alternative Indigenous and local theory challenges these assumptions, showing that there are other ways of living, belonging and contributing that challenge this dominant paradigm.

💬 Summary

- Sociology seeks to expose a wide range of social processes and explain the basis of inequalities with the aim of providing theories that will help develop the human condition and lead to a more socially just society.

- There is no such thing as 'theory-free' facts – theory aims to establish the what, how and why of any social phenomena.

- Social class has been a central feature of youth sociology and remains at the core of much theorising of young people's lives.

- 'Intersectional' perspectives are important for understanding how categories of oppression overlap, such as gender, sexuality, race/ethnicity and class.

- Historically, the Global North has been the site for knowledge-making in the social sciences. This affects how youth are understood in different parts of the world.

✏️ Exercise: The sociological imagination

Each person's identity and journey through life is shaped by the social and cultural forces of the time and place they were born into. If you were to 'zoom out' and look at your life and identity, what factors do you see as crucial in shaping who you are? What is your 'position' in society in terms of gender, class, race/ethnicity inequality and privilege, and how does this affect your view of the world?

📖 Key readings

Aapola, S., Gonick, M. & Harris, A. (2005) *Young Femininity: Girlhood, Power and Social Change* (New York: Macmillan).

Cuervo, H. & Miranda, A. (eds.) (2019) *Youth, Inequality and Social Change in the Global South, Perspectives on Children and Young People* (Springer).

France, A. (2007) *Understanding Youth in Late Modernity* (Milton Keynes: Open University Press).

Harris, A. (2013) *Young People and Everyday Multiculturalism*, vol. 13 (Routledge).

McRobbie, A. (2007) 'Top Girls? Young women and the post-feminist sexual contract', *Cultural Studies,* vol. 21, no. 4, pp. 718–741.

Nayak, A. (2017) 'Young People, Race and Ethnicity' in *Handbook of Youth and Young Adulthood*, 2nd ed. (Routledge).

Roberts, S. (2014) *Debating Modern Masculinities: Change, Continuity, Crisis?* (Springer).

Roberts, S. (2017) 'Young people and social class' in *Handbook of Youth and Young Adulthood*, 2nd ed. (Routledge).

Wright-Mills, C. (1959) *The Sociological Imagination* (Oxford: Oxford University Press).

3 EDUCATION AND IMAGINED FUTURES

> ## In this chapter you will learn about:
>
> - The changing nature of the post-16 education and training sector
> - The major drivers of recent changes to the sector
> - How far the changes have increased or widened participation
> - How inequality has been maintained and socially reproduced
> - What has been happening to graduate employment.

The massification of post-16 education

🗨 Thinking point

- How many people from your network of family and friends have attained a university-level degree?
- Would you consider university to be a normal or even majority experience for young people in your home country?

At the level of everyday 'common sense', education systems are understood as being necessary for readying individuals for the world we live in, and as having significant effect on the direction of their lives. Youth sociologists are keen to understand, document and analyze the student experience, to determine how attainment, **aspirations** and attitudes to education are formed, and to interrogate the ways in which educational institutions are managed and organized. All this is done with the aim of better understanding the *relationship between* education and society.

As we noted in Chapter 2, education is typically framed as a critical site where young people are engaged in making the 'transition' to adulthood. Education is positioned as crucial in providing young people with the knowledge and skills to become independent citizens and workers – key characteristics of having 'succeeded' in transitioning from youth to adulthood. As we also highlighted, since the 1990s, the routes into adulthood have been radically reconfigured, and this is especially the case with the expansion of post-16 education and training. If we are to understand more about young people's lives then we need greater insights into the changes and their impacts on the education system.

Aspirations: In education research this usually refers to a young person's ambitions to participate in higher education. It is also used to think about a young person's desired employment outcome. In both cases, *aspiration* is not the same as *expectation*.

Social mobility: The movement from the social class one is born into to another social class. Education is often described as being the key to upward social mobility. Sociologists are critical of how much upward mobility can be achieved.

Education is seen as the 'great leveller' of life chances, offering the opportunity for anyone who engages in it to improve their personal situation. Our chief consideration as youth sociologists, though, is to ask critical questions and to challenge commonsense assumptions about education's capacity to remedy social divisions and increase **social mobility**. In other words, borrowing from C. Wright Mills again, youth sociology is concerned with '… which varieties of men and women come to prevail in society and how does education influence this'. In this chapter, we consider these questions mostly by exploring the field of post-compulsory education and training. We will make occasional reference to compulsory schooling and studies about school-aged pupils, but predominantly we look at structures, experiences and outcomes in the post-compulsory schooling domain. This reflects the growing impact of this field in the lives of young people today, and youth sociologists' predominant interest in the 'youth and young adult' age bracket, from 18 to 30 years of age. We start our discussion by looking at the recent changes that have taken place in the post-compulsory education sector.

'Massification'

Across the globe, young people's encounters with education have both extended and increased. Since the 1990s, we have seen a major transformation of education systems in many of the Organisation for Economic Co-operation and Development (OECD)

Massification: The dramatic change in OECD countries that saw participation in further (particularly higher) education shift from being a destination for a limited, often privileged few, to being a widely accessible 'mass' experience. This process involved expansion, with the provision of new universities and new courses.

member states, based on a huge expansion of the post-school sector and efforts to increase participation across all social groups. Higher education became accessible as a 'mass' experience, referred to as **massification**. In short, this means that young people are increasingly encouraged to complete their upper secondary schooling at 17 or 18 and then to participate in the tertiary education system, either at university or in the further and/or vocational education sector. This compares starkly to most students' parents' or grand-parents' generation where, up until the late 1970s, large proportions of people in industrialized nations left school at age 15 or 16, for the most part moving into paid employment pretty much simultaneously (France and Roberts, 2017; see also Chapter 4). In those days, only a small proportion of people, often those from more privileged families, stayed at school or college for another year of two, and fewer still went on to university.

The routes taken in those days were extremely gendered, with young women tending to follow normative practices of leaving school early with the expectation of domestic servitude in a marriage, or undertaking courses that would lead to gender-typical roles as secretaries or nurses. Meanwhile, most young men focussed on jobs in the manufacturing or heavy industries, while those who stayed on at school were most likely to find work in the professions. Under such circumstances there was an understanding (and maybe a hope) that one was entering a job for life. Today, finishing compulsory schooling would not give the majority of young people the qualifications they need to find work. As a result, we have seen massively increased numbers of young people entering post-16 education and training.

This is not to say that all – or even most – young people go to university; this is a common error in popular thinking. The field of post-16 education and training includes a wide range of vocational courses that teach trades and basic skills. Many young people go into vocational training, and some do still go straight into work (or unemployment). Indeed, while university participation has increased dramatically over the last 20 years, we have also seen a massive increase in vocational training courses across OECD countries. For example, New Zealand increased its apprenticeships annually between 1995 and 2008. Similarly, Australia's Technical and Further Education (TAFE) system had over 1.8 million people taking vocational training courses across Australia; this continued to expand year on year, driven by increasing numbers of apprenticeships, which grew by 28 per cent between 2004 and 2012.

Global gaps in children and young people's educational participation

In 2000, the World Education Forum in Dakar gathered representatives from 164 countries and produced the ambitious 'Education for All' agenda, setting targets to improve the global equity of access to and participation in early childhood, primary, secondary and post-school education by 2015. The progress report (UNESCO, 2015a, 2015b) found almost all targets set had not been met, though improvements had been made in some areas. In 2015, around 57 million children were not in school, and almost half of those will never go to school. Considerable gender disparity exists: 48 per cent of out-of-school girls are likely never to enrol, compared with 37 per cent of boys. The highest percentages of children who had never attended school were in sub-Saharan Africa. The poorest girls continued to be most likely never to have attended. In Niger and Guinea, for example, approximately 70 per cent of the poorest girls had never attended school – notably higher than the share of the poorest boys – compared with less than 20 per cent of the richest boys.

New global education targets now include an international benchmark of at least 9 years of free, equitable and compulsory primary and lower secondary education. There are stark global inequalities affecting which countries are likely to achieve this target. For example, in 54 of the 164 countries, mostly from Central Asia and Central, Eastern and Western Europe, almost all children enrolled in primary school will reach the last grade. At the other end of the spectrum, in 32 countries, mostly in Sub-Saharan Africa, at least 20 per cent of children are likely to drop out early and not reach the last grade.

While going to university is seen by many in wealthy OECD countries as a normative, or almost prescribed, course of action for young people, it is not a statistically dominant status (Roberts, 2011). In addition, as we see later in this chapter, some groups are more likely to dominate at university (i.e. the middle class) while others will dominate in the vocational sector (i.e. the working class). This is an important point to stress, as it reminds us that a comprehensive understanding of youth in education and training is achieved only by assessing the complexity they face at this stage of their lives. Of course, we also have to remember those young adults on the outside of the education track, as well as those within it. This is a group we will discuss further in the next chapter.

The skills revolution

More young people than ever are engaging with some form of education between 16 and 24 years of age. One of the implications of this is that young people are dramatically increasing the level and number of qualifications they hold. For example, the number of young people who have at least upper second secondary qualifications has been increasing year on year. While there can be variations across countries, it is commonly accepted that leaving school without some form of qualification is now very unusual. In fact, since 2007 the number of young people without such qualifications has dropped from 20 per cent to 15 per cent across the OECD countries. There has also been considerable growth in the 'non-academic' qualification market where diplomas and a variety of 'certificates' have also been recognized as relevant in a changed economic climate. This is especially the case for the young unemployed or low skilled, who are reliant on using such qualifications to 'signal' their employability to potential employers (Allen and Ainley, 2010). Accordingly, many countries, including the UK, Australia and New Zealand, have set about increasing the 'basic skills' of the unemployed or 'upskilling' and 'reskilling' the employed (Tomlinson, 2013) through a process of 'education for employability' (Allen and Ainley, 2010, p. 41). This tends to take place in schools or further education colleges, whose focus is recruiting academically unsuccessful and/or poor or problematic populations.

University qualifications have seen unprecedented, massive growth in recent decades. A substantial number of young people now attain tertiary-level qualifications across most OECD countries, at, just below and often above the Bachelor's degree level. The growth has been extraordinary: between 1992 and 2012, global tertiary enrolment among young people aged 18–24 shifted from 14 per cent to 32 per cent (Brooks, 2016). Across OECD countries, young adults with tertiary qualifications now make up the biggest share of young people (44 per cent) (OECD, 2018). It is also important to recognize the growing number of young people who are now taking postgraduate qualifications. For example, the most recent census data from Australia show that more people than ever are achieving postgraduate qualifications: between 2011 and 2016 the number of people with such qualifications grew from 631,000 to 921,000 – a staggering 46 per cent growth in five years. One of the major consequences of this 'skills revolution' is that young people today are more educated than any other generation:

> In most OECD countries, younger adults (25–34 years old) have attained higher levels of education than older adults (55 to 64 year olds). On average 82 per cent of younger adults have attained at least upper secondary education compared to 64 per cent of older adults. Younger adults also have higher tertiary attainment rates than older adults by about 15%. (OECD, 2013a, p. 31)

Human capital and the growth of the knowledge economy

The massive expansion of the post-16 education and training sector occurred particularly from the late 1980s onwards. Prior to this, the global economy was going through a period of readjustment or reconfiguration that saw technological developments and neoliberal economic policies shift the emphasis from an industrial economy (or what was called a 'Fordist' economy) to a post-industrial economy that was built on high-level products, services and high-end technologies. Paid work, especially in industrial and primary industries, declined, and claims were made that work as we knew it was changing dramatically. This economic transformation of the late 1980s also had a massive impact on young people's employment outlook, and, subsequently, their relationships with the education system. For example, in the UK, Australia and New Zealand, as well as many other countries, the youth labour market collapsed as the jobs that would ordinarily absorb school leavers no longer existed (France and Roberts, 2017). Governments then responded to the prospect of large number of workless youth by rolling out a variety of educational opportunities and youth training schemes (see Chapter 4 for more detail). Indeed, what we see is the emergence of what Mizen (1995) calls the 'training state'.

The knowledge society

It is claimed a 'new society' is emerging where paid work is not about making 'stuff' with your hands but about what is in your head. The knowledge society thesis rests on several ideas about modern economies:

- Ideas/innovation and the production and use of information and knowledge is central.

- Information and knowledge are replacing capital and energy as primary wealth-creating assets.

- A new stage of capitalism – a shift from land, labour, capital and energy to knowledge and information economies – has created a need for high skills.

- With technological developments, information and knowledge can be transported instantaneously around the globe, generating a very competitive environment.

- To gain economic advantage, a company or nation will need to continually innovate through market and technology know-how and the creative talents of knowledge workers, to help solve problems and develop new products.

Governments around the world proposed that these trends gave strong indications that the value of knowledge was critical to the future of work. As a result, they proposed and achieved investment in what was called **'human capital'**. If nation states wanted to remain productive in the future they would have to produce a highly qualified workforce, which would in turn, through a kind of virtuous circle, create a more highly skilled economy. It was suggested that the 'new' **knowledge economy** would stimulate an expansion among high level, high skill

Human capital: Related to knowledge, this denotes the economic principle that skills, attributes, intelligence, training, experience can all be certified and measured through qualifications, and that more qualified populations will produce economic benefits.

Knowledge economy: An economy supposedly centred on growing levels of highly skilled, information-based employment. Usually cited as a key motivation in government drives to have more people gain university degrees.

jobs; a steady number of intermediate, technical skilled roles; and a diminishing lower end of the labour market, where low skills and low wages would gradually disapp.ear. It was therefore proposed that employment in knowledge-based economies would be underpinned by increasing demand for more highly skilled workers (OECD, 1996).

During the 1990s, linked to the human capital doctrine and Third Way politics, there was a sharp turn towards a skills agenda, and its attendant policies. This became a crucial component of the growth of post-compulsory education. The skills agenda represented a direct effort to facilitate the transition from an industrial-based economy to a so-called knowledge-based economy. Policy makers in many Western countries emphasized that such a de-industrialized economy, filled with technology and service-based employment, would demand a highly skilled, flexible workforce. In the UK, for example, the 1997 election of Prime Minister Tony Blair saw New Labour commit to 'three' priorities during their time in government: 'education, education, education'. While broadly linked to a range of social issues, the education commitment was quickly and unequivocally established as related to the knowledge economy as Blair made a bold policy target (which was never achieved) of ensuring that 50 per cent of young people participated in university-level study by 2010. This commitment to the skills agenda was evident in the words of the then first Minister for 'Lifelong Learning', Kim Howells, who in 1997 stated:

> If we do *not* create a learning society – if we do *not* find the means of generating the appropriate skills and craft and expertise, then we will fail to develop our most important resource – our people – and we will fail as an economy in this increasingly globalised market. (Kim Howells, 1997, original emphasis)

Such thinking was widespread. The Australian Federal Government had also identified increasing university participation as the major plank in expanding post-16 education (Gale and Tranter, 2011). In fact, much of the agenda was driven by a desire to 'widen' participation, with concerted efforts, at least in political rhetoric, to enhance higher education participation among those young people from under-represented, or what were then described as non-traditional groups. Such expansions saw university enrolment in countries across OECD increase significantly. For example, in Australia, participation rates increased by 15 per cent between 2003 and 2008 and a further 23 per cent between 2008 and 2013 (Peacock et al., 2014).

The impact of the changing nature of education

So far, we have outlined the major changes in the post-16 education and training field. But what have been the impacts of this on the lives of young people?

From public good to private responsibility

A key central theme in the claims of governments was that expanding education in the post-16 sectors required individuals to take charge of their own trajectories and careers, and to be wholly aware of the need to adapt to rapidly changing work environments and requirements. It was also important that the 'user' of the post-16 education systems needed to pay. This modification in the framing of both labour market and educational policy is important, and while on the surface it may feel intuitive or logical, it represents a significant shift in direction. It reveals that, while policy makers talked about how 'they' needed to create a learning society, the onus of taking up opportunities was increasingly placed on the individual. This agenda was thus about further entrenching neoliberal imperatives that were initiated by the 1980s New Right governments in the USA, the UK, Australia and New Zealand. This was an agenda of reducing state expenditure and re-distributing the risk of investment to individuals in myriad ways.

A core imperative of the neoliberal approach was the need to 'responsibilize' the individual to take educational matters into their own hands. This included passing on financial obligations to students who would, in most advanced nations, begin to be referred to as 'consumers'. As a result there has been a shift, meaning that education is seen not as a 'public good' but a 'private responsibility'. In this sense, education was designated as a commodity that one personally purchases as a means to achieving personally desired employment outcomes. As a result, we start to see major changes in higher education which suggest it is like any market. In this context we see the **marketization** of universities, changing the student experience. For example, we see education being strongly structured around the notion of 'consumer choice'. That said, most countries' post-16 education systems would be defined as quasi-markets. This notes that education is paid for by both government subsidies and private tuition fees, but the principle is aligned with market-based ideas. Here, the student is able to choose from many providers; in so doing, the idea is that quality will rise and be controlled and accountability will be delivered as institutions in the market compete to attract the consumer's 'spend', while at the same time reducing the cost of education for the state. Not only is there a market of providers in the higher education (HE) system in this model, but also a market within institutions, with departments and courses competing against one another for students. This is especially important when, as is the current case in Australia, government funding of student numbers is capped for each institution.

Marketization: The introduction of market-based principles into the newly expanded higher education system, including league tables, student satisfaction evaluations, and reconfiguring of students as fee-paying 'consumers'. Education institutions compete with one another for students, who have to pay increasingly high fees. Within individual Higher Education Institutes, departments and courses also compete against one another for students.

This has of course paved the way for a complex array of fees for going to university and/or entering training programs. The cost of studying varies from country to country, sometimes from state to state, and often from course to course. For example, in England, since 2012 fees have been capped for domestic students at £9250 per year, for any university course. This represented an almost three-fold increase since 2006, and an almost nine-fold increase since 1997. From 2018, this fee cap was intended to rise in line with inflation (though at the time of writing there is debate about reducing the fee). Consumers usually pay these fees by accessing student loans, which can be extended to cover costs of living. The net result is that the average student debt upon graduation with a three-year university degree in England is over £50,000. These loans require no repayment until a graduate begins to earn more than £25,000 per year (as of April 2019), at which point the consumer has a percentage taken out of their salary directly by the Inland Revenue Service.

However, student debts also attract interest premiums. Indeed, UK student loans now have interest rates of over 6 per cent per annum, sitting in sharp contrast to New Zealand, where there is now no interest charged on student loans. As a result, we are seeing country-specific systems of student financing and a spiralling level of student debt caused by student loans. In the USA alone, outstanding student debt sits in excess of 1.5 *trillion* dollars (Friedman, 2018). In the UK, outstanding student debt sat at a high of just over £105 billion in 2018, but is forecast to reach over £450 billion by the 2050s (Bolton, 2019). Australia's student debt is currently estimated at around $54 billion AUD (Ferguson, 2018), while New Zealand, with its much smaller population, had a nominal value of all student loans of $15.7 billion NZD in 2017.

All of what is described in the previous subsection is deeply reflective of the shift towards individualization, understood by Beck (1992, p. 88) as being a situation where the individual has the responsibility of choosing and changing their social identity as well as taking the risks in doing so (see also Chapter 2). It is also clear that, as Black and Walsh (2019, p. 36) comment, the 'social possibilities of higher education [are now] largely subsumed by economic purposes'. The notion of education as a public good that works to the benefit of many, not just its 'consumer', by enhancing intercultural competence and moral obligation to social justice and to others, has been abandoned. Education has become a private matter, and its success is measured only in terms of the employability of individuals, with liberal arts subjects (such as the humanities and social sciences) especially coming under attack for a presumed inability to offer the right 'skills'.

VET programmes: 'churning' and 'warehousing' the young

A second issue that we need to recognize is that the expansion of vocational education and training (VET) training courses has also seen an increase in lower skilled young people being 'warehoused' and 'churned' through the system. This tends to be more relevant to the unemployed and low-income earners in a variety of short-term programs. Researchers have found that a high degree of 'churning' between employability qualification programmes and low paid work is becoming common practice (Tomlinson, 2013). We have seen the deliberate creation of a system largely concerned with managing the unemployed when work remains scarce. It has been argued that at least some parts of the VET system have been left to '… fill the vacuum left by the decline in youth jobs and traditional industrial apprenticeships that arise as a result of the post-industrial changes' (Allen and Ainley, 2010, p. 41). More scathingly, Atkins (2010) has illuminated how the general discourse around the VET system in the UK is bound up with negative sentiment:

> [The discourse] frames these young people in need of or heading towards such programs as 'low achievers with low aspirations', routinely dismisses them as non-academic, yet claims to offer opportunities in the form of a vocational education which, according to the rhetoric, will lead to a lifelong nirvana of high-skill, high-paid work, personal satisfaction and opportunity (providing they continue to engage in lifelong learning) and this is something which many young people take on trust.

There is a vivid classed reality here. VET courses have never been especially attractive to the middle classes, and young people from lower social class backgrounds are over-represented in the VET sector. For instance, Australian data from the mid-2000s (Foley, 2007) show that the VET participation rate was greatest in low socio-economic areas (12.7 students per 100 population), and significantly higher than the national participation rate (10.8 per cent). In contrast, high socio-economic areas recorded a significantly lower participation rate (8.7 per cent) by comparison with the national average and other socio-economic regions. VET participation was also disproportionately higher among young people based in regional and rural locales. Newer Australian data (Webb et al., 2017) complicate this somewhat, showing that more middle class young people are now entering into *higher* vocational qualifications than their lower social class counterparts. Nonetheless, Webb et al. (2017, p. 156) contend this is due to the process of high SES or middle class students 'redressing their weak school performance by accessing new degree provision' and as such taking steps to maintain their **positional advantage** and avoid downward social mobility. Webb et al. explain that this process can be seen to mirror wider trends where tertiary expansion appears to have, inadvertently or otherwise, served to benefit middle class young people more than working class or lower SES young people (see Furlong and Cartmel, 2007; Elias and Purcell, 2012). We shall return to this in our discussion of the impact of these changes on **widening participation**.

Positional advantage: The need to stand out in the crowd as a result of the 'massification' of higher education.

Widening participation: A policy aimed at increasing the numbers of people with higher education qualifications, especially those from backgrounds with traditionally low levels of university participation.

Widening participation

Social class inequality

Despite, or perhaps because of, its expansion, the experience of young people in post-16 education is highly differentiated. This is sometimes masked in discussions of the absolute growth of the sector, but is an issue central to the research of youth sociologists. In this section, we will explore contributions on how inequality continues to be socially reproduced throughout the system.

Thinking points

- Who are the main social groups that enter university?
- What percentage of university students are from the working class?

Inequality operates in terms of social class, gender and ethnicity. For example, in OECD countries, young people's attainment and patterns of participation are affected by the class location of their parents (OECD, 2018). Parental education, sometimes a proxy for class position, is particularly influential. Across OECD countries, young people with highly educated parents are between two and six times more likely to complete tertiary education. Chesters and Watson (2013) found that, in the Australian context, men with a university-educated father were 2.8 times more likely to have graduated from university than other men, and that women with a university-educated father were 3.7 times more likely to have graduated from university than other women. Other interesting facts derived from international research show that elite and prestigious universities are less likely to admit young people from poorer backgrounds. For example, in the UK, Oxford and Cambridge have long recruited disproportionately from those who have attended elite private schools. Despite those private schools educating only 7 per cent of the UK population, their students represent 60 per cent of the student body at these elite universities. It is also the case that the odds of a child at a state secondary school who is eligible for free school meals in year 11 being admitted to Oxbridge by the age of 19 are almost 2,000 to 1 against. By contrast, the odds of a privately educated child being admitted to Oxbridge are 20 to 1 (Social Mobility and Poverty Commission, 2013).

There is also an internally differentiated market within higher education, in which different intuitions and different types of degree have a status hierarchy. As above, more prestigious and research-intensive universities, such as the Russell Group in the UK and the G08 in Australia, recruit far more middle class students than do the newer universities. Additionally, traditional degrees, at the aggregate level, are taken up far more by middle class students, and newer degrees, which are offered more in newer or less elite institutions, and which have less social esteem, are disproportionately taken up by working class students. Clear class divides exist within the university sector.

But it is not simply in the university sector where class operates. Within the VET sector, students from disadvantaged backgrounds are overrepresented in *lower-level* VET qualifications and under-represented in higher-level qualifications, particularly in diplomas and advanced diplomas. Most VET qualifications do not offer routes into typically

---

SES definition as a measure of social class

In Australia socioeconomic status (SES), '...refers to the social and economic position of a given individual, or group of individuals, within the larger society. Socioeconomic status is usually, but not always, conceived of as a relative concept and can be measured for the individual, family, household or community/area. The Australian Bureau of Statistics defines 'relative socioeconomic advantage and disadvantage in terms of people's access to material and social resources, and their ability to participate in society' (ABS, 2018, p. 5) As a measure it can be used as a proxy for a person's social class. It can include data on a person's economic resources, such as income and wealth ownership or whether they are on benefits; their type of housing tenure; their level of education; and whether they receive free school meals. One of its weaknesses is that what is included can vary by country and over time. As a result, comparisons both between and within countries are hard to achieve.

---

middle class jobs, and despite many new entry pathways being developed to facilitate transitions between the VET and university systems, lower level VET qualifications, in contrast to those at the higher level, offer no prospect of pathways from VET into higher education (Wheelahan, 2010). This means that, once students are embedded in vocational training, they become 'locked' into a pathway, 'escape' from which is unlikely. Even where students are increasingly undertaking vocational training in universities, this tends to occur in the lower-ranked, lesser-esteemed universities, rather than the elite universities, which are likely to better enhance future prospects. The key point here is that evidence from the UK, Australia and other Western countries all shows that the VET sectors are disproportionately populated by students of lower SES, and the highest SES groups are under-represented. In addition, despite an emphasis on work-related training, the VET sector predominantly leads to lower-level skills and low pay. What we see is that the 'human capital thesis' as a driver for educational expansion is both perpetuating and remaking inequality within the post-16 education and training system.

Gender and inequality

Prior to the 1990s, there were on average more male than female students in HE across OECD member countries. Since then there has been a 'revolution' in almost all countries, as women in most industrialized societies have become more likely to participate in HE. Women accounted for 46 per cent of students in higher education in 1985 (1.2 men for every woman). However, the faster increase in female participation in higher education has reversed the trend in OECD member countries (but of course not in most of the rest of the world). For example, in New Zealand, women make up 62 per cent of the higher education participation rate (https://www.educationcounts. govt.nz/statistics/tertiary-education/participation). Accordingly, young women now have a higher propensity to study at HE levels and a corresponding higher propensity to obtain degrees (OECD, 2018). The widening of the gap between men and women does not reflect a decline in the number of degrees awarded to men but rather the higher rate of growth in the percentage of women graduates.

💭 Thinking points

- Are young men or young women more likely to go to university and why?
- What subjects do you think are dominated by young women and why?

Measuring gender in university participation

The statistical data on university participation by gender are very limited and tend not to record many of the LGBTIQ+ categories. It usually does not allow for people to identify themselves outside of the fixed gender boundaries of male and female, reinforcing the gender binary.

Gender presents us with interesting, seemingly paradoxical, issues. Despite being more likely to repeat a grade, drop out of school, and not attain a tertiary education, young men still have better employment and earning outcomes than young women (OECD, 2018). It is also the case that, after nearly 20 years of increased participation in universities, women still earn, depending on country and occupation, between 10 per cent and 20 per cent less than male workers. These disproportionate employment outcomes and incomes extend to the higher education setting, where men are vastly over-represented at the level of professor and in the highest management positions. There also remain continuing inequalities in terms of access to degrees. Barone's (2011) quantitative analysis of international data showed that, across eight advanced Western countries, gender segregation in terms of subjects studied remains entrenched. Young women tend to choose education, the arts, humanities and health, while young men do sciences, engineering and medicine. Not only this, but when young women do study some of the male-dominated subjects, they tend to be from the most affluent families (Barone, 2011). In terms of VET programmes, we see similar trends for young women. For example, in both the UK and Australia, traditionally VET programmes were targeted at young men. More recently we have seen more young women entering apprenticeships. For example, in the UK, nearly 60 per cent of all apprenticeships are held by young women (Fuller and Unwin, 2013). However, similar to university, subject segregation is significant, with women disproportionately participating in childcare (96 per cent women), hairdressing (90 per cent) and health sector training (86 per cent), compared with young men, who dominate areas such as engineering (97 per cent men), construction (97 per cent) and IT and telecommunications (91 per cent). We also see pay differentials even worse than the national average, being 21 per cent in favour of males (compared with the 11 per cent national average).

Ethnicity and inequality

Finally, it is critical to recognize that inequalities exist in the post-16 education and training field for different ethnic groups. In the UK, a major trend in participation has been the significant rise in the number of young people from different ethnic backgrounds. In fact, the massification of higher education has resulted in those from an ethnic background being 10–15 per cent more likely to go to university compared with the White population (Crawford and Greaves, 2015). English as a first language and proximity to London increase the chances of young minority ethnic people going to university, and their low SES status is less of an indicator compared with young White British people. However, the increased participation of different ethnic groups in higher education does not translate into significant improvements in their employment positions after leaving university. For example, young people from Black Caribbean backgrounds have the lowest rate of professional employment six months after graduation, and this gap continues over the next four years (HEFC, 2015).

In countries such as Australia, New Zealand and Canada, the 'race question' is strongly shaped by their histories of colonization. These countries have large Indigenous populations that have historically been marginalized and exploited due to colonialism. As a result, the involvement of young Indigenous people in universities has historically been low. While governments have claimed to be addressing these low numbers, low levels of participation have remained entrenched. For example, on average only about 5 per cent of all young people of Aboriginal and Torres Strait ancestry aged 18 and 19 enter university, compared with 30 per cent of the White population of Australia. A similar pattern exists in New Zealand and Canada. We also see high attrition rates for Indigenous populations and a concentration of Indigenous students in arts and humanities courses, with small numbers in science and engineering courses. We also see that more Indigenous students are involved in VET programmes compared with the White populations of these countries.

Causes of inequality in post-16 education and training

A substantial body of work has emerged in youth sociology, looking at the inequality in post-16 education and training that draws, particularly, on the ideas and theoretical and practical tools of Pierre Bourdieu. As we saw in Chapter 2, Bourdieu's work is having a major impact in youth sociology, and it is in the field of post-16 education where we start to see his approach operationalized and offering a way of understanding how inequality is being socially reproduced.

Thinking points

- Why do you think some social groups are more likely to go to university than others?
- What factors operate to give some groups more opportunities than others?

A lack of 'aspiration'?

Much of the blame for the ongoing low numbers of working class young people entering university has been laid at the door of 'low aspiration'. Such a claim is problematic as it constructs the problem as one of individual failure and weakness. That said, it is clear that most young people from middle class or elite backgrounds have what Ball et al. (2002, p. 69) call 'deeply normalised grammars of aspiration' (p. 69). This means that, for most such young people, going to university is embedded in their culture and language. The low representation of certain groups at university is claimed to result from a lack of appropriate educational aspirations amongst the poor. Such an approach, while sometimes emphasizing the financial burdens involved, does little to foreground social-structural factors, and instead locates barriers to participation at the level of the individual. Research has, however, repeatedly illustrated that the 'low aspirations' discourse is predicated on a myth (Roberts and Evans, 2013). This debunking has been achieved by both quantitative and qualitative research. For instance, Berrington et al. (2016) analyzed a representative large-scale survey in the UK and revealed that, while there were class, ethnicity and gender gaps in higher education aspirations, across all groups the majority of teenagers did aspire to go to university. In the Australian context, Gore et al.'s (2015) large-scale analysis also found relatively small differences in aspirations between socio-economic groups. These researchers also 'caution against both simplistic policy directives and superficial educational interventions in a field where complexity prevails' (Gore et al., 2015, p. 177). A crucial point here is that there is a gap between young people's aspirations, which are usually high, and their *expectations*. Kintrea et al. (2015) explain that, because young people's self-efficacy, self-esteem, confidence and motivation are affected by social and economic circumstances, expectations can become reduced, and this can shape or re-adjust aspirations, or even lead young people to refrain from talking about their 'real aspirations'. In other words, aspirations are socially and culturally framed by the context young people find themselves in. A good example can be found in Mullen's (2009) research in the USA. This shows that concerns about elitism at universities led students from less privileged backgrounds to consider a place at prestigious Ivy League institutions as out of the realm of the possible and somewhere they would not fit into. This contrasted strongly with students from wealthy backgrounds, whose choice of an Ivy League university place functioned more as an expectation, normalized by parental ideals and explicit high school positioning. It seemed natural for them to apply to such an institution.

Thinking point

Reflect back to when you made your decision to come to university – what influenced your choices and why did you take the degree that you did?

Lastly, this body of work has also shown how 'incitements to aspiration and the implications of these are gendered' as well as classed (Allen, 2014, p. 762). This is particularly clear in accounts of aspiration that situate young working class women, who might perhaps opt for motherhood over higher education, as 'ungovernable, excessive, and immoral…[and] the failing femininity of the ideal neoliberal subject' (Allen, 2014, p. 762). Alternatively, elite schools can and do foster 'a habitus which [is] grounded in a strong self-belief and high levels of self-esteem, a confidence and sense of efficacy about the self and the future' (Forbes and Maxwell, 2018). In this context, aspiration is highly structured.

Choice-making mechanisms for young women for deciding whether to go to university, or which university to attend, can also be greatly influenced by their class. For example, class and gender combine to produce particular consequences for the location of the institution of choice. In Evans' (2009) study, young women from a working class background tended to prefer to remain closer to home in order to retain their wider contribution to familial caring roles and duties. These factors often go overlooked and might instead be presumed to be the province of mothers (such as a role, however small, in caring for older relatives or younger siblings). Simultaneously, elite institutions were viewed by working class young women as middle class (often masculine) spaces from which working class girls are symbolically excluded. Evans comments that, to the young working class women of her study, the 'elite' university felt like 'Hogwarts' because of formal dinners, the attire of teaching staff (e.g. gowns), and paintings of old middle class White men. These institutional settings discouraged young working class women from going to the top universities. But why then, even if they enter university, do most young women end up on courses that are highly gendered?

Research with children as young as primary age and their parents has shown that science subjects are understood as unfeminine and thus undesirable (Archer et al., 2013). Archer et al. (2013) note an enormous body of existing research evidence that indicates most children are aware that mathematics and/or science (but particularly the physical sciences) are 'for boys'. Young women are then likely to perceive STEM subjects as an unrealistic prospect, or experience rejection and/ or hostility from their male peers and friends for choosing STEM subjects (Leaper, 2015). Women who do physics and engineering wrestle with the tension of being esteemed as *both* a competent scientist *and* a woman, such that they erase their femininity to be taken seriously. To avoid this stigma, STEM subject are less likely to be chosen (Archer et al., 2017). Alongside this perception of the culture of science, teachers and even the curriculum are features that ensure a '... pervasive alignment of science with masculinity... [which] creates an identity gap that prevents many girls/women – particularly those from minority ethnic and/or socially disadvantaged backgrounds – from identifying with science' (Archer et al., 2017, p. 90). The outcome is that young people internalize arbitrary ideas like 'physics is masculine', 'physics is hard' and 'boys are better at hard subjects like physics'. These ideas are not 'truths', but are perceived and understood as such. The effect of this internalization is that there are 'formidable barriers and blocks to girls/women's progression through from compulsory to post-compulsory education, higher education, and into scientific workplaces' (Archer et al., 2017, p. 90).

'Being a fish out of water' at university

Beyond access to and choices of university, the *lived experience* of being at university is highly classed. This is especially the case in the UK. This can happen because of a wide range of factors, including '... university decision-making processes, funding strategies, and struggles to compete with middle-class peers' (Bradley and Ingram, 2013, p. 68). A number of examples exist. Lehmann (2012) shows that those lacking in sufficient economic and social resources face exclusion from culturally enriching extra-curricular activities while at university and so longstanding inequalities become reinforced. Often, even financial resources will not suffice; Allen and Hollingworth (2013) consider how middle-class young people are able to deploy a range of social, cultural and economic resources to access placements in the creative industries. These are *required* efforts to try to stand out from peers in a period of social congestion, produced by a complex amalgam of political decisions and social processes. Navigating this highly contested terrain can also be a problem for middle class young people, as accruing the right capitals to do well in such a positional competition is not a level playing field. Therefore, the middle classes are also increasingly engaged in a secret war for positional advantage.

Young working-class people have also been observed to suffer from the 'closure' behaviours of class-based groups. This prevents proper integration into the university setting and constrains the development of social capital, potentially undermining equality of experience. Even where more 'successful' working-class experiences have been documented, substantial identity work is often required for working-class students to 'fit in' after entering elite institutions (Reay et al., 2010). Of course, support networks are also important while at university. Families without a history of university struggle to be an effective resource. Those working class families who have never been to university do not always have knowledge of or familiarity with university systems. The lack of past experiences means such families tend to provide what we might term 'in the moment' support, which is more practical and emotional.

Thinking point

When you arrived at university did you feel like 'a fish out of water' or a 'fish in water'? Why might that be?

Family support: cultural, social and economic capital

Beyond this discussion of how one *feels* in the HE setting, researchers have also been keen to consider the role parents and other family members play in helping young people navigate the education and training system via financial (or related material) contributions. The level and type of support parents might provide clearly varies by social class practices and financial income. Given the shift in how education is now funded, young people find themselves with higher costs, greater risk of debt and limited means to pay their own way. As a result, parents are now making greater monetary contributions compared with previous decades. What we find is that students who received most from families '… tended to be from more "traditional" student backgrounds: they were younger, white, living away from home.' (West et al., 2015, p. 26). Parents not only make contributions towards fees and accommodation costs but also everyday shopping, train fares, laptops, clothes and leisure items such as gym membership. This is sometimes further supplemented by grandparents and other family members. Australian research, meanwhile, shows co-residence is a significant form of support. Most young people in Australia will attend a 'local' university and remain living in the family home as a major way of keeping the costs of university low (Cobb-Clark and Gørgens, 2014). However, those young people from families receiving welfare support are less likely to live at home as it creates an extra cost for the family that is hard to manage.

Thinking points

- What kind of support do families give to their young people while at university?
- How might it differ by class, gender and ethnicity?
- How can this support be understood as social and cultural capital?

Class, work and study

Another critical factor in creating a differentiated university experience is whether or not young people (need to) pursue paid employment during their studies. The distinction between work and education has become blurred, and the two fields now exhibit some intimate overlaps; as the number of young people in university has grown, so too has the proportion of students who combine work (most often part-time) and study. For UK students, this figure is over 50 per cent, and this is similar in Australia and New Zealand. Tuition fees, first through their introduction and then various and quite dramatic increases, are one part of the explanation. However, increased fees are only part of the story. There has been a steady abolition of state maintenance grants, and while they have been replaced with loans and a wide range of bursaries, the cost of being a student requires more than just fee payments: rent, bills, food and drink, costs for books, materials and/or extracurricular activities, travel, clothing and socializing. In short, students have significant living costs, like everyone else.

Recent research by Jewell (2014) is telling in that it demonstrates that term-time employment is more likely to be undertaken for financial reasons than for enhancement of transferrable skills, and that people with such motivations are more likely to be 'from lower socioeconomic backgrounds, [have] less financial support from their families and [have] therefore a higher expected debt on graduation' (2014, p. 10). She explains the advantages of not having to work, stating unequivocally that 'those who are obliged to work, or who work with a greater intensity [...] experience the larger negative effects on their academic performance'. Some research points out complexities, such as how working-class students present their jobs as opportunities to build a sense of belonging or even leadership skills, but ultimately their employment results in their being less likely to engage in valuable extracurricular activity. Employment during studies is not problematic per se, but the need to work and the amount of time committed is an issue, and motivations to work longer are very often associated with needing to deal with pressures; i.e. they are classed pressures.

The critical point here is that, because those from marginalized social backgrounds are more likely to seek part-time employment, student employment risks exacerbating inequality. Roberts and Li (2017) highlighted how middle class students deploy their parents' economic capital to cushion the blow of joblessness, meaning that the quality of their diets, social activities and efforts at extra-curricular cultural enhancement are not sacrificed. The opposite was found for working-class students, whose lack of capital left them vulnerable to lack of access to many valuable capital-building enterprises. These students also lacked the luxury of even contemplating the idea that, for example, the exam period should be a time when job searching can be allowed to become less of a priority. Middle-class students were willing and able to choose to avoid employment when it was deemed detrimental to their studies.

> ☁ **Thinking point**
>
> Think about your own experience and that of your friends. Have you had to work while at university – if so why and how much? Do you think it has affected your study?

Why are fewer young men going to university?

So far, our discussion has concentrated on either the classed or gendered experience of going to university, but it is also important to take an intersectional approach. The issue of young men's under-representation in higher education is also of interest to sociologists. A critical feature of this debate, one which sometimes goes unstated, is that it is working class boys and young men who make up the largest proportion of non-participating males. Indeed, as we have stressed already, despite its growth and expansion, HE participation 'continues to be monopolized by those from higher socio-economic classes' (Loveday, 2015, p. 570).

> ☁ **Thinking points**
>
> • Why do you think men's participation in university is dropping?
> • Why might they see it as a 'risk' compared with young women?

A key point here is that what appears at face value to be a question of gender is, in fact, also a question of class. Indeed, even when persuaded to talk about the lack of participation from boys from 'poorer' backgrounds, the full scale of the impact of class is usually watered down. This is because, as Ashley (2009, p. 181) neatly summarizes, 'gender often has a smaller effect size than race or social class, yet it is boys to whom the media often turn first for good stories'. Nonetheless, sociological research has offered a range of insights into the relationship between masculinity and working class young men's decisions not to go to university. First, it is important to acknowledge that working class boys achieve, on average, lower levels of qualifications at school. These educational profiles can make it difficult to gain entry into university. Indeed, qualifications form part of young people's **'horizons for action'** (Hodkinson, 1998) as they finish their compulsory education. These horizons are partly determined by the availability of external opportunities but also partly by internal subjective perceptions of what seems possible and, importantly, 'what might be appropriate' (Hodkinson, 1998, p. 304). Furthermore, Ball et al. (2002) have illustrated that young people with access to particular types of social, cultural and economic capital are likely to be 'embedded choosers', for whom entering university is deemed to be part of a normalized process of transition and a necessary bridge between education and employment. Alternatively, young people from working class and other less advantaged backgrounds can only make decisions about engagement with university after giving due consideration to overcoming various barriers. Research has shown that current available finances and material circumstances and/or future projections of personal debt have a central role in deciding

Horizons for action': The internal subjective perceptions of what seems possible and 'what might be appropriate' for an individual's educational journey.

whether to study locally and live in the parental home or to move away – or indeed whether to go to university at all (Abrahams and Ingram, 2013).

Sociological research has made it very clear that, for many working class young people, university participation is seen as an 'investment risk' (Reay, 2017). Young men's particular decisions to avoid higher education can be better understood through this lens, which allows us to see that they do not always make a totally technical, rational, calculated decision. Instead, post-16 options are pursued as part of 'the socially constructed and historically derived common base of knowledge, values and norms for action that people grow into and come to take as a natural way of life' (Hodkinson, 1998, p. 304). Here, working class masculinity can be added to the mix to help make sense of men's low rates of HE participation. Some have argued that working-class masculinity has not fully caught up with the demands of the globalized, technology-led world (Marks, 2003), while others have suggested that working class men retain an understanding that 'women learn and men earn' (McGivney, 2004). Some men might emphasize the importance of being a breadwinner, while many will prioritize achievable economic returns, and minimize related risks (Roberts, 2018). Given a perceived high risk of educational failure, and in a context in which they are required to transform their identity and commit to a difficult and often impossible transition from struggling to successful learner, the attitudes and apprehensions exhibited become more understandable (Reay, 2017; Roberts, 2018).

Beyond material needs and potential risks to incomes, risks for young men also pertain to socially sanctioned identities. Studies illustrate that 'doing' working class masculinity often requires that working class men prioritize their male peer group; emphasize 'doing' heterosexual hegemonic masculinity; being social 'leaders'; playing football; chasing girls and having fun (Archer et al., 2001). University is often cast as a feminized terrain; something that can compromise one's masculine identity as it is associated with a less appropriate version of masculinity – the so-called geek or boffin – and reflective of the old understanding that, as above, 'women learn and men earn'. Nonetheless, Roberts (2018) suggests that the assumed rejection of the education system as a feminized one is an oversimplification. Instead, greater attention must be paid to how 'men's disadvantaged positions within interconnecting power relations renders participation a less feasible and realistic route' (Archer et al., 2001, p. 446).

Graduate employment

The 'broken promise'

So far, our discussion has focussed on questions of access to post-16 education and training and the 'university experience'. In the next chapter, we will discuss young people's relationship to paid work in more detail, but here we want to focus on outcomes and how inequality within the graduate labour market influences the future trajectories of young people.

It is important to start our discussion by thinking about what has happened to the economy in terms of jobs for highly educated and skilled young people, especially those who have invested in getting a university degree. As discussed earlier, in the 1990s it was proposed that the future economy would be built on knowledge not manufacturing, and making 'things with your hands' would not be core to the types of jobs being created. Future generations, it was claimed, would need to have relevant 'human capital' and new skills. The 'knowledge economy', as an idea, is embedded in education and economic policy around the globe. However, the very notion of the knowledge economy has been heavily criticized by a wide range of academic research, with contemporary labour markets representing what Brown et al. (2011) describe as the 'broken promise'. In essence, this suggests that what was promised has not 'arrived' and a clear mismatch exists between the skill levels of young people and the types of jobs that are now available. The massive investment by governments in expanding the education system, the array of policies geared towards growing and widening partici-pation, and the almost relentless rhetoric around the need for individuals to engage in skill development and/or become 'knowledge workers' has produced a highly trained and skilled workforce. However, the contemporary economic reality is at odds with these demands, and 'the qualifications that [young people] are accumulating do not always guarantee them the future they are seeking' (France, 2016, p. 85), let alone what they were promised.

As suggested by the knowledge economy thesis, higher paying, highly skilled jobs that require thinking, planning, creativity and emotional intelligence have opened up at the top of many advanced economies, but economies have also massively expanded in terms of lower skilled jobs at the bottom. In both cases these tend to be the types of jobs that are less easy to automate, including not only skilled professional and managerial jobs, but also things like shelf stacking, and most customer-facing, front line interactive service roles in cafes, restaurants, shops, and aged and disability care.

This troubles some of the basic tenets of the human capital thesis that are so important to the knowledge economy arguments. Indeed, despite the policy emphasis on encouraging participation in tertiary education, there are now many highly edu-cated young people in so-called advanced societies who are unemployed or working in low-skill, low-pay jobs (MacDonald, 2011; France, 2016). Indeed, Spain and Greece, countries with the highest unemployment rates in Europe, have the most highly edu-cated young people in Europe (Roberts and Antonucci, 2015). Meanwhile, the MENA countries (Middle Eastern and North African nations such as Morocco, Egypt, Jordan and Saudi Arabia) have much higher rates of unemployment among tertiary graduates than among those with basic qualifications (Drine, 2017).

The last piece of the puzzle of the broken promise of education relates to graduate career outcomes. A broader discussion of employment is offered in Chapter 4, but here we draw out those connections between the investment made in education under the auspices of the human capital/ knowledge economy approach that was sold to students, and the subsequent reality of the 'pay off'. Green (2017, p. 40) summarizes the problem: 'Compared to their parents' generation, all groups have, on average, received more years of schooling and gained higher level qualifications but this does not necessarily translate in better job prospects'. As we noted in the first half of the chapter, one half of the promise made to young people has come to fruition. Even if we put aside the inequalities in access, experience and outcomes, the expansion of education has made it a 'mass' experience in advanced nations. But a significant 'bro-ken' element in the promise of the knowledge economy relates to graduates' labour market outcomes.

Inequality in the graduate labour market

Graduate qualifications are purported to provide an array of protections, such as reduced chances of being unemployed and higher salary returns over the working lifetime relative to less highly educated peers. Correspondingly, however, graduate returns and experiences are highly unequal and the better point of comparison is *between* graduates. Research on the differences in outcomes of those who attend university has been sparse, although a growing body of evidence confirms that significant differences exist among graduates in terms of who benefits most from going to university.

Thinking point

- Reflecting on your own circumstances, are there activities you get involved in with the aim of improving your chances of getting into the type of work you want when you leave university?
- What types of things are done by others you know, and is everybody able to undertake such activities?

Graduates from advantaged or privileged backgrounds (and particularly those who had been privately educated) achieve employment in higher-status occupations and earn higher returns from their degree than their working class peers (Friedman and Laurison, 2019). Being privately educated is significant and creates a premium over and above doing a degree. Crawford and Vignoles (2014) showed that graduates who attended private secondary schools earned approximately 7 per cent more per year, on average, than state school students 3.5 years after graduation, even when comparing otherwise similar graduates and controlling for differences in degree subject, university attended and degree classification. Relatedly, Britton et al.'s (2016) analysis of major administrative data showed that parental income remains the most significant feature in determining the future career trajectories and incomes of young people after university. As a result, the average gap in earnings between students from higher- and lower-income backgrounds is £8,000 a year for men and £5,300 a year for women, ten years after graduation (Britton et al., 2016).

The status of the university attended also contributes to maintaining this inequality in some countries. As noted above, when young people from working class backgrounds attend university, they often cluster in particular university types. Variations in future incomes exist between those who attended elite and high-performing universities, for example between the 'Russell Group' universities and the 'new' universities in the UK. Given that most working-class young people attend the lower status universities, earnings after leaving university are often significantly lower. This is much less clear-cut in Australia. The body of evidence in Australia has produced mixed results, but the most recent analysis by Caroll et al. (2018) finds that, while there is a starting salary/wage premium for graduates from Australia's elite Go8 institutions, it is relatively small, ranging from 4.3 per cent to 5.5 per cent. Moreover, these researchers have determined that large chunks of this wage premium are related to the higher than average **ATAR** scores of the students these institutions recruit.

ATAR: Is a national based percentile ranking based on upper secondary performance of an entire school year cohort.

Social and cultural capital and CV building

Various studies show how these classed processes create different types of educational experience that enhance differentiated opportunities both within and after university. One example is the ability of those from wealthier backgrounds to develop their CV during and beyond university (Health et al., 2007). For example, the 'gap year' is seen as an important form of cultural capital for bringing added value to graduate CVs. Traditionally the 'gap year' was seen as 'time off' or a chance for personal growth, but the contemporary competitive environment has led to the professionalization of travel, and a sense of instrumental purpose (Snee, 2013). Rather than the 'gap year' being about 'unproductive' fun and leisure travel, neoliberal discourses place greater value on 'career development' possibilities and the production of a 'public image' of self that is appealing to employers. However, 'gap years' remain dominated by the middle class and elite, who have both the economic resources and family support to facilitate these ventures (King, 2011; Haverig and Roberts, 2011). As these types of activities gain greater institutional recognition, they prove to be a form of social distinction (King, 2011). For example, Heath (2007) suggests gap years are a middle-class response to the widening participation agenda in higher education, in that they help produce new forms of embodied cultural capital in the form of '… soft skills, greater maturity, enhanced self-awareness and increased independence' (Heath, 2007, p. 100; see also Snee, 2013). This is advantageous when seeking graduate work, and is part of the effort to accrue positional advantage (Brown et al., 2011).

Access to the best internships

The ability of young graduates to use their social and cultural capital to advantage themselves in the labour market is also evident in getting access to the best internships. Grugulis and Stoyanova's (2012) study of the film and TV industry is a good example. They explained how social capital advantaged White, middle-class men and ensured that middle-class signals came to be proxies for the most sought-after jobs. This kind of process often starts in universities, with middle-class students using their family embedded social capital to be able to access the best internships (Shade and Jacobson, 2015; Bathmaker et al., 2013), and then within those same internships further strengthen their networks. Internships, indeed, have been identified across many nations as being critical for maintaining and developing advantage. Shade and Jacobson's (2015) study of Canadian graduates showed that those from privileged backgrounds dominate internships in the 'creative sector'. Such opportunities tend to be 'employment based', and lead to paid and more permanent work, yet there is a strong bias in who gets access to the best internships. Leonard et al.'s (2016) observations of complex rationalizations and mixed motivations for undertaking internships are important here. They found that, for young people, internships were becoming the 'new degree' and the new 'must have' form of differentiation for accessing good jobs.

This is not simply about the ways young people and their parents use their capital(s) to gain advantage, but also about employers. For example, even though the number and diversity of university graduates have increased substantially, employers recruiting in the financial sector still recruit interns from the elite group of universities (Brown et al., 2011). Graduate recruitment agencies tend to target the most selective institutions, which are dominated not only by the highly educated, but also the wealthiest (e.g. Cambridge, Oxford, the London School of Economics, UCL and the University of Manchester). This is relevant in terms of ensuring employment, for these groups, in some of the key professions that not only have greater influence in decision making in the state but also have greater security of tenure and career opportunities (Social Mobility and Child Poverty Commission, 2013). Once again, class is critical to the process of graduate recruitment.

The 'class ceiling'

One final point that is important to note relates to what Friedman and Laurison (2019) call the 'class ceiling'. Allied to this is research on wage returns among upwardly mobile graduates in the UK (Friedman and Laurison, 2019). Friedman and colleagues demonstrate that significant wage inequality also exists *within* elite occupational groups. Focussing on just the highest occupational social class, they show a clear gradient that implies a working class background produces a wage penalty relative to those who were born into and remain in the highest social class upon entering the labour market. They also found clear classed compositions of workforces, with the more traditionally middle class professions tending to recruit predominantly graduates of middle class origin, compared with technical industries, such as IT or engineering, which recruit more diversely.

Thinking point

Can you think of any other employers whose objective recruitment criteria use social magic to obscure exclusionary process? Use your internet browser to search for some advertising material on graduate employment opportunities. Can you apply the 'social magic' conversion table to this material?

Tholen (2017) adds to this understanding of how the graduate market operates against those from working class backgrounds. He suggests that, while more working class young people have become graduates, they have not become more socially mobile. Instead, they remain concentrated in recently professionalized occupations, in part because of the practices of symbolic closure produced and practised in combination by middle class students and families, elite educational institutions and elite professions and occupations. This complicity in the process of how inequality is maintained is highlighted in the practices of Harvard and Stanford, where students are funnelled into highly prestigious employment. Ultimately, those from less privileged backgrounds are not only less likely to enter elite universities; they may also have fewer cultural resources to legitimize their own educational and social trajectory (Binder et al., 2016).

'Social magic' and the pre-hiring of graduates at Google

Ingram and Allen's (2018) analysis of the 'pre-hiring' practices of Google and Price Waterhouse Cooper (PwC) used a notion called 'social magic' (popularized by Pierre Bourdieu).This process shows how personal capacities designated as 'objective' and 'natural' operate to give advantages to certain groups. The table below shows how Google (and other graduate recruiters) use seemingly objective criteria in their 'talent spotting' recruitment process (the left column), but that this is achieved by denying the socially structured measures they are really testing for (the right column). (ECAs are extracurricular activities that can enhance your CV) (Table 3.1).

Table 3.1 Ingram and Allen's (2018) 'Google' social magic conversion table

'Objective' criteria	Socially structured 'Capital'
Strong educational credentials	Degree from an elite global university
Passion and natural curiosity	'Good' ECAs; interesting leisure pursuits
Highly-motivated	Internship (ideally with Google); financially supported by parents and sourced through family social networks
Go-getting self starter/ entrepreneurship	Entrepreneurial activity undertaken in spare time; supported by available economic capital
Quirkiness, like-mindedness	At ease in interview setting; supported via institutional assessment preparation and family networks
Committed to the 'Google Family'	Able to participate in work social activities; unburdened by caring responsibilities or other commitments

These kinds of processes work to further exclude people from specific backgrounds, and prioritize the recruitment of others. Such unwritten and unspoken advantages in the graduate labour market are argued to contribute directly to the classed and gendered inequalities that are so visible in graduate labour market outcomes.

 ## Summary

- The post-16 education system has expanded massively in the last 30 years. This applies to vocational education and more particularly to university education.

- Governments in most OECD countries have followed a path of 'upskilling' their populations because of a commitment of the central tenet of the 'knowledge society' – it assumes today's jobs demand a highly qualified population.

- While education is thought to be a way to promote upward social mobility, very often it works to reflect, reproduce or entrench existing societal inequalities.

- Gender, class and race all remain big influences on access to 'elite' educational institutions and/ or the type of degree studied.

- Educational attainment, aspirations and attitudes are all shaped by social processes and social forces; they are not simply a result of individual aptitudes and efforts.

- Those with the best composition of cultural, social and economic 'capital' are advantaged in the competition for graduate employment. It is a highly unequal 'playing field'.

Exercise: The sociological imagination

Compare your experience in higher education with that of your parents or older family members. Did they attend university? What work did/do they do? Consider the impact of changing social and cultural norms of gender, and what role social class might play in your experience of higher education today.

Key readings

Allen, K. & Hollingworth, S. (2013) '"Sticky subjects" or "cosmopolitan creatives"? Social class, place and urban young people's aspirations for work in the knowledge economy', *Urban Studies*, vol. 50, no. 3, pp. 499–517.

Archer, L. et al. (2017) 'The exceptional" physics girl: a sociological analysis of multi-method data from young women aged 10–16 to explore gendered patterns of post-16 participation', *American Educational Research Journal*, vol. 54, no. 1, pp. 88–126.

Brown, P. Lauder, H. & Ashton, D. (2011) *The Global Auction: The Broken Promises of Education, Jobs, and Incomes* (Oxford University Press).

Ingram, N. & Allen, K. (2018) '"Talent-spotting" or "social magic"? Inequality, cultural sorting and constructions of the ideal graduate in elite professions', *The Sociological Review*, 0038026118790949.

Loveday, V. (2015) 'Working-class participation, middle-class aspiration? Value, upward mobility and symbolic indebtedness in higher education', *Sociological Review*, vol. 63, no. 3, pp. 570–588.

McKay & Devlin. (2014) '"Uni has a different language … to the real world": demystifying academic culture and discourse for students from low socioeconomic backgrounds', *Higher Education Research & Development*, vol. 33, no. 5, pp. 949–861.

4 YOUTH, WORK AND UN(DER)EMPLOYMENT

In this chapter you will learn about:

- The important role that paid work plays in the lives of young people
- The growth of interest in NEETs (those not in education, employment or training) and how different governments are responding
- The growing development of underemployment and the collaborative economy and its impact on young people's relationships with paid work
- How we can understand young people's relationships with unemployment.

Work for the young in contemporary times

🗨 Thinking point

- What role does work play in your life currently?
- If you are working, does your current job relate to your future employment plans?
- Do you have a 'career plan' – a sense of what type of work you want to do in the future?

In this chapter, when talking about work, we use the term interchangeably with **employment**. There are different types of activity that are also definitely work – such as the unpaid labour most often undertaken by women in relation to caring for children and/ or other relatives – but our primary focus is young people's formal relationship with what we might describe as the formal economy that involves work for monetary compensation, or wages. Sociologists have for many decades been keen to focus on young people's transition from education into the workforce. Research by Norbert Elias in the 1960s aimed to understand how young people integrated into employment, especially their experience of workplace socialization and the adjustments that new young workers had to make to fit into a new social world. Beyond this, though, youth sociologists have long recognized that, in capitalist economies, employment is a pivotal foundation that underpins the broader transition to adulthood and independent living.

> **Employment:** A specific relationship between an employee and an employer, referring specifically to being paid to execute a task as the basis of some sort of contract. The term is not synonymous with 'work', which is a much wider term that incorporates both paid and unpaid work, domestic and household work.

When young people (or any of us) do paid work, we sell our labour power to an employer, and the wages we receive in return permit us (in theory, at least) to do things like exit the family home and make steps into the housing market, perhaps on our own, with a partner or with friends or others. We, of course, do not simply choose who we will work for and how much we will be remunerated. This has long been made evident by research in youth sociology, as exemplified by Roberts' (1968) proposition that we ought to shift our understandings of young people's 'occupational choice' towards an understanding of the *limits* to choice brought about by the employment 'opportunity structure'. This idea was further developed by Ashton and Field (1976), who explained how experiences at home and school intertwined with social class position to produce a relatively narrow set of career alternatives.

Paid work, or a lack of paid work, is about more than the transition to adulthood: having the means for survival, the means to flourish, to achieve status, to develop an identity, to be an active consumer. Paid work is also bound up with issues of respect, subordination, opportunities, commitment, feelings of alienation, pride, dignity or esteem, and is a realm linked to health and wellbeing. How young people fare on all these themes is of interest to us; that is, research on the world of work is about much more than the counting up of employment 'destinations' among young people after they finish their education. Indeed, the notion of destination holds less and less relevance. On one hand, the divide between education and work is becoming progressively blurry, as increasing numbers combine part time work with full time studies in high school and tertiary education. On the other hand, young people are much less likely than their parents' generation to start with a job, or even an occupation, that they will retain for their whole working life. Changes in economic conditions and their impact on social norms and the experience of work are a crucial element of this chapter. Before we move on to that, we first briefly discuss the broader, institutionally sanctioned inequalities that affect all young people in the world of work.

Inequalities for youth at work and the issue of youth wages

Young people occupy a very interesting and somewhat unique position in relation to employment. As we discuss later in this chapter, they're more likely to be unemployed than the general population, a trend that is amplified during economic recessions, with the recent Global Financial Crisis being no exception (France, 2016). Young people are subject to a range of other detrimental experiences. For example, young people are more likely to experience non-payment, especially for attending meetings or training; to be underpaid; to miss out on meal breaks; to work illegally long shifts; to feel pressured to work overtime; to lack adequate health and safety protections; and, as has been the case for decades, to have higher chances of workplace injury (Furlong et al., 2017). There is also the legitimated discrimination that occurs in relation to **youth wages**, which reflect an institutionalized process of paying young people lesser rates than their adult counterparts. This legal discrimination is enshrined in many national minimum wage legislations (France, 2016).

Youth wages: The institutionalized form of underpayment that allows employers to pay young people less than adults. This is usually a graded system, with the gap between adult and youth wages shrinking as a young person passes each birthday.

Thinking points

- Do you think young people are treated fairly in the labour market?
- Do you think young people should get paid the same as adults in the workplace?

In countries such as Turkey, Ireland and Portugal, young people are entitled to a specific fraction of the full adult minimum wage. However, other countries have very different and sometimes complex approaches. Australia, for example, as of July 2018, had a minimum wage of $18.93 AUD per hour, but the minimum wage for young people is less than this. Australia uses a gradational system, where the proportion of the adult wage that a young person is entitled to goes up with every birthday between 16 and 20. The minimum pay rate is $8.95 AUD at age 16, $10.94 AUD at 17, $12.93 at age 18; $15.61 at age 19; and $18.49 at age 20. The UK, New Zealand and a wide range of other Western nations operate on broadly similar lines. Young people are paid less than older people simply because of their age.

One thing that may have come to mind is the argument that young people lack the skills and experience of their older counterparts, which means suffering a wage and jobs penalty is to be expected. However, this economic principle and its rationality have been critiqued by academics. Price (2011) propose that we ought to remain aware that the labour market itself is *socially constructed*. The argument here is that young people are perceived and *constructed* as lacking in value and skills. Yet, rather than limited experience meaning having no skills, we might instead think of young people's skills and contributions to workplaces as being undervalued or even unrecognized.

The changing landscape of young people's working lives

Beyond these relatively consistent types of inequality that young people are subjected to in terms of their working lives, a central focus for youth sociologists has been the changing nature of work and its impact on youth transitions in contemporary times. The social and economic climates shaping young people's current experience of work is vastly different from previous generations. So, what exactly has changed, why has it changed and what consequences does it have for the young?

When talking about labour market change and young people, the usual point of reference is the period beginning just after World War II and lasting to around the middle to late 1970s. This period, sometimes referred to as the 'golden age of youth transitions', marked a change from previous decades, and was characterized by *predictability* and *linearity* with regard to young people's engagement with work. What this means is that, generally speaking, school to work transitions happened for the vast majority of young people at the school leaving age, and their journey to the labour market was relatively uncomplicated. Some stayed on at college and far fewer (mostly middle class people) stayed on to go to university (see Chapter 3), but the move from education to employment was a mass experience. Furthermore, because the period in question was a time when many countries' government policies were supportive of full employment, and jobs were in plentiful supply across low skilled sectors of the economy in manufacturing, getting a decently paid job was not especially difficult even with few or no qualifications.

This one-step, uniform process has been positioned by some researchers as overly romanticized. Vickerstaff (2003) and Goodwin and O'Connor (2005) draw on data from the UK to remind us that, even in such 'golden' times, the experience of work itself was not necessarily easy, with poor working conditions and low wages being the experience of some young people who had extended periods of being junior apprentices. Nonetheless, this period, as above, was marked by a relatively smooth fit between the education system and the manufacturing-dominated labour market. Transitions to stable work were understood as being the foundation of standardized life trajectories, which were easy to follow because one's parents and peers (in the same social class or locality) acted as communal points of reference. The period is sometimes called the era of 'Fordism', with the name noting the influence of the factory design implemented by Henry Ford (the car maker), where the standardization of working techniques was translated into the lives of young workers, creating standard rhythms and patterns of working weeks. It also notes that young people came straight out of education and into work in a fashion not dissimilar to a well-synchronized factory production line. The predictability of young people's engagement with work, however, began to crumble towards the end of the 1970s.

A combination of globalization, technological advancement and occupational change – alongside the steady erosion of welfare state protections informed by neoliberal political decision making across much of the Western world – worked together to rapidly transform many economies. While the labour market had absorbed many unqualified young people into the large number of unskilled jobs that existed up until the late 1970s, the outsourcing of much manufacturing and heavy industry to countries with lower operational and wage costs ensured that youth unemployment become a reality. This trend continued for several decades and was also accompanied by a turn to service-based employment. The industrialized nations are now often referred to as service- or consumer-based economies, having once been called production-based economies. This economic shift had profound consequences. Service-based economies were, and indeed still are, more strongly associated with part time and flexible work, 24/7 shift patterns, low wages, short-term, insecure, precarious or temporary work and, crucially, fewer protections in the form of trade unions and collective bargaining.

The political rhetoric deployed in many countries as these transformations were occurring focussed on the positive. The move from an industrialized era of work to a **post-Fordist economy** was argued to be centred on high-level products and services, high-end technologies and the development of a so-called knowledge economy, an argument that underscored drives across industrialized nations towards the 'massification' of higher education (see Chapter 3). Highly skilled 'knowledge intensive' jobs have opened up at

Fordist economy: This term denotes a type of economy centred on factory production lines, where tasks have been broken down into small specific details so they can be repeated to save time. A post-Fordist economy is one where products made on factory production lines have become a relatively small part of what the economy produces.

the top end of the labour markets, in banking, finance, and new technologies, but intermediate-level and technical jobs appear to have been increasingly sucked out of the economy, and there has been an expansion of manual or low-skilled jobs. In Australia, for example, despite 24 years of sustained economic growth, these structural changes in the Australian labour force have ushered in more low-wage and low-skilled work. American economists Goos and Manning (2007) explain that, in practice, labour markets have become characterized by a polarization between 'lovely jobs', characterized by stability and decent pay and conditions, and 'lousy jobs', those with few protections, high instability of tenure and low wages. Ending up in one or other of these jobs (as we return to below) is a classed form of social reproduction (Friedman and Laurinson, 2019).

These changes have had a massive and ongoing impact on the 'social timetable' of young people's lives, with youth transitions radically restructured, and entry to work being later and increasingly protracted. Indeed, instead of the largely one-step transitions that were common among those young people who had gone before them, youth transitions from the 1980s onwards were increasingly non-linear and instead a 'set of movements which are less predictable and involve frequent breaks, backtracking and the blending of statuses' (Furlong et al., 2003, p. 24). Not only did youth transitions become less predictable, the changes in employment also meant that the achievement of previous markers of adulthood, such as cohabitation or moving out from one's parents' home, became difficult and thus delayed. A good, stable income was central to building an independent life, and now those wages were less readily available, at the same time as the cost of living, and of housing, started to rise. This is still, and increasingly, the case today, where house prices, and even private rents for solo living, are often far beyond what a young adult can afford, and where young people are expected to wait for longer periods of time after they finish their education before getting the kinds of jobs they desire and are for which they are trained.

Young people and unemployment

What is young people's relationship with unemployment?

Unemployment:
Does not simply mean 'workless' or 'jobless'. The official definition of unemployment is that one must be able and willing to work, being of an age that is officially designated as between the official start of working age up to the age of retirement in the relevant jurisdiction, and being actively engaged in the process of searching for a job in the last four weeks.

As we noted at the beginning of the chapter, another feature of young working lives in contemporary economies is the heightened risk of **unemployment**. To be unemployed is, as defined by the ILO, being able and willing to work, being of an age that is officially designated as between the official start of working age up to the age of retirement in the relevant jurisdiction, and being actively engaged in the process of searching for a job in the last four weeks. This is different from the wider definition of joblessness or worklessness, which includes people who are labour market inactive through choice, such as opting to be stay-at-home parents, or circumstance, such as inability to work through illness or disability. The unemployed have always represented a small proportion of those who are workless. When it comes to young people's unemployment, statistics are usually (but not always) published in relation to those aged 15–24. This is the standard age bracket used by the Organisation for Economic Co-operation and Development (OECD).

Thinking points

- Why do you think young people are more likely to be unemployed than any other age group?
- Why do you think minority ethnic and Indigenous groups of young people are more likely to be unemployed than any other social group?

Young people have, on the whole, a highly unequal relationship with unemployment. This has historically tended to be the case in some regions of the world, such as North Africa and the Middle East, where youth unemployment rates in excess of 20 per cent have been common for several decades. Since the late 1970s and early 1980s, the developed nations have also seen quite dramatic growth in youth unemployment, and this has been exacerbated by the impacts of the 2007 Global Financial Crisis. The youth unemployment rate is often up to three times higher than that of the adult population (France, 2016). This was the case in Australia in January 2018, when youth unemployment was 12.2 per cent, more than twice the overall rate (5.5 per cent), and three times the rate for those aged 25 and over (4.1 per cent) (BLS, 2018a).

This sensitivity of young people to being unemployed is underpinned by a range of interconnected reasons. First, the primary issue is that of aggregate demand (O'Higgins, 2016). This means how many jobs there are available and how this relates to the supply of potential workers. For instance, in Australia, in 2017 there were five times as many jobseekers who were only qualified for entry-level jobs as there were entry-level jobs advertised nationally (Anglicare, 2017). This is the macro context. The other interconnected issues are somewhat easier to understand when we consider economic contractions or recessions, when, as France (2016, p. 113) tells us, in response 'young people tend to lose their jobs more quickly than any other social or economic group ... and they suffer most from long term bouts of unemployment'.

In economic recessions, as at the onset of the 2007/8 Global Financial Crisis, and indeed the recessions of the early 1990s and early 1980s, jobs are lost and young people often find themselves victims of 'last in, first out' approaches. Employers often prefer instead to retain their more experienced members of staff, with the rationale that more experienced workers are more productive, and because it is usually easier and cheaper to make younger workers redundant than older workers. This is because young workers cost businesses less in redundancy payments and the young are also less likely to be members of a trade union and thus lack protection. Correspondingly, and to make matters worse for young people, entry-level recruitment is usually scaled back. The key here is the focus of employer's demands for work experience, something that is obviously in short supply among new labour market entrants, even when they are adequately qualified educationally. This means that young people fall into a trap, commonly described as a vicious circle, where they need a job to get experience, but cannot get experience without getting a job.

Young people's unemployment is often amplified through what is known as the '**scarring effect**', which refers to how the pockets of time where one is out of the labour market are perceived by potential employers as signalling something negative and not being employment-worthy. This can lead to even longer periods of unemployment, and long-term unemployment has an even deeper scarring effect. This is the case, for example, when employers begin recruiting young people again. They are likely to take those fresh from school or college rather than those who have been left unemployed for some time. Those suspicions about the absence of paid work translate into a negative impact on future employment prospects, and even future earnings for those who do get back into work. Crucially, economists have found that this scarring is '…induced by negative signalling and not by human capital depreciation' (Cockx and Picchio, 2013, p. 951). This means that employer perceptions, rather than a diminishment of people's qualification or skills, are a central issue. These realities are often the basis for concern that there will be a 'lost generation' of young people who will forever be excluded from productive employment.

> Scarring effect: The negative impact of a period of unemployment on future employment prospects.

What is crucial to note here is that, while youth unemployment is especially pronounced during economic down turns, there is a worrying trend towards growing gaps between youth and general population unemployment even when economies are in recovery. In the UK for instance, Green (2017) identified that 'age gaps in unemployment rates seem to rise even during periods when youth unemployment is declining and overall unemployment is lower (at around 5 per cent between 2000 and 2007)'. This is reiterated in the work of Furlong et al. (2017), who also document that the UK's youth unemployment as a proportion of total unemployment continued to rise during the presumed 'good times' prior to the global recession. This underlines the changing nature of the labour market and serves to remind us of the hostility of the conditions that young people face, relative to the adult population.

As we have stressed throughout the book, there is a clear and largely intuitive link between being unemployed and its impact upon other elements of the transition to adulthood. But unemployment does more than limit a young person's choices in terms of, say, moving out of the parental home. Having paid work is seemingly essential for that, but unemployment also has a variety of other significant consequences that are felt at both the individual and societal level. For example, UK and European studies point to considerable evidence showing that unemployment may influence health and wellbeing, including psychiatric illness during young adulthood, psychological health, increased likelihood of smoking; and lower general satisfaction with life. Similarly striking, using a large-scale 28-year data set from the Eurobarometer Survey, which surveys all EU member states at least once a year, Blanchflower et al. (2014) investigated the relationship between unemployment and wellbeing. Using the rate of inflation (i.e. the rate at which the cost of living increases) as a comparator, they found '…a 1 percentage point increase in the unemployment rate lowers well-being by more than five times as much as a 1 percentage point increase in the inflation rate' (Blanchflower et al., 2014, p. 117).

An important sociological perspective here is again present in the writing of C. Wright Mills, and his concept of the sociological imagination (see Chapter 2). Rather than thinking solely about the individual, their choices, or even their education profile, Mills insisted that sociologists look at unemployment as more than a private *trouble*, and instead consider it as a public *issue*. Thinking about the high and unequal rates of unemployment faced by contemporary young people, Mills' words on the issue of unemployment from more than 60 years ago still seem pertinent:

> ... we may not hope to find its solution within the range of opportunities open to any one individual. The very structure of opportunities has collapsed. Both the correct statement of the problem and the range of possible solutions require us to consider the economic and political institutions of the society, and not merely the personal situation and character of a scatter of individuals. (1959, p. 4)

We can and should, however, think about how some individuals, and indeed social groups, are more likely than others to be at risk of unemployment. This is another major calling of sociology noted by Mills; to make clear which 'varieties' of people are likely to face advantage or disadvantage. While unemployment is something that can happen to people from any social background, the level of risk is dependent on factors such as class, geographical location, gender and ethnicity. For example, the US Bureau of Labor Statistics reported that in July 2018 the unemployment rate for young men (9.8 per cent) was marginally above that of young women (8.6 per cent) (BLS, 2018a). The stepwise difference among those from different 'race backgrounds' is even more striking, with youth unemployment rates being 7.6 per cent among White youth populations, and 8.4 per cent among young Asians, 10.8 per cent among young Hispanics and 16.5 per cent for young Blacks – well over double the rate of their White counterparts. Similar disparities are visible in the UK (McGuiness, 2018).

Furthermore, Indigenous young people are substantially disproportionately likely to be unemployed – indeed, compared with non-Indigenous youth, Indigenous youth or First Nations youth are three times more likely to be unemployed in Australia, twice as likely in New Zealand and a third more likely in Canada (France, 2016). The situation is amplified by young people's geographical location. Youth unemployment in remote or regional locations is disproportionately high, and this is doubly problematic for Indigenous youth, given that they are more likely to reside in such locations. This disadvantage is clear when we consider, for example, that, even after emerging from the economic downturn, New Zealand still had growing rates of Maori youth unemployment, even as the general population unemployment rates were falling (France, 2016). It is important to realize, though, that unemployment varies in urban areas, from city to city and even within cities. Some regions, cities or districts within cities stand out as what are commonly called unemployment 'blackspots' or 'hotspots'.

Thinking point

Take a moment to imagine where the unemployment 'hot spots' are in your home country, city or region. What makes you think they would be the hot spots? Undertake a quick internet search to see how accurate you were …

The task of the youth sociologist is thus to resist and critique justifications that situate some groups as lacking in effort, and instead to give proper consideration to the barriers that are faced by people with regard to, for example, their ethnic background. We know that racial discrimination is rife in labour market recruitment. Research across a wide range of Western countries has repeatedly found very clearly that adjusting names on CVs to more 'White sounding' names substantially increases the possibility of a call back for interviews. These potentially implicit biases work in tandem with other issues, such as inequalities in education.

The 'risk' without qualifications

Qualifications (or the lack of them) are a big predictor of unemployment risk. Early school leavers and those with no to few qualifications are particularly vulnerable to unemployment, and unemployment during this time period can be especially bad for long-term employment prospects. Low-level qualifications are associated with lower wages and with working in a job that has a higher chance of being curtailed. Even in an economic climate where graduate job prospects are of enormous concern, those with tertiary level education are on average better protected against the risk of unemployment in comparison with non-graduates, and even years after graduating, as unemployment rates fall for both categories, they still remain relatively well protected in comparison with non-graduates. Data from the OECD countries make this very plain, noting that on average, among young adults, 'the unemployment rate is almost twice as high for those who have not completed upper secondary education: 15 per cent compared to 8 per cent for those with upper secondary or post-secondary no tertiary education. The unemployment rate of tertiary educated young adults is only 6 per cent' (OECD, 2018, p. 73).

The emergence of NEETs

Given the stark relationship between education and labour market outcomes, and indeed the long-term decline of youth labour markets in many industrialized nations, it is perhaps no surprise that this is a major theme of attention for policy makers across the globe. Yet, rather than focussing squarely or solely on unemployment, attention instead has turned to the numbers of young people identified as '**NEET**'. This acronym implies the status 'not in education, employment or training'. The term derives to another term, 'status zero', which was used by researchers Rees et al. (1996) in South Wales (UK). Status zero was the moniker for those young people outside of the labour market and education system and who, for

> **NEET:** This is an acronym for the status 'not in employment, education and training'. Similar to but wider than the measure of unemployment, it measures young people's engagement in work and/or education.

those authors, were 'going nowhere'. This negative connotation was perhaps something to be avoided, but the idea of both counting and (re-)engaging disconnected young people who were outside the system of employment and education was seen to be an admirable ambition. Since its conception, the notion of NEETs has become central in policy-making discourses in most European countries, as well as Australia and New Zealand, and in supranational bodies such as the World Bank, the European Union, the ILO and the OECD (France, 2016).

Thinking point

Why do you think some young people might not be in employment, education or training?

The NEET category is an umbrella term, focussing on all those who are disengaged, and is thus a conscious deviation from the ILO definition of unemployment towards recognizing both those who are labour market active and those who are inactive. This means the category contains young people with various characteristics and dispositions. More than this, being NEET is associated with a range of 'social ills', including an increased risk of involvement in crime, drug use and teenage parenthood, as well as a greater likelihood of long-term unemployment, poor health and a range of other social problems. In that sense, governments have been keen on the construct because it allows for a fuller understanding of vulnerability beyond unemployment (France, 2016).

Researchers have pointed to a number of problems with the NEET construct. For instance, they highlight the conflation of young people with different experiences and conditions – such as disabled young people and those who might simply be taking a gap year – into a single category as being particularly problematic and not especially helpful, given that each group may require different and particular approaches to help re-engage them (Furlong, 2006). Such a collation, which includes those who choose to disengage for a wide range of reasons and those who do not, 'promotes a state of confusion' (Furlong, 2006, p. 555) about who is at a disadvantage and why. For example, in Australia, by the end of the 2015 there were around 580,000 15–29 year olds classified as NEET, but only one-third of these were unemployed and actively looking for work. The remaining two-thirds were classified as labour market inactive and educational non-participants. Beyond this, the category excludes those who are in education and who are still actively looking for work – this distorts the figures considerably, as students often make up a significant minority of the unemployed (Roberts and Li, 2017).

Breaking the NEET population down into sub-groups, such as those seeking work, teenage parents, teen carers and young people with a disability or illness, would better refine our understanding of these young people to some extent. Even then, though, because the numbers of people who are NEET is measured cross-sectionally, at a single point in time, the construct offers only a static view of young people's transitions. It does not capture the dynamic experience of the processes that take them in and out of differing types of engagement from education, to unemployment to work and then back again, over any given period of time (MacDonald, 2011). There are further issues to consider with the measurement of NEET status because several groups of young people who are not in education, employment or training are simply not in the estimates because of the survey methods used to count them. Examples include the homeless (including rough sleepers and those sofa surfing), some young people in care or leaving care, those in prison, in hospital or other forms of institutional care, travellers and other hard-to-reach groups (Coles, 2014). Beyond these issues of measurement, a more overriding concern is that NEET status is cast in moralistic terms and, in official discourse at least, neglects the social and economic inequalities that underpin the status. As the focus falls on the individual rather than the circumstance and conditions they face, attention shifts from the problem of NEET status *for* young people towards the 'NEET status as a problem *with* young people' (MacDonald, 2011, p. 431; emphasis in original).

Although the NEET category is a flawed construct, it is not without value. One significant benefit is that it has helped to keep the issue of youth unemployment on the political agenda. Furthermore, just like other statistics, it can highlight inequalities if measured over a longer term. For example, an NCVER (Stanwick et al., 2017) study in Australia showed that being classified as 'persistently NEET' (with the status lasting six months or more) was strongly correlated with non-completion of year 12, having a child, and coming from a more disadvantaged socio-economic background. In this study, young men were more likely to meet the ILO definition of unemployment and thus be actively looking for work. Young women were more likely to be designated inactive, with the majority of female persistent NEETs identifying that they were mostly engaged with home duties or caring for children (although we might want to challenge the idea that raising a child is being inactive!). Using an older cohort, the NCVER study also showed that being persistently NEET from the ages of 15 to 19 years is associated with further persistent NEET spells at ages 20–24, as well as being correlated with poorer education outcomes by age 24.

A very NEET solution?

To try to combat this conundrum of young people's complete disengagement, governments have made efforts at 'early intervention', to try to predict and prevent NEET status, and they have also turned to 'active labour market policies' (ALMPs) or 'welfare to work' programs. France (2016, pp. 141–147) provides a detailed account of how those early intervention strategies have been built into education and training policy (see also Chapter 3). Here we want to focus on ALMPs and welfare to work approaches. While ALMPs take many forms, the crucial point is that they sit in contrast to so-called passive policies, such as simply providing unemployment benefits. Increasingly, states have turned towards 'conditionality' as a driver, with job training opportunities or job readiness activities offered, but also mandatory if one is to receive a welfare benefit. The ambition of such policies is to disrupt what politicians refer to as a 'culture of dependency'. The discourse on, and efforts to tackle, 'welfare cultures' or dependency cultures is a very familiar sound bite, and likely something that readers will have heard or read in the news.

These ideas are not new, having been present in political rhetoric for about forty years. In the UK, the early 1980s saw the start of a shift in policy towards a requirement for the unemployed to be available for any work and to be actively job searching.

The late 1980s and mid-1990s saw subtle shifts in the language of benefits that helped promote these ideas further, with the birth of the 'Job Seekers Allowance' carrying a different message to the 'Income Support' it had replaced, which itself had replaced 'Supplementary Benefit', the mechanism for unemployment benefits since 1966. Similar welfare reforms took place in Australia and New Zealand, also starting in the 1980s, which were also aimed at scaling back welfare spending. In both cases, just like the UK, reduced benefit rates and the eventual abolition of a benefits entitlement for those under 18, accompanied a push towards conditionality, characterized by the need to be actively job searching or engaging in labour market preparedness. Governments initiated youth training programs for young people to join, and joining them often meant that unemployment figures were massaged or disguised. These schemes were strongly criticized by academics and young people themselves. For instance, the UK's Youth Training Scheme (YTS), initiated in 1983 as part of the effort to address growing youth unemployment, was perceived as being no substitute for proper jobs, and lacked credibility with young people, their families and employers.

Regardless of the country in which such policies are deployed, these approaches to moving from welfare to 'workfare' have several unifying characteristics. As Kildal spells out, workfare programs: 'oblige able-bodied recipients to work in return for their benefits; on terms inferior to comparative work in the labour market; and are essentially linked to the lowest tier of public income maintenance system[s]' (Kildal, 2000, p. 3). The responses to the perceived issue of youth disengagement have only accelerated in the last 15 years, with ALMPs becoming more common. Rather than consider these approaches modern or necessarily advanced, researchers have argued that they are in fact retrograde. Dean (2006, p. 10) notes that 'the idea that social benefits or 'relief' should be made conditional upon the performance of labour – such as breaking stones or picking oakum – is one that dates back to the Poor Law era'.[1]

Across those policies, which are aimed specifically at tackling the 'dependency culture', there is a strong emphasis on coercion. For example, the compulsion to participate in initiatives like the UK's 'Work Programme', and the penalties for not taking part, are quite clear. In the case of the UK and Australia, the state uses 'carrot and stick' approaches, with state-subsidized childcare, for example, offered to help (mainly) women back into the labour market. Benefit payments are at risk if obligations for searching for work, including meeting with job search advisers, are not met. This is highly controversial as there is no evidence that benefit sanctions actually work to motivate claimants to engage with the support on offer or to look actively for work and thereby move into work. In fact, *The Welfare Conditionality Project* (2018), a large-scale, UK-based five-year study involving more than 30 researchers across six universities, concluded in its final report that:

> Benefit sanctions do little to enhance people's motivation to prepare for, seek, or enter paid work. They routinely trigger profoundly negative personal, financial, health and behavioural outcomes and push some people away from collectivized welfare provisions.

1   The English Poor Laws were a system of giving relief to the poorest in society that existed up until the end of the Second World War. It involved means-tested benefits with harsh criteria.

The report also makes clear that, even when people do take up the conditions, the support they get is of little or limited value.

Underemployment and the growth of the collaborative economy

Underemployment

A major development in recent decades has been the growing problem of underemployment. **Underemployment** refers to two issues: *time-related* underemployment and *skills-related* underemployment. The first is a measure of those who lack the working hours that they want or need; the second is a measure of people who face a mismatch between their skill level and the skill required for their job (sometimes also called 'over education'). Both are important, because they each allow us to shift attention away from solely the (very important) issue of unemployment towards a better understanding of how employment is not necessarily a safe haven. A full understanding of youth requires more than knowing whether people have experienced unemployment or transitioned straight from education to work. Instead, attention needs to be directed to the internal quality of jobs that young people inhabit (Roberts, 2011).

> **Underemployment:** Time-related underemployment is a measure of those who lack the working hours that they want or need; skills-related underemployment is a measure of people who face a mismatch between their skill level and the skill required for their job (sometimes also called 'over education').

Thinking points

- How do you think underemployment differs from unemployment?
- How might you measure it?

Underemployment in terms of time and hours is the definition that dominates academic and policy debates. This form of underemployment is bound up with the emergence of a service economy and the growth of part time work that is associated with industries such as retail, hotels and restaurants. This suits many people, and the majority of part time workers in most industrialized countries do so voluntarily. However, there is now an ongoing shift towards higher rates of *involuntary* part time working in OECD countries (Streeck, 2016). This is of particular concern for young people because opportunities, for them especially, but also for other younger adults, to undertake full time work have sharply declined over the last 30 years. Even in recent years when economies started to recover after the 2007–2008 recession, it has been part time work that has been the major area of growth in OECD countries, and most of this increase in part time work is because of a shortage of opportunities for full time employment (OECD, 2015).

Correspondingly, the jobs and industries that young people tend to work in are those where part time work is highly prevalent. This is not a surprise: more than ten years ago, Ken Roberts, a longstanding prominent figure in youth sociology, contended that 'underemployment is the 21st century global normality for youth in the labour market' (Roberts, 2009, p. 4). Despite these warnings, youth underemployment seem to have been a slow-burning crisis that has sneaked up on us before getting sustained attention from policymakers and researchers quite recently.

We can turn to Australia as a case study to make this clear. The stark reality is that young people are disproportionately likely to bear the brunt of both unemployment and underemployment relative to older age groups in Australia. Young people aged 15–24 represent nearly double the numbers of those underemployed in other age categories. This is in part reflected in their higher than average rates of part time employment, to which the young are the biggest contributors. Part time employment does not in and of itself mean one is underemployed. This is observable in the low rates of underemployment in the 55+ age group, who still are highly represented as part time workers. However, the youngest age group makes up the biggest proportion of part time workers, and this age group has the highest rates of involuntary underemployment (ABS Labour Force Report, 2018)

It is commonly assumed that the growing number of students leads to increases in part time work; this might seem reasonable given that many young people do combine employment with their studies. However, in Australia, around 260,000 young people aged 20–24 who are *not students* work part time (BLS, 2018b). Analysis by the Reserve Bank of Australia (RBA, 2018) shows this reflects a pronounced increase in involuntary underemployment for this particular group. Furthermore, this same analysis shows the gap between the underemployment rate for younger workers and the overall underemployment rate has widened recently.

Of further interest is the trend towards youth underemployment. In Figure 4.1, the top line (grey) shows, over a 20-year period, the youth under-utilisation rate,

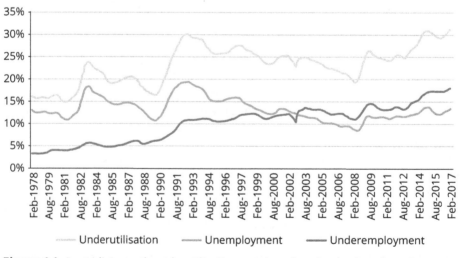

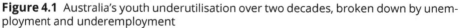

Figure 4.1 Australia's youth underutilisation over two decades, broken down by unemployment and underemployment

Source: ABS 2017, **Labour force Australia,** *February 2017, Cat. no. 6202.0, Table 22, trend data.*

which is the youth unemployment and underemployment rates combined. There is clearly an upward trend. Of note, though, is that the lower two lines show that, while unemployment was in decline until the Great Financial Crisis in 2007, underemployment had overtaken unemployment as the biggest contributor to youth under-utilisation nearly five years *before* the onset of the GFC.

The emergence of the 'collaborative' economy

Related to underemployment is the rise of the so-called **collaborative economy**. Driven by technological change, mobile technology apps have become a key component in linking consumers and services, with individuals working independently on a task-by-task basis for various companies. Popular and well-known examples include Uber, deliveroo, Foodara and Airtasker. In most cases, the technology service is not an employer, meaning that those who do these jobs are self-employed, and are simply 'collaborating' or 'sharing' the delivery of the goods or services with the tech company. This kind of collaboration has many other names. It has been called the sharing economy and the pairing economy, both of which

Collaborative economy: Also called the 'sharing economy', this refers to the sectors of the economy that rely on independent contractors working with (but not for) technology companies. Examples include Uber, Airtasker and Deliveroo.

emphasize the relationship between worker and an 'app company'; it has also been called an 'access economy', signalling the means for customers to access cheap goods and services, and, more pertinently, the 'gig economy'. 'Gig' work can occur offline or online via apps, but the online world tends to receive particular attention. Indeed, in a report for the UK Department for Business Energy and Industrial Strategy, Lepanjuuri et al. (2018, p. 4) defined the gig economy as follows:

> The gig economy involves the exchange of labour for money between individuals or companies via digital platforms that actively facilitate matching between providers and customers, on a short-term and payment by task basis.

🗯 Thinking points

- What do you understand by the terms 'gig economy' and 'gig work'? What types of jobs might it include?
- Are these forms of work most common amongst young people?

The types of work done can vary, and can include technical and specialized tasks such as the creation of a logo, proof reading and editorial work, or even marketing tasks (this is often called 'crowd work' or 'crowd sourcing'). Most often though, these apps are about work 'on demand' in the form of 'micro tasks', which are relatively menial and monotonous, such as cleaning, transporting food or people, household tasks or running errands (De Stefano, 2016).

The gig economy conjures the image of 'workers living like musicians, living from gig to gig' (Morgan and Nilligan, 2018, p. 6). Broadly, this reflects a significant move away from the standardized model of paid work with an employer, towards greater volumes of short-term contracts, temporary and freelance work. A characteristic of such work is that workers have little control over how much work they get; also, they are paid on a one-off or job-by-job basis. Such work also features a complete lack of the established benefits of permanent work, such as income security, guaranteed minimum wages, accident insurance, pension provisions and paid leave. All this represents a significant transfer of risk from employer to individual. By this we simply mean that the app company, for example, is not responsible for the health and safety of the individual, nor for ensuring a minimum wage, and is less likely to be held accountable for things like unfair dismissal (Friedman, 2014).

Pinning down the exact numbers and characteristics of gig workers is extremely difficult. Although government statistics departments are beginning to collect data, there is little available at present. Researchers across and within different countries often produce estimates using different methods and definitions of measurement, resulting in a patchy and often contradictory evidence base. Nonetheless, some data suggest it is still a relatively small proportion, ranging between 1 per cent and 3 per cent of the workforce (Wood et al., 2019). There is a common assumption that young people are at the front of the gig economy. A quick internet search will return numerous news and magazine articles, as well as academic commentaries, that will attest to this. Similarly, and notwithstanding the problems with methods as above, some research suggests that young people under 30 are the bulk of the freelance digital platform gig workforce (Martin, 2018). This is echoed in most reports, which indicate '[t]hose involved in the gig economy were generally younger than the rest of the population' (Lepanjuuri et al., 2018, p. 5). We should not, however, underestimate the number of older workers in this economy. Uber, for example, has a large and disproportionately older workforce.

Given the bias towards the youth population, there are important questions to ask about young people's engagement with such an economy. There tend to be two discrete schools of thought on this matter. First, we have the view that young people choose and benefit from 'gig work'. This is a common position in business and economic magazine literature and commentary. For instance, a 2016 'thought leader' paper by the Australian Industry Group states that 'Many workers (particularly those of Generation Y) are disenchanted with their 9 to 5 routine and have an increasing need for flexible and diversified work.' (Ai Group, 2016, p. 4). This echoes a variety of other forums, with a recent commentary in Forbes (2019) online magazine declaring that 'Millennials, the generation credited with disrupting everything from housing to marriage, are gravitating towards gig work for the promise of greater work-life balance'. Choice is writ large in such accounts. It is not just magazines that run with these kinds of stories. Economics research by Carleton and Kelly (2016) in the USA concludes that workers are 'more satisfied with jobs that provide more control over their work day than with regular salaried job', and thus point to 'happiness bumps' for people in the gig economy.

Such work of course also allows people to top up their primary earnings through gig work. According to a survey of 8,000 people across Europe and the USA by the

McKinsey Global Institute (Farrell and Greig, 2016), as many as 40 per cent of independent workers are 'casual workers', who use such work as a way to supplement their regular salary. Note that the McKinsey research is actually a study of *independent* workers, not gig workers per se, who are only a small subset of this research. Indeed, the McKinsey report (Farrell and Greig, 2016, p. 3) states that 'online marketplaces are used by 15 per cent of independent workers'. However, the research, and other commentaries about gig work, often conflates gig workers and independent contractors. Even disregarding this, a more sociological critique might lead to greater interrogation of whether 'casual workers' who use such work to top up the main income are also operating from a position of constraint. Working a second job to top up a first is, arguably, partially aligned with the motivations of those who do gig work because they are 'financially strapped'.

The second take on gig work is captured primarily in discussions of 'bogus self-employment'. Crucial to the distinction between genuine self-employment and bogus self-employment is the existence of a relationship of subordination. This crucial definition is an issue at the centre of contemporary legal battles. In a recent case in Australia, food courier company Foodora was determined by the Fair Work Commission to have held a subordinate relation over their riders. As riders were required to wear a uniform and the company determined when staff could or could not start their shift, the staff were seen as being not genuinely self-employed, independent contractors. The implications of this are being tested in a variety of legal cases, but at the time of writing the UK has recently determined that Uber drivers should be entitled to various industrial protections.

The situation here, where worker choice and benefits are overplayed, is well captured by Friedman (2014), who argues

> While the rise of this 'gig' economy is praised by some as a response to the wishes of a more entrepreneurial generation, it is more likely that it is driven by the concerns of businesses to lower wages and benefit costs during business down-turns while also reducing their vulnerability to unfair dismissal lawsuits.

Thinking point

How attractive do you find gig work? What pros and cons might come to mind? Do you think this might change if you were older?

Understanding young working lives in contemporary times

The 'individualization thesis' or 'choice biographies'

Throughout this chapter it has become increasingly obvious that young people's relationship with work has been undergoing radical restructuring. Notably, the changes that have occurred provide the core evidence for Wyn and Woodman (2006) contention that contemporary young people grow up under a generationally specific set of social, political and economic conditions and that transitions are not a useful way of understanding young people's lives today. Moreover, the experience of these changes can also be viewed through the lens of what is called individualization, which according to Beck Gernsheim (1998, p. 3) is a 'historical process that increasingly questions and tends to break up people's traditional rhythm of life'. This notion of a change to the rhythm of life can be related to the relatively later entry into the work force that young people now experience as a result of education policy, and to economic realities that mean acquiring full time, decently paid work after leaving education, whether at university or school leaving age, is far from certain.

The individualization thesis sees young people being detached from any comprehensible reference points and increasingly left to be the architects of their own lives and careers. For example, Manuela Du Bois Reymond (1999), writing at the turn of the millennium, used Beck's ideas to make it clear that young people are forced to adapt to the changing demands of the labour market. However, she also pointed out that, with few frames of reference, and less collective movement as occurred in the mass transitions of previous generations, young people feel increasingly responsible for constructing 'choice biographies'. Indeed, the normalization of choice biographies has led some researchers to argue that labour market (and educational) 'failure' is felt at the level of the individual, with young people sometimes blinded to the structural barriers they have to overcome (such as intersecting social characteristics of class, gender, race and even the basic realties of whether there are enough jobs available; see Furlong and Cartmel, 2007). This is an artefact of what Kelly (2006, 2017) describes as the neoliberal requirement to be an 'entrepreneurial self', so that in the face of tricky economic conditions young people must strive to be 'rational, autonomous, choice making, risk aware, prudential, responsible and enterprising' (Kelly, 2017, p. 57), and consider their lives a project that requires ongoing management. This is somewhat reflected in the understanding that young people will less likely have stable 'careers' for large chunks of their working life and instead have a 'portfolio' of jobs up until their retirement. In Australia, for example, the Foundation for Young Australians (2017) estimated that the average 15-year-old can expect 17 jobs across five different industries over their working life. Meanwhile, Berger's (2016) analysis of LinkedIn user account data in the USA shows that each 5-year cohort experiences increased rates of job change within the first five years of college graduation (see Figure 4.2).

Although evidence seems to suggest that the complexity of the world of work is driving young people to be active participants in the process of 'choice biographies', its weakness is its failure to address the structured inequalities that remain at the core of how different groups experience the labour market. A number of writers have been highly critical of the concept of 'choice biographies' because it fails to engage with embedded structural inequalities. Furlong and Cartmel (2007) explore this thesis in their work on social change in late modernity. They show, across a range of areas, that structural inequalities still remain in education and employment, and in terms of future trajectories (and outcomes), issues of class, gender and racial background still have a significant impact on young people's pathways through life. In their conclusions they reflect upon the 'choice biographies' thesis by talking about the dual nature of the experience. On one hand, the evidence shows a substantial level of change taking place, and they argue that the 'process of individualisation represents a subjective

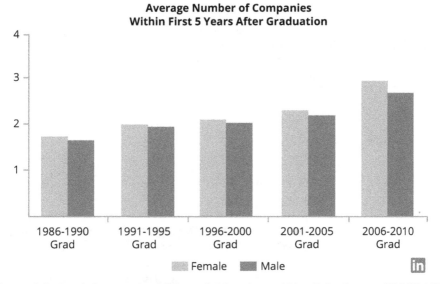

Average Number of Companies
Within First 5 Years After Graduation

Figure 4.2 Graph from and publicly available at https://blog.linkedin.com/2016/04/12/will-this-year_s-college-grads-job-hop-more-than-previous-grads

weakening of social bonds due to the growing diversity of life experiences'. But, on the other hand, they suggest that there is a growing expectation and perception that choice is more freely available and that this may mask the underlying structuring of young people's lives.

For some groups of young people, choice may be more readily available as something that emerges as a result of their class position, but the types of choices are clearly differentiated by structural differences between groups. Living in North-East England, on one of the poorest housing estates in the country, where very few employment opportunities exist, limits what is possible (MacDonald and Marsh, 2005). Of course, historically young people have always thought they have control of their lives; Paul Willis's (1977) lads thought they were in control, although as he went on to show their destinations were 'pre-determined'. Young people make the best of their structured opportunities, but their lives are shaped by the local context.

Young subjectivities and affective labour in the service economy

Studies by Farrugia (2019) and Farrugia et al. (2018) explore how young people's identities and styles produce value in the particular employment and economic conditions termed 'post-Fordist'. Theories of post-Fordism state that people's identities and enactments of social relationships are critical (yet often invisible) dimensions of labour *required* for the job. Affective labour describes the way sensations, emotions or embodied experiences constitute the true 'product' of the work. Farrugia et al. studied the way young people doing bar work contribute to the production of affective atmospheres, or the sensations of ease, pleasure and enjoyment that are offered to the clientele of boutique bars. They suggest this focus is important for youth studies and efforts to better understand the power dynamics informing young people's actual working practices in post-Fordist economies.

The precariat

A second argument that tries to explain the impact of the changing nature of young people's relationship with work can be found in the work of Guy Standing (2011). Standing emphasizes the growth of precarious work and how it has produced an emergent new class that he calls the '**precariat**'. The precariat are situated somewhere between 'an army of unemployed and a detached group of socially ill misfits' (Standing, 2011, p. 65) beneath them and, above them, a shrinking core of old working-class manual labourers, a professional technical class; a 'salariat' characterized by stable, full time, well-rewarded employment and, at the very summit, a ruling elite. Standing offers his explanation in class terms, and targets neoliberal policy-making choices as being responsible for the emergence of the precariat. More pertinently, he explains that, while anyone can fall into the precariat, 'the most common image is of young people emerging from school and college to enter a precarious existence lasting years' (Standing, 2011, p. 65).

The precariat: A group of people united by precarious conditions of work, such as inadequate income-earning opportunities, short-term or zero hours contracts, and limited opportunities to develop or make use of competencies.

Thinking points

- What is precarious work, and how is it different from other forms of employment?
- Do you think young people are more vulnerable than other age groups to precarious work? Why / why not?

This approach has, however, been criticized on a number of fronts. Firstly, Standing seems to indicate that this condition is relatively new. There is no denial that neoliberal policy making, which began the deregulation of employment and the freeing up of international markets from the late 1970s, has been influential in producing at least some of the current working conditions that young people face. However, Judith Bessant (2018, p. 788) usefully advocates for a longer view of history as a way of testing the theory to the full, arguing that 'precarious employment is not new nor is it solely due to the advent of globalisation or neoliberal policy'. This is a point that chimes with the thoughts of others, who have stressed that precarious work has long been a feature of working class lives, and that this was well understood by Marx, Durkheim and other sociologists nearly two centuries ago (Kallberg, 2009). Furlong (2017, p. 7) also suggests that researchers should be mindful that 'the realities encountered by young people more or less confirm their expectations'. He also notes that, because the parents of many contemporary young people themselves left school in the late 1970s and the 1980s, they will most likely be familiar with the prospect of potential unemployment and unfavourable conditions. This does not make it easier for young people but is a salutary reminder to youth researchers not to overstate either the newness or the uniqueness of young people's experience of harsh economic realities.

The point here, though, is not to deny the significance of the contemporary context. An epidemic of low wages and growth in atypical work arrangements such as part time, short-term or zero hours contracts, has meant that even paid employment cannot guarantee safety from poverty. Low paid work is common across the kinds of sectors that young people find themselves working in, such as hotels and restaurants, IT, finance and services, and wholesale, retail and transport jobs. The emergence of the gig economy and its associated job-by-job characteristics leaves open questions about whether young people can develop skills or even a track record that is a useful stepping stone to more desirable careers in the future while they cobble together ways to get by, often juggling several jobs.

The key here is to think carefully, and consider the evidence, about whether processes of casualization have a disproportionately negative impact on those who are least well resourced to shelter themselves from such changes. One reason that this is crucial is that young people might also be trapped, destined for a lifetime of low level jobs with little skill development or potential for upward progression even when they are employed. Indeed, Gallie and Paugam suggest that 'employment does not guarantee social integration: in the longer run, poor quality jobs are likely to make many people highly vulnerable to job loss and to eventual labour market marginalisation' (2002, p. 62). This is something that we would do well to remember when we see government leaders and policy makers talking up reductions in unemployment. Unemployment figures might go down, but alone this tells us little about the internal job quality and contract conditions, or their associated consequences. This is of particular pertinence during the youth period, when experiences tend to solidify social disadvantage and shape future patterns with respect to work, housing and domestic transitions.

A second issue with the notion of the precariat, one that sometimes also applies to generational analyses, is the broad-brush approach it relies on. This applies to the supposed unity in young people's feelings of anger about and their experiences of precarity, which somewhat understates the role that different social, economic and cultural resources play in helping to navigate the contemporary landscape. In other words, while the term 'precarious' can be applied to the experience, and even captures the feelings of the experience for many young workers, it does not make them a class of any sort. Threadgold (2017, p. 182) captures this well, suggesting that a 'migrant domestic cleaner in Hong Kong has a very different subject position than a British, zero-hours contract commercial pilot'. Indeed, research shows how flexible work and short-term contracts can afford middle class, high earners a variety of possibilities. This includes taking time out of the labour market to relax or helping facilitate moves to different locales. Meanwhile, the relatively poor and working classes are often subjected to the considerable difficulty of a life in a 'low-pay, no-pay cycle' (Shildrick and

MacDonald, 2012). As we saw earlier in our discussions on changes, churning from one low paid job to another, including periods of worklessness, is not only increasingly common, but is very damaging in the medium to longer term, operating as a kind of trap that ensures young people can remain on these trajectories well into their adult life. Thomson (2015) researched the impact of 'churning' by following, over a four year cycle, a group whose earnings were less than two thirds of the median hourly wage, which is the standard definition of low pay. Thomson found '… almost a quarter of low-paid workers (24.3 per cent) cycle between employment, worklessness, and back into employment over a four-year period, with a further 14.1 per cent leaving employment and not returning to work' (p. 4).

Youth sociologists have offered nuanced re-workings of Standing's concept of precarity. Threadgold (2017) has usefully brought to our attention how precarious work has been a calculated choice by some young people, even in the face of difficult financial circumstances. In his study of people doing 'DIY careers', he explores how some young people deliberately opt out of the formal and well-trodden trajectories through education towards the labour market. Instead, these young people opt for 'creative, cultural modes of existence' and come to accept the relative poverty that results from careers punctuated by otherwise highly enjoyable gig work. In these accounts, Threadgold reveals a variety of ways in which young people struggle to practise a more ethical and satisfying life. Importantly, Threadgold positions these choices in the context of and as a reaction to precarity. This reaction is therefore a rejection of the seemingly mandatory investment in conventional notions of career, premised on their own recognition that such a career is unachievable. There are strong resonances here with Willis's (1977) study, where working class school-boys constructed a subjectivity premised on the rejection of school and its ethos because they figured out for themselves that a commitment to education would not change their lives for the better. These examples show the importance of detailed sociological analysis in making sense of the patterns of inequality shaping young people's education and employment trajectories.

💬 Summary

- Young people in most OECD countries are subject to legal wage discrimination.

- The structure of labour markets has changed hugely in the last forty years: youth labour markets, for 16–18 year olds, rarely have opportunities for full time, meaningful work.

- Contemporary economies are dominated by service-based employment, often in industries that require large numbers of low-skill, low-pay, part time work.

- Experiences in the home and at school combine with social class and gender to produce a relatively narrow set of career alternatives for large numbers of young people.

- Youth unemployment is usually much higher than unemployment rates among the wider general population.

- Unemployment is a classed phenomenon: people from poor backgrounds and those who leave school with fewer qualifications are disproportionately likely to be unemployed.

- Governments' use of 'labour market activation schemes' and welfare penalties fail to recognize the lack of quality and quantity of jobs available.

- Underemployment and precarious work has become more central to the work experiences of the young and it remains on the rise

- The rise of 'gig work' and the so-called collaborative economy is a growing concern and has the potential to increase young people's precariousness in the labour market.

Exercise: The sociological imagination

Talk to some of the older people in your family about their experience of leaving school and going to work. How does it compare with your own understanding and experience of work? Critically reflect on why this might be and what changes have taken place that seem to have changed the nature of work.

Key readings

Bessant, J. (2018) 'Young precariat and a new work order? A case for historical sociology', *Journal of Youth Studies*, vol. 21, no. 6, pp. 780–798.

Farrugia, D., Threadgold, S. & Coffey, J. (2018) 'Young subjectivities and affective labour in the service economy', *Journal of Youth Studies*, vol. 21, no. 3, pp. 272–287.

France, A. (2016) *Understanding Youth in the Global Economic Crisis* (Policy Press).

Furlong, A. (2006) 'Not a very NEET solution: representing problematic labour market transitions among early school-leavers', *Work, Employment and Society*, vol. 20, no. 3, pp. 553–569.

Furlong, A., Goodwin, J., O'Connor, H., Hadfield, S., Hall, S., Lowden, K. & Plugor, R. (2017) *Young People in the Labour Market: Past, Present, Future* (Routledge).

MacDonald, R. & Glazitzoglu, A. (2019) 'Youth, enterprise and precarity: or, what is, and what is wrong with, the 'gig economy'?' *Journal of Sociology*, online first pp. 1–24.

Morgan, G. & Nelligan, P. (2018). *The Creativity Hoax: Precarious Work in the Gig Economy* (Anthem).

5 YOUTH CULTURES AND IDENTITIES

> **In this chapter you will learn about:**
>
> - The significance of the study of youth cultures and subcultures in sociology
> - The way that youth subcultures have been theorized, researched and critiqued
> - Post subcultural approaches such as taste cultures, neo-tribes and scenes
> - Debates on the influence of leisure and consumption practices for understanding young people's lives.

Youth cultural practice

Thinking point

- What comes to mind when you think of *youth culture* and subcultures?
- How are youth cultures portrayed in the media?

'Coachella' in the USA, 'Glastonbury' in the UK, 'Splendour in the Grass' in Australia, 'Summer Sonic' in Japan, 'Clockenflap' in Hong Kong, 'Deichbrand' in Germany, 'Pukklepop' in Belgium. Many readers will recognize some or all of these as names of some of the world's most famous annual music festivals. Regardless of whether you have ever attended one of these or other similar events, or even if attendance would be an attractive proposition, it is likely that you can create a mental picture of such spaces. What comes to mind? Maybe you thought of particular types of music, certain styles of dress and fashion, widespread consumption of alcohol, crowds of young people, perhaps? Such an image would make sense, and these kinds of events are often commonly considered a part of **youth culture**. What we mean by this is the ways of being for young people, where there may be some shared norms, values and dispositions that are connected to consumption and leisure practices. Youth sociologists are interested in how young people construct their identities through consumption and leisure practices, and how these practices are shaped by structural forces including class, gender, ethnicity and place. The things that young people 'think and do' tend to be thought of as being at least somewhat distinctive from the societal mainstream, adult or 'parent' culture, and are sometimes denoted by the term 'youth subcultures'. The relevance of this term to the lives of the young is subject to intense theoretical debate in youth sociology (as outlined in Chapter 1).

> **Youth cultures:** Young people's everyday or 'mainstream' leisure and consumption practices.

However, the term retains meaning in everyday discussions and is sometimes used interchangeably with the term 'youth culture'.

Let's briefly return to that imagined music festival. There is no question that music festivals have great appeal to young people, and the 18–24-year-old demographic makes up large proportions of the audiences at such events. However, it might surprise you to know that the average age of attendance at music festivals is rising. In 2016, almost a quarter of all music festival goers in Europe were over the age of 30 – with many of these aged between 40 and 60. The *average* age of attendees at the UK's 2016 Glastonbury festival was reported as 36 years and 8 months. As well as tweaking our imagined view of festivals, this revelation prompts a number of questions that speak to some of the core issues of this book;

- Is this evidence of the 'extended' nature of the youth period?

- Is there still such a thing as a distinctive youth culture or subcultures, or is popular culture something that engages all age groups?

- How are such activities mediated by social forces such as place, race, class and gender?

- What role does youth (sub)culture have in shaping youth identities?

- What roles do consumption and leisure have in young people's lives?

Before thinking about such issues, it is first important to consider how youth sociology has researched and theorized young people's cultural practices over time. Historically, youth sociologists have been concerned with particular *conditions* that give rise to certain types of youth culture and have asked how young people engage with and create cultural practices within these limitations. Contemporary youth sociologists see this process as crucial for understanding how young people's identities are shaped. The capacity for young people to shape their own identities, and the social forces such as class, gender and ethnicity which shape the *conditions of possibility* for young people's lives, are a central point of debate among youth sociologists. The key tensions here revolve around questions of social change and inequality. How much or how little control do particular groups of young people actually have in shaping their identities, or being shaped by social and cultural forces? This question links to the structure/agency debate we introduced in Chapter 2. Sociologists aim not only to describe the world, but also to understand and challenge inequality. Understanding these dimensions of youth cultures and identities is a major priority in youth sociology.

Theorising youth (sub)cultural practice

Youth is about much more than the experience of school or the reality of employment destinations. As noted in previous chapters, these settings tend to represent the focus of one-half of the youth sociology research binary – the youth transitions perspective. The other strand of youth research has long paid attention to young people's cultural practices and engagement in the world.

Firstly, we need to think about what we mean by culture. It is a pretty common word, but its meaning can be complex and controversial. Raymond Williams defines culture as:

> ... a particular way of life, which expresses certain meanings and values not only in art and learning but also in institutions and ordinary behaviour. The analysis of culture, from such a definition, is the clarification of the meanings and values implicit in a particular way of life, a particular culture...the characteristic forms through which members of the society communicate .... (Raymond Williams, 1961, p. 57)

In this definition, culture includes ordinary and everyday activities. It acknowledges the diversity of culture including activities such as opera, ballet and art galleries and also TV soaps, alternative theatre and music festivals. Culture can also be a 'way of life' of being and doing. For example, in New Zealand, Māori life worlds and cultural practices are underpinned by Tikanga, which is a set of cultural practices and customs that operate to guide and give meaning to everyday life for young Māori. For example, the concept of *Tapu* is defined as 'sacred', containing a strong imposition of rules and prohibitions. A person, object or place can be *tapu* and may not be touched or, in some cases, not even approached. *Noa* is the opposite of *tapu*, and includes the concept of 'common'. These concepts embedded in Māori culture require young Māori to behave in a certain way in particular situations and settings. Culture can thus be a signification that expresses certain meanings and values implicit in a way of life. It is a form of social activity, a set of linguistic practices and/or cultural artifices, and its values are expressed through the meanings given to them in any context.

So what is *youth* culture? In the previous chapters we had a strong focus on education and work, showing how the changing context is affecting young people's everyday lives. When it comes to the study of youth culture, the emphasis is more on how young people might define their own lives and worlds and how they might produce as well as respond to social change. The notion of youth culture makes a distinction between the cultural orientations, interests and affiliations of young people compared with those of adults. This tends to imply a degree of homogeneity, which is shaped by (social) age. What we mean by this is that being young might involve shared norms, values and dispositions that are separate from those of adults. Youth culture, then, is about much more than the experience of education or the reality of employment destinations. Andy Bennett (2014) explains this as young people's efforts at 'play'. This framing extends to include 'the various resources – musical, stylistic, technological, spatial, and so on – [that young people use] to make their lives meaningful' (Bennett, 2014, p. 784). Play is thus seen as being far more than a simple analysis of leisure and is instead seen as 'core to the identity, politics and lifestyles of youth' (Bennett, 2014, p. 784). Consumption is also a crucial aspect of 'play' in youth subcultures. This means that, to understand youth identities and lifestyles, we need also to understand their consumption practices. Youth sociologists are interested in how young people construct their identities through such 'play' and how these practices are shaped by structural forces including class, gender, ethnicity and place. One final point to note is that the 'cultural' view tends to be more focussed on the 'being' aspects of youth, and a separation, and sometimes hostility, exists between 'transitions' and 'cultural' perspectives. This is something we will return to at the end of the chapter.

The emergence of youth (sub)cultures

The first significant sociological work that focussed on youth *culture* emerged out of the Chicago School in the USA in the 1930s. It was here that a group of scholars were investigating crime and delinquency among young people in urban settings in Chicago. They argued that young people created and engaged in alternative cultures, which broadly speaking involved having different ways of life and patterns of existence from those of adults. These were referred to as subcultures, a term that indicated that young people deviated in various ways from what was customary. Such an idea became popular in criminology and was picked up by a wide range of now world-renowned scholars. For example, Albert Cohen (1955) argued that a youth subculture was a *reaction* to the situation within which young people found themselves. This 'reactive' component was core to the idea of subculture, and its distinctiveness from youth culture more generally, at this time and for many years to come, as we explore below. For Albert Cohen, if young people could not achieve societal goals, this led to 'status frustration' and underscored delinquent activity that appeared on the surface to serve no purpose, such as petty vandalism. Importantly, Cohen emphasized subcultures as a form of collective behaviour, and stated that deviant behaviour by working class boys could be seen as *logical and understandable* as a result of their position in the social structure and the feeling of failure this brings about. Cohen described such behaviour as stemming from 'subcultural values', which were different from and a rejection of a society's dominant cultural values.

🗨 Thinking points

- What is the difference between youth cultures and subcultures?
- What contemporary youth cultural practices can you think of that could be considered 'deviant'?

The CCCS and the British 'subcultures' tradition

As we saw in Chapter 1, the Centre for Contemporary Cultural Studies (CCCS, sometimes known as 'the Birmingham School') was a major influence in youth sub-cultural studies. The theorizing of deviance as normal and logical was transferred to the UK through the work of the CCCS in the mid-1970s, particularly its extension of the idea of subcultural practice. While drawing on the ideas of the Chicago school as well as the work of Albert Cohen, the CCCS offered a more explicitly Marxist, macro-sociological account of young people's style and behaviour. Using a form of analysis called **semiotics**, the CCCS focussed on young people's forms of style and their attachments to specific types of music that were newly emerging in the post-WWII period. They argued that these newly emerging youth formations were produced by,

Semiotics: The study of how social meaning is created through use of symbols.

a commentary on, and a resistance to, wider class-based inequalities. Thus, while young people's new stylings and musical tastes tended to be defined by the general public, the media and some commentators as delinquency, the CCCS wanted to draw attention to how young people used style as a creative response to the contradictions and conflicts in their lives, especially in a period of rapid social change. In this context, culture was the way in which groups 'handled' the raw material of their social and material 'experience' and specifically their class experience.

In the post-war era, increased affluence was very much a real thing. Teenagers became associated with '… coffee and milk bars, fashion clothes and hair styles, cosmetics, rock 'n' roll, films and magazines, scooters and motorbikes, dancing and dance halls' (Frith, 1986, p. 9), in which consumption became a central act of leisure. However, the starting point for CCCS scholars was to challenge the idea that this new affluence associated was indicative of dissolved social class differences. The thirty years after WWII was a period that gave rise to the emergence of a wide range of youth groups, such as 'the mods', 'the rockers', 'teddy boys', 'skinheads' and 'Rastafarians'. Making sense of these post-war developments became central to the research programme of the CCCS scholars. Much of this work can be found in *Resistance through Rituals* (Hall and Jefferson, 1976), one of the most famous books in 20th century youth sociology. In order to offer a fuller and more sophisticated theorization of the styles that were so characteristic of these emerging youth subcultures, CCCS writers drew on a concept devised by the neo-Marxist writer Antonio Gramsci: '**hegemony**'. This concept was offered as a way of understanding power relations in contemporary societies. Gramsci made clear that dominant groups maintained power not through force or coercion but through their capacity to ensure subordinated groups were complicit in or accepted their own subjugation. This was achieved through presentation of power relations being simply 'the way things are', as being natural and unavoidable and thus producing a form of 'false consciousness'. The key point for CCCS scholars was that the subcultural style and activity were vividly against the grain of mainstream culture, against this 'hegemony' of 'how things should be'. Hence, young people *resisted* disempowerment through *rituals* of dress, speech and music, 'hanging about on street corners' and engaging in drug use as a rebuttal to social control and a symbolic challenge to authority.

> **Hegemony:** A concept by Italian Marxist philosopher Antoni Gramsci, meaning the 'cultural, moral and ideological' leadership of a dominant social group.

The teddy boys

Teddy boys re-interpreted and re-contextualized the traditional dress of past eras with that of the present. They appeared in the mid-1950s in Britain and were associated with American rock and roll. They appropriated the Edwardian style of their grandparents, drawing upon important formal dress styles to make themselves distinctive. Popular clothing included waistcoats, drape jackets or zoot suits, usually with velvet trim collars. They usually wore 'drainpipe' trousers (tight to the leg) that exposed their socks, and crepe-soled shoes known as brothel creepers. Their hair style was distinctive, being long, strongly

> moulded and greased up, with a quiff at the front and what was known as a 'duck's arse' at the back. Their counterparts the teddy girls were also distinct with their long jackets, cigarettes, and often masculine styles, though these young women have often been drastically overlooked in research and historical accounts. A parallel youth culture emerged in Australia around the same time, with Bodgies (young men) and Widgies (young women) stylizing and behaving in similar ways to the Teds.

In all cases, the aesthetic styling, the speech or slang patterns, the demeanour and values associated with groups such as the Teds, Mods, Rastafarians, Skinheads and others were part of a method of defining oneself as a member of a collective and reflected the group's reaction to its invisibility or marginality. While subculture is in more recent times 'defined as that which constructs, perceives and portrays itself as standing apart from others in an isolated, defined and bounded group' (MacDonald et al., 2001, p. 152), the pivotal point for the CCCS was that the material conditions of existence and social class divisions were crucial in producing subcultures. These challenges were seen by CCCS as collective rather than individual practices and as a form of finding 'solutions' to the problems faced in young people's everyday lives.

The collective expression of subcultural identities was argued to, in some ways, constitute a challenge to authority. Clarke et al. argued, however, that their impact in producing social change was entirely 'imaginary', and did not actually *change* anything in particular:

> There is no 'subcultural solution' to working class youth unemployment, educational disadvantage, compulsory miseducation, dead end jobs, the routinisation and specialisation of labour, low pay and the loss of skills. (Clarke et al., 1976, p. 47)

Class distinctions and disadvantages remained very real at the material level, and some argued that a subcultural sensibility offered only a temporary relief, with few tangible benefits. For example, the affluent-looking stylings of the teddy boys, as mentioned above, might have evidenced young people's new-found capacity to be active consumers in hitherto middle class ways. Instead, though, CCCS scholars explained that teddy boys and, indeed, teddy girls were actually still relatively poor:

> Far from being a casual response to "easy money" the extravagant sartorial display of the Ted required careful financial planning and was remarkably self-conscious, a going against the grain, as it were, of a life which in all other respects was, in all likelihood, relatively cheerless and poorly rewarded. (Hebdige, 1979, p. 70)

Thinking point

Williams (2006, p. 174) explains that '... music is seen as consequential in the creation of subcultures as well as a consequence of them' – what kinds of music are you familiar with that appear to be representative of a (modern or historical) subcultural group? What do the lyrics and sounds tell you about the subcultural group you have in mind?

Consolidating knowledge: the skinheads as a case of intersectional complexity

Youth cultures should not be understood as a homogeneous mass. Instead they are 'a complex kaleidoscope of several subcultures, of different age groups, yet distinctly related to the class position of those in them' (Brake, 1985, p. ix). Youth subcultures themselves are also composed of different strands and can evolve in a variety of directions. To make this a littler clearer, we focus on the skinhead subculture in the UK. The early 1970s saw a decline in the need for well-paid skilled labour in traditional working class industries and businesses. Additionally, working class people found themselves in the midst of a complex, multidimensional community 'redevelopment'. This redevelopment included an altered population structure resulting from the accommodation of new waves of migrants (from the West Indies and other parts of the Commonwealth), and also included changes to housing tenure through the building of and movement into tall tower blocks of social housing. These transformations had profound impacts, producing an environment that broke up the traditional neighbourhoods and facilitated a negative perspective of collective spaces (P. Cohen, 1972a).

It was from such conditions that the skinhead culture emerged. In its early iteration, rather than having the racist or far-right connotations that might commonly spring to mind, the subculture was influenced by the peaceful intermingling of young people from English backgrounds with their peers newly arrived from parts of the Commonwealth. The music and style of dress associated with Jamaican 'rude boys' was drawn upon and shared by working class young men who became the first 'skins' (Pilkington et al., 2010). In combination with reggae and 'ska' music, skinheads opted for a fashion consisting of Doc Marten boots, drain pipe jeans, braces, simple t-shirts and short, cropped hair. The black and white 'two-tone' or 'chequer board' imagery that became associated with 'ska' music is thought to be representative of this intercultural blending (Gidley, 2007). This was an inversion of style (if not musical influence), which sat in contrast to subcultures who had come in the years before them, such as the 'Teds', whose outfitting had been more self-consciously flamboyant and proudly expensive, or the 'hippies'. The skins' outward display was argued to reflect a stylized reassertion of working class '[culture and] traditional working class community as a substitution for the real decline of the latter' (Clarke et al., 1976, p. 99).

The skinhead subculture in the next two decades fractured – one strand becoming commonly associated with both football hooliganism and racist violence, and the second with neo-Nazi subcultures, co-opting the style that was born from the first-wave 'original skins'. While neither of these should be understated in terms of being criminal and social problems, they both remained a search for and defence of community. Racism was also a symptom of rising tensions around increasing unemployment and scarcity of jobs and resources. Asian youth were subjected to racist violence as a result of a combination of the perceived 'double threat' of being 'visible' economic competitors and more overtly cultural 'others', and having a seemingly closer association with White middle class cultures.

There is no doubt that, even today, the concept of the skinhead is as a global cultural resource that articulates particular hatreds and fears at both local and national levels (Pilkington et al., 2010). However, this dominant depiction of skinheads as violent and racist only tells part of the story. There have in fact long been different 'types' of skinheads, including 'skinheads against racial prejudices' (sometimes called redskins) and gay skins. Pride, loyalty and unity – often seen as traditional working class sensibilities – became important catchwords for the various strands of the subculture, often with a rejection of violence and hate. Gay skins in particular offer a very interesting counter to the dominant negative representation of skinheads' association with the far right. Healy (1996) documented the presence of gay men in the skinhead community right back to the 1960s and argues that 'gay men' and skinheads were problematically represented as symbolizing two extremes of what men 'shouldn't be', and so the idea that the two identities could be occupied simultaneously was mostly unthinkable, leading to gay men's invisibility in both academic and popular accounts of the subculture.

Thinking point

- What do you make of the CCCS analysis of youth subcultures as responses to class inequality?
- Do you think it resonates for contemporary youth cultures?

Critiques of the CCCS theories of youth subculture

The influence of the CCCS on theories of youth has been enduring in a variety of ways, but it is far from uncontested. Even during the heyday of the CCCS, it was justly subjected to critique internally about its serious short sightedness with regard to gender. Angela McRobbie led the charge here (McRobbie and Garber, 1976; McRobbie, 1980), pointing to an unmistakably masculinist orientation that led the mostly male researchers to render young women almost entirely invisible. McRobbie and Garber, who were members of the CCCS, agreed that these would have often been male-dominated subcultures, but argued that accounts that either spoke nothing of girls or briefly talked of them as background noise, or afterthoughts in comparison with men (as girlfriends for example) were the result of a total lack of a desire to canvass girls' experiences. McRobbie and Garber (1976, p. 108) note for example that in the mod subculture 'there were certainly thousands of mod girls who made their appearance in the nightclubs, on the streets, at work and even upon the fringes of clashes between mods and rockers'. A further influential issue raised by McRobbie and Garber (1976) was related not just to the absence of girls in the analysis, but also to the lack of analysis of girls' cultures more broadly, and particularly how 'girls interact among themselves and with each other to form a distinctive culture of their own' (McRobbie and Garber, 1976, p. 111).

To this end, McRobbie and Garber insisted on the need to engage with the sphere of the family and the domestic realm if researchers were to avoid excluding the experiences of young women. They offered the example of 'teeny bopper culture', and pointed to a range of 'negotiated processes' that showed girls as active agents of the gendered hegemonic norms, rather than just passive consumers/fans of a manufactured pop culture. Teeny bopper culture was explained as being used by girls as a way to resist or (temporarily) ignore the boring demands of school and work; to offer a route into a sexual and otherwise off-limits imagery; and, through the process of developing tightknit peer groups, to buy time from sexual encounters that they sought to put off. Such attachments to and use of music and associated paraphernalia have been explored in more contemporary youth research, too, notably in Sian Lincoln's (2005) work on how teenage girls use music to transform their bedrooms into dynamic cultural and social spaces that facilitate identity development and offer a challenge to mundane realities and authoritarian structures.

> **Teeny bopper culture:** The cultural activities of young people in their early teens (10–13-year-olds), usually associated with mainstream pop music and fashion.

A number of other critiques emerged over the CCCS approach. For example, the CCCS has, quite rightly, been accused of 'over-reading' the actions of the young. In many ways, the CCCS was a political project that was driven by a particular Marxist ideology and desire to put class back onto the research agenda. As a result, researchers and writers had a tendency to overemphasize and interpret the actions of the young, putting meaning where it was not necessarily present. For example, would the Teds see themselves in the way their actions and motivations were portrayed by CCCS scholars? How did teddy boys themselves understand their own actions? What was really going on with and for punk rockers? By not asking the young people themselves, the CCCS tended to 'over-romanticize' these actions and to relegate them to 'cultural dupes'.

A further issue was that most of the work of the CCCS concentrated on the most spectacular and exciting aspects of youth culture, highlighting those groups that were predominantly visible and in the media. Mods, rockers, teddy boys, skinheads, punks, and finally goths were all identifiable yet not necessarily mainstream to the ordinary everyday experiences of the majority of young people. While the CCCS wanted to show these actions as creative forms of youth culture, they also concentrated efforts on the most visible sections of the population. CCCS scholars had little or nothing to say about 'ordinary youth' – those who did not join different subcultural groups or express their identities in such public ways. Whole sections of the youth population were ignored because they apparently conformed. The everydayness of life was missing. For example, in focussing their gaze on 'the frozen moment in which styles are born' Clarke argued that such research 'restricts the resulting politics of youth to a flash-point of rebellion' (1982, p. 2). By this he meant that the majority of working class youth were not really part of the equation and the specificity of the youth period was reduced to consumption, rather than offering more attention to the particular structural location of young people in society, or even indeed how styles become incorporated into the lives of working class young people beyond the moment of the subculture's inception. Clarke (1982, p. 30) ultimately argued that researchers ought to instead pay more attention to what young people actually do – 'such as hanging around chip shops, babysitting, and part time jobs.' CCCS scholars were considered too full of admiration for the subcultures they studied, and, in determining which subcultures were 'authentic', had perhaps sought out those that somehow reflected the academics' own desires for more progressive, class-conscious politics. In doing so, the sexism and racism so often apparent in the accounts of subcultures was, for Clarke, played down and not adequately held to account.

Others argued the CCCS had substantially overlooked the fact that style was likely to be transient. That is, for every one person who was totally committed to the style and the lifestyle of a mod, punk or rocker, there were 'hundreds of working class kids who grow up on a loose membership of several groups' (Frith, 1983, p. 219). Frith also noted that style held the potential of being played with for fun; this was similar to another point made by Clarke (1982, p. 27) that the CCCS paid no heed to 'the pleasure of dressing up'. This idea was developed further in a later critique by Miles (1995), who proffered that the CCCS had made a mistake in simply collapsing consumption with resistance, with his argument underscored by the absence in CCCS accounts of young people's own subjective understandings and interpretations of their style and consumption.

The British-centric nature of the CCCS studies was also discussed as a limitation to proposals that subcultures were a universal response to class oppression. Work by Blackman (1995), while sympathetic to the theory of subculture, still noted the risk of the term not being able to account for local variations. Not only was this seen to offer a partial reading of working class youth in the UK context, but as other writers noted, it was difficult to transpose the concept of subculture to different international settings (Bennett, 2014).

Finally, one last contention, though somewhat more recent, was postulated by Bennett, who pushed back against CCCS claims that subcultures were consolidated class reactions:

> It could rather be argued that post-war consumerism offered young people the opportunity to break away from their class based identities, the increased spending power of the young facilitating and encouraging experimentation with new, self-constructed forms of identity. (Bennett, 1999b, p. 602)

This notion of breaking away from the constraints of class-based identities, alongside many of the other critiques above, was pivotal to a major development that emerged in the 1990s – the body of work loosely labelled post-subcultural theory. This strand of theorizing retained a commitment to the importance of consumption for youth cultures, but in essence, as Bennett's words above make clear, flipped the CCCS scholars' understanding of consumption on its head.

Reframing youth subcultures

Post-subcultural youth and the 'rave' generation

As social and cultural changes gathered pace in the decades following the CCCS analysis of subcultures, sociologists sought new approaches to understand new forms of leisure and consumption. In youth sociology, rave and club cultures became a focal point. Subcultural theory was situated as having little to offer in understanding the significance of '**rave**' because 'rave culture' represented such a fusion, collage and eclectic mix of pre-existing youth cultural forms that it was impossible to attribute it to any underlying structural determinations (Redhead, 1990). Cultural artefacts were borrowed, repositioned, realigned, juxtaposed and given new meanings at such an alarming rate that looking for their underlying meaning was bound to fail. For example:

> **Rave:** A major cultural phenomena of leisure and dance that emerged in the 1980s. It was initially seen by national governments as illegal.

- Rave appropriated the smiley face of the hippy movement and created it as a symbol of the rave movement.

- Raves were defined as 'house parties', and it is thought this was because the first 'raves' took place in people's houses.

- Once they grew in size, raves were not held in formal venues but in warehouses – this was against the backdrop of the disintegration of much of British industry.

- Participants took and used a new generation of designer drugs and also used mundane items such as whistles, Lucozade and lollipops as accessories to their dancing.

- It claimed people flaunted sexuality yet often appeared highly asexual in the sense that people went to dance and not chat up others.

- Raves involved highly socialized gatherings, yet turned inwards to celebrate the individual experience of dance, drugs, and music.

- Rave was eclectic and innovative, borrowing music from the ghettos of Chicago, the 1970s disco of East Coast America, northern soul and funk, and mixed White culture with Black culture.

- Rave used state of the art technology to create ever more eclectic sounds, which drew from a vast array of cultural resources, including borrowing samples or beats from old songs, mixing them together with other sampled sound bites, extracts from speeches or any other sound that just seemed to go.

The sheer eclecticism of such a cultural form and its rapid tendency to shift, to change, to reconstitute itself in new ways, was argued to move us beyond the idea that youth subcultures existed, and therefore it was suggested that a new era of post-subculture theorizing was necessary.

Club cultures

Others developed this approach and expanded it to talk not just about 'rave culture', but 'club culture'. Thornton (1995) argued that the notion of subculture had lost its significance and relevance (both theoretically and analytically). She instead turned her attention to 'taste cultures' in clubbing. Similar to Redhead, Thornton emphasized that raves and clubs are home to diffuse and fluid communities with few boundaries to access. Despite rejecting the CCCS formulation of subculture as 'empirically unworkable', Thornton used the language of subculture, referring specifically to subcultural capital and subcultural ideologies, to explain hierarchies of taste. These were not about class, nor about outcomes of political struggle or social relations. In fact, Thornton argued that 'class is wilfully obfuscated by subcultural distinctions' and that subcultural distinction 'relies on the fantasy of classlessness', referring to how some middle class people change their accent during their clubbing years (1995, p. 12).

Thinking points

- What do you think is the difference between youth subcultures and 'club cultures'?
- Are there other types of youth culture activities that neither of these terms explain?

What is at stake for clubbers is, however, the hierarchy of values and what is or is not cool (in Thornton's book she uses the term 'hip'). Subcultural capital 'reveals itself ... by what it empathically isn't'. This starts with a concrete rejection of mainstream culture, with many clubbers seeing themselves as alternative or underground. It is worth noting that later work by Pini (2001) and Hutton (2006) also drew attention to the ways that women rejected mainstream clubbing because it represented oppressive traditional gender relations. In such research, the 'underground' scenes were deemed safer because of the emphasis on dancing and recreational drugs, and a feeling of being 'freed' from the 'cattle markets' of conventional nightclub spaces that are home to excessive alcohol drinking and men's sexual aggression. Beyond this, Thornton points out a variety of sources of subcultural capital such as the importance of the right haircut, appreciation of particular music, or being 'in the know' about how to perform at contemporary dance events. This subcultural capital, importantly, also included the need not to ask; that is, having a second nature understanding of the phenomenon was a necessary component of being 'hip'. This school of thought recognizes that taste cultures 'drive and gatekeeper music scenes, steering the material actions individuals perform, and the experiences they recall and document' (Bennett and Rogers, 2016, p. 63). In other words, subcultural capital permits some clubbers to claim authority and authenticity and thus position others as inferior.

Neo-tribes and scenes

Extending the work of Redhead and Thornton, Andy Bennett has been enormously instrumental from the late 1990s through until today, especially in producing a theoretical vocabulary that offers a sophisticated challenge to the CCCS concept of subculture. In perhaps his most influential piece of work, Bennett (1999b, p. 605) described the use of the term 'subculture' by the media and scholars as a 'convenient "catch-all" term used to describe a range of disparate collective practices whose only obvious relation is that they all involve young people'. For Bennett, the term 'subculture' imposed a top-down logic, such that youthful lifestyles and consumption were somehow part of a fixed and given form of identity that emerged from being working class. Bennett countered that instead 'fluidity [is]... characteristic of the forms of collective association which are built around musical and stylistic preference' (1999b, p. 599).

Building on the work of postmodern theorist Maffesoli, Bennett offers the concept of neo-tribes, contending that 'the musical and stylistic sensibilities exhibited by the young people involved in the dance music scene are clear examples of a form of late modern "sociality" rather than a fixed subcultural group' (Bennett, 1999b, p. 599). The concept of the neo-tribe, for Bennett, allows us to understand how young people hold loose affiliations with any particular grouping, style or musical preference, rather than a staunch commitment to one group or associated style at any one time. Discussing young people's engagement with the urban dance music scene, he argues that clubbing, even in one event or venue, is defined by 'a series of fragmented, temporal experiences as they move between different dance floors and engage with different crowds' (Bennett, 1999b, p. 611).

At the fore of this argument is that 'the individual is free to choose, not only between various musical styles and attendant visual images, but also how such choices are lived out and what they are made to stand for (Bennett, 1999b, p. 614). Bennett uses another concept, called 'lifestyle', as a way of explaining how the individual goes about '… choosing certain commodities and patterns of consumption and in articulating these cultural resources as modes of personal expression' (Bennett, 1999b, p. 607). The concept of lifestyle differs from the notion of a way of life, because the latter indicates individuals are 'locked into particular "ways of being" which are determined by the conditions of class', while the former provides the image of choices that might be '[in] no way indicative of a specific class background' (Bennett, 1999b, p. 607).

The active nature of the consumer, and the ways that one's identity is actively *constructed* rather than passively given, are central here. This corresponds with the broader discussion of style put forward by Polhemus (1997, p. 150), who argues that 'like tins of soup lined up on endless shelves, we can choose between more than fifty different style tribes.' This also accords with the work of Muggleton, who describes contemporary young people as living by a sensibility, which manifests itself as 'an expression of freedom from structure, control and restraint, ensuring that stasis is rejected in favour of movement and fluidity' (Muggleton, 2000, p. 158).

A second development, again using and defining music as a central site for cultural activity of the young, has been the emergence of what has been defined as 'scenes'. Based on the work of Canadian cultural theorist Will Straw (1991), music 'scenes' are situated fundamentally as spaces that allow individuals to come together, bonded not by class or community but by musical tastes and aesthetic relationships. They are in constant evolution and are transient in their nature. Straw's focus was on rock music and how it was cross-cutting in membership groupings, showing how class and gender are irrelevant to participation. Scenes, though, have been associated with the idea of locality and geography, suggesting that they can be differentiated and bring together different groupings within a particular region and city around particular tastes that give a local dimension to cultural practice. One example is the way jazz music became established in New Orleans and rock and roll in Memphis in the USA. This gives taste and cultural practice around music clear linkages to local cultural histories and practices. Alternatively, 'scenes' can operate outside of geography and structure and provide a more global analysis. For example, Harris (2016) argues that heavy metal participation/identification is not bounded by geographic or class lines; rather, it operates across time and space, creating and recreating a wide range of texts, institutions and cultural practices that individuals can access and be a part of from afar. In this context, scenes not only cut across class, gender and racial divisions but also geographical locations.

The impact of these two approaches has been to construct youth cultural practice as being more fluid and driven by taste and choice, rather than structure. As Bennett (2011) suggests, the analysis of youth culture should not be understood or explained through a 'structural lens' but as a 'fusion zone' where the lens is focussed on the cultural practice to see whether and how 'structure' might influence it. The question then becomes how structure is reflexively managed by young people through the creative appropriation of cultural resources.

> ### 💭 Thinking point
>
> - Would you describe your own stylings, musical tastes or other cultural prac-
>   tices as corresponding to post-subcultural theorizing?
> - Why do you reach these conclusions?

Critiques of post-subcultural theory

Post-subcultural theory (PSCT) is also not immune from interrogation. Indeed, PSCT scholars have been subject to quite stinging critique, matching the ferocity PSCT aimed at the CCCS. The debates between the two poles are not yet resolved, so here we lay out some of the substantive arguments of those who have engaged with the PSCT work. A starting point for many scholars is that PSCT has underplayed the role of structural factors such as race, gender and especially class.

Hesmondalgh (2005) is fiercely critical of the PSCT evidence base, claiming that the ethnographic methods that PSCT scholars have used cannot speak so confidently to questions about musical cultural tastes and their correlation with variables such as age, class, gender and ethnicity. Concurring with this argument, Shildrick and MacDonald (2006, p. 133) suggest that PSCT scholars miss in their analysis that 'social and economic constraint reverberates through the youth cultural and leisure experiences of less advantaged young people'. These critics suggest that, while some working class people may be present in the samples of Bennett, Redhead and others, for the most part, genuinely marginalized and disadvantaged young people are 'wholly absent', with the flamboyant, stylistically spectacular young people who are documented tending to reflect the lives of 'the more privileged sections of dominant cultural groups' (Shildrick and MacDonald, 2006, p. 129). These writers are in effect positing the very same argument that was used *against* the CCCS conceptualization of subculture: post-subcultural theory is also based on the 'stylistic art of the few'. The net result is that, for Blackman (2004, p. 120), PSCT research misses an important, and perhaps the most important, issue for youth sociology, which is to 'address or critique the relation of dominance and subordination exercised through social and cultural structures of society'.

Hesmondhalgh (2005) suggests the post-subcultural approach also fails to acknowledge that 'traditional' or original subcultural groups do still exist and are a powerful force in shaping the lives of some young people: goths, for example (Hodkinson, 2011, 2012). Hodkinson suggests that, as a subculture, goth has remained fixed and of significance to a whole range of young people. It generates a level of commitment beyond other groupings, a distinctiveness, and substance of meaning to participants. Questions still remain over how typical these sorts of movements are and how much they are built on nostalgia for a lost age of collectivism, rather than having real significance. However, it does suggest collective subcultures still have meaning and relevance.

A final point that we would stress is that at least part of the PSCT critique of the CCCS is problematic. The CCCS scholars were in fact very aware of the limits of focussing on specific sections of the working class, and they did not overstate the prevalence or segregated nature of subcultures and styles. Indeed, the introduction to *Resistance Through Rituals* states very clearly:

> the *great majority of working class youth never enters a tight or coherent subculture at all. Individuals*, in their personal life careers *may or may not move in and out of one, or indeed, several such subcultures.* Their *relation to the existing subcultures may be fleeting* or permanent, marginal or central. The subcultures are important because there *the response of youth takes a peculiarly tangible form....* (Clarke et al., 1976, p. 16)

More recent scholarship has extended some of these points, illustrating how accessing and engaging with multiple subcultures is entirely logical and not necessarily evidence of the need for post-subcultural theorising. For example, US-based researchers Ulusoy and Firat note young people's tendency toward multiple and even 'eclectic, fragmented, and paradoxical subcultures', but also stress that this makes sense because 'each subculture provides a distinct escape from different oppressions perceived in the mainstream' (2018, p. 21). Contemporary analyses of youth must be able to approach young people's engagements with subcultural practices as involving dynamic rather than fixed forms, styles and boundaries. What all subcultures have in common is a desire, at least, to oppose or escape the oppressions of the mainstream.

Contemporary subcultures

Contemporary global youth subcultures are now very diverse, and have flourished in the social media age, enabled through the immediacy of new forms of connectivity (Robards and Bennett, 2011). The study of youth subcultures in sociology tends to still revolve around musical forms, and forms of bodily presentation.

The straight edge subculture

'Straight edge' adherents are a group of young people who are committed to a 'clean living' ideology alongside an engagement with the hard-core punk music scene. In this, 'members abstain, completely, from drug, alcohol and tobacco use and usually reserve sexual activity for caring relationships, rejecting casual sex' (Haenlfer, 2006, p. 10). For these young people this is not something experienced

---

as simply passing through in an ephemeral way. There are also strong notions of subcultural resistance, with such behaviours representing a rejection of 'both mainstream adult and youth cultures' (Haenlfer, 2006). Beyond a large black X (inked or tattooed) on the back of the hand, the style of dress, relatively cropped hair, hoodies and t-shirts emblazoned with band names, and the even the style of dancing, are not entirely distinct from other strands of the hard-core music scene. The lyrics of the bands speak to core components of straight edge identity, and the music is fast, distorted and dense. Engagement with the music is characterized by almost a loss of control and a sense of abandon. While there is a lack of overt emphasis on class in the research on straight edge, both the online practices as well as the documented real-life behaviours, stylings and commitments of adherents appear to confirm the presence of a subculture, despite post-subcultural analysis questioning whether subcultures even exist.

Hip hop is, in many ways, indicative of a global youth culture. It also has a multitude of localized variants, where young people have synergized the local and global (this is sometimes described as '**glocal**'), and are influenced by existing complexes of host cultures and histories of migration (Hesmondhalgh and Melville, 2002). For many people, hip hop might be described as at least in part as inescapably related to mainstream youth culture and an important part of wider capitalist markets, in much the same way that punk moved from being subversive to the commodified mainstream. Its roots, though, are firmly grounded in issues of race, inequality and the *structural location* of minority ethnic people in US society; That is, while hip hop has a hugely significant racial dimension, the intersection of race and social class location is vivid.

Glocal: A term used to describe the interaction between global and local culture.

Born in the Bronx in New York, hip hop culture is mostly often associated with the experiences of African American youth, though scholars have frequently also foregrounded the cultural contributions of Puerto Ricans and people of other Latino backgrounds. Similar to some of the subcultures described above, the origins of the music and stylings associated with hip hop have been located in rising inequality and the transformation of the economy. As Pough comments, 'jobs were scarce, and factories and businesses were leaving the area. The future looked bleak...' (Pough, 2004, p. 7). Another similarity is that hip hop was set against the dominant culture, and moreover in 'defiance of the white establishment' (Rahn, 2002, p. 2). MC-ing, DJ-ing, rap music, graffiti art and breakdancing became some of the hallmarks of a subculture that rebelled against hegemonic norms and sought to combat the exclusion of Black and other minority ethnic people from public space. This was achieved through a strategy of legitimating minority cultural expressions and making it visible in public spaces. As a male-dominated (though not exclusively) form of resistance, with its own language, slang, symbols, and form of expression pitted against 'the system', these early origins of hip hop appear to have many parallels with the subcultures set out in the work of the CCCS.

While hip hop is now a huge commercial enterprise with widespread appeal and massive uptake among lots of young people across racial and class boundaries all over

---

Hip-hop, resistance and female rappers in Iran

Hip hop as a musical form and cultural practice is illegal in Iran, as it violates the traditional and religious practices of the dominant Muslim culture. Yet, as Elham Golpushnezhad writes, Iranian hip hop has flourished over the past two decades: 'Hip-hop became a platform for the expression of young people's political view-points, as female rappers targeted issues of gender, sexuality, religion, language and identity' (2018, p. 261). Many rappers must use international networks, and reside outside of Iran, coming together at international festivals such as Rhythm of Change, held in Sweden in 2008. No political rapper resistant to dominant Islamic culture or female rapper living in Iran can openly rap to express his/her concerns. More recently, hip hop has been used by rappers to articulate and emphasize Islamic values of chastity, faith, martyrdom and jihad in their songs. Political and resistant hip hop artists must retreat 'underground' as this new style of Islamic hip hop gains financial and state support.

---

the world, research still points to the significance of underground or non-mainstream production and consumption of hip hop for many young people who suffer from being at or near the bottom of the social and/or economic hierarchy. This form of unity of appeal is described by Osumare (2007) as 'connective marginalities'. Echoing this idea, Dimitriadis (2009, p. xiv) argues that hip hop 'has become a vehicle for disenfranchised youth to articulate their own needs and concerns', and points to its uptake by Arab youth in France, Afro-Germans in Berlin, Maori youth in New Zealand and First Nations young people in Canada and Australia. On the latter, Morgan (2015) has studied the appeal and production of 'underground' (non-mainstream) hip hop subcultures for Indigenous First Australian youth. Such young people are familiar with systems of oppression that parallel the plight of young Black men in the USA, such that hip hop offers 'an account of urban racism, police persecution and a sense of living in the ghetto, but one that is glocalized, transformed and provided with local meanings and inflections' (Morgan, 2015, p. 70). The localized re-working of hip hop has also been identified as a significant element of White working class young people's cultural affiliations in North East England (Bennett, 1999a) and for disaffected Japanese youth who feel alienated from their country's cultural mainstream (Condroy, 2001), among others.

Modifying the body is another way contemporary youth subcultures can be expressed. For example, Derek Roberts' (2015) online ethnography of body modification in the USA, UK, Canada and Australia highlights that, as many readers might guess, tattooing has become an acceptable form of expression among young people. This on the one hand connotes that the practice is not subcultural at all, appealing to people from different class backgrounds. However, Roberts (2015) reminds us that it is important to differentiate between modifications that are always visible and those that can be hidden. This is key to understanding what he found to be the difference between 'modified people' and 'people with modifications'. The latter represents the mainstream, while the former, for Roberts, represents a committed, authentic subculture, one that requires its adherents to have extensive tattooing, for example, and accept that they will be financially penalized by not being able to access jobs *because of their style*. That is, people with tattoos and other very visible body modifications experience labour market discrimination because of mainstream lack of acceptance of this visual style, resulting in high rates of unemployment. In turn, though, the modifiers reject mainstream culture, preferring to seek employment within the subculture (e.g. in tattooing parlours). The class backgrounds of the modified community in Roberts' study are also of interest. Roberts suggests that, using education as a proxy for class, the committed members of this subculture held an education level below the level of a college degree, indicating working class status. Tranter and Grant (2018) in Australia confirm this relationship between body modifications and social background, pointing to a higher prevalence among younger, less educated, working-class, non-conservative people.

The fetishization of youth in Japanese gay male media

Japan's gay male subculture, like many others around the world, is highly stratified by class, body type, age and gendered identity. Thomas Baudinette's (2015, 2016) research in the Shinjuku Ni-chōme district in central Tokyo explores the ways idealised body types appear in this district, which is the source of most Japanese gay male media, including gay magazines, pornographic videos and online dating agencies. He argues, 'these media play an important role in rendering gay male desire as a commodity, reducing gay men's identities to patterns of consumer behaviour' (Baudinette, 2016). In this subculture, these identities are known as 'types' (taipu), which refers to the alignment with a stereotypical identity category based upon ideas of an idealised body type and modes of consumption, such as 'cute guy', 'sporty guy' or 'body builders'. Types are expected to participate in particular forms of consumption associated with each 'scene' in Ni-chōme. Baudinette's research shows how consumption of media is central to young Japanese gay men's conceptualizations of their gay identities and desires.

The dominance of Northern theory

As we suggested in Chapter 1, much of the debate over subcultural theory and post-subcultural studies has been dominated by work that has emerged in countries in the Northern Hemisphere, and especially the UK, although the influence of these ideas as a way of constructing and understanding youth cultural practice has broadened to countries such as the USA, Japan, Canada and Russia. It is also the case that the theories that are used to make sense of young people's cultural practices emerge out of theorists that are influential in what is called Northern theory. Relatively little attention has been paid to how and whether subcultures operate outside of these contexts in mainstream journals, but this is not to say it does not exist. We know, for example, that across all countries, young people are continually engaged in a wide range of cultural activities. As was suggested at the beginning of this chapter, youth cultural practice is young people's 'effort at play' (Bennett, 2011) and brings them into practices that involve music, dance and performance, in a wide range of settings. It can also involve dress and style and consumption. These are not unique to the Western nations where research has dominated, but are also prominent in India, China, Southern American and African countries, and basically everywhere in the Global South. We need to acknowledge that young people, regardless of their location, are involved in such cultural practices.

For example, in the Republic of Congo, subcultural groups called 'le sape' (see https://haenfler.sites.grinnell.edu/subcultures-and-scenes/sape/) are a collective who take styles and clothes, such as Yves Saint Laurent suits, Yamamoto jackets, Marcel Lassance suits, Gresson shoes and Cacharel pants, from their French colonisers as a way of making anti-colonial statements. Similarly, in South Africa there is the Skhothane subculture (Inngs, 2017), with roots in dance like Pantsula. They appropriated the uniforms that Black South Africans were forced to wear during apartheid as a statement against apartheid. In China, there is 杀马特 Shā mā tē. (http://blog.tutorming.com/expats/5-fascinating-chinese-sub-cultures), a youth subcultural group that is both popular and hated in China. They wear dark eyeliner and black clothes with spiked hair. They tend to be from rural areas and from poorly educated groups. They are working in urban jobs, being paid low wages and form gangs. These three are examples of subcultural groups that exist in countries that are not always recognized as having such cultural diversity in their youth populations. Not only do they exist, they have long existed, and as Global South scholarship shows us, their existence both aligns with and sometimes troubles the subcultural tradition. For example, there is Mooney's (2005) elaboration of the 1950s South African 'ducktails' subculture, comprised of White young men whose styling challenged the hegemonic norms of adults, but who at the same time enacted racist violence towards Black youth, which perpetuated racialized hegemonic power relations, rather than resisting them.

Identity, youth popular culture and consumption

Young people's engagement with **popular culture** is studied as a key dimension of youth cultures in youth sociology. Practices of consumption are recognized as central to understanding contemporary youth, as the youth market has expanded significantly over the last 40 years (Best and Lyn, 2016). For example, entire markets have emerged around 'the girl as a consumer', celebrating femininity and targeting girls and young women as consumers; a market worth over $9 billion in the USA alone (Best and Lyn, 2016). Many working within a post-structuralist framework focus on how

> **Popular culture:**
> Usually a term used to describe young people's involvement in more mainstream cultural activities that impacts more on the majority. It has *mass* accessibility and appeal.

the young do not passively accept commodities, but instead use them in creative ways that are often not intended; and ways which allow them to actively construct their own cultures and identities in new and challenging ways (see e.g. Loh (2016) on 'tween' girls' fashion choices in Singapore). One of the first such studies was Angela McRobbie's work in the 1980s. This demonstrated how girls do not just passively accept the dominant culture and ideology of femininity but attempt instead to appropriate it and to give it new meanings. She argues that girls' reading of the teenage magazine *Jackie* was a way of taking a commodity and with it generating their own sense of what it means to be a girl, and to deliver self-empowerment. Reading a magazine is, therefore, not just buying a commodity and passively absorbing the intended content and messages, but is an active process of engagement and creativity. McRobbie's work also showed that the ultimate act of consumption is shopping. In this, girls are not just passive beings, subordinated to the market or the empty purchase of meaningless and often useless things. Shopping represents an important sphere of activity for girls because it allows them access to the public world in ways that are normally denied. It is through the act of consumption that girls can exercise some degree of choice, autonomy and independence through the creation of their own identities. That is, girls and young women can exercise some degree of choice over who and what they want to be. Youth culture here operates to offer young people ways of doing things differently, of stepping outside dominant notions of gender, and to radicalize their conduct to create new ways of life that offer them real alternatives.

Thinking points

- How important is consumption to young people's social identities?
- To what extent do you think young people are 'creative innovators' in their engagement with commodities?
- How important is it that you buy new items of clothing? How often is it necessary and why?

Paul Willis's (1990) work on 'common culture' shows that the act of consumption can produce a vastly different range of youthful subjectivities and identities. Willis, too, argues that young people consume commodities in creative ways that often have little or no meaningful relationship to the 'original' role of that commodity, so that young people are always involved in the creation and recreation of their own cultural life. He described this as a process of bringing one's own specific 'grounded aesthetic to bear on consumption' (Willis, 1990, p. 85), showing how young people make their own judgments and rearticulate supposed orders and rules. Through their daily interaction with each other and the market, young people engage in a process of symbolic exchange and role-playing that continually defines and redefines what it means to be young. Under contemporary conditions, young people's identities are derived primarily from the creative ways in which they consume.

The expansion of mass, multi- and social media over the past two decades has huge implications for the current generation of youth. We explore these dynamics in depth in Chapter 6. Young people do not passively receive messages about products, or passively absorb social media messages. They decode and de-construct the cultural messages around the product. Young people become discriminating consumers, able to articulate what they like about some things and what they dislike about others. Young people's acts of consumption are therefore seen as more complex than mere passivity, offering an important source of individual activity and, seemingly, an infinite number of possibilities in which they use choose and use such commodities for their own ends. For example, Danah Boyd's (2007) work shows that young people's engagement with social media is critical to the development of both identities and youth communities. She describes social media sites as 'networked publics' through which young people can 'write themselves and their communities into being' (p. 120).

A critical insight here is that people have to 'do things' with commodities, since commodities are the only things most people possess, and it is in doing things with these commodities that young people generate their own peculiar experiences of consumption, leisure and thus lifestyle. Willis talks about the ways that, historically, youth culture has used home taping, re-recording and mixing as a creative force, and young people have used the commodities available to them to create new and innovative cultural forms, through the use and development and use of sound systems, DJ-ing, 'toasting' and rapping. Being young therefore is constituted through a constant process of interaction and borrowing, as youth is constantly creative in refashioning what it actually means to be young.

These perspectives position young people as crucial actors in producing their own distinctive identities, which are built through the use of the market and commodities. In this sense, young people have embraced the post-modern condition in a way that academics, politicians and others have failed to recognize, and through this they are recreating new and innovative ways of living. This even extends to relatively poor young people. For instance, Willis (1990) noted that, while stylistic consumption for the unemployed young person can seem like an unnecessary luxury, many relatively poor young people still find ways to make style central to their identity (Willis, 1990). Young people, in engaging with consumption so prolifically, demonstrate that they abide within the dominant ideology of the need to be a consumer, but with a pluralism of styles.

Celebrity culture and contemporary youth

Mendick et al. (2019) explore young people's engagements with celebrity culture as an important component in the social and cultural contexts that shape young people's identities, and how 'social divisions and hierarchies are reproduced within celebrity' (p. 13). Drawing on celebrity examples including Beyonce, Kim Kardashian and Justin Bieber, the authors see celebrity as both a freely chosen engagement with popular culture, and as a way of reading the limits of the narratives of austerity and aspiration also informing their identities. Their discussion helps to further unpack the influence of celebrity on young people's perspectives on work, authenticity, success, happiness, money and fame in relation to their own lives. Thinking about celebrities as a 'cultural text', Mendick and colleagues (2019) explain how they regulate possible ways of being in any given socio-historical context. This allows us to understand how 'structural factors ... shape young people's sense of desirable and achievable aspirations, and their opportunities for realizing them' (Mendick et al., 2019, p. 5). The ways that inequalities of class, gender and race play out in this context are made clear, with a vivid rejection of the idea that young people's aspirations are a 'project of self-fashioning' (Mendick et al., 2019, p. 14). Instead, young people's engagement with celebrity as a text of popular culture is a valuable resource as it delivers insights 'about young people's current circumstances and for how it mediates their sense of possible and desirable future' (Mendick et al., 2019, p. 165).

Thinking point

Think about your friends and extended networks. How much 'choice' do young people really have in shaping their self-presentations or styles? How are 'choices' made in the context of already limited options regarding class and socio-economic status, gender, race or ethnicity?

The intersection of youth culture and youth transitions

Beyond these ongoing and very important debates among those looking at youth culture, researchers have more recently turned towards trying to bring the youth transitions and youth cultures traditions into productive dialogue. Woodman and Bennett (2015) have gone so far as to say that trying to mark out any neat division between young people's transitions and their cultural lives is out of step with reality. After all, both 'transitions' and 'cultures' perspectives are embedded in cultural and social practice themselves. Recent work in youth studies has acknowledged the need for more critical encounters between the 'transitions' and 'cultures' fields. Transition studies need to be more 'culturally rich', while youth culture studies need to be more aware of 'spatial divisions' (Valentine et al., 1998) and socially segmented consumption patterns among youth (Hollands, 2002, p. 154). Hollands (2002) and Miles (2000) point out that youth transition studies need to incorporate aspects of youth culture studies because it is 'young people's cultural experiences [that] represent the actual area within which they seek to cope with, and at times defy, the ups and downs of structural change' (Miles, 2000, p. 65).

Summary

- Youth sociologists are interested in how young people construct their identities through consumption and leisure practices, and how these practices are shaped by structural forces including class, gender, ethnicity and place.

- Historically there has been a strong focus on class and the structural conditions of the young.

- Feminist writers have been highly critical of subcultures that marginalize young women.

- Post-subcultural studies also challenge structural approaches seeing young people's participation in subcultures as more diverse.

- Critiques of post-subcultural studies challenge its emphasis on agency.

- Popular culture and consumption practices have increasingly become important in shaping young people's social practices and lives.

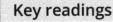

Exercise: The sociological imagination

Ask someone a generation older than you about the youth subcultures or cultures that were around in their youth. What were the characteristics of these groups (e.g. bodily presentation, political message and musical style)? How did these groups align with or challenge dominant culture at the time? Compare with your own experience or knowledge of youth cultures and subcultures in your generation.

Key readings

Allen, K. Mendrick, H., Harvey, L. & Ahmad, A. (2017) 'Cultural transition: celebrity and young people's aspirations' in Furlong, A. (ed.) *Handbook of Youth and Young Adulthood*, 2nd ed. (London, Routledge).

Bennett, A. (2011) 'The post-subcultural turn: some reflections 10 years on', *Journal of Youth Studies*, vol. 14, no. 5, pp. 493–506.

Dimitriadis, G. (2009) *Performing Identity/Performing Culture: Hip Hop as Text, Pedagogy, and Lived practice* (Peter Lang).

Haenfler, R. (2006) *Straight Edge: Clean-Living Youth, Hardcore Punk, and Social Change* (Rutgers University Press).

Hall, S. & Jefferson, T. (eds.) (1976) *Resistance Through Rituals: Youth Subcultures in Post-War Britain*, pp. 209–222 (London: Hutchinson).

Hodkinson, P. (2017) 'Young people's fashion and style' in Furlong, A. (ed.) *Handbook of Youth and Young Adulthood* (2nd edition) (London, Routledge).

McRobbie, A. (2000) *Feminism and Youth Culture* (London: Macmillan).

Shildrick, T. & MacDonald, R. (2006) 'In defence of subculture: young people, leisure and social divisions', *Journal of Youth Studies*, vol. 9, no. 2, pp. 125–140.

Woodman, D. & Bennett, A. (eds.) (2016). *Youth Cultures, Transitions, and Generations: Bridging the Gap in Youth Research* (Singapore: Springer).

6 YOUTH, SOCIAL MEDIA AND DIGITAL LIVES

In this chapter you will learn about:

- Different perspectives on 'digital natives', 'digital immigrants' and the 'digital divide'
- How young people use the digital world to help create and establish their identities
- The risks young people face on digital media
- Political economy perspectives on the implications of the digital age in social life.

Youth, the internet and digital lives

Thinking point

- How much time do you spend on the internet each day?
- How important is connectivity in your daily life, and why?

Technological developments associated with the internet and digital media over the past two decades have fundamentally altered the ways people communicate and interact. Young people are positioned at the forefront of debates about the impacts of digital and **social media**. Whilst social media can allow possibilities for progressive social transformation, transparency and access, they can also incubate forms of public shaming, dissemination of false information, discrimination and hate speech. Digital platforms can reinforce barriers of gender, sexuality, class, ethnicity, race, religion and ability/disability. Sociological perspectives are therefore crucial in thoroughly interrogating and exploring the wide-ranging implications of digital developments in young people's daily lives.

Social media: Broadly refers to different forms of social interaction that we do online, and also incorporates a variety of online platforms that facilitate exchange or connection in some form; for example, *Facebook*, or *Instagram*.

The 'net' generation: 'digital natives' and 'digital immigrants'

In Chapter 1 we touched upon the idea that we are seeing the emergence of a 'new' generation. One of the major areas where this debate has taken place is in the growth of digital media. It has been said that we are seeing a revolution for the young because developments in digital media are providing a vehicle not only for massive social change, but also for the meaning of what it is to be young today. This was first claimed by Prensky (2001), who introduced the idea that we are seeing the emergence of a new generation of '**digital natives**' who are different from previous generations ('**digital immigrants**'). Digital natives are those young people who have grown up with new media and, as a result, have a very different style of interacting with them. Digital natives are characterized as craving interactivity, valuing graphics over text and operating at 'twitch speed' in video games and social networking sites. Prensky suggests there is a form of evolution going on in which members of the digital generation are adapting to new environmental conditions. Digital immigrants, on the other hand, are people in their later years who were not brought up with digital technology. They are still working on step-by-step logic and are characterized as struggling to adapt.

> **Digital natives:**
> People who have grown up with new media and who use it with familiarity and comfort in their everyday lives.

> **Digital immigrants:**
> People who have not been brought up with digital technology, and have learnt how to use digital devices and platforms as adults.

🗨 Thinking points

- Do you think there is a generational divide over the use of the internet?
- Do you think older people misunderstand how young people use technology?

As a result it is argued there is an increasing 'generational divide' between 'digital natives' and 'digital immigrants'. It is claimed that 'digital immigrants' lack the skills and understanding needed for the new digital age, which is creating a 'them' and 'us' situation, '...where adults and institutions are rendered obsolete by the rise of the digital native' (Selwyn, 2009, p. 369). This, it is argued, is creating conflict between the generations. Concerns about 'generational conflict' regarding technological developments, however, are certainly not new. Commentators are prone to idealize the potential of a 'net generation' who could harness the new access to information to overthrow the old hierarchies. Tapscott (1998) for example describes the N-Geners as 'hungry for expression', articulate, creatively inquisitive and as having a social conscious. Using this technology is as natural as breathing. Alternatively, others bemoan the current generation of youth, who are seen to be 'disengaged' from the 'real world', or 'dumbed down' by the technology (Selwyn, 2009).

There are criticisms of the digital native thesis. For example, while the internet is important, traditional media activities, such as watching TV and films, still remain a major leisure activity of the young. In fact, watching TV and films is the most common leisure activity amongst the N-Geners (or digital natives). The internet has created new ways of consuming traditional media. We can see this when we watch TV programmes on mobile devices or computers using providers such as Netflix, Amazon and Sky. We are able to stop, rewind and replay live TV, and decide what and when to watch. In short, the internet and new technology is important, but 'old media' remain a major form of leisure activity for young people.

The 'digital native' thesis also ignores, and fails to recognize, the banality of much media usage. As Sonia Livingstone (2009) reminds us, in reality many young people's engagement with technology is often passive, solitary, sporadic and unspectacular. What is not always acknowledged is that the large majority of young people's interactions on the internet are not 'spectacular', 'creative' and 'innovative'. 'Cyber kids' may exist, but they are not typical of the majority of users. Most interaction on the internet by the young relates to the consumption of music and films, or social networking. It is also important to remember that most young people do not necessarily have the most recent technological hardware. Generally, such equipment would only be available to the wealthy few. Rather, they have the technology that allows them access to the relevant online spaces. The degree to which digital technology is a driving force in young people's lives remains questionable. For many, as we saw in the previous two chapters, there are far more pressing matters; for example, getting a good education, getting a job, leaving home, starting (and ending relationships) or becoming financially independent. All of these needs and desires require substantial investment in the offline world. In reality, technology tends to be a 'tool' for 'doing life'. Ultimately, descriptions of digital natives and digital immigrants are part of a broader discursive argument that wants to frame the young as a 'problem' that needs to be managed (Livingstone, 2009). In many ways, these divisions are used simplistically to construct the young as 'tech savvy' while the older population is not.

Who is not a part of the digital revolution?

One of the major debates over social media and the internet relates to what is called the '**digital divide**'. Ragnedd and Muschert (2013) define this as '... the unequal access and utility of internet communications technologies'. (p. i) In the early days of the internet, the digital divide was very much characterized in terms of access to internet infrastructure and hardware. If you did not have a desktop computer, and you did not live in a place that had the necessary infrastructure, then you could not go online. Today, this still remains central and is particularly evident in geographic regions with limited economic means to invest in such infrastructure and with populations that are similarly constrained.

> **Digital divide:** Refers to unequal access to the internet and digital technologies, including physical access to hardware and infrastructure, as well as exclusion based on socio-economic dynamics.

🗨 Thinking points

- Who do you think does not have access to the internet?
- What types of factors can influence the extent and quality of access?

One way of recognizing the geographical divide is seeing how people across the world can, or cannot access, the internet. It is not just an 'in country' issue. For example, the highest rates of internet use as of 2018 are in North America (95 per cent), followed by Europe (85 per cent). The regions with the lowest rate are Africa (35 per cent) and Asia (48 per cent), although developing regions have shown the greatest rates of growth over the last eighteen years (2000–2018). Africa has exhibited the most growth, followed by the Middle East (Internet World Statistics, 2018). Proliferation and user rates are not evenly spread across continental or national boundaries, however, and an expanding diversity of users increases the dynamics of change already associated with the internet. It is difficult to compare internet up-take rates across countries because of differing data collection methods and measurement categories.

The geographical divide also exists within countries. For instance, in Australia, access is greater among city dwellers than those living in more remote areas (ABS, 2014–15). In some instances, this can be attributed to a lack of infrastructure, such as mobile networks or cellphone towers. Commercial telecommunications companies struggle to service large geographic areas with small populations. The issue of the rural/urban divide is significant worldwide. Even in countries such as the UK and the USA, where infrastructure coverage is high quality, large sections of the population remain unconnected (Internet World Statistics, 2018).

However, when we examine the digital divide, it is important to recognize how it impacts different groups as well as geographies. As Selwyn (2009) reminds us:

> … research studies suggest that young people's abilities to access digital technologies remain patterned strongly along lines of socio-economic status and social class, as well as gender, geography and the many other entrenched "social fault lines" which remain prominent in early twenty-first century society. (p.371)

While the 'digital divide' still exists, whereby access is predicated on hardware, infrastructure and geography, the divide has reduced. This is because schools are now providing both the technology and time for students to work online at school, and new technologies, such as smart phones, are much more accessible. More and more young people, regardless of their social economic status, are therefore able to access the internet in different ways. However, differences in regard to access at home have remained strong. For example, in 2012, an OFCOM survey found that access at home had grown from just over 50 per cent to 70 per cent for those in the lowest SES groups. In contrast, access for the highest SES groups had reached 98 per cent.

It is also now recognized that the digital divide has moved to a 'second level divide' (Lichy, 2011) that is increasingly related to usage. There is a body of evidence suggesting that, while access is increasing, there are still divisions along class lines (Lichy, 2011). For example, in their work in Indonesia, which has a relatively low degree of internet diffusion, Utomo et al. (2013) found that, of those who had used the internet, 85 per cent reported that they did so on a daily basis, mostly using mobile phones. However, the level and type of internet access was strongly shaped by socio-demographics such as gender and education.

The digital divide amongst children and young people

A study by Livingstone and Helsper (2007) found significant classed dimensions of internet use and access. Those who were 'non-users' were more likely to be from working-class households and from the 9–11 or 18–19-year-old groups. Only half of non-users had access to the internet at school, and very few had home access or access elsewhere. Occasional users were more likely to be working class, though over half had home access, and most had access at school. Their quality of access was poorer than more frequent users (in terms of broadband, and bedroom access). Like the non-users, they explained their low use in terms of difficulties of access and lack of interest. Those who went online at least weekly were spread across different SES groups. Most had access at home, school and elsewhere, and they spent longer online than occasional users. They used the internet for school work, information, games and email.

   The daily users came from more middle-class homes and were a little older than weekly or occasional users. They also benefited from better quality internet access. They had been online for longer than the other groups as well, and spent more time online each day. They also considered themselves more skilled (self-labelling themselves 'advanced' users). Over half used it for school work, information, email, instant messaging, games, music and looking for cinema/theatre/concerts.

The impact of the digital age in the forming of social identities

The growing usage and influence of social media

The growth of what we now call 'social media' has been central to recent technological development. While it seems as though social media have always been a major part of young people's lives, they actually represent a continuously changing and adapting collection of technologies that have emerged slowly over time.

Thinking point

- What forms of social media do you use in your everyday life, and why do you use them?
- Do you think you could you live without social media, and how much does it impact on your daily life?

Facebook is perhaps one of the most popular and recognizable social media platforms and has been particularly popular among young people. Other social networking sites preceded *Facebook*; for instance, the once popular *MySpace* and *Friendster*. The current landscape is now filled with many different platforms that represent a variety of ways to both talk to people online and exchange content. For example, *Instagram*, *Snapchat* and *YouTube* are now the most popular sites with the young, and *Facebook* is increasingly less popular with the younger generation than it once was.

These social media platforms are sites that young people visit multiple times per day to entertain themselves, and interact socially with others.

Social media is a concept with many different meanings, and layers. It encompasses different forms of sociality, including collaboration, community or communication, and can be broadly understood as '…engaging with different forms of sociality on the internet in the context of society.' (Fuchs, 2017, p. 7). Such a broad definition includes the variety of online platforms that we are familiar with, which facilitate exchange or interaction in some form. Information on user rates, including who is using what, and how often, has been collected in numerous surveys in different countries. In the USA, a survey conducted by the Pew Research Centre (Smith and Anderson, 2018) found that, while *Facebook* and *YouTube* have endured as popular platforms over the last eight years, young people are commonly using other apps such as *Snapchat* and *Instagram*. In this survey, 71 per cent of 18–24-year olds reported using *Snapchat* multiple times per day. In the same age group, 71 per cent also reported using *Instagram*, and 45 per cent were using *Twitter*. The researchers found that young people tended to visit these sites quite frequently as well, with 74 per cent of *Facebook* users reporting daily use, and 63 per cent of *Snapchat* users and 60 per cent of *Instagram* users indicating they visited the sites daily. Further, younger uses (18–24) were more likely to report multiple daily visits. In terms of perceived importance, just over half of the young people in Smith and Anderson's report (51 per cent) indicated that it would be difficult to give up social media.

A younger cohort (13–17 years) reported using *YouTube*, *Instagram* and *Snapchat* the most, with *Facebook* the fourth most popular. Anderson and Jiang (2018) suggested that the increasing near-ubiquitous rates of Smartphone ownership contributed to this trend; indeed 95 per cent reported having a Smartphone, or being able to access one. In the survey, 45 per cent of the young respondents said that they were online nearly constantly (Anderson and Jiang, 2018). As we showed above, those households containing young people under 15 years of age have consistently represented the highest proportion of internet connection. For example, in Australia in 2016–17, 86 per cent had internet access at home (ABS, 2016–17). Of those aged 15–17 years, nearly all reported having access to the internet (98 per cent) while those aged over 65 years had the lowest rate of access of all the age groups (55 per cent) (Figure 6.1).

As we explored in the preceding section on the digital divide, internet access and up-take rates necessarily differ between regions and countries. For instance, compared with Australia or the USA, China has a much lower degree of internet reach (53.2 per cent are online). But Chinese 'netizens' represent one of the largest groups online, equalling the population of Europe (CNNIC, 2017). Microblogging is a particularly popular genre in social media, with 45 per cent of users engaging in the activity (Qin et al., 2017). As of 2016, the instant messaging app WeChat was the most common online destination, with 79.6 per cent of internet users using the site (CNNIC, 2017). China, the USA and Australia are just three contexts that represent some of the different ways the internet has spread across developing and developed nations. A clear trend is that young people represent one of the largest groups online compared with the rest of the population. This trend has inspired many researchers to explore and explain how and why young people go online.

YouTube, Instagram and Snapchat are the most popular online platforms among teens

% of U.S. teens who ...

	Say they use ...	Say they use ___ most often
YouTube	85%	32%
Instagram	72	15
Snapchat	69	35
Facebook	51	10
Twitter	32	3
Tumblr	9	<1
Reddit	7	1
None of the above	3	3

Note: Figures in first column add to more than 100% because multiple responses were allowed. Question about most-used site was asked only of respondents who use multiple sites; results have been recalculated to include those who use only one site. Respondents who did not give an answer are not shown.
Source: Survey conducted March 7-April 10, 2018.
"Teens, Social Media & Technology 2018"

PEW RESEARCH CENTER

Figure 6.1 Most common social media platforms

What do people do on social media sites?

Social networking sites are being seen as not only about technological change, but about cultural change. For example, Miller (2011) suggests that technologies are having significant impact in our 'offline' lives by increasing our social networks and therefore, our social capital. Technology helps young people make, keep and manage their relationships while helping to create a sense of community, which may be missing or limited in other parts of young people's lives. As boyd (2014) and Lincoln (2014) explained, social technologies can transform young people's relationships with privacy and affect their relationships with time, space and place (see also Waite, 2019). Users are able to communicate across large spatial masses (for example, from New Zealand to the UK), crossing time zones as well as geographical boundaries.

Thinking points

- What do you think are the main activities that young people undertake while on social media?
- Do you think social media are important in constructing young people's social identities? If so how?

More recently, *Facebook* has introduced a number of new features such as the time-line, 'look back videos', 'year in review' and 'on this day'. These new features create a portal for users to document their everyday lives, which can function as a life diary. In some cases, users can feel that they are bound to the platform because leaving the network would mean losing a record of this history (Robards, 2014). Social networking sites also include dating sites and apps such as *Tinder*, *Grindr* and *Scruff*, which have become more popular amongst the young (Smith, 2016). As a result, opportunities to form relationships and to work on ways to present themselves to others are increasing (Waite and Bourke, 2015a).

The Pew Centre (2018) recently identified some of the key activities that young people engage in on social media. As we can see in Figure 6.2, social media have become places where young people can share their accomplishments. While there is a continuous flow of social interaction, they remain significant sites for presenting themselves. Therefore, we need to recognize social media as a central site for identity

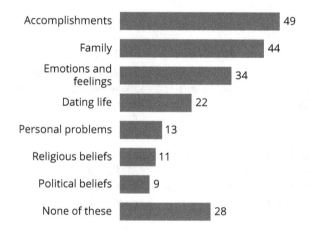

While about half of teens post their accomplishments on social media, few discuss their religious or political beliefs

% of U.S. teens who say they ever post about their___ on social media

Accomplishments	49
Family	44
Emotions and feelings	34
Dating life	22
Personal problems	13
Religious beliefs	11
Political beliefs	9
None of these	28

Note: Respondents were allowed to select multiple options. Respondents who did not give an answer are not shown.
Source: Survey conducted March 7 -April 10, 2018.
"Teens' Social Media Habits and Experiences"

PEW RESEARCH CENTER

Figure 6.2 Common posts online

construction. One major opportunity to display identity is through profiles and pictures. The representations seen here are a way of presenting to friends and peers, especially to those known locally. Of course, a number of difficulties have emerged through this process; for example, young people presenting themselves in ways that are seen as inappropriate to parents or employers, such as getting drunk, taking drugs and being sexually active.

These approaches or 'identity announcements' posted through social media platforms project visual or narrative images of the person whose profile it is. Lots of pictures of the person having fun or pictures with lots of friends may be used to suggest you are a fun person who is popular. This can be enhanced with other blogs or announcements on the 'wall' of Facebook, making claims about who you are. A person's cultural identity can also be developed through the identification of their 'bio'. This allows young people to set out preferences in books, films, music, TV programmes and personal interests, which all present a cultural identity. As we shall see in the discussion that follows, the degree to which this process is creating new spaces for people to construct 'new' identities needs to be examined with care. With the convergence of friends, workmates and others online, being able to construct different selves becomes harder to achieve.

The digital age and social identities

In the previous discussion we raised several questions about the relationship between digital media and social identities. These questions have been central to discussions about digital lives. The unprecedented proliferation of digital media in the 1990s solicited academic interest, seeking to make sense of the impact new technologies had on people's lives. An early writer in the field was Howard Rheingold (2000). In his book *The Virtual Community*, he reflected on seeing himself '… participating in … a new kind of culture … a kind of speeded-up social evolution' (2000, p. 3) during the early 1990s. He painted a hopeful vision of the potential of online communities where information could be requested and supplied, and emotional support unquestioningly offered. The social support and connection of a traditional, face-to-face community was invoked, and the advantages of collapsing geographic boundaries with the obscurity offered by the screen were characterized as improvements on traditional communities. Here, the virtual community was seen as a place to meet new people, irrespective of the constraints of physical co-presence. The bonds forged in the virtual community were 'real' according to Rheingold, and he talked about becoming friends with those he met online.

🗨 Thinking point

Do you think that your online self is different from your offline person? Think about how you represent and respond on social media in comparison with how you might react when meeting someone offline.

Sherry Turkle (1996) was also interested in how the internet, as a discrete sphere, was separate from 'real' offline life. In her book, *Life on the Screen* (1996) she, like Rheingold, was keen to understand the impact this increasingly pervasive technology was having on everyday life. Turkle's particular interest was in the communities that had grown online, and the types of activities that she believed provided users with the potential to 'become someone else' online. Turkle argued that entry into the online world enabled people to shrug off physical or social constraints that might shape their offline selves. In virtual spaces people could potentially re-construct a new self and experiment in utopian cyber-worlds without the risk of needing to commit to any one identity position. New selves could be forged online, and alternative identities could be developed: 'the obese can be slender, the beautiful can be plain' (Turkle, 1996, p. 158).

Turkle drew on examples where users construct a radically different persona in online spheres. She discussed immersive online games like 'Second Life' and other online multiplayer games that offer a channel through which alternative selves can be formulated and expressed. Ducheneaut et al. (2009) also researched virtual worlds that allowed people to experiment with identities. The researchers had a specific inter-est in the types of **avatars** players designed for themselves and why. They found a strong trend of players experimenting with 'digital bodies' that were very different from their own, although online personas were more likely based on the play-ers' own personalities, albeit an idealized version of them.

> **Avatars:** Are digital representations that people can design for themselves when playing games on line.

Buckingham (2008) further explored these questions by looking at the way young people were engaging in and navigating their way through new technological environ-ments. These researchers were interested in understanding the impact such environ-ments were having on participants' social practices and identities. For example, danah boyd (2008) developed the concept of 'networked publics'. Focussing on the changes digital technology created in the ways we negotiate and conceptualize privacy, boyd (2008) explored how young people navigated the virtual 'publicness' created by tech-nological developments and the associated risk of privacy breaches that emerged. boyd outlined four unique 'properties' of networked publics as they relate to young people using social networking sites: 'persistence, searchability, replicability, and invisible audiences' (boyd, 2008, p. 120). boyd is grappling with what it means to be 'public', that is to speak in public, and to be in a public space in the physical offline sense and to reflect on how this might change in the online context. boyd contends that digital spaces fundamentally and irrevocably change the way people interact with each other and that such interactions have become much more complex.

What is the relationship between online and offline lives?

More recently, attention has shifted toward the question of the interrelationship between online and offline social identities. What is really happening when young people go online, and how does it relate to the offline world? While Turkle (1996) quite rightly asked about how people present themselves online, the key question is: what is the relationship between offline and online lives? There are of course many different platforms that users engage with to achieve different ends; for instance, some seek social interaction, while others are seeking information or entertainment. On the whole, different platforms and interfaces emerge across different devices, with a range of affordances.

The term 'affordance' is used to describe the ways we use different devices and platforms, and refers to the possibilities or resources that users obtain by using particular technologies (Hutchby, 2001). For example, a key affordance of *Facebook* is being able to chat with school friends who have been 'accepted' as contacts and are on the 'friends' list. But, depending on how and why you use the site, a key affordance might also be reaching out to a large, geographically dispersed interest community. The range of affordances change, and this is because many of these platforms are user driven (boyd, 2014). There is a certain flexibility built in that allows people to craft highly individualized, customizable forays into online spaces.

What we start to see is a close interconnection between the online and offline activities of the young. While their main motivations may be to engage in social interaction with their friends or to listen to music, source videos or stream movies and television (Anderson and Jiang, 2018), what does become clear is that young people also take part in these activities in their everyday offline lives (Waite and Bourke, 2015b). For example, a social activity in the offline world is talking to friends about their online activities. This can include sharing funny items they come across online and talking about them at school or when out with friends. Watching downloaded content, or streaming movies and TV together, in each other's homes, is a way of physically being together, while also being online. In this sense the relationship between online lives and offline realities is an intimately embedded one (Waite, 2019). Separating these realities into 'virtual' versus 'offline' ignores the intersections between them.

As we know, the construction and performance of identities draws on a wide range of cultural and social, symbolic and material resources, which the internet can clearly contribute to, but it is not the only source. In many ways, the relationship between online and offline identities is blurred (Waite and Bourke, 2015b). A simple reading that sees identity as being 'split' or 'dichotomous' ignores the complex process of how young people navigate their social and cultural lives. In fact, it is clear that offline, 'real life', remains a significant feature of young people's lives. As we suggested earlier, seeing young people as a new digital generation who live their lives on the internet is to deny the importance of their everyday activities.

Digital youth cultures in small town and rural Gujarat, India

In their research on young people living in rural India, Pathak-Shelat and DeShano (2014) reflected on utopian 'hopeful' narratives suggesting that access to the internet will increase their individual mobilities. What the researchers found, however, was that digital technologies were usually seen as relatively peripheral. The young people reported maintaining strong ties that were embedded in close geographic locales, and their lives continued to be shaped by pre-existing structural divisions and cultural practices. For the young respondents, digital technologies were just one component of a larger, rich social existence that was necessarily limited and constrained.

Of course, there is a certain amount of fluidity and malleability afforded within the online world that differentiates it from offline lives in important ways. For instance, there is increased flexibility for users to present themselves in more flattering, or alternate ways, than might be possible in more face-to-face contexts (Donath and boyd, 2004). However, the social cues used to convey information, while presented in a virtual context and susceptible to greater levels of manipulation, are still often based on users' offline, everyday identities. Users post and tag pictures of themselves, but these can be idealized selves (for instance through optimized poses, stylized lighting, or filters) showing how they want to be seen. Comments and chats can be carefully considered responses, or they can resemble a fast-paced back-and-forth conversation in real time. Further, interactions can be continued at a time and place convenient to the user and are not reliant on physical or temporal co-presence in the way traditional face-to-face interactions are. How people present themselves can be a mix of controlled performance, alongside the representation of real emotions and feelings which reflect their offline lives. The relationship between online and offline lives and identities therefore needs to be characterized by representing online and offline as thoroughly embedded. This is an approach that highlights the regular, daily forays young people make online and sees these as reflective of their everyday lives. For example, Kate Davis (2012) illustrates how pre-existing offline friendships help young people to mediate and understand what acceptable and unacceptable forms of behaviour are. The presence of offline friends functions to help young people maintain consistency between their online and offline selves in how they represent themselves to other online friends. This is because they are keen to present themselves in ways that their offline friends can recognize.

Experimenting with sexual and gender identities online

While we need to recognize that offline and online selves may not be irrevocably separated, the internet has been a site for expression, and experimentation. For instance, research into social network sites has focussed on how young people use it as a way of exploring their gender or sexual identity. In some cases, social network sites are seen as being able to provide a safe space for trialling creative expression and as a means to struggle against restrictive gender norms or expectations (Kanai and Dobson, 2016). Such work suggests that the internet offers new ways that people can 'be themselves'. However, stories of free gender identity exploration have become increasingly intersected with regulation and control (Kanai and Dobson, 2016).

One context in which access to online spaces can afford important opportunities to source identity resources is that of LBGTIQ+ young people living in rural areas. In this literature, coming out stories are a common way to frame young peoples' negotiation of queer identities. In many instances, the internet is cast as a space through which young people can gain vital information and knowledge to support identity development and experimentation in supportive environments. Gray's (2009) work in a rural town in a southern American state (Kentucky) explores the experiences of a cohort of young people negotiating diverse sexual identities. Online spaces were a key arena in which these young people gained social knowledge about LBGTIQ+ lives. Media texts found online, such as non-commercial sites fostering discussion among young people themselves, or advertisements on for-profit websites, provided young people living in rural areas with '… materials for crafting what it means to "come out"' (Gray, 2009, p. 1165). While popular media narratives were familiar to the young people living in the country, these tended to characterize queerness as fundamentally out of place in rural spaces, and more natural in the city. Therefore, young people were forced to venture away from their rural homes to find representations that would enable them to develop and articulate queer identities (Gray, 2009, p. 1164).

The internet is also seen as a relatively safe space where young people can 'experiment' with their sexual identities. Opportunities to explore alternate identities in more anonymous online settings, as well as the ability to experiment and be creative, were seen as a positive benefit of the internet (Craig and McInroy, 2014). Being able to find and access online information about sexuality and sexual identities was relatively easy, and could be done without the risk and stigma that they would find in offline contexts. Being able to see others who were similar to them, and who were going through similar challenges in their lives, was also a key form of information. That said, identities developed and explored online are still closely intertwined and informed by everyday offline lives (Craig and McInroy, 2014). Digital media were less an opportunity for forming entirely new identities and communities crossing vast distances, and more a space to consolidate relationships and networks spatially embedded in the young people's everyday lives (Gray, 2009).

Importantly risk does not disappear completely when young people go on line do not disappear for young people online. While some have explored the positive experiences of young people in rural areas using the internet and social media to access opportunities to experiment and explore alternative identities, the story is rarely without more negative experiences. Young LBGTIQ+ people have reported diverse experiences, such as being the targets of **cyberbullying** attacks online (Varjas et al., 2013).

> **Cyberbullying:** Refers to a phenomenon in which traditional forms of bullying are enacted, and sometimes amplified, through new technologies. Cyberbullying can include posting images online that victimize others, posting negative comments directed at another, or sending hate messages.

Risks in the digital age

Some positives of the digital age

As we have already seen in the discussion above, there are key benefits to going online. For example, within virtual spaces, the limits of geography have been found by some to no longer be a limitation for young people (Ei Chew et al., 2011). Such perspectives are reflective of Rheingold's vision of a global community that collapses the barriers of geography and education to bring all like-minded people together. For instance, imagine a school student living in a regional town looking for information to finish a school assignment. Before easy access to online spaces, this student would have been limited to what they could source locally. Introduce an internet connection however, and suddenly their ability to find information and knowledge for their assignment is no longer limited to the local library. Now they can visit an online community, post a question for people to answer, look up *Wikipedia*, check *Google Books* and get information from others from anywhere in the world. Information sourced online may be written by someone on the other side of the world, or equally by someone nearby. We also saw above that, in addition to accessing information, going online can provide a veil of anonymity and the potential for identity expression and experimentation. This is particularly pertinent among young people who may feel a sense of isolation from those around them in their everyday life or who are trying to work out who they are, and where they fit in the world. Connecting online can be a way to gain social support from a community of likeminded people who may encounter similar challenges.

Thinking points

- What do you think are the main risks that young people encounter online?
- How do you think they protect themselves?
- Are there positive benefits of social media?

Chinese youth performing identities and navigating belonging online

For young Chinese people, spending time on social media platforms like *Weibo* and *WeChat* (these are Chinese social media platforms similar to Facebook) can foster sociality while also allowing them to experiment with their sense of self. Fu's (2018) research into Chinese young peoples' use of the internet found this operated across a number of sites. *WeChat* tended to be the site in which normalized identity performances took place that closely reflected offline selves, while *Weibo* provided opportunities to mould a different self. It supported a greater sense of privacy where the likelihood of friends and family closely following interactions was lessened. It was in this space that the research respondents tended to craft alternative online identities. These tended to be more outspoken, value-orientated identities. Young people felt safe enough to reach out to a geographically dispersed community of like-minded others based on mutual understandings. *Weibo* was a site on the internet that was a '... relatively free space for people's experimentation and formation of alternative identities ...' (Fu, 2018, p. 12).

However, the idea that the internet is an information utopia, in which any question can be posed and satisfactorily answered, or a space in which entirely new identities can be 'tried on' and appropriated for short-term periods, is overly optimistic. Indeed, in many respects, the internet reflects those lines of power we see in the offline world (see Pathak-Shelta and DeShano, 2014). While young users can find information that they might not otherwise be able to access, the source and form of the information may bear little critical reflection. And while there are identity resources that can be accessed online, it is often not possible (or desirable) to become someone else online. Going online does not always represent opportunity and positive engagement for young people.

What risks do youth face online?

In Chapter 8 we will explore the idea of risks and risk taking in more detail, but it is important for us to recognize that, embedded within digital media are risks and dangers that young people have to manage and navigate. However, we also need to acknowledge that risk is a social construct that is socially and culturally defined and can be seen as having a role in creating regulation and control of the young (Douglas, 1966). Within this process, how risks are understood, managed and regulated is fuelled in part by adult anxieties and concerns about the impact of digital media on the everyday lives of young people. Sonia Livingstone in her book, *Children and the Internet* (2009) reminds us that there are three factors driving this anxiety:

> First, the extraordinary rapidity of the internet's development and diffusion, outpacing adults' ability to adjust; second, an endemic cultural fear of the new, encouraged by media panics framing the internet as an unmanageable source of threat to children's safety; and thirdly, the novelty of a reverse generation gap whereby parental expertise and authority is exceeded by children's ability to use technology and to evade adult management. (Livingstone, 2009, p. 151)

Historically, adults' fears for children and young people have always focussed on matters of morality, sexuality and aggression. Childhood is seen as a 'period of innocence' that can be corrupted by technology and particularly media. These anxieties are not new; in fact, similar anxieties arose over the arrival of earlier technologies such as print media, the radio and television (Criticher, 2008).

Recent adult anxieties around young people's use of digital media emerge in fears about the 'groomer', the 'cyberbully' and 'the addict'. These can be seen as constructions of a media that feeds on the anxiety of others to source news stories to sell newspapers or increase hits on a webpage. But are these purely constructions or should we recognize that there are real dangers that we need to protect young people from online? Historically, sociologists and other social scientists have been unwilling, or reluctant, to engage in such claims because they are seen as contrary to the objectives of a socially just approach to evaluating the lives of the young (Livingstone, 2009). Livingstone goes on to argue that we have a responsibility to recognize that the risks are real (and not simply constructions) and that we should bring this to the attention of policy makers and practitioners: '… we must (engage with risk) if we wish to recognise children's own experiences and give them voice.' (p. 153).

However, we still need to be cautious about accepting risks as endemic because there remains uncertainty about the extent of many of the 'risks' we discuss below. Public opinion can be highly informed by unreliable information that can create moral panics, which aim to increase regulation and control of the internet. However, we should, as Livingstone suggests, not deny that real risks exist for young people and that '… new types of deviance and unpredictable behaviour' online cannot be dealt with using traditional legal or ethical means (Ibrahim, 2008, p. 245). In this sense, the threats associated with going online are ever-present for the young. These are real problems, seen to be directly enabled by the lack of transparency in online spaces: '… with every hour they log online, they are leaving more tracks for marketers or pedophiles for that matter to follow' (Palfrey and Gasser, 2008, p. 7). The internet can facilitate anonymity for those who want to do harm, or exercise control over the vulnerable. It can also protect perpetrators with bad intentions and lead innocent young users unwittingly into danger.

Watching harmful and illegal content

So what types of risks are young people encountering online? One of the main issues for young people relates to the type of content they encounter while on the internet. Young people are consistently being bombarded with images of material they do not want to see. For example, findings from OFCOM in the UK (2018) found that 32 per cent of young people in the UK aged 12–15 had encountered something online that they found worrying, or nasty in some way that they did not like. This can range from sexually explicit content (pornography for example) to violence. International surveys in countries such as the UK, Norway, Sweden and Ireland have found that over a quarter to a third of 9- to 16-year-olds had accidently seen violent, offensive, sexual or pornographic content online (Livingstone, 2009). Other studies confirm that young people are also continually having to manage unwanted advances. These might include unwanted sexual solicitations, often from acquaintances rather than strangers, and growing requests for young people to provide nude or sexually explicit photos of themselves (Livingstone, 2009).

The internet is also a site that is renowned for creating opportunities for sexual grooming. This refers to '... a process of socialisation through which an adult engages with and manipulates a child or young person for the purpose of online sexual abuse which may include offline aspects' (Livingstone et al., 2017, p. 47). This can take place in online chats where the groomer adopts an alternative, inoffensive identity. While little research is available about the extent of such grooming and its relationship to offline sexual abuse, research with young victims shows how they can become drawn into abusive relationships (Webster et al., 2012). More recently, there have been major concerns about young people being groomed and recruited to religious fundamentalism (see Callimchi, 2015; Wilkinson, 2015). Media reports describe how young people are being persuaded to leave their families, and their countries, and fight for the Islamic State. Grooming occurs online, via *Twitter* and *Facebook*, away from the protective gaze of parents and guardians. Again, how extensive this is remains unclear, but clearly the internet has become an important tool for those who want to try to recruit young people to activities that are illegal.

Bullying online

Bullying is now recognized as a major risk that young people are encountering online (Livingstone et al., 2017). This has been described as 'cyberbullying', 'sexting' and/or 'trolling'. Definitions of such terms remain ambiguous, but all highlight the growing body of evidence suggesting that new technologies are creating opportunities for traditional forms of bullying to exist online. It also acknowledges that there can be complex connections with 'traditional' forms of bullying, which aggravates the risk of victimization online (Livingstone and Haddon, 2012). Such activities can include having an image posted online that aims to victimize someone, having negative comments posted on an online picture, or receiving hate texts and messages. How extensive such activities are remains difficult to identify, but a body of research increasingly shows that online bullying is a growing risk to the young. For example, a study by Lilley et al. (2014) found that 28 per cent of the sample reported an experience that had upset or bothered them when using social network sites. Of this group, 37 per cent reported experiencing trolling, 22 per cent had been excluded from a social group online, and 18 per cent had experienced aggressive and violent language. Of those who had been cyberbullied, 11 per cent reported that this happened every day and 55 per cent at least once a month. In total, 19 per cent reported being affected by upsetting online experiences for a few days or a week, and 12 per cent for a period lasting weeks or months.

More recently, concerns have focussed on sexting. Sexting describes the practice of sharing sexualized images, or other media, in online contexts using digital technologies. Within this broad definition, the term 'sexting' covers a range of activities experienced by young people. Some commentators and scholars have described the practice as a form of crime, while others argue for a more middle-ground approach. When 'minors' are involved, such as those aged under 16, sexting can be characterized as a crime (Livingstone and Görzig, 2012). In such instances, sexting comes under child pornography statutes and can also intersect with other illegal practices including child solicitation, or coercion (Salter et al., 2012). Due to risqué humour, rude jokes and sexual experimentation, it can be difficult to identify and maintain a boundary separating what is acceptable and fun, and what is harmful. Because of this difficulty, there is a significant amount of commentary on the topic. In many cases, sexting can be seen as a form of communication among young people interested in experimenting with sexual self-representation (Albury and Crawford, 2012) and be seen as a harmless way of flirting (Livingstone and Görzig, 2012). This issue is also discussed in relation to young people's mental health in Chapter 9.

The political economy of digital life

Big business

We must of course recognize, when thinking about digital life, that it is very much a big business focussed on making money. It is easy sometimes to forget the amounts of money global companies such as *Google*, *Facebook* and *Microsoft* make as a result of our activities online. For example, *Alphabet* (GOOGL), the parent company of *Google*, reported in 2017 that it made $100 billion in annual sales, the highest revenue in *Google's* 20-year history. *Alphabet* posted $32.3 billion in sales in its fourth quarter, pushing total annual revenue to $110 billion. That's up from about $90 billion in 2016. Similarly, *Facebook* made more than $40 billion in revenue in 2017, approximately 89 per cent of which came from digital advertisements.

Thinking point

- Across a wide range of media, a number of major issues are being raised about the relationship between big business and social media. Think about what some of these issues are and how they impact on your own use of social media. Do you have concerns about the way big business is involved in owning social media sites such as Facebook and Instagram or servers such as Google?

The political economy of digital life describes a new way of doing business in the digital age that young people are intimately caught up in. One such development has seen large businesses, such as *Google*, perpetuate utopian narratives that characterize the internet as a space of 'opportunities', which subverts traditional structures. Such narratives suggest that the traditional divisions that have traditionally structured people's access to markets and opportunities to make money have become flattened. Online markets such as *Etsy.com* and *Ebay* are popular platforms that enable individuals with something to sell to easily connect with buyers. Crucially, sellers can circumnavigate the traditional 'middle men', or those structures that have traditionally only allowed established business with adequate networks access to local or international markets. The popularity and success of these platforms highlights the significant changes to the way business operates in the digital era.

A number of processes have been developed with regard to broad-scale access to markets online. For example, the ways that products are marketed and advertised has changed significantly. Companies can improve their access to consumers by drawing on existing online communities with an interest in a particular product. By disseminating information about the product and shaping the potential future purchases of a targeted group, the traditional approach to broadcasting advertorial content to mass audiences is radically altered. In this way, it is information about, and surrounding, the product, including interested online communities, that becomes commodified, rather than just the product itself (Lupton, 2014).

The growth of 'prosumers'

The political economy of digital life also highlights the collapse of traditional producer/consumer binaries. A portmanteau of the words 'producer' and 'consumer', prosumers are those who produce content, while also being consumers. Prosumers are people who create content to share online, for instance writing a blog post, making a celebrity fan page, writing comments, making memes or gifs. These in turn can be used in marketing and advertising or to promote products (Beer and Burrows, 2010; Lupton, 2014). Participatory web cultures, such as the community we see on *Wikipedia*, as well as on social media like *Facebook*, represent prosumer developments in online cultures. These developments are geared towards 'user-generated content' that results in a 'blurring of production and consumption' (Beer and Burrows, 2010, p. 6).

This idea was first raised by Ritzer in his book *The McDonaldization of Society*. He outlined how more and more of us are being put to work in the production of the things we buy. A new way of selling products, such as hamburgers, now requires us to be part of the production process (for example, we fill our own cups, collect our own salt and pepper and carry our food to a table). As a result, this mode of consumption has now become a central part of the process of production. In the digital world we can see an example in the open-source software movement. It is here where people are able to collaborate, share and build on what others have created by contributing to new software or hardware. In many cases this is done for free, or for a minimal fee.

Social media have been characterized as an opportunity for individuals to become prosumers, and to promote creative endeavours in a relatively free manner. However, there are limits to this freedom because power structures continue to constrain such endeavours in the background (Lupton, 2014). The notion that this form of commercial online agency operates outside of traditional capitalist markets is somewhat erroneous. Various actors and traditional power structures seek to exploit and use such prosumers for their own ends (Lupton, 2014). Indeed, '… people's creative efforts … have become harnessed to the media and data industries, but many of them might not be fully aware of this …' (Lupton, 2014, p. 31) because platforms are often vague about how uploaded content is sold on, or used in other capacities. We shall return to this point below in the discussion on big data.

The role of influencers

In this changing environment we are also seeing the emergence of 'influencers'. These tend to be celebrities, or what have been termed 'micro-celebrities', who represent an example of the brands and consumer products aimed at young people, although sometimes in vague and obscured ways. For example, in her ethnographic investigation into influencers and micro-celebrity in Singapore, Abidin (2016) looks at a cohort of (mostly) young women and the 'visibility labour' that they engage in as influencers and followers of influencers. Abidin explains that content created by the influencers is a form of advertising that brands can take advantage of, but with little remuneration for those engaging in the marketing labours. Indeed, the work of influencers is '… quietly creative but insidiously exploitative.' (Abidin, 2016, p. 86). The advertorial content created by influencers on social media is ultimately beneficial to large business interests.

Influencers, who are often young women, narrate their everyday lives on social media with comments and text, alongside photos of themselves wearing or using various consumer goods. Followers of influencer accounts then 'model themselves after' these individuals, and become '… a network of advertorial capillaries by duplicating, amplifying and multiplying the Influencer content to their own circle of followers and personal friends.' (Abidin, 2016, p. 89). Here, what is essentially advertorial content is disseminated between followers, from consumers to other consumers in a form of 'word of mouth' marketing. Essentially the labour of the influencers and followers serves to promote the profits of other business interests. Importantly, the followers who participated in advertorial dissemination did not frame their work as 'labour'; rather it was a form of 'tacit labour' (Abidin, 2016). The participation of influencers, and their followers, in the interests of larger, traditional business is consistent with a political economy of digital life in which prosumers take part in a new form of commercial activity where business interests are obscured and marketing content is disseminated among social networks.

Big data

Big data: Refers to the huge amounts of information that result from our interactions online, which are collected with a view to strengthening predictive opportunities, and to improving different aspects of our lives.

One major development is the recent growth of '**big data**'. While 'big data' is a common term, its meaning is a little ambiguous. Lupton explains that '… big data are viewed as offering greater precision and predictive powers to improve efficiency, safety, wealth generation or resources management.' (Lupton, 2014, p. 93; Andrejevic, 2014). The knowledge that can be gained by analyzing the vast stores of information collected is understood as a particularly powerful opportunity for organisations such as *Facebook* and *Google*. Big data is more than just a collection of data points; it refers to a significantly expanded quantity of digital data produced via the collection of information resulting from our interactions online (Lupton, 2014; Andrejevic, 2014). Data are the outcome of exchanges, transactions and uploading content online. For instance, big data might be compiled from information on who we call on our smartphones, the websites we visit, the Instagram accounts that we follow, the searches we conduct, GPS locations on our movements or what we purchase at the supermarket (collected via customer loyalty discount schemes). The information is constantly updated, and offers very detailed reflections of people's online lives. Companies like *Facebook, Google, Microsoft, Amazon* and other commercial entities, as well as governments, use data sets like this to better tailor and market their products and services.

But there is some uneasiness about 'big data'. There is an 'anxiety about the ubiquity and apparent uncontained nature of digital technologies and the data they produce' (Lupton, 2014, p. 107; Andrejevic, 2014). Andrejevic's (2014) research into the topic found that respondents indicated feeling powerless in terms of how big data is collected and structured. While respondents were aware of commercial interests shaping the information they accessed online, they felt a loss of agency in light of the fact that the only way to avoid such meddling was to withdraw from the internet altogether, which is unrealistic for the majority (Andrejevic, 2014). Further, claims that 'big data' is all powerful and able to predict future behaviours are not always borne out. In spite of some claims to the contrary, it cannot always be used to fully understand the complexity and contradiction often inherent in human behaviour (Lupton, 2014).

As the above discussion on influencers demonstrates, our interactions online have become commoditized, and constitute pieces of data that are aggregated into huge datasets. This has engendered a 'new information economy' whereby people's everyday labour online is what generates income, rather than physical labour exchanged for income that characterized more traditional economies. The new economy has then resulted in a power shift from a previously top-down model in which power hierarchies tended to be relatively stable. The new system has engendered a 'horizontal, rhizomatic, fluid and dynamic' distribution of power (Lupton, 2014, p. 22). In his work on big data, Andrejevic (2014) also traces uneven power dynamics between those who collect and use the data and those who are targeted for data collection in the first place. More than a shift in power, Andrejevic sees a continuing power imbalance (as does Abidin, 2016). Primarily, the power imbalance lies in the fact that it is difficult, and sometimes impossible, to know how the data will be used in the future, how it will be sorted, and what the outcomes will be. Andrejevic argues that ultimately the empowering promise of the internet is sacrificed for the obscured, sometimes vague interests of big business and/or government.

Within this, young people have expressed disquiet about surveillance of their online interactions, and the impacts on audiences including school, family, educational institutions and potential employers. They are responding to anxieties about big data and online surveillance by self-disciplining and changing their online habits. Responses include managing online selves by adapting privacy settings, controlling what is put online, and using fake names, or altered names for social media profiles (Duffy and Chan, 2019). Given the pervasiveness of data mining, such strategies are unlikely to shield users from the commercial interests outlined by Lupton and Andrejevic. However, the more personalized gaze of education, family or employment can potentially be mitigated in this way.

New strategies for advertising and disseminating marketing information are replacing traditional 'top-down' structures, which have undergone a blurring of key relationships and power dynamics. The interests of big business are increasingly obscured, and advertorial content is passed between followers and social networks as 'word of mouth'. Information is personalized and targeted to specific interest communities online, who in turn become commodities in and of themselves. Big data describes the emergence of huge data sets comprising detailed and constantly updated information tracking users' interactions and activities online. The mining of such data sets, and the predictive knowledge derived from them, has then been used to serve business and/or government interests, while creating disquiet and anxiety among young internet users, and the community more broadly.

💬 Summary

- Young people engage with the digital world in complex ways which are not adequately captured in generational terms such as 'digital natives'.

- While the digital world is an important site for the creation and experimentation of social identities, we need to recognize that online and offline worlds are closely interconnected.

- While the risks young people encounter in the digital world can be constructed or perceived as a form of moral panic, we need to acknowledge that many risks young people have to manage are real.

- Celebrities, influencers and prosumers are becoming important in the way that products are promoted to the young.

- The digital world, while providing resources and opportunities for young people to be creative, remains a significant site where business makes huge profits. It is important that we do not ignore these processes when trying to understand young people's engagement online.

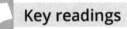

Exercise: The sociological imagination

The impacts and significance of social media in young people's lives are a central issue in youth sociology. Can you think of examples where social media expands your understanding and engagement in social issues? Or do you think it often re-affirms rather than challenges social divisions such as gender, class and race? How different do you imagine your life would be if you had been born in your parents' generation when there was no internet?

Key readings

boyd, d. (2014) *It's Complicated: The Social Lives of Networked Teens* (New Haven: Yale University Press).

Craig, S. L. & McInroy, L. (2014) 'You can form a part of yourself online: the influence of new media on identity development and coming out for LGBTQ youth', *Journal of Gay & Lesbian Mental Health*, vol. 18, no. 1, pp. 95–109.

Fuchs, C. (2017) *Social Media: A Critical Introduction* (Sage).

Hogan, B. (2010) 'The presentation of self in the age of social media: distinguishing performances and exhibitions online', *Bulletin of Science, Technology & Society*, vol. 30, no. 6, pp. 377–386.

Ibrahim, Y. (2008) 'The new risk communities: social networking sites and risk', *International Journal of Media & Cultural Politics*, vol. 4, no. 2, pp. 245–253.

Kanai, A. & Dobson, A. (2016) 'Digital media and gender' in *The Wiley Blackwell Encyclopaedia of Gender and Sexuality Studies*, pp. 1–4.

Livingstone, S. (2010) *Children and the Internet* (Cambridge, UK: Polity Press).

Lupton, D. (2014) *Digital Sociology* (Routledge).

Smith, J., Skrbis, Z. & Western, M. (2013) 'Beneath the digital native myth: understanding young Australians' online time use', *Journal of Sociology*, vol. 49, no. 1, pp. 97–118.

7 YOUTH, SPACE AND PLACE

> **In this chapter you will learn about:**
>
> - What is meant by the terms 'space' and 'place' in youth sociology
> - How youth sociology has researched the spaces and places young people use
> - The differences and relationships between rural, urban and global spaces and places
> - The way different social groups (e.g. classes, genders and ethnic groups) experience or use social space and places.

The importance of space and place

> ### 🗨 Thinking point
>
> - How important is the place where you grew up in shaping your own personal journey through youth to adulthood?
> - What are the limitations, opportunities and contexts of your 'place', and how have these shaped your life so far?

In the previous chapters we explored a number of institutional contexts of young people's lives. For example, we have looked at their relationships with education and work settings, as well as cultural spaces, and we have explored a wide range of activities including listening and playing music, dancing and being involved in subcultural practices. We can already see that the sites of engagement for these activities are important (for example, school, college or university). In this chapter we turn our attention to the idea of spaces and places in more detail, especially how young people might relate to their neighbourhood, community or locality. What we know is that the locations where young people live and experience their everyday lives is important, not only to their sense of who they are but also for future trajectories. It is where they start their lives and their journey towards independence and adulthood. This following discussion, therefore, focusses on the micro aspects of their interactions in what sociologists call 'space' and 'place'.

For many, space and place are the taken-for-granted 'background' of everyday life. Youth sociologists are very interested in **space** and **place** because these introduce key explanatory mediums through which we can better understand society and young people's position within it. Human geographers have long been interested in the nature of space and place, and the meanings people attribute to them. In a way, '... everything that we study is emplaced; it happens

> **Space:** This can be understood in terms of freedom of movement and openness and as lacking the type of meaning that generally characterizes place. However, definitions of space differ according to the approach applied.

Place: This can be understood as the material manifestation of locations, and cultural terrains occupied and reproduced by particular groups that have acquired or been given particular meaning by people. However, definitions of place differ according to the approach applied.

somewhere and involves material stuff' (Gieryn, 2000, p. 464). Gieryn explains that place and space are more than just backdrops to social life; rather, 'place saturates social life', and therefore is of significance to sociologists. Drawing on Appadurai's explanation (1996), social life is indeed embedded in, and mutually co-constituted through material locales and their meanings. Social life is therefore implicated in, and intimately interwoven with, how we understand, and how we construct space and place.

Cresswell (2015) also helps us think about the everyday relevance of space and place by explaining some of the mundane intersections between society, space and place. For instance, the ways in which mapping software on our smartphones help us get around, and navigate to new places, represent a mundane convergence of information technologies, places and people. Police are also interested in the links between place and people; in particular how this might relate to crime and crime prevention. Marketers, and those interested in selling things, are also invested in the particular sites in which we encounter information and consume products. Indeed, the list of everyday intersections is long, and also includes protesters choosing a site to perform resistance, to religious sites of significance. Ultimately, these all represent ways of coming together, forming meaning and using the spaces we inhabit to amplify it (Cresswell, 2015). The terms 'place' and 'space' are words that we all use on a regular basis in our daily lives, yet they can be difficult to pin down as important dimensions of sociological analysis of young people's lives. For this reason, it is important we clearly define 'space' and 'place', and how they are used in analysis in social science research.

Conceptualizing space and place

It is important to be clear what we mean by the somewhat nebulous concepts of 'space' and 'place' because there are many interpretations across different disciplines and spheres of social life. However, it is possible to loosely categorize approaches into two broad groups. **Structural** accounts represent more objective, tangible interpretations and are perhaps more familiar because of their prominence in government classifications. A second broad approach involves social constructionist accounts. These are mainly concerned with the ways that place and space are subjectively experienced, and are associated with the work of Henri Lefebvre, and human geographers such as Doreen Massey, among others. The following sub-sections attempt to untangle these approaches. However, these each represent much larger debates, and you can find out more about them in the recommended reading list.

Structural approaches: In which definitions of particular locales are based on descriptive or structural parameters, for instance by population or dominant industry.

🗨 Thinking points

- How do different perspectives of space and place give us different insights into their significance in shaping young people's lives?
- What is the relationship between community, space and place?

Differences between space and place

While conceptually similar, place differs somewhat from the analogous, sometimes synonymous concept of space. Social scientists and human geographers explain that, where space tends to be conceptualized in more abstract terms, place is given meaning and value over time as it becomes more familiar to those who reside within it (Tuan, 1979; Cresswell, 2015). Links to individual people or particular communities, practices, objects or representations are more commonly thought of as being ascribed to places than they are to more abstract spaces (Gieryn, 2000). A variety of scholars also understand place as the material manifestation of locations and cultural spaces occupied and reproduced by particular groups (see Clayton, 2009). Places are made up of 'location, material form, and meaningfulness' (Gieryn, 2000, p. 465).

On the other hand, space has been conceived in terms of freedom of movement and openness: 'if we think of space as that which allows movement, then place is pause; each pause in movement makes it possible for location to be transformed into place' (Tuan, 1979, p. 6). That is, if place is that which has acquired, or been given particular meaning, then space can be understood as conversely lacking that same form of meaning. Once meaning has been attributed, and an attachment formed, then previously abstract space becomes personally meaningful place (Cresswell, 2015). However, conceptual divisions separating 'place' from 'space' have been critiqued (Merrifield, 1993). Ultimately, boundaries separating space and place are blurred, and it can be difficult to untangle them. In many ways, they can be more usefully defined in relational terms, which we will discuss below.

Differences between 'community', 'place', and 'space'

The term 'community' also has much in common with 'space' and 'place'. The concept of 'community' has an enduringly '... powerful position as a term denoting social connection and shared experience' (Panelli et al., 2002, p. 111). The concept highlights social relationships as a key component. However, crucial differences mean that the terms cannot be used interchangeably. Most importantly, place focusses attention on material locality first and foremost, while space is concerned with more abstract interpretations of locality. This is the anchor of the analytical gaze. On the other hand, the concept of community is primarily concerned with groups of people. While material locations often embed such relations, they are not the defining feature. Indeed, communities can expand beyond physical locality and encompass material sites beyond immediate locales to include symbolically defined spaces (Liepins, 2000). Therefore, community can refer to 'imagined communities of nations, and alternative or counter-culture communities ...' (Liepins, 2000, p. 32) in which geography plays a more contingent role.

Structural approaches to space and place

Space and place have also been understood as the absolute, immutable and unchanging surroundings and environments, irrelevant to the subjective, changing world of society. They have been characterized as a 'container for objects and processes ...' (Heley and Jones, 2012, p. 209). Such perspectives are consistent with structural approaches to space and place, and this approach has been dominant in many disciplines in the past, and remains strong today. Examples of structural approaches to conceptualizing space and place can be seen in government classifications (see for example ARIA, 2014; AIHW, 2011). A country such as Australia, with a relatively small population living in a geographically extensive continent, relies on structural divisions as a means to carve up and gain knowledge of the cartography of the country. For example, ARIA is the Accessibility and Remoteness Index of Australia and is described as an 'objective process for classifying Remoteness Areas' (ABS, 2018). ARIA provides an objective measure that contributes to analyzing census and statistical information used to inform service provisions to Australia's dispersed population.

Under structural paradigms more broadly, definitions of particular locales are based on descriptive or structural parameters; for example, by population or industry, or, in the case of rural or regional places, by distance from urban places (Heley and Jones, 2012). Structural approaches are perhaps more common outside of youth sociology. Indeed, structural accounts have attracted criticism from sociologists because these definitions ultimately do not provide a sufficiently thorough account of what locales are and what they are not (see Amin and Thrift, 2002). While structural accounts have a vital role in approaches to space and place, they do not offer detailed descriptions related to the qualities of place and people's engagements with these in their daily lives.

Relational approaches

Relational approaches: In which space and place are understood less in terms of absolute criteria as in structural approaches, and more in relative terms, for instance, compared with perceived similarities to other familiar places.

Relational approaches to understanding space and place are another common way to investigate and clarify these concepts, particularly within youth sociology. This type of approach has been used in a range of research agendas within the social sciences (see Rye, 2006; Farrugia et al., 2014; Amin and Thrift, 2002; Goodwin-Hawkins, 2014; Walsh, 2012). In plain terms, relational places are understood according to what they are, while being defined by what they apparently are not. This is because such places are 'opposed to something else and derive from other, already produced' places (Appadurai, 1996, p. 183). The term 'relational' has become a shorthand way to refer to this approach. Relationality is demonstrated in understandings of place based less on absolute criteria, such as pre-defined population or structural parameters, or specific distances from other places, and more on perceived similarities to other familiar places. That is, a town might be understood as 'rural' because it is relatively smaller, and more distant from larger cities, but not as 'remote' because there are other even more distant localities that residents are familiar with. The increasing influence of post-modern and post-structuralist stances are clear in the relational approach. There has been a movement from structuralist descriptive understandings of particular places towards a growing recognition of their increasingly connected, socially and culturally constructed nature. Relational approaches are newer and have been criticized as 'under-developed', yet they are being used increasingly to add knowledge about the significance of people's meanings and experiences of place and space in making sense of their lives (Heley and Jones, 2012).

Experiential approaches

Finally, space and place have been understood through an '**experiential**' lens, which includes sensations that we experience in place and space. This perspective has been used to think about some of the more difficult to explain aspects of young people's relationship with space and place. Human geographers such as Thrift (2008), Tuan (1979) and Seamon (1979) explain that material worlds are not created independently from those who occupy them; they do not necessarily exist as we know them in discrete forms separate from people. Rather, places are formed when they are occupied by people and constructed through their experiences of them. Experience comprises information and interpretations gathered from our physical senses, including taste, touch, smell, vision and how we feel when we are in particular places. For example, a home town is a place often associated with particular feelings that might involve an affirming sense of belonging, a sensory experience that might include particularly familiar smells and sensations, as well as a neighbourhood or house comprised of material structures (Waite, 2018). Experiential approaches to understanding place help illuminate some of these more sensory experiences and identify the role they play in our complex understanding of place and space. Experiential approaches have also attracted similar criticisms to relational approaches. That is, it is claimed that the focus on experience and sensory perception is difficult to capture, and is inherently subjective.

> **Experiential approaches:** In which space and place are understood through our experiences of them, which includes sensations like touch and smell.

It is clear that there is no straightforward definition of concepts such as space and place. That does not mean that they need to remain nebulous and opaque. Rather, their meaning can be derived contextually, while being informed by the disciplinary lens that is applied. In the research context, we can further narrow definitions according to the types of research questions and aims that are guiding the project. As youth sociologists, often this means leaning towards more social constructivist approaches, such as relational or experiential perspectives. The section below explores how each of these approaches is used in youth sociology.

Young people in the context of space and place

'Spectacular' youthful places

Over the last three decades, the ways in which young people use space and places have become a major theme in youth sociology. Within this, much research has focussed on more **spectacular** groups and behaviours; for instance youth gangs, drug-taking, homelessness, delinquency and low-level violence. Many of these relate to crime, and the construction of

> **Spectacular youthful places:** Refers to the tendency for youth researchers to focus on more remarkable groups and behaviours of young people, such as petty crime or drug-taking.

young people as socially deviant (explored in the next chapter). For example, early work in studies such as Howard Parker's (1974) *View from the Boys,* which followed a group of Liverpool lads involved in car crime, had a strong tendency to give attention to the spectacular and resistant characteristics of young people on the streets. Other such examples can be found in the discussions in the previous chapter. Work by the CCCS, for example, focussed on the spectacular activities of subcultural groups on the streets of working class communities. Such a tradition continues today, with many community-based studies focussing on the spectacular and high profile activities of the few. For example, Kraack and Kenway (2002) trace the reaction that emerged in a rural town around a small group of young people who were perceived as engaging in dangerous driving practices, and their seemingly ominous 'loitering' in public spaces.

Thinking points

- What types of activities do you associate with young people's use of space and place?
- How important are different spaces and places for young people's 'transitions' or cultural practices?

This focus on 'conflict' and 'resistance' is unsurprising given young people's experiences and frustrations with regard to constraints on their physical mobility, spatial autonomy and punitive experiences when in public spaces. Matthews et al. (2000) point to the fact that young people's presence in public spaces can represent significant tension between adults and young people and this can lead to or exacerbate apprehensions about their presence in public places. MacDonald and Marsh (2005) show how young people's leisure activities in a highly deprived area of the UK were a consistent focus among public policy makers and local adults. This created significant risks for the young insofar as 'hanging about' brought the threat of police attention. It is claimed that young people actually share a unique, age-based relationship with spaces more commonly conceived as 'adult spaces', such as the shopping mall, or the local neighbourhood (Matthews et al., 1998).

A second core theme in much of the work on young people's use of space in their neighbourhoods relates to the 'carving out' of space. In spite of controls on the ways young people occupy and move through space, they are usually seen to assert themselves and embrace youthful 'agency' by making choices and everyday decisions to circumvent some of these constraints. Young people are commonly described by social scientists investigating space and place in terms of their need to 'carve out' their own space among adult-centric and adult-controlled spaces in public, at home, in the city, on the street and at school. Indeed, '… young people face mounting tensions and surveillance at home, on the street or in the park as they seek to capture what adults already possess; their own place' (Shildrick et al., 2009, p. 457). This enduring theme in youth research on place and space speaks to a broader marginalization of young people in society.

Of course, tendencies to focus on 'spectacular lives' and 'choice' often mean that the more mundane, everyday dynamics that constitute the majority of young people's experiences are neglected (Cieslik, 2003). Much of young people's engagement with leisure practices on the streets and in neighbourhoods tends to be 'boring', lacking structure and opportunities for fun. As Paul Corrigan in his 1977 book, *Schooling the Smash Street Kids*, argued, '... the largest and most complex youth subculture is young people hanging about and doing nothing' (p. 103). Much research that concentrates on street life therefore tends to focus on 'things that are happening', rather than the boring and mundane activity of just doing nothing. Focussing on the spectacular also tends to shift attention away from how choice is increasingly limited due to the power dynamics of adults and mechanisms of regulation and policing (France et al., 2012). In spite of an extensive body of work critiquing such approaches, the power of these representations is pervasive and they emerge time and time again (Cieslik and Simpson, 2013). The overlapping influence of a range of social structures means that young people's relationship with, and construction of, local place is rarely so straight-forward, or predicated on taking part in deviant, or spectacular activities.

Youth and urban space

Historically, understanding young people's relationship with space and place has been dominated by the urban experience. David Farrugia (2014) argues that the historical relationship of spatialized analysis in youth sociology has arisen out of work on urban contexts. A vast diversity of research has investigated young peoples' relationship with, and construction of, city spaces. Indeed, many assume urban locations to be almost the natural site for youthful interaction, giving limited attention to the rural context of growing up (Farrugia, 2014).

Of course, in discussions about different forms or categories of place, such as 'rural' or 'urban', it can be difficult to know what these are referring to. Inevitably, urban or rural spaces emerge not so much as absolute, discrete geographic territories, but rather as heterogeneous, pluralistic spaces, problematic to define according to dichotomous conceptions. While much of the research on young and urban living has been dominated by the negative images of 'problematic youth', there is also a body of research that highlights the important roles that young people play in the development of cities and city life. Young people play an important role in shaping and constructing urban spaces, while the specific structures and dynamics of cities underscore and inform their lives. Young people are intrinsic contributors to the production of urban spaces; spending time, hanging out, meeting friends, going to the local park or shopping mall, or taking part in subcultural activities like attending music festivals. These constitute key practices through which the urban geographies of cities emerge and develop. Further, the ways in which young people move around the city using public transport, driving (alone or with adults), walking or cycling, are another domain of spatial practice. In many ways, everyday activities such as these can challenge the dominant, mainstream uses of urban space and serve to re-appropriate it for youthful practice (Horschelmann and van Blerk, 2013).

Skelton (2013) introduces us to the idea of understanding youth mobilities within cities. Urban living in large international cities around the world requires people to be mobile and navigate city spaces. Drawing on her research in Auckland in New Zealand, she shows how young people access and use modes of transport. What she shows is that, '… their ability to move into, through and out of urban spaces is an important element of their independent geographies' (p. 469). With public transport being 'unreliable' and 'expensive', young people increasingly focus on becoming independent in how they develop modes of transport. Moving away from the 'parent taxi' is a central feature, while driving a car is a necessity.

Place-narratives characterizing large cities also imagine spaces as sites of opportunity, enterprise and innovation, intersected by intense global flows, and with vibrant cultural scenes. They are areas with highly concentrated populations and infrastructure. Further, city spaces are often symbolically representative of the future, and of moving forward. We can see this future-narrative reflected in the way that the study of young people has been heralded as a means to ascertain broader processes of social change into the future (Farrugia, 2014). Indeed, urban spaces, particularly progressive inner-city neighbourhoods, have been associated with youthful demographics. The classic 'face' of the youthful city is of a night-time district, frequented by young people engaging in activities popularly associated with youth: hanging out, drinking, sexual encounters, drug-taking or dancing for instance (see Chatterton and Hollands, 2003). Indeed, such nightlife scenes are popular and are seen as the core domain of youthfulness.

A less 'spectacular' facet of youthful city life, though no less common in its prosaic characterization of suburban life, is presented in Mäkinen and Tyrväinen's (2008) investigation into young peoples' experiences of suburban green spaces of Helsinki. They found that young people used these spaces in a unique way, and valued green spaces not only as an aesthetically pleasing environment, but also in terms of opportunities to engage in outdoor activity, including mundane activities like hanging out with friends. Further, challenging perceptions of outer-ring housing estates as inherently family friendly, Robson (2010) considers young people in their teen years negotiating change within their suburban communities and reflects on the ways suburban space can be improved for its young residents. In many ways, the city, and its suburbs, represent another sphere of experience for young people that disrupts more stereotypical urban imaginaries.

Thinking about more inner-city areas, stylized accounts rarely account for the diversity of these sites; nor do they reflect the variety that exists within urban environments. Downtown areas differ substantially from suburban neighbourhoods, and young people's ability to participate in the utopian range of opportunities seen to be available similarly differs. The intersecting structural dynamics explored in the above section highlight many of those paths leading to opportunity, exclusion and challenge. Stereotypes that paint city spaces as particularly progressive, or global, or replete with opportunity can be accused of being overly deterministic. Such accounts attribute too much influence to place while neglecting the role that broader structures and individuals play. It is also important to remember that city-scapes can, and do, exclude the young. Horschelmann and van Blerk (2013) described this in terms of young people being 'designed out' of urban space. Others have shown how gentrification of urban spaces is limiting young people's opportunities to be included in new forms of redevelopment (Raia-Hawrylak, 2005). We also have to remember that cities are central sites where young homeless people visibly congregate and where violence is most prevalent for the young.

Lost youth in the global city

In their research, Jo-Anne Dillabough and Jacqueline Kennelly (2010) focussed on young people who live at the margins of urban centres, and where they are on the 'edges'. These are the sites in which low-income, immigrant and other disenfranchised youth are living. Their research concentrated on those who have seemingly lost out and suffered in urban spaces, and who are increasingly subjected to new levels of inequality. They explored the ways in which these young people, who are marked by substantial economic disadvantage as well as ethnic and religious diversity, are trying to navigate these new urban contexts and terrains. In so doing, what they found was that these young people have created new ways of seeing themselves and managing their everyday lives in urban centres.

Regional and rural areas

Rural places have often been characterized as 'idyllic', seen as closer to 'nature', and as safer and more inclusive. Positive aspects are usually expounded, including a stronger sense of community, perceived tranquillity, the aesthetic appeal of the natural environment and greater security (Benson and Jackson, 2012). However, in addition to being seen as 'idyllic', regional or rural places have also been represented as conservative and racist, as well as more static, isolated and removed from the impacts of **globalization** (Goodwin-Hawkins, 2014). In youth sociology, there has been a propensity to reaffirm the notion that rural communities are likely to have stronger connections and social capital. This can be seen, for instance, in work tracing the motivations of amenity migrants moving to the countryside from the city. The motivations of those moving from the city to the country reflect some of those more positive concepts of rural places. For example, they want to move to the country because such places are seen to be more cohesive, supportive and community friendly for families, and more secure for children and young people (Osbaldiston, 2010).

> **Globalization:** The movement of people, products and ideas flowing at a global level, but impacting places and communities at a local level.

💭 Thinking points

- Why might it not be useful to characterize rural and urban as a dichotomy?
- How do rural places afford particular experiences for young people, and how might this be different for young people living in cities?

Others apply a more negative lens in terms of young people living beyond the city. Young rural residents have been characterized as being significantly disadvantaged as a result of geographic isolation (Bourke et al., 2010). Somewhat reminiscent of the isolation and stasis sometimes associated with rural spaces, disadvantage is usually measured in more structural terms. Negative impacts are rated against a range of indicators, including lower incomes, fewer employment opportunities, limited public transport and reduced access to health services. The impact for young people living in rural communities is then seen to be even greater, with key transitional pathways in the form of employment and education sometimes not readily available. Such conditions oblige youthful migration towards urban places (see Gabriel, 2006).

This discourse however, has been interrogated and criticized for not taking account of the complexities of disparate rural communities (Bourke et al., 2010). Conceiving of rural places wholly in terms of disadvantage or advantage neglects and simplifies the dynamics of social disadvantage that are not always related to geography, but rather to broader dynamics such as socio-economic status. The work of David Farrugia (2016) is important here. He, like Skelton (2013), wants to highlight the importance of mobilities in rural areas. Farrugia argues that young people who live in rural areas need to be mobile in order to access the resources they need to build biographies and to manage their transitions into adulthood. But he reminds us that the distinction between urban and rural is not 'natural'. Rather, differences are formed through a complex process involving the structural, symbolic and personal dimensions of young people's dispositions and identities. In terms of the structural, he wants to draw our attention to how the relationship between the city and rural has been constructed:

> As flows of capital are accumulated and agglomerated in cities, the relationship between the city and the country has been reshaped ... this has taken place differently in different places, but the global fluidity of contemporary capital has created a strong mobility imperative for rural youth. (p. 841)

For example, the collapse of the youth labour market in rural settings is a result not only of deindustrialization, but also of the increasing vulnerability of agriculture and primary industries as a result of global capital flows. Alongside this, unlike in cities, the growth and expansion of services has been limited. This means that opportunities for 'new' jobs have become increasingly limited. Further, how young people feel they 'belong' is shaped by the interrelationship between their embodied selves, their sense of place and their abilities to adapt (or not adapt) to new environments. The example he gives is of the struggles young people from rural areas have in adapting to urban spaces, where they describe feeling 'uncomfortable', and a 'disturbed' feeling of being 'out of place'. Moving out of rural areas into urban areas is difficult for many young people.

Space, place and indigeneity

So far, our discussion on space and place has focussed on a range of literature and ideas that emerged from Western social science. As we described in Chapter 2, such an approach constructs our knowledge and understandings of concepts such as place and space in particular ways. For example, Barker and Pickerill (2019) remind us that social geographers have had a significant part to play in colonization and imperialist encounters around the world. However, they also recognize both this and the continued struggles of social geographers to include in their analysis concepts that are important to Indigenous people. While there is much engagement with critical development studies, '... there remains a reluctance to fully embrace the decolonialism of geography' (Barker and Pickerill, 2019). From this position Barker and Pickerill (2019) argue

> Place in Indigenous contexts is not an object of study but an ever present member of a wider, more than-human community, with wants and needs of its own and dynamic and unknowable aspects beyond human comprehension. (p. 9)

What they mean by this is that we need to understand and recognize that 'place' is more than a physical thing, in that it goes beyond being simply about human relationships with each other. Land, for example, has agency because it lives as 'ancestral' land (with a history and role in defining the people who live on the land). It includes animal and plant life (as well as having its own ecology) and it speaks to, creates, and teaches us (Johnson et al., 2016). Place has a special significance for Indigenous people in that it is given life through stories of the ancestors, the spirts of the land and the sea and the cosmos, which require present and future generations to act as guardians and custodians.

Recently, in New Zealand, this special relationship of place has been enshrined in law. A new law was passed giving legal personhood to the Whanganui River. This gave it the same rights and protections that people receive under the law. The aim of the New Zealand government was to recognize the essential food source it provides, and the deep spiritual connection between the local iwi (tribe) and the river. It has been the life blood of their community for centuries, and the law aims to protect it for future generations.

Colonialism, post-colonialism and place

It is important to recognize that, at the heart of colonization was the theft of land from Indigenous peoples. This happened worldwide in countries such as Australia, New Zealand, Canada and the USA, to name just a few. This 'displacement' and breaking of connections to the land has had massive implications for Indigenous groups. Not only did they lose their homes and sources of food and livelihood, but they lost connection with their ancestors and their history (Walker, 1996). While countries such as New Zealand and Canada have created mechanisms such as, respectively, the Waitangi Tribunal and the Truth Commission, for compensating or returning lands, the fact remains that irrevocable damage has been done to generations of Indigenous people. The impact of colonialization is still present today in a wide range of ways. One example is found in the growth of urbanization and particularly the gentrification of international cities. This has seen Indigenous people further displaced and marginalized. As Wall (2016, p. 301) states, 'Cities operate to regulate Indigenous people to certain neighbourhoods, usually peripheral to mainstream civic life.' Alongside this, spatial planning and development reflect the existing and historical colonial relationships, ensuring that both the needs of Indigenous people and their cultural representations are marginalized in the growth of new urban environments.

The 'battle' over Ihumātao

In New Zealand, young people led a protest over the selling of land that had originally been owned by Māori. The land at Ihumātao has always been seen as important and sacred land and an important historical site. The land was confiscated under the New Zealand Settlements Act in 1863, thus breaching the 1840 Treaty of Waitangi agreement. The land was then sold by the state to a private owner whose descendants held on to the land for more than a century. The land was recently sold to a large building company in New Zealand who had permission to build over 480 houses on the land. SOUL (Save Our Unique Landscape) was formed by a number of young Māori who argued that Ihumātao matters '… because its stories, relationships, built heritage, ecological values and archaeological sites are critical to our understanding of the histories and futures of our city and country. For mana whenua (local Māori), this place embodies sources of identity and wellbeing as well as family, community and tribal relationships'. https://www.protectihumatao.com/. Tensions were raised as the local iwi had been compensated in its tribunal pay out and an agreement had been made between it and the large building company to provide 'affordable housing' for Māori on the land. Agreements had been made, but many young people felt that this was not an acceptable outcome and believed that the land should be returned to Māori. At one level this was portrayed as a 'generational conflict' between young and old, but the protesters resisted and rejected such an representation, saying that their movement had a broad spread of people of different ages. What is clear is that the actions of the state over 160 years ago in taking the land from Māori are having repercussions on young people today. This is an example of the lasting legacy and impact of colonialism.

Globalization and local – the importance of the glocal

In terms of the question of space and place, one final area we need to consider is the impact of globalization on young peoples' lives. Globalization has had, and continues to have, an important impact on place, particularly with regard to young people's spatial embeddedness and relationships with place. Globalization is widely understood as the movement of people, products and ideas, flowing at global level but impacting places and communities at a local level. Globalization represents a shrinking world in which time and space do not act as barriers in the same way they did previously. In many ways, '… globalisation comes to represent the crystallization of the entire world into a single space' (Nayak, 2009, p. 4).

Thinking points

- Give some examples of globalization that might impact young people's everyday lives.
- Can you think of examples of how the 'local' and the 'global' have interfaced to influence young people's cultural practices?

Globalization occurs through the linking of the world via 'thin networks' which connect diverse places because '... nowhere can be an 'island' (Sheller and Urry, 2006, p. 209). Appadurai (1996) conceptualizes the movement of various material and intangible flows on a global level as a series of 'scapes'. By this he means that, in the global world we now live in, our cultures intersect and overlap all the time. This is influenced by a wide range of 'scapes' that are loosely grouped around the transnational flow of people, media images, technologies, economic resources and ideas. Some of the critical questions about globalization include: does it have a homogenizing impact on local places, and will we end up with a loss of local difference in lieu of a universal sameness across the globe? These questions articulate fears that have been expressed by many in discussions about globalization.

Doreen Massey (2005, p. 81) describes disruptive impacts as amounting to the 'total unfettered mobility of free unbounded space.' Here, globalization creates a wholesale disconnection of people and place. Movement across territories might previously have been understood as bounded, and interconnected, but is now totally uninhibited. As Relph (1993) states: 'in a world of multi-national corporations, universal planning practices and instantaneous global communications, we have to take seriously the argument that sense of place is just another form of nostalgia and that places are obsolete' (p. 25).

Despite early fears that increasing rates of globalization might result in a homogenization of social, cultural and ethnic difference, the reality is more complex. It cannot be denied that global flows do permeate local places. However, globalization is better understood as contesting and creating challenges for relationships between place and the people. It can also impact on people's self-identity as well as understandings of difference. Rather than a broad-brush, universal relationship between the local and global, the connection is bumpy and contradictory, with local cultures and places responding differently, and incorporating or adapting global cultures unevenly (Nayak, 2017). Nayak uses the metaphor of painting, and the application of paint to an uneven surface to explain the relationship:

> ... globalization has not followed a basic 'painting by numbers' schema designed around predictable colour charts and anticipated natural finishes. Closer inspection reveals a gloss that is patchy and spread unevenly by the sweeping, roller-brush of change as it comes into direct contact with the unexpected surfaces, ridges and contours of locality and identity. (Nayak, 2017, p. 5)

Harris and Wyn (2009) present a similar argument. For them, negotiations between place, people and global flows are much more complex than the dichotomous, linear conceptions often assumed. They suggest that particular places remain important for the young, and while global narratives and discourses around products, goods and services are important, they are negotiated with the local. They become '... forged within the mundane spaces of household, family, school, peer group and neighbourhood' (Harris and Wyn, 2009, p. 335). This idea has drawn upon the term 'glocal', which is where young people draw on global and local resources to construct their cultural practices. For example, based on research on Russian youth cultures, Pilkington (2004) shows that young people, who are peripheral to the core of global forces, do not act culturally on a purely local basis. In fact, the 'global' and the 'local' are resources that young people draw upon that help them develop youth cultural strategies that shape their cultural practice in ways that are both a reflection on globalization and embedded in cultural ways of doing things. This creates a unique set of practices that are neither purely global nor purely local; rather they are a 'hybrid' and draw upon a wide variety of international, national and local knowledge.

Other examples from youth studies on the relationship between the local and global include greater access to information flows via digital media (Valentine and Holloway, 2001), or the movement of jobs and industries into, or out of, particular regions (Lashua and Kelly, 2008). While changes driven by global forces have occurred, these have not necessarily been consistent with fears of wholesale cultural and ethnic homogenization (Nayak, 2009). For example, access to global information flows in the form of social media technologies among young people in rural England were interpreted and used within the embedded, culturally and socially specific context of their everyday lives (Valentine and Holloway, 2001).

On the relationship between global and local for young people in particular, Nayak explains that '… young people are also active agents who participate, albeit unequally, in the global economy. They are cultural innovators and consumers involved in a complex negotiation with social transformations.' (Nayak, 2017, p. 4) Nayak explains that, while cultural or information flows intersect across the globe, young people inevitably consume and interact with these from the perspective of their own socio-cultural positioning. In his ethnographic exploration of a particular youth subculture in the post-industrial site of his northern UK study, young people's cultural identity was put together with global and local identity sources. The mainly White participants of the study sought to keep up with the 'cultural excess of global times' by incorporating consumption from four areas: sport, fashion, hairstyles and music. This constituted a form of experimentation using embodied identity positions that moved beyond and re-conceptualized the traditional confines of place and nation.

Globalization is also epitomized by social media technologies. With high usage rates across many countries in the developed world, digital technologies serve as a reminder of the shrinking world in their ability to deliver ready access to information flows from a range of cultural and national contexts (Cieslik and Simpson, 2013; Nayak, 2009). Indeed, in many ways, digital data flows serve to collapse geographic boundaries, and thus shrink a subjective sense of distance and geographic discreteness (Nayak, 2009). As a result, under the contemporary conditions of globalization, place and space are indeed seen to have changed irrevocably.

It is not easy to quantify the impacts of globalization on place, nor the differential distribution of such impacts, or people's subjective sense of their relationships with place (Massey, 2005). Indeed, constructions of place change significantly over time, and vary across demographic populations, including younger and older people, culturally and linguistically diverse groups, as well as according to gender and socio-economic positioning (see Massey, 2005). Ultimately however, under the disruptive conditions of globalization, localities provide a source of meaning, authenticity or identity for those who occupy and move within them (Massey, 2005).

The importance of class, gender, sexuality and ethnic identity

Social class, place and space

So far, our discussion has concentrated on identifying how space and place can be different as a result of urban, rural and global forces. It is important to recognize that the ways people use and access spaces and places can be shaped by their class, gender, sexuality or ethnicity.

Thinking point

- Can you think of any particular spaces or places which might be used or experienced differently by different social classes, genders or ethnic groups? Why might this be?

As we highlighted above, much attention in both public discourses and social science has concentrated on those groups of young people that are perceived as social problems. What we see is a literature, and a body of knowledge, that aims to associate problem youth with particular spaces and places. This interest has driven a massive research programme, funded by governments, to identify the causal factors embedded in the ecology of neighbourhoods, localities and/or communities that may be influencing and shaping the problem behaviours of young people. These explanations can range from environmental factors such as poor lighting and badly planned housing areas, to more social and cultural dynamics such as low levels of policing, poor parenting and anti-social or criminal cultures. What is being suggested in much of this work is that where young people live, as well as the places and spaces they use, is in some way criminogenic; that is, they are places that are likely to cause criminal behaviour.

A classic study relating to crime and place was the work of the Chicago School in the 1930s. This study identified a number of zones in the City of Chicago, between the central business district (CBD) and the outer rings of respectable working- and middle-class suburbs, including a suburb that they called the 'zone of transition'. This was inhabited by the poorest in society and included ethnic minorities and migrants in transition. The researchers argued that this was where the most deviant youth lived. Such an idea remains entrenched in much policy and in research. We shall come back to this issue in Chapter 9 when we look more closely at young people's relationships with crime.

But how young middle and working class use spaces and places can be very different. For instance, middle-class youth have greater access to social and economic resources that allow them to 'carve out' youthful spaces within the private domain (Pickering et al., 2011). There are also fewer risks for middle class youth and more opportunities for them to be mobile in the city. Having the resources to either use public transport or have access to cars increases their ability to be mobile and access a wider range of social and cultural activities. It is also normal for middle class parents to give their children opportunities to be engaged in a wide range of formal activities, such as after-school sports, music lessons or horse riding. These are all controlled and regulated activities accessible to the middle class.

Working class youth, however, have been found to be relatively embedded in local neighbourhoods and other public places (Pickering et al., 2011). Young people from working-class backgrounds are more likely to be present at various times of the day, experience greater spatial freedom at the neighbourhood level, and are more lacking in resources that would allow them to exercise their freedom within the private sphere (Pickering et al., 2011). 'Hanging about with mates' on the streets in their local communities is a major activity of working class youth, which makes them both visible and vulnerable.

Adopting a subcultural lens, Tolonen (2013) explores the lifestyles of young people as they are mediated through a range of localities in urban Helsinki, Finland. In particular, social class plays an explanatory role in the range of shared habitus and cultural practices that are produced within different lifestyles. Indeed, Tolonen argues that specific places afford certain classed performances and these are not spatially interchangeable; rather they must be enacted in particular localities. Classed differences between a middle-class school and one in a more working-class area of the city were distinguished through stylistic performances, music consumption, occupation of space, leisure activity such as sports or theatre, and use of alcohol and other drugs. While the young people themselves were less likely to identify a particular class identity, classed lifestyles in terms of borders and inclusion were writ large.

Gender, space and place

Gender is a significant influence on young people's experience of place. Indeed, it is difficult to paint a picture of young peoples' spatial relationships without reflecting on the role of gender. Researchers have extensively investigated young men's and young women's experiences of moving through space and constructing places of meaning. For example, young women are said to experience 'affective geographies' where public places can come to be associated with male domination (Bondi and Rose, 2003, p. 233). Embodied risk and fear, including harassment or violence perpetrated by an unknown other, become a feature of being in public spaces (Green and Singleton, 2006). In some cases, this has meant that young women feel that they cannot be in certain public spaces at certain times of day. Dunkley (2004) contrasted the experiences of male participants to those of female participants in her North American study. Young men reported being able to frequently move from their workplace, their home, and entrainment establishments without any worries for their safety. Young men also tended to be more in control of their mobility because they were more likely to own cars. By comparison, young woman faced more restrictions and reported feeling uneasy about using public transport and being in certain public spaces, especially at night. Parents also expressed concerns and insisted on picking up their daughters after dark, or setting times to return home that were seen as safer.

🧠 Thinking point

- What everyday public spaces do you use which might be experienced differently by someone of a different gender or sexual orientation than you?

How young women use night-time spaces and places has, in more recent times, undergone significant changes. As we highlighted in the previous chapter, rave culture and the growing practice of engaging in night-time drinking has become a popular activity of young people. What we see in this process is that more young women are engaging in what has been called 'active girlhood' (Nayak and Kehily, 2013). This involves young women seeing themselves as 'can do girls' who are out seeking pleasure and fun. Young women's involvement in the night-time economy is now far more visible. Hen parties, girls' nights out and birthday celebrations in the city are now far more common, and girls see being involved in the night-time economy as a core part of their lives (Nayak and Kehily, 2013).

Of course, others have highlighted the need to recognize that girls' uses of place and space can be significantly different from those of young men. Teenage girls in the 1990s were more likely to get together in private spaces such as their bedrooms. McRobbie (1978) for example, introduced the notion of 'bedroom culture' as way of addressing the gendering of space. It was here that young women met their friends and had fun enjoying a range of 'girly' activities such as experimenting with fashion, playing popular music, dancing in front of the bedroom mirror and talking about romance. Since this work, others have continued investigating girls, space and place. Lincoln (2004) showed how girls continued to use private space as a way of being cultural. The bedroom is a private space, away from prying eyes; it is a space where girls sleep, daydream, read magazines and listen to music. The bedroom is also a place where they meet with their friends and are social, in addition to being a biographical site that contains posters, photographs, books, magazines and a wide range of other cultural possessions.

Nayak (2006) explored some of the gendered dynamics that arose in a post-industrial UK city in the north-east of the country. In particular, he investigated the transition to work among working class young men from different backgrounds, namely from communities with high unemployment, and those from skilled labour backgrounds. The post-industrial city has a history that has seen a profound transformation in terms of labour from skilled manufacturing towards a more service-based economy, and this plays a role in the young men's lives. For Nayak, social class played a central role in the construction of urban places by young men, and the relationship is evident via a number of practices and discourses: 'social class is rendered visible through a mobile economy of signs, discursively mapped onto the cartography of the post-industrial city and the working and non-working bodies that lie therein' (Nayak, 2006, p. 827). Despite rapid economic and social change however, regional identity remained strong among the young participants of Nayak's (2006) study.

Young men's masculine cultures further shape their relationships with place. For example, Kenway et al. (2006) show that maintaining, fixing and racing cars represents a spatially embedded subculture where young men express a wide range of masculine practices. Joelsson's (2015) research on young men in regional Sweden also identified a highly gendered zone constructed by the local 'greaser' clique. The young men would regularly converge in a public car-park to spend time and work on their cars, thereby forming a gender- and youth-specific sense of place. While strongly associated with masculine participation in subcultures, young women were also occasionally active participants in the car subcultures, although they remained on the fringes.

Queerness

An added dimension in the extensive literature on the gendering of public places is the experiences of those with diverse gender and sexual identities (Skeggs, 1999). City space has been delineated, carved out, and territories have been termed 'gay villages'; these are imbued with political meaning. Cases from different spatial contexts, in both urban and rural areas, highlight diverse experiences. Some afford affirming and positive experiences, while others do not. Systems of oppression and overt control are evident; however, young people go about their lives with a greater or lesser degree of freedom in most cases.

Schroeder (2012) investigated the construction of spaces for queer young people in US city schools. In particular, the research identified the mechanisms that support young people to negotiate heterosexual spaces, as well as the contradictory 'safe spaces' delineated by adult advocates. Spaces within school grounds were constructed discursively, and adults were found to (re)produce heteronormativity within them. With regard to the intersecting role of religion, a study into queer-friendly churches in the UK looked to the ways that religion and sexuality are shaped and articulated in a range of spaces (Taylor, 2016). While religion has been characterized as incongruent with queer sexual identities, Taylor found a much more complex, nuanced relationship that is realized through the medium of certain religious spaces, such as churches.

Moscow, in Russia, represents a much less affirming experience for young LBGTI people than in Taylor's (2016) study. While Moscow has been positioned as an emerging global city, it is nonetheless characterized by institutionalized homophobia and violence directed towards the queer community (Stella, 2013). There are significant and hostile responses to the visibility of queer and LBGTI communities in the city. Stella (2013) explored the ways people carve out spaces within the city under such anti-LBGTI regimes. In particular, the study focussed on 'the scene', or a collection of commercial and community spaces frequented by the LBGTI community in Moscow, as well as Pride events, as an appropriation of urban space. This latter form of spatial appropriation is highly contested, and much more fraught than in other urban contexts. Stella found that commercial locations were generally subtly signified as queer (i.e. with small rainbow plaques at the courtyard entrance). More broadly, community initiatives also shared minimal public visibility, and relied on word-of-mouth. However, low visibility did not necessarily mean that there was not a thriving queer community in Moscow, even if it was completely hidden from public view.

Moving from urban contexts, Gray (2007) describes her young respondents' relationship with space and place in a rural town. The young people in Gray's study displayed non-normative genders and sexualities in their rural homes, countering notions that such visibility is only present in more accepting city spaces. In the context of rural spaces, Gray's (2007) young respondents seemed to enjoy relative freedom in their traversal of rural geographies; however, their experiences were not without tension and some experienced verbal abuse. Indeed, young LBGTI people's embeddedness in regional terrains is often one fraught with anxiety, and the fear of encountering violence shapes and bookends their experiences of place (see Hubbard et al., 2015). Familial and social embeddedness, alongside implicit acknowledgement of diverse sexual identities, underscored the accounts of rural young people in Kazyak's (2011) study. Interestingly, rurality was found to support non-normative sexual identities rather than confine them.

As we can see from the diversity of research from the UK, Moscow and the USA, ranging from those in urban spaces to those in rural locales, place affords a vast range of contexts for young people to practise gender-diverse identities and engage in queer communities. What is also clear, however, is the necessity to consider a suite of shaping influences, along with their intersecting relationships (i.e. class, religion, gender, culture, state sanctions), to gain a comprehensive view of young people's relationships with place.

Intersectionality and cultural difference

Young people's cultural background, as well as their gender or sexuality, is a further shaping factor in relationships with space and place. This is particularly salient for cultures in which young women are expected to moderate their behaviour in public spaces (Wattis et al., 2011), although the gendering of public spaces emerges in a range of cultural contexts. For example, among the South Asian community in a UK town, young women engaged in heavy self-policing in response to their visibility within their community while in public areas of the town. However, the young women were still able to negotiate public spaces to manipulate and reduce the likelihood of being seen by other community members. In this way, they could protect their reputations, adhere to behavioural expectations and still engage in activities, such as spending time with friends, or meeting young men, that might involve spending time unaccompanied in public (Green and Singleton, 2006).

Watson and Ratna (2011) also highlight the importance of the intersections of South Asian and British culture in the production of leisure spaces in the north of the country. Cultural difference and a sense of belonging were negotiated and claimed via public parks as sites of mutually constructed sites of leisure (in the manner of Tolonen's work on social class in the section above). Relating a range of observations and experiences during a 'Bollywood'-inspired cultural event, Watson and Ratna highlighted intersecting gendered, cultural and classed relations among the attendees. The researchers explained that these ultimately served to produce a space that was both inclusive and exclusionary of some bodies. Indeed, young women were found to be somewhat less visible throughout the culture event, though this may be because their spatial practice was less 'spectacular' and therefore less noticeable.

Acknowledging the changing, dynamic nature of cultural identities, Harris (2016) focussed on the cultural diversity that characterizes Australian urban communities and the role it plays in young peoples' sense of belonging and place. For the young, urban participants, place was a 'dynamic environment of proliferating differences' (Harris, 2016, p. 365). Indeed, they were able to 'achieve belonging by positioning themselves as one of the many equal differences present in the community and participating in its cultural mix' (Harris, 2016, p. 365). The young people spoke of local neighbourhoods and other spaces where cultural diversity was a mundane, taken-for-granted aspect of daily life, and they contrasted this with more exclusionary spaces. Harris argued that this form of 'unremarkable' negotiation of difference played a key a role in their ability to take part in local and national belonging, and ultimately in positioning them within the 'multiple spaces of belonging… in multicultural Australia' (Harris, 2016, p. 371).

The discussion about cultural background and young peoples' spatial embeddedness is abundant, and the studies discussed in this brief section represent a small slice of it. Minority cultural background among young people in the UK mediates and shapes their spatial embeddedness, while diversity more broadly fosters a sense of belonging among Harris's respondents. Acknowledging the intersectional nature of the ways young people relate to and make places, however, shows us that focussing on just one structure can sometimes mean neglecting a broader perspective in which many social structures intersect, and play a role in our relationship with space and place. For example, cultural background intersects with gender and social class, while gender and sexuality intersect with religious identity. These social structures exist in relation to each other, rather than in a vacuum. Nonetheless, applying a single lens can help direct our analytical gaze, as we have shown in this section.

In many instances, it is those groups in a given community who retain the greatest degree of power, in the form of cultural, social or economic capital, who are in a position to legitimately shape and occupy public places with the most freedom. Benson and Jackson's (2012) analysis of a middle-class UK suburb demonstrated the symbolic power wielded by those sharing a relatively powerful class position. It is this form of power that is mostly denied to young people as a whole, irrespective of their class positioning. However, the contours of social class, alongside place-history, gender, labour relations and subcultural practice, help illuminate the complexity of young peoples' experiences and construction of place. Ultimately, accounting for young peoples' various structural positionings (see Davis, 2008; Watson and Ratna, 2011) supports a more complex, detailed understanding of the constraints and enablers that young people experience related to their age, and their relative positioning according to different structural parameters.

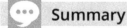 **Summary**

- Space and place are important concepts in youth sociology, and our understandings of them have been strongly influenced by social geographers.

- Spaces and places can be seen through a number of different lens i.e. structural, relational or experiential.

- Youth sociology has tended to concentrate on the spectacular and cultural aspects of young people's use of space and place, ignoring the mundane and the normal.

- The impact of globalization and its relationship with the local is influencing and shaping young people's cultural practices.

- In analyzing space and place there is a need to understand the complexity and interconnection between terms such as urban, rural and the global.

- Spaces and places have an important role in shaping the experiences of those from different classes, genders, sexualities and ethnicities.

✎ Exercise: The sociological imagination

What spaces and places do you move between as you go about an 'ordinary week'? What are the different characteristics of those spaces (e.g. Are there zones where you feel more or less safe at particular times? Who are the people you encounter? Do you perform your identity differently in particular settings?) Try to pinpoint some social and cultural forces shaping the spaces you inhabit in your everyday life.

📖 Key readings

Baker, A. & Pickerill, J. (2019) 'Doings with the land and sea: decolonising geographies, indigeneity and enacting place-agency', *Progress in Human Geography*, Early online view, pp. 1–24.

Cresswell, T. (2015) *Place: An Introduction* (Oxford, UK: Wiley).

Farrugia, D. (2014) 'Towards a spatialised youth sociology: the rural and the urban in times of change', *Journal of Youth Studies*, vol. 17, no. 3, pp. 293–307.

Lashua, B. D. & Kelly, J. (2008) 'Rhythms in the concrete: re-imagining relationships between space, race, and mediated urban youth cultures', *Leisure/Loisir*, vol. 32, no. 2, pp. 461–487.

Massey, D. (2005) *For Space* (London, UK: Sage).

Nayak, A. (2009) *Race, Place and Globalization: Youth Cultures in a Changing World* (Oxford: Berg).

Watson, B. & Ratna, A. (2011) 'Bollywood in the park: thinking intersectionally about public leisure space', *Leisure/Loisir*, vol. 35, no. 1, pp. 71–86.

Woods, M. (2007) 'Engaging the global countryside: globalization, hybridity and the reconstitution of rural place', *Progress in Human Geography*, vol. 31, no. 4, pp. 485–507.

8 YOUTH, RISK AND RISK-TAKING

In this chapter you will learn about:

- The 'risk society' and its implications for young people today
- Major theories of risk and risk-taking
- What we know about young people's use of drugs and alcohol
- How risk-taking can be understood as an interplay between the individual, cultural and structural context of social practice.

The normality of risk?

Thinking point

- What types of risks are popularly associated with young people?
- When you were younger, what types of risks did you take?
- Did you see them as 'risky' at the time?

The issue of risk and risk-taking amongst the young has always been a great concern to adults. In many ways it is not a new concept or something that we should be surprised about. As we have seen in previous chapters, the 'youth question' has always been dogged by anxieties about the behaviour and activities of young people. Panics emerge and create societal responses. Some are supportive and aimed at dealing with the welfare needs of the young, while others are more intrusive, controlling and punitive. When it comes to risk and risk-taking, much of the literature concentrates on trying to find causes and focusses on young people's individual behaviours rather than the socio-cultural contexts framing young people's actions. The literature is strongly influenced by work of psychologists who are looking for inherent problems that are linked to youth (or child) development. For example, in Chapter 1 you were introduced to the neuroscientists or brain scientists, who claim that young people have defective cognitive reasoning until their late 20s, and link this to risk-taking behaviours. Sociologists are highly sceptical of 'brain in a jar' approaches for understanding young people's behaviour, as they effectively separate an individual entirely from their social context and provide overly simplistic causes for what we know to be highly complex issues (see Kelly, 2012).

When thinking about the above questions, you may have started by looking at forms of behaviour that are seen as dangerous, illegal or threatening, such as **binge drinking**, drug abuse, stealing cars and fighting. But you might also have considered risk as more

> **Binge drinking:** A popular term that is used by the media and the public to define excessive drinking patterns. It is usually associated with the young. Its definition is contested and can have different meanings in different countries and contexts.

positive and a part of 'natural' social development. For example, our personal growth depends on our taking risks. Children have to learn about boundaries, and they have to develop. Taking their first steps, or going down a slide in the playground for the first time, are massive risks for a child. These are key stages in a child's development. A second issue you might have considered is that risk-taking can be very much an accepted part of everyday life and in fact is not only considered normal but also pleasurable and fun. For example, people undertake endurance challenges such as climbing mountains or sailing solo around the world; or they gamble at the race-course or in the casino.

Risk operates in a wide range of places and practices in society. For example, we can also associate it with financial management and entrepreneurial activity in the marketplace. Insurance companies and banks are all about risk management. When insuring houses, insurance companies assess the 'risk' of accidents (floods or storms for example) that might happen alongside the history of the house and of the person asking for insurance. They then create a price to cover this as a fee. The less risk, the lower the price (supposedly). Similarly, investors and hedge fund managers in the financial sector are continually assessing risk in the 'money market' when buying and selling shares. And of course those setting up businesses are involved in taking risks in starting new ventures, and usually, to get funding, they have to have a business case that deals with risk management. Risk is and has always been central to how our societies operate. Given the fact that risk and risk-taking have always been normal in most societies, why is there so much concern about young people and their risk-taking?

The risk society thesis

The growth of the 'risk society'

One explanation is that contemporary conditions of social life mean we are subject to greater 'risk' than ever before. Ulrich Beck's (1992) concept of

> **Risk society:** A new era of rapid changes has led to traditional social systems becoming largely unpredictable and uncertain. As a result, risks have been increasing in society.

the **'risk society'** describes this. Beck argued that we are in a period of historical transformation (what he called a shift from 'modern' to 'late modern' society), mainly as a result of rapid scientific and technological development. He argued that these rapid changes have led to traditional social systems becoming largely unpredictable and uncertain. In the 'risk society', new hazards such as global warming, environmental pollution, food shortages, cybercrime and terrorism become a normal part of everyday life. We all feel far more vulnerable and uncertain about our safety and security. At an individual (as well as societal) level we are continually confronted by new risks that are dramatically re-shaping the world around us. Many of these risks are created and manufactured by governments, private industry and financial capital. For example, the growth of pollution in the atmosphere arises through a wide range of industrial activities such as farming and the burning of fossil fuels. While individuals can and do contribute to this process (for example, we drive cars or dump rubbish and plastic), the structural operations of technologies and (lack of) regulation of industries cause large-scale damage, such as gas emissions that harm the planet's ozone, or the sale and usage of plastic, which ends up in the ocean, choking ecosystems.

Thinking point

- How might recent changes in society increase risks for the young?
- Are there things that business, governments and other institutions are doing that might be making life more 'risky' for the young?

But it is not just at the macro level that we are confronted by more risks. Increased risks also manifest at the individual level. As we saw in Chapters 3 and 4, major change has taken place in the ways in which education and the workplace are structured, which affect young people's everyday lives. There are also growing concerns over the safety and security of spaces and places within our communities. For example, since the Global Financial Crisis of 2008, there have been growing anxieties about the ability of our once-trusted institutions to manage financial risks. There is also growing concern about the risk of our personal data being used by marketing companies or criminals stealing our identity. As a result, we have seen major restructuring of social, economic and political life. According to Beck (1992), we have been moving into a period of **detraditionalization** where the old systems and frameworks that helped us manage life are changing. Social relationships have become 'disembedded', for example, through increased mobilities (see Chapter 11), meaning that families and friends may be spread across national borders. The institutions and individuals we traditionally relied upon to help protect us (such as the welfare state, or banks) may no longer be trusted in the same way as before. People start to feel more vulnerable and less certain about what the future holds for them.

> **Detraditionalization:** Where old systems and frameworks for helping us manage life are changing and are less reliable.

Clearly, we live in a period of rapid change, in which things that previous generations took for granted, such as a 'job for life', have now disappeared or changed considerably. Some, however, argue that Beck's claims are 'exaggerated' (Adams, 1995), pointing out that risk has always been contextual at different times in history, and that navigating risk has always been part of the human condition. Beck disagrees, suggesting that the conditions of the 'risk society' are qualitatively different, because of the global scale and nature of contemporary risks.

The 'biographical project' in the risk society

As we saw in Chapter 4, the work of Beck (1992) has had a major impact on youth sociology. He introduces is to the idea of the **'biographical turn'**. For him, the growth of reflexivity as a core social task is a key dimension and a consequence of the risk society. Individuals must now become more adept at navigating the increased social and personal risks that are emerging at a range of levels. They must try to take control over everyday risks as a way of managing the increasingly uncertain social and

> **Biographical turn:** In the 'risk society' we are confronted by more risks, and young people are expected to make more decisions and to take more responsibility for themselves.

economic conditions they face. As we are confronted by more risks, we are continually expected to make more decisions and to take more responsibility for ourselves. Of course, young people with the most social, economic and cultural capital have more of the resources needed to successfully navigate the risk society, while those with the least are most vulnerable and face the consequences of a proliferation of contradictory and changing rules and guidelines. MacDonald and Marsh (2005) showed that, because of young people's class and location in disadvantaged neighbourhoods in the North East of the UK, risk was very high. Not only do such young people lack the resources to avoid the risks of high unemployment and poverty, but also the opportunities available to them are structured by wider decisions being made in corporate business about where to locate and provide work. Risk is therefore a creation of society, but its impact is not experienced equally. In the context of unemployment and poverty, young people's inability to manage risks effectively is seen by some governments as 'their problem'. In this context they are blamed for their 'failure' to get work, avoid being poor or make successful transitions. Risk discourses can have a significant role to play in placing blame and failure on the individual (Kemshall, 2002).

Thinking points

- To what extent do you think young people plan out their lives?
- Do you think young people are consciously creating their own biographies?

Risk, governmentality and neo-liberalism

The roles of the state and government policies are crucial in understanding how the 'risk society' impacts young people (Kelly, 2001). As we have seen in previous chapters (and will discuss further in Chapter 10), how the state defines the 'youth problem' can have significant implications for how policy both responds to and affects the everyday lives of young people.

> **Governance** (can be called 'governmentality'): is the disciplining and regulatory role of the state and is a key function of government as a way of making people behave in certain ways.

The risk society has significantly changed how society is governed (Zinn, 2019), which has in turn influenced youth policy across a wide range of areas. **Governance** and the disciplinary and regulatory role of the state is a key function of government that needs us to behave in certain ways. Historically, governance, especially after the Second World War, tended to be more about protection, dealing with needs, and wealth creation for the many. It aimed more at gaining compliance and regulation with a set of norms and behaviours linked to inclusion and collective good. But in the 'risk society', government policy tends to be less about working towards the collective good, and more geared towards the displacement of risk management onto the individual citizen.

Neo-liberalist policy is closely aligned with the risk society. It draws upon and uses risk to justify its politics of regulation and control and can be active in helping create the 'neo-liberal subject' (Kelly, 2001). Neo-liberalism gives recognition to individual action and behaviour over collective endeavour, while regulation and compliance becomes a significant objective of the state. Individual conduct is constructed as entailing choice, life planning (biographies) and the creation of purposeful pathways through life. Individuals are increasingly expected to bear the responsibility (and cost) of managing themselves and their risks in society – what Steven Webb calls 'the privatisation of risk and risk management' (Webb, 2006). What we have seen in the new era is the removal of the paternal welfare state and universal social services, replaced by individualism and rationalization that reinforce freedom and choice but centralize individual responsibility. Governance in a neo-liberal society also happens at the 'micro level' where citizens are required to self-regulate towards a particular set of norms. In a risk society, those who are troublesome and problematic, and who are not self-regulating and conforming, are identified as 'risky subjects' who need policing and managing in particular ways. This can then lead to their being excluded, marginalized and demonized;

> 'Risk therefore exists not as an external reality but as a calculative rationality' of governance, through which particular groups and individuals may be identified as 'at risk' or 'high risk' and thereby observed, managed and disciplined. (Sharland, 2006, p. 255)

Across the welfare/social policy nexus, we see this notion having significant weight in youth policy in areas such as youth justice, social work, education and health policy (Bessant, 2001).

Crime, early intervention and prevention

Risk factor analysis (RFA) emerged from research by academics in the fields of developmental life course research and criminology (Farrington, 1996). It had a major impact on the development of early intervention programmes for young people and children 'most at risk' of future offending. It was taken up at policy level in countries such as the USA, the UK, Australia and New Zealand. Building on longitudinal research, it claimed that there are a number of key risk factors that increase the likelihood a young person will offend. These risks seem to correlate with individual malfunctioning or personality problems such as lack of cognitive reasoning skills or control skills. While it does not claim to predict future offenders, it argues that, by targeting those with multiple risks, policy makers are *more likely* to reduce future offending.

Such an approach has seen the growth of early intervention programmes with 0–5-year-olds and young people deemed most 'at risk' of being future offenders. Risk factors help governments find 'solutions' to problems such as youth crime, yet RFA has a number of methodological limitations. It constructs the problem as one of individuals, and while not denying the ecology of offending, it marginalizes the context and gives it less relevance. More importantly for our argument, it also creates a view of risk where the state is less interested in needs and more focussed on managing risk factors and 'risky individuals'. It becomes an important 'social marker' of otherness, by which certain groups and populations are defined as outsiders and social problems. Such an approach creates a negative view of certain groups of young people and justifies both intensive intervention/attention and, if necessary, punishment. This acts to help maintain social control and the status quo (Kelly, 2001; Bessant, 2001).

Theorizing risk-taking

Artefact, realist and social constructionist theories

So far, our discussion has concentrated on how 'society' and/or government are central in creating the risks young people encounter or have to manage, but such a position does not explain *why* young people might take risks and *why* in some cases they actively seek out risk-taking as a social activity. As we outlined at the start of the chapter (and in Chapter 2), the dominant ways of understanding and making sense of young people's risk-taking tend to come from psychology and are defined as an artefact and realist approach. This means that risk-taking is seen as being driven by the failings and problems of the individual; they are seen as having something wrong with their development such as lack of self-control, poor judgement or low education. It is embedded in empiricist scientific proof and a realist epistemology with regard to the study of risk. For example, as we saw in the box on the previous page, the conceptualization of risk is epitomized by the pursuit of statistically valid and predicatively useful risk factors. Risk is a social fact; i.e., young people take a range of risks, which can be measured and, theoretically, reduced. In this context it is psychology that has driven our understandings. Such an approach has its problems as it does not emphasize the social context of risk-taking, or explanations from young people themselves about why they take risks. Such an approach is useful in highlighting the types of risk young people might take but fails to understand the motivations or the social contexts informing young people's actions. 'Artefact' approaches to understanding risk-taking therefore locate the risk in the failings of individuals.

An alternative approach to understanding risk-taking is the 'constructionist' position. It suggests that our understandings of risk depend on how it is socially and culturally constructed (Lupton, 1999). A strong social constructionist approach to understanding risk position is advocated by scholars working in cultural theory, and it recognizes that 'risk is always a social product' (Douglas, 1992).

The work of Mary Douglas

Mary Douglas, a British anthropologist, has explored how risks operate culturally to shape people's responses and choices. Her main interest is in how certain forms of behaviour are defined and constructed as 'risky' in different contexts. She is focussed on how social groups, organizations or societies construct and maintain boundaries between self and others, how they deal with deviance and how they achieve social order. She suggests that cognitive arguments and probability or psychometric risk measurement approaches, as discussed above, fail to understand the lay perspective and why people make the choices they do. Behaviour can only be understood in its social context. In her approach, she argues that individuals learn about risks through shared cultural definitions based on communality rather than the individual. Douglas's approach can also take into account the mutual obligations and expectations embedded in particular cultures and ways of life.

Douglas's most famous work explored themes of 'purity and danger', explaining how taboos act in cultural frameworks to protect people in societies from behaviours that threaten them. For example, the notion of 'dirt' and related concepts such as contamination, pollution and defilement are all embedded with risk and danger, yet in different contexts they have different meanings in different cultures and can create and raise different taboos. What these concepts mean and how people deal with them vary by context and culture. Such concepts set boundaries, classifications and categories, and if these are then broken or transgressed, people are breaking taboos or committing a sin and can face vilification or exclusion, which thus act as a form of social control.

An interpretivist approach to risk-taking

A final position (which fits under the umbrella of 'constructionist' approaches to risk) has been developed by Jens Zinn (2019), who takes what is called an interpretive approach to risk and risk-taking. This approach acknowledges that the meaning of risk is socially and subjectively framed and that the choices and decisions people make can only be understood in their social context. He suggests that decision-making and risk-taking are not the same thing. This approach acknowledges that people have explanations and motivations for why they take risks (even bad ones). As we know, risk-taking may conflict with expert advice. For example, we all know that smoking cigarettes is bad for our health (the risk is high), but large numbers of people continue to smoke, against expert advice. Zinn (2019) argues that risk-taking as a voluntary activity is deliberate and involves a degree of reflexivity. People also believe that in taking a risk they have an element of control or agency in making the decision. Of course the notion of 'voluntary' can be problematic in that it assumes 'free choice', while in reality, all 'choices' originate in social conditions and contexts.

Zinn (2019) suggests there are three main social motivations. Firstly, there is risk 'as an end in itself'. By this he means that taking a risk is the dominant driver of the activity. The example he gives is the work of Steven Lyng (1990) on '**edgework**'. Lyng suggests that, rather than avoiding risk, many people engage in risky activities for positive self-development and the 'thrill' or the 'pleasure' of an activity. Risk-taking is in many ways about negotiating and navigating the 'edge' of the boundary between 'life and death' or 'order and disorder'. Such activity is highly emotive, relying on body sensations such as a 'rush of blood' or the 'drive of adrenaline'. A second motivation Zinn defines is 'risk as a means to an end'. This refers to aiming for material or personal gain or value (for example, investing money on the stock exchange or gambling – although some of this could be seen as 'edge work'). Zinn describes people who volunteer for overseas aid work in risky places, who are willing to take these risks on the basis that for them the contribution they make is for the betterment of the human condition. People accept the risks, which are largely out of their control, because they value the activity and it gives them a feeling of social worth. A third, final motivation Zinn describes is one where people are in unbearable situations or have limited resources to resist or avoid them. In this sense he suggests people take risks in response to vulnerability. These may include situations where there are competing high risks that are beyond a person's control. His examples include refugees paying people smugglers, and the illegal selling of a kidney to pay off high debt, or illegal abortions. These are high risks, which must be

> **Edgework:** Where people engage in risky activities for positive self-development and the 'thrill' or the 'pleasure' of an activity.

understood in the context of significant vulnerability caused by global patterns of disadvantage, hardship and inequality.

Risk-taking as 'habit', 'routine', 'learned' and 'normalized'

Most understandings of risk tend to locate risks as originating from a 'rational actor'. This position has only a limited understanding of the 'social' drivers of risk-taking. While this perspective does extend attention from individuals to their immediate circumstances, it does not focus on the social patterns of disadvantage that shape these circumstances. The rational actor paradigm focusses on the interaction between the 'propensity' of the individual to react to 'temptations' or 'deterrents' located in the various settings s/he enters. Influenced by a rational choice model, it emphasizes an interactive approach and an examination of the social mechanisms that influence the individual's routines and decision-making processes. Individual agency is seen as central (Clarke and Cornish, 1985), and the research focus is limited to the decision-making of individuals, rather than patterns of social context.

So, what role does social context play in risk? Firstly, it is important to recognize that risk-taking can be deeply embedded in the everyday practice of social life. Torbenfeldt Bengtsson and Ravn (2018) show that much of young people's risk-taking is trivial and ordinary, and does not involve a search for a 'thrill' or excitement'. Risk-taking is 'habitual' and 'routine' (Crawshaw and Bunton, 2009) and is strongly influenced by localized understandings, past experiences and future anticipations. Torbenfeldt Bengtsson and Ravn (2018) argue that risk-taking can be part of the 'routine' of young people's everyday lives. In this sense, risk-taking is culturally defined and shaped by the context and histories of a place. They also emphasize that risks involve not only the mind, through 'decisions', but the body through learned and habitual practices. In this sense, risk-taking is always embodied and is connected to feelings and perceptions of both the past and future.

Similarly, Crawshaw and Bunton (2009) draw on Pierre Bourdieu's concept of social practice to note that risk-taking must be understood through social practice at the intersection of habitus, history and culture. They explored why young men in highly deprived communities took risks that were dangerous. They found that these young men grew up in 'high-risk environments', which became a part of their habitus (personal history and sense of selfhood). They were aware that their social location (place) was stigmatized as a 'risky community', and they had to manage the risks of living in deprivation and with high levels of crime on a daily basis. Risk and risk-taking was then learned and normalized as routine, unremarkable and expected as a part of their everyday social practice. It created a logic of its own and was taken for granted as the 'way things are done' in their community spaces and with friends. These young men had a different view of risk and risk-taking from adults and policy makers. Their concerns were more with how they managed themselves in risky environments and coped with the consequences of failure. In many cases, there was a hierarchy of risk, and different strategies were developed as a way of remaining safe. This logic of risk was embodied in both their habitus and their everyday experiences. Being able to reject it and move away from it was described by these men as itself a risk, which could attract punishment and reprisal.

'Risky practices': young people and drug and alcohol use

In the previous discussion we introduced different approaches to understanding why young people might take risks. In this section, we are now going to turn our attention to looking in detail at what a sociological approach to young people's relationship with risk-taking looks like in practice. We are doing this by focussing on two major examples of risk-taking behaviour that are always seen as a major concern to adults and policy makers. The first is young people's risk-taking with drugs. The second is alcohol, especially 'binge drinking'.

Thinking point

- As you read the discussion that follows, think about how drug and alcohol use can be understood from the social constructionist and interpretivist approaches we explored in the previous section.

The social context of drug use

It is important to recognize that the notion of 'drug use' or 'drug abuse' are themselves problematic terms. What is a 'drug', and when is it being 'abused'? For example, caffeine in coffee and tea, nicotine in cigarettes, and alcohol are all recognized as drugs that many people take as a part of their everyday life. It is generally accepted that these drugs can be harmful, yet they are not seen as 'problems' as are other drugs. They are legal and are not controlled or regulated other than by age. What we do have to acknowledge is that these drugs can do significant harm, but they are given the status of being legal and thus socially acceptable.

A similar issue exists around prescribed drugs. These are seen, in the main, as legitimate and as 'doing good', yet we know that prescription drugs can cause harm and be used in ways that were not intended. Young adults aged 18 to 25 have the highest annual and monthly rates of nonmedical use of prescription medications (NUPM) of any age group in the USA, including the use of opioid, stimulant, tranquilizer and sedative medication (Tapscott and Schepis, 2013). In college and university settings, the primary motivation for this type of drug use is to enhance academic performance. However, attention from the media and politicians is primarily focussed on users of illegal drugs, rather than on the misuse of legal, prescribed drugs.

Of course, what is defined and classified as a legal drug is a contested and political issue. The regulation of drug use tends to be a core responsibility of governments through legislation; however, more recently it has become increasingly challenging for governments to know what a drug is and how to regulate it. How a drug is managed determines its legal or illegal status. An interesting example is in New Zealand. In the early part of the 2000s, the drug benzylpiperazine (BZP) or 'party pill' as it became known, was very popular. This drug was legal and was manufactured as a method for decreasing methamphetamine addiction, which at that time was a growing concern to the public (Kerr and Davis, 2011). Research showed that 40 per cent of 18–29-year-olds had used it at some point in their lives. As a 'legal high' it was available from local shops and had no restrictions on its use. Following its increase in popularity and usage, the government produced a review of the risks it created. The results of this suggested it was 'low risk' and that government should put an age requirement (over 18 years) on its use and advertising. The following year, new evidence was presented to government suggesting it be redefined as 'moderate risk'. After wider public consultation and debate, it was then classified as a class C drug (the same as cannabis) and effectively made illegal (Kerr and Davis, 2011).

One of the major consequences of this experience in New Zealand was that the 'appetite' of young people for '**legal highs**' increased. 'BZP-free' pills such as the 'Elements' range (www.evolvetech.co.nz) and 'Go-E' (www.cosmiccorner.co.nz) replaced the illegal BZP products on the shelves. These pills, containing dimethylamylamine (DMAA; often defined as 'geranium extract') were widely marketed in New Zealand following the ban. By 2010 there was major growth in the selling of 'legal highs' in local shops, which created significant problems for the New Zealand government. Trying to legislate became extremely difficult. Once a 'legal high' was seen as being dangerous or of moderate risk, it was 'banned' or made 'illegal', but with some minor changes to the ingredients and a new name, it could be back on the market again as a 'legal high'. As a result, the New Zealand government, through the *Psychoactive Substances Act* (PSA), established the world's first regulated legal market for 'low risk' psychoactive products (Wilkins, 2014). This legislation requires producers to prove, through toxicology or clinical trials, that the product they are selling is 'low risk'. From 2013, New Zealand saw the outlets for selling legal highs drop dramatically from over 4000 to 156 specialist shops. It also saw the number of products available on the market drop from 200 to 46. Ambiguity exists over products that may have dual usage, for example those used in dietary or therapeutic products that may also have psychoactive impacts (Rychert and Wilkins, 2016).

> **Legal highs:** Drugs that are manufactured and available to be purchased over the counter in shops, which give people a similar feeling to some illegal drugs but are not categorized as illegal.

History of drug regulation and moral panics

The issue of 'drug abuse' by young people is clearly emotive, particularly for adults and policy makers. Shane Blackman, in his book *Chilling Out* (2004), argues that in late modern society we seem to have a 'historical amnesia' about drugs. He suggests we have tunnel vision about the present that denies the past, creating an ahistorical perspective of young people's usage of drugs. His analysis shows that, in most previous decades, concerns about drugs have at some stage reached fever pitch, which led to greater regulation and control of those drugs. For example, in the 1890s there was a moral anxiety in Victorian England over the growing use of opium that was being important from China and Asia. How extensive this was or how much of a social problem it was remains unclear; however, new legislation criminalized its use. Similarly, in the 1920s, there was a moral panic about cannabis use, which led to its being made illegal. We can see how, historically, drugs shifted from being socially acceptable and legal to objects of concern and were reclassified as illegal. These 'panics' increased after the Second World War. For example, in the early 1960s, concern was focussed on the 'mods' and their taking of speed and purple hearts; in the 1970s, it was the 'hippies' and their use of cannabis, LSD and amphetamines; in the 1980s, it was 'yuppies' and cocaine use; in the 1990s, the focus was on the recreational use of 'E' or ecstasy and its variants. More recently, in Australia, concern has centred on the methamphetamine drug 'Ice', and the liminal status of 'legal highs' produced using synthetic products such as Kronic. The point to acknowledge here is that there is a long history of panics about 'drug use', and that in the majority of cases they are linked to youth and their cultural activities. As Blackman reminds us, not all anxieties about drugs are based on evidence or rational arguments. Public concerns about youth drug use are often based on moral outrage or fear, yet they feed into a wider discourse about 'dangerous or decaying youth' and 'the problem with our young'.

Thinking points

- What do you think is the rate of drug use in youth?
- Why do you think young people take drugs?

Patterns and rates of use

So, what is the pattern of drug use by the young? In exploring this question we need to firstly look at drug usage in young people aged 11–15 years and 16–24 years. Data are collected differently for these two age bands. In terms of the 11–15-year-olds, a number of studies from around the world show that about a quarter of young people in this age group have tried an illegal drug at some point in their lives. This figure tends to be higher amongst the older age group (15-year-olds), with little difference between genders. For example in the UK, in 2016, 24 per cent of 11–15-year-olds had tried illegal drugs at least once (NHS, 2017). This varied by age in that 17 per cent of 12-year-olds said they had tried illegal drugs once compared with 37 per cent of 15-year-olds. Interestingly, drug use in this age group has been declining, especially since 2009. Evidence shows that in 2001 over 29 per cent said they had tried drugs. The figure peaked in 2004 then started to decline. By 2014, the figure had almost halved (16 per cent). In 2016 there was a sharp increase (to 24 per cent) because of the reclassification and introduction of 'legal highs' and synthetic cannabis, which only explained a 3 per cent rise. It is worth noting that, when questions are asked about 'regular usage', most young people who have tried drugs tend to say they have only used them once; or in more regular users, only once a month (NHS, 2017). The most common drug used has always been cannabis, with the use of most other drugs being small in comparison. Again, at certain historical times, some drugs have been more popular than others. For example, ecstasy was more popular in the 1980s and glue and solvents were more popular in the 1990s. These drugs have since dropped in terms of use, with psychoactive substances growing in popularity.

Levels of drug use tend to increase in 16–24-year-olds. In fact, it is usually in this age group where we see the highest levels of drug use (Office of National Statistics, 2013). By the age of 25 it starts to decline. The group with the highest level of drug use is the 20–24-year-olds (21 per cent) followed by the 16–19-year-olds (16.5 per cent). Again, similar to the 11–15-year-olds, usage of drugs by 16–24-year-olds has been declining over time. In this age cohort, men (24 per cent) are more likely to be taking drugs than women (14 per cent). This age group are also more likely to be using class A drugs, although again men were higher users than women. Lifestyle factors are important in that those more likely to go to pubs and clubs have increased levels of drug use; this was measured as being ten times higher amongst those who visited nightclubs at least four times per month. Again, those going to pubs and night clubs more regularly were also more likely to use class A drugs (Office of National Statistics, 2013).

Risk, pleasure and protection in drug-taking

What do young people say about why they take drugs? Many studies recognize that drug-taking is both a social activity (done with friends) and one that is about pleasure and fun (Farrugia, 2016). Getting 'stoned' with your mates for the 'buzz' and 'the laugh' is not an uncommon justification, especially amongst the younger age group. Yet many of the large quantitative studies are not able to capture the more nuanced perspectives in the way young people operate and manage the risks. A more detailed and interesting analysis comes from the work of Geoffrey Hunt and his colleagues in the USA (Hunt et al., 2010). They undertook a research programme with young people in a North American city in the mid to late 2000s, looking at the relationship between recreational drug use, risk and pleasure. Hunt et al. suggested that the heightened feeling of the extraordinary feelings that many young people get from taking drugs helps them overcome the mundane and routine of life. It becomes a way of escaping the routine of ordinary life and replaces it with feelings of autonomy, control and self-actualization. In a consumption-led society, this form of pleasure-seeking through the consumption of drugs helps users establish new forms of identity that show them to be 'cool' or 'cultural leaders'.

Young people also raised issues over how 'expert knowledge' was used, suggesting that the science they encounter in adult and public discourses around drug use over-exaggerates the 'reality'; in fact a disconnection exists between how the experts see risk and young people's personal experiences. Young people have a huge knowledge of the risks that are involved in drug-taking, and in many cases even when they are unsure of the risks, they are more than willing and capable of looking them up on the internet. For example, the arguments about the impact of ecstasy on a person's health, as promoted by science, were understood by many young people, but their own personal knowledge and networks (and actions) suggested that they experienced regular and safe taking of ecstasy, in a measured and controlled way, which was not dangerous. In fact, many young people developed their own 'harm reduction strategies' when using drugs.

Young people also highlight that there is an over-emphasis in adult discourses on 'risk and danger', ignoring the importance of 'risk as pleasure'. The messages that scientists and professional educators ignore are in fact the key motivators for young people to take drugs; they can be pleasurable and fun. By ignoring this reality, the professionals' messages are discarded as ill-informed and not matching with reality. Young people talk about weighing up risks with pleasure, suggesting that if they follow simple rules the benefits outweigh the risks. They in fact engage in a process of negotiation in judging whether the 'risks are worthwhile'. Young people then use numerous strategies to maximize pleasure and minimize risk, often optimizing the setting (where to take drugs and how to make sure they are safe). They limit risk through harm reduction strategies, for example, by drinking water and taking breaks from dancing. They also consider the potential risks from combinations of drugs and operate around moderating the dosage and considering the source.

Where young people take drugs is also very important to the pleasure they get from the drug, and some places are recognized as 'riskier' than others. Nightclubs and parties can have heightened levels of risks because clients have limited control over this environment and over issues such as the levels of ventilation and access to water. Certain settings can also be inductive to 'a bad trip', although large crowded venues can be a place of safety (for trying out combinations of drugs and having safety in numbers). However, recreational drug-taking is a social activity for large numbers of young people. Not only does this enhance the pleasure; it also helps them manage the risks. Being amongst friends while taking drugs creates a source of protection. If they are surrounded by friends they can trust, this can also increase the feeling of pleasure.

Young people, alcohol and risk-taking

Similar to drugs, young people's alcohol drinking was typically framed through a lens of 'risk' and harm. Recently, much of this has focussed on binge drinking and how the young take risks with their health and safety as a result of 'being out of control'. Pictures in the media of young people falling about on the street have driven anxieties about the young and their drinking habits. But what are young people's drinking habits, and how do they manage the 'risks'? Similar to the findings in studies of young people's drug-taking, their use of alcohol has also been on the decline. Since the mid- to late 2000s, evidence from across a number of major economies has shown that young people aged 11 to 24 are either drinking less or abstaining altogether. For example, in the UK the number of 11–15-year-olds who have ever drunk alcohol fell from 60 per cent in 2003 to 44 per cent in 2016. Similar patterns exist in those who stated they had drunk alcohol in the last week (a drop from 25 per cent to 10 per cent). Drinking amongst the older age group (18–24-year-olds) has also been on the decline. For example, in Australia the levels of abstinence among 18- to 24-year-olds has been increasing, and figures for regular alcohol usage have also been in decline (Australian Institute of Health and Welfare, 2018). In the UK the proportion of 'teetotal' young adults (16–24-year-olds) increased by over 40 per cent between 2005 and 2013 (Office of National Statistics, 2013).

🗯️ Thinking points

- Do you think there is a culture of binge drinking among young people today? If so, what is the evidence and why might they do it?
- Do you think that young people today drink more alcohol than previous generations?

But is this the full story? While evidence shows that young people's relationship with alcohol is declining, there are concerns about those who remain regular drinkers taking increased 'risks'. Historically, this has been defined as 'binge drinking', although more recently it has been described as 'high risk' behaviour or 'hazardous drinking'. In the UK, recent evidence has found that, although those aged 16 to 24 years showed a decline in regular alcohol use, when they did drink they were the group most likely to 'binge' (Office of National Statistics, 2017). In New Zealand, this group also had the highest level of 'hazardous drinking' with 32.9 per cent of 18- to 24-year-olds engaged in an alcohol drinking pattern that carried a risk of harming their physical or mental health or having harmful social effects on the drinker or others (Ministry of Health, 2017). Similarly, in Australia it was found that 18–24-year-olds were most likely to report risky drinking behaviour, with 47 per cent reporting more than 4 standard drinks on a single occasion and 33 per cent reporting having consumed over 11 or more standard drinks. These figures were higher in rural and remote areas (Australian Institute of Health and Welfare, 2018). So, while young people are drinking less at the aggregate level, risky drinking is still occurring and is seemingly concentrated in sub-populations of the youth cohort (Roberts et al., 2019).

International definitions of 'binge drinking'

- The Alcohol Advisory Council of New Zealand (ALAC) defines adult binge drinking as seven or more standard drinks consumed in one drinking session.

- The NHS in the UK defines binge drinking as 'drinking lots of alcohol in a short space of time or drinking to get drunk'. ... The definition used by the Office of National Statistics for binge drinking is having over eight units in a single session for men and over six units for women.

- The Health Canada guidelines for heavy drinking state that heavy drinking refers to males who reported having five or more drinks, or women who reported having four or more drinks, on one occasion, at least once a month in the past year.

- The National Institute on Alcohol Abuse and Alcoholism in the USA defines binge drinking as a pattern of drinking that brings a person's blood alcohol concentration (BAC) to 0.08 g/dL or above. This typically happens when men consume five or more drinks or women consume four or more drinks in about two hours.

- The Australian Bureau of Statistics defines binge drinking as more than seven drinks a night for men, and more than five for women.

Where and why do young people drink?

It is generally assumed that young people under 18 years of age drink with their friends on the street, usually to get drunk, yet all the evidence shows that this not a true representation of the facts. A substantial amount of drinking, especially by young people under 15, is undertaken with parents and relatives in the family home. For example, 59 per cent of young people (11–15-year-olds) in the UK (NHS, 2017) said they drank with their parents. Sixty-two per cent also said the most usual place to have a drink was in the family home, with only 13 per cent saying they usually drank on the street. These levels of drinking at home were also assessed by age, and this indicated that 15-year-olds were less likely to drink at home with their parents compared with 11-year-olds, although the numbers still remained high, with 59 per cent of all 15-year-olds still saying they were more likely to drink at home with their parents than in any other setting. That said, drinking at parties was a significant activity, with 43 per cent of all participants saying they usually had a drink with friends at parties, although again age was a factor in that the figures were highest for 15-year-olds (52 per cent compared with 14 per cent of 11- to 12-year-olds).

When young people are asked to explain why they drink, it becomes increasingly evident that alcohol consumption is a social activity and one that is connected with relationships with friends and social activities. In a 2012 study in New Zealand, young people aged 11–15 years explained their reasons for drinking alcohol. In total, 77 per cent said they drank alcohol to have fun while 56 per cent said it was to enjoy parties and 41 per cent did so to get drunk. Alcohol could also be used to control feelings, with 35 per cent saying they drank alcohol to relax, to feel more confident (22 per cent), to forget things (21 per cent) or to deal with boredom (21 per cent). Only 7 per cent drank alone, and 21 per cent admitted to drinking only because their friends did it. Drinking amongst this age group appears to be a very sociable activity, linked mainly to pleasure and having fun.

Risk-taking across generations

Does the current youth generation differ from previous generations with regard to drinking behaviour? Valentine et al. (2010) explored young people's 'drinking cultures' through an intergenerational lens. They conducted research in urban and rural communities in the UK, exploring the different motivations and practices of three family generations (children, aged 18–24 years; parents of children, aged 34–54 years; and grandparents, aged 65 plus) across a range of family types to explore their relationships with alcohol consumption and risk-taking in their teens. There were striking similarities across all generations in terms of their early encounters. Many started drinking more regularly between the ages of 15 and 17. Parents and the family home remained an important source of their early introduction, while streets and pubs became more common as they got older. Drinking 'behind your parents' back' in public spaces, or furtively elsewhere, was also common, as was drinking 'under the legal age'.

The study did, however, find three major differences between generations. Firstly, accessibility of alcohol in the home and parents' attitudes towards drinking at home had changed. For older generations, alcohol had tended to be present in the family home only for special occasions during their teens, but with the increase in trade sales by supermarkets and other forms of retailing, the availability of alcohol in the home has increased substantially. For example, UK research has shown that 45 per cent of all alcohol consumption in the UK is now done in the family home (Office of National Statistics, 2013). A second significant difference among the study participants was that the products that young people consumed were very different from those drunk by older generations. While those from the older and middle-aged groups started their drinking careers by consuming lager, beer and cider, young people aged 18 to 24 started drinking with vodka and other types of shots alongside alcopops. This in effect means that the current generation of youth is consuming far more alcohol in absolute terms than their older relatives did in their teens, because of the higher alcohol content in such drinks, and the increase in the 'normalization of drunkenness'. This is not surprising given the massive expansion of the alcohol industry and the production of 'youth-friendly' products, which have increased opportunities to consume alcohol inexpensively at home.

A final difference they found was in attitudes and motivations to drink. Major differences existed in the role that alcohol plays in the lives of young people compared with previous generations. The younger generation described how they deliberately set out in an evening to 'get drunk' or 'wasted' and to increase the risk and fun of drinking. Having a 'good time' was only achievable if they had consumed large quantities of alcohol and engaged in various forms of risk-taking behaviour. This created significant peer pressure, as those who did not participate could be ridiculed and accused of being 'boring' or 'unsociable' and young people risked being ostracized and excluded from peer groupings. This culture can include excessive 'round buying' and drinking games that increase the speed of a group's drinking. Such activities were seen as helping them to relax, lose their inhibitions and as intensifying the sense of fun. Young people also explained how alcohol operated to give them self-confidence in romantic and sexual encounters.

A 'culture of intoxication' in the 'night-time economy' and risk-taking

Culture of intoxification: A term that is used to explain recent economic and social policies that have promoted and supported a growing culture of excessive intoxication amongst the young.

This idea of a new **'culture of intoxication'** amongst young people has been further expanded upon by Measham and Brain (2005). They argue that this culture is a result of broader social, cultural and political changes in economic and policy frameworks. They suggest that recent economic and social policies have promoted and supported a growing culture of excessive intoxication amongst the young. New policy and legal developments, influenced by neo-liberal thinking and approaches, have 'freed up' the market and deregulated social spaces, especially in urban centres at night, giving young people greater access to cheap alcohol. Cafes, dance bars and themed pubs encourage drinking and intoxication by providing initiatives like 'two for one' drinks and 'happy hours', suggesting high consumption of alcohol is a normal part of a 'good' night out. These changes

Psychoactive consumer: A person who actively seeks out the consumption of substances and alcohol to get feelings of being high.

have been supported by marketing and alcohol services appealing to hedonistic ideals of what they call 'psychoactive consumption'. This competition for the **'psychoactive consumer'** has led to new, high-strength alcohol products such as alcopops targeting the young. Risk and risk-taking is therefore inherent in this culture, being a core driver for increased forms of pleasure seeking.

Night-time economy (or nightscapes): A term that is used to describe the spaces in large urban environments that aim to accommodate the consumption of alcohol.

Chatterton and Hollands (2003) support this by showing how the urban **night-time economy (or nightscapes)** have been restructured. Their focus is on the 'ordinary' activities of young people (not just the 'thrill seekers'). Clearly, youth leisure activities are diverse, and while much research has concentrated on activities such as clubbing and the music scene, this seems to give it prominence it does not deserve, as large numbers of young people participate more in drinking cultures in urban city spaces than anywhere else. Chatterton and Hollands' study looked at the processes of capital accumulation and restructuring in the North East of England's night-time economy, focussing on the production, regulation (both state and private sectors) and consumption practices of the young. They identified how young people's experience of alcohol consumption was being framed and shaped by large scale multi-national corporations who are able to construct and order urban landscapes. As they state '… corporate control in the urban entertainment and night-life economies is usurping and commercialising public spaces, segmenting and gentri-fying markets …' (p. 20).

Branding and marketing within the consumption industries are also important in shaping the cultural attitudes and drinking behaviour of the young (Szmigin et al., 2008). The marketing industries' continual association of night-time drinking and risk-taking with pleasure reproduces and creates messages that suggest 'fun' can only be had if you are intoxicated. Much of this emphasizes the importance of drinking to excess and suggests that being drunk is humorous and pleasurable (Szmigin et al., 2008). Taking more risks by drinking more is seen as not only 'cool' but also an acceptable way of 'doing' leisure. Alongside this, much of the advertising also gives strong sexual messages that link intoxication with sexual pleasure. It suggests that drinking large amounts of alcohol heightens the sexual experience and creates greater opportunities to have a broader range of sexual partners. In this context, risks and risk-taking are a central part of the night-time economy, and while the perception is constructed by others, it is central to shaping how young people have to behave (as seasoned and skilled drinkers who position themselves as risk-takers).

'Calculated hedonism'

While the young have to be seen to take risks as a part of the night-time economy, they also learn how to balance the risks with harm. Young people are active in the process of managing and negotiating the risks of 'drinking to intoxication'. Griffin et al. (2009) showed that, in the process of 'heavy drinking', young people operated on what they called a **'calculated hedonism'** or a form of 'controlled loss of control'. In other words, young people's risk-taking was undertaken usually within the boundaries of time (the weekend) and in certain spaces, such as clubs, bar and private parties that felt 'safe', and in certain company such as supportive friends. Similar to the research on recreational drug-taking, we see that young people try to balance the potential risks. While they want to reach a certain stage of intoxication, thus showing they are 'having fun', they must also work to avoid an 'undesired state' of excess, sug-gesting they are 'out of control'. For example, they continually try to avoid 'embar-rassments on the dance floor', and 'the casualties of the toilet floor', which may lead to the loss of social credibility. 'Getting it right' suggests a 'seasoned drinker' and 'risk taker' who is in control and having fun. However, even if they fail to maintain this balance, the narrative and story of the drunkenness and being 'out of control' can also be a critical part of the cultural practice of drinking (Griffin et al., 2009). The impor-tance of the story and a narrative of 'fun' can increase the credibility of the story-teller, especially after the event. Even experiences of vomiting, waking up in hospital or

> Calculated hedonism: When young people's risk-taking is calculated and taken within the boundaries of time and certain spaces.

losing consciousness can become an important part of the 'fun', relived and reflected upon after the event, which then creates a sense of 'community' and 'binding' that holds their friendships together.

Diversity and the issue of life course drinking patterns

A final point for us to consider is the relationship between 'drinking cultures' such as those discussed above, and diversity and changing patterns over the life course. Firstly, it is usually assumed that youth drinking cultures are homogeneous or singular, and they are always believed to be excessive. However, there is significant diversity and disparity between different groups in how and when they drink alcohol. For example, in New Zealand we see significant diversity between white Pākehā, Māori and Pacific young people (McCreanor et al., 2005). It is also the case that patterns of drinking are strongly influenced by religious affiliations, such as being Muslim (Jayne et al., 2010). However, it is also important to recognize the way that drinking patterns can and do change over time. For example, it is interesting that more young people are now abstaining or drinking less and that by the age of 22 there is a large decline in alcohol use among a wide range of young people (Seaman and Ikegwuonu, 2011). What this suggests is that broader social changes and lifestyle patterns may well be influencing the drinking cultures of the young. For example, Woodman (2012) showed that the growing influence of 'non-standard work', such as evening or weekend work, was having a major impact on the opportunities for young people to be 'social'. This could lead to the young drinking less because of time constraints or engaging in more intensive drinking within shorter time frames as a form of coping strategy. New drinking cultures and patterns are therefore also greatly influenced by lifestyle factors and changes in young people's lives across the life course.

💬 Summary

- 'Risk' is a historical and social process, rather than merely a set of problematic behaviours associated with young people within an age category.

- Traditional ways of conceptualizing risk-taking as 'problem behaviour' that emerges from psychological or 'brain' development operates to see decision-making as irrational and/or de-contextualized.

- How young people mange risks in the 'risk society' is greatly affected by a young person's access to resources.

- Many risks are constructed by broader external forces, and these impact on how young people encounter and have to manage risk in their everyday lives.

- Much risk-taking involves young people in an interactive process that can be habitual, routine, learnt and normalized.

- Illegal drug-taking and binge drinking can only be understood in context. Young people construct different forms of social practice as ways of managing risk.

✎ Exercise: The sociological imagination

Issues of risk and risk-taking have become major areas of research for youth sociologists. One of the interesting discoveries is that risk-taking in areas such as drug-taking and alcohol abuse has been on the decline. Such trends can also be seen in involvement in crime, smoking and teenage pregnancy. What are some of the social and cultural factors that might explain these trends?

📖 Key readings

Crawshaw, P. & Bunton, R. (2009) 'Logics of practice in the "risk environment"', *Health, Risk & Society,* vol. 11, no. 3, pp. 269–282.

Hunt, G., Moloney, M. & Evens, K. (2010) *Youth Drugs and Nightlife* (London: Routledge).

Kerr, J. R. & Davis, L. S. (2011) 'Benzylpiperazine in New Zealand: brief history and current implications (Links to an external site.)', *Journal of the Royal Society of New Zealand,* vol. 41, no. 1, pp. 155–164.

Measham, F. & Brain, K. (2005) '"Binge" drinking, British alcohol policy and the new culture of intoxication', *Crime Media Culture,* vol. 1, pp. 262–283.

Torbenfeldt Bengtsson, T. & Ravn, S. (2018) *Routines of Risk: A New Perspective on Risk-Taking in Young Lives* (London: Routledge).

Valentine, G., Holloway, S. L. & Jayne, M. (2010) 'Generational patterns of alcohol consumption: continuity and change. (Links to an external site.)', *Health Place,* vol. 16, no. 5, pp. 916–925.

Zinn, J. O. (2019) 'The meaning of risk-taking – key concepts and dimensions', *Journal of Risk Research,* vol. 22, no.1, pp. 1–15.

9 YOUTH AND CRIME

In this chapter you will learn about:

- Historical and contemporary trends in youth crime
- The relationship between youth crime, the media and moral panics
- How youth crime has been theorized historically, and contemporary developments
- The importance of approaches that emphasize culture and territoriality
- The importance of the relationship between youth crime, class, gender and ethnicity.

Do we have a youth crime problem?

Thinking point

- How involved are young people in crime, and how much of a problem do you think it really is?
- When you were younger did you or any of your friends get involved in criminal activity, and if so what were your or their motivations?

There is a very powerful view that youth crime is a major problem in most advanced countries in the world. When the public are asked if they think there is a 'youth crime problem', it is not unusual for them to claim that the young seem to be out of control and there is a serious problem with youth crime. For example, in a UK survey, 75 per cent thought that youth crime was on the increase when in fact the number of incidents requiring police attention was actually falling (Hough and Roberts, 2004). International studies consistently show that public opinion is at odds with evidence of the 'real' levels of youth offending (Australian Institute of Criminology, 2007). So what is the real story? How much crime are young people actually involved in, how much of a problem is it, and should we be concerned?

Measurement of crime

It is very difficult to accurately and 'absolutely' measure crime. Official police data relies on reporting of a crime and/or prosecution of an offender. The introduction of self-report measures as a means of understanding experiences and actions has been highly significant in providing more detail about the extent of offending in a given population. Both victim and self-report surveys have been found to be a more reliable measure of crime than reporting or prosecution data (Qureshi, 2016). Probably one of the most influential has been the Crime Survey for England and Wales (2015).

However, this large national survey does not normally include young people aged under 16. This is because they are seen as either unreliable or a difficult population to access. A final source of knowledge about young people's relationship with crime can be found from longitudinal research studies. These have been very popular in criminology and health. Such studies usually aim to capture the behaviours and events in the lives of children and young people that contribute to future social problems. Such studies have been very influential, particularly in providing evidence aiming to show causes and factors that lead to future problem behaviour. They have also been used in the policy making process (France et al., 2012).

Youth offending data

So what does the data on youth offending say about young people's involvement in crime? In New Zealand, the recent statistics (Ministry of Justice, 2018) show that youth only account for 5 per cent of all people prosecuted for crime annually. It shows that 1,884 children and young people (60 in every 10,000) were prosecuted in 2017. If we look over a longer period, there has in fact been a long-term decline. There were 25 per cent fewer prosecutions than in 2013 and 63 per cent less than in 2007. Prior to this, the numbers prosecuted had been increasing gradually since 1992. Such trends are not unique to New Zealand. In fact, evidence from England and Wales (Youth Justice Statistics, 2018), Australia (Australian Bureau of Statistics, 2017), Canada (Malakieh, 2017) and the USA (Hockenberry and Puzzanchera, 2019) all show similar trends. The peak of youth crime prosecutions was in 1992, and since then there has been a gradual (and then dramatic) fall. However, it is important to recognize that there remains, across all of these international examples, an imbalance around ethnicity. In New Zealand, Australia and Canada, the imbalance occurs for Indigenous populations, and in America, England and Wales, for Black, Asian and/or Hispanic groups. This trend is not unique to the current time period. Historically these groups have been overrepresented in the youth justice system worldwide. However, if we are to take youth prosecution figures as a reliable measure of youth crime, we can conclude that youth crime is clearly not the social problem that it once was or as significant a social issue as the general public perceives it to be.

🗨 **Thinking point**

Rates of crime among youth are declining. What do you think could explain this?

Self-report and victim studies provide a more in-depth picture of the extent and types of crimes young people engage in. The following points are some of the key issues they raise:

- Across a wide range of self-report studies, between 50 per cent and 75 per cent of young people admit to having committed a crime over their lifetime.

- The types of crimes young people tend to be involved in are usually petty offences, i.e nuisance offences such as low-level vandalism, petty theft, small-scale shoplifting, drinking alcohol and fighting.

- For the majority of young people who admit to a crime, their offending is not persistent. That is, most young people will only break the law once or twice in their teens.

- The peak age for offending is usually between 13 and 18. This can vary by country. For example in the Netherlands, UK and Spain, the peak age was between 15 and 18 years of age.

- Most young people tend to 'grow out' of any form of criminal behaviour from the age of 18. By their early 20s most young people have stopped any form of illegal behaviour.

- Boys and young men are more active in crime than girls and young women.

- Boys are more active in crime than girls, although it is not as marked a difference as we would think. It is not until the age of 17 that major differences emerge, with boys and young men are more likely to commit crimes than girls.

- Boys and young men tend to be more involved in crimes like fighting and vandalism, while girls and young women tend to be more involved in shoplifting and buying stolen goods.

- While it would seem that social class should be a high predictor of offending, the evidence suggests that middle class young people are just as likely to be involved in minor forms of criminal activity as those of lower SES.

- The relationship between ethnicity and crime remains unclear in self-report data, suggesting that the high rates of prosecution are more likely to be a result of policing strategy and/or actions of the courts.

What we see is that many young people, at some point in their teens, engage in low-level criminal activity and that by the time they reach their early 20s they have moved away from such activity. In fact it is estimated that young people only account for 20 per cent of all crime, while adults account for 80 per cent (Simmons and Dodd, 2003). However, there is evidence suggesting that a small group of young people commits a large number of crimes and tends to be involved in more serious crimes. These young people also tend to continue with their offending in later life. Moffitt (1993) for example showed that there are two distinct categories of individuals who each have different relationships to anti-social behaviour. The first engage in anti-social and criminal behaviour throughout the life course, starting early in childhood; the second and much larger group are only involved during adolescence.

It is important to recognize that, while youth crime is clearly not the problem people think it is, large numbers of children and young people are more at risk than adults of being victims of crime. For example, the Howard League for Penal Reform survey (2007) found significantly higher levels of victimization, showing that 95 per cent of all young people (3000 in the survey) had been victims of a crime at some point in their young lives. Half (49 per cent) had property stolen from them at school, and 57 per cent had property deliberately damaged. Almost half (46 per cent) of those surveyed had been called racist names, and 56 per cent reported that they had been threatened on at least one occasion. Nearly three-quarters of children in this survey had been assaulted (hit or kicked). There are two main reasons why this is the case, especially for older young people. Firstly, evidence shows that young people aged 16–24 years (young men in particular) are more likely to be victims of violent crime than any other group in society. This is because they are more likely to be out in public spaces. The second is that young people who are offenders themselves are at greater risk of being victims of crime than any other group of young people (Roe and Ashe, 2008).

Thinking point

- Why do you think young people are more likely to be victims of crime than other age groups? What might put them more at risk?

The growth of digital media and crime

So far our conversation has concentrated on the more traditional forms of crime, which bring people into personal contact and/or involve activity in public spaces and places. However, what is increasingly obvious is that, in the world of social media and the internet, criminal activity has moved into the online worlds of young people. As we saw in Chapter 6, young people in advanced economies are accessing the internet on a regular basis. In terms of young people being offenders online, one key area that has grown is 'hacking'. It is defined as 'unauthorised use of, or access into, computers or network resources, which exploits identified security vulnerabilities in networks' (McGuire and Dowling, 2013, p. 5). However, it is hard to find reliable and detailed evidence of the extent of hacking taking place by young people as it is a relatively new phenomenon. One study in 2015 reported on cyber-fraud offences committed by people under the age of 18, suggesting it had risen by 26 per cent in the previous two years, and 84 per cent in the previous three years (Harris, 2015). Similarly, The National Cyber Crime Unit (NCCU, 2017) stated that the average age of suspects arrested in cybercrime investigations is 17, and there have been several recent cases in which the perpetrators were children.

Other areas of online activity that are also associated with young people include activities such as cyberbullying, sexting and trolling as well as 'grooming' and sexual abuse (see also Chapters 6 and 9). The relationship of these behaviours to criminality is ambiguous. For example, cyberbullying and trolling are not always criminalized in the way that petty theft or assault are, yet they can in some cases result in criminal activity (e.g. grooming by sexual predators). While there is significant ambiguity over these terms, and what is reported or recorded, it is claimed that young people are at higher risk of being victims on the internet than other groups. For example, an online questionnaire by Lilley et al. (2014) found that:

- 28 per cent of the sample reported an experience that had upset or bothered them when using social networking sites (SNSs) in the last year.

- Of this group, 37 per cent reported experiencing trolling, 22 per cent had been excluded from a social group online, and 18 per cent had experienced aggressive and violent language.

- 11 per cent of those who had been cyberbullied reported that this happened every day and 55 per cent at least once a month.

- 19 per cent reported being affected by upsetting online experiences for a few days or a week, and 12 per cent for weeks or months.

Data on the prevalence of 'sexting' also varies widely, although it is an area of growing concern. Sexting describes the practice of sharing sexualized images, or other media, in online contexts using digital technologies. Within this broad definition, the term 'sexting' covers a range of activities experienced by young people. Some commentators and scholars have described the practice as a form of crime, while others argue for a more middle-ground approach. When 'minors' are involved, such as those aged under 16, sexting can be characterized as a crime (Livingstone and Görzig, 2012). In such instances, sexting comes under child pornography statutes and can also intersect with other illegal practices including child solicitation, or coercion (Salter et al., 2012). Woods (2017) in his study found that 38 per cent of 14–17-year-olds had sent sexual images to a partner and 48 per cent had received them. Twenty per cent of these felt pressured to do it, and 32 per cent had also reported that images had been shared more widely without their consent. The gendered and heterosexual dimensions of power relations shaping young people's sexting practices and potential harms are discussed further in Chapter 10.

When is sexting a crime?

Sexting describes the practice of sharing sexualized images, or other media, in online contexts using digital technologies. Within this broad definition, the term 'sexting' covers a range of activities experienced by young people. Some commentators and scholars have described the practice as a form of crime, while others argue for a more middle-ground approach. When 'minors' are involved, such as those aged under 16, sexting can be characterized as a crime (Livingstone and Görzig, 2012). In such instances, sexting comes under child pornography statutes and can also intersect with other illegal practices including child solicitation, or coercion (Salter et al., 2012). Due to risqué humour, rude jokes and sexual experimentation, it can be difficult to identify and maintain a boundary between what is acceptable and fun, and what is harmful. Because of this difficulty, there is a significant amount of commentary on the topic. In many cases, sexting can be seen as a form of communication among young people interested in experimenting with 'sexual self-representation' (Albury and Crawford, 2012). In others, sexting can be a harmless way of flirting (Livingstone and Görzig, 2012).

One final point we need to consider with regard to young people as victims online is the growing risk they face around sexual abuse and 'grooming'. The levels of sexual abuse that arise as a result of a young person being groomed remain unknown, but it is clear that this has become a major concern to detection agencies. While little research is available on the extent of grooming and its relationship to offline sexual abuse, research with young victims shows how they can become drawn into abusive relationships through this process (Quayle et al., 2012). Webster et al.'s (2012) research with convicted groomers also suggests that offenders deliberately target young people perceived to be vulnerable.

Representations of youth crime

🗨 Thinking point

The media tends to misrepresent the levels and types of crime. Why do you think this is, and what impact might it have in society?

Youth crime and moral panics

Symbolic interaction-ism: Explains social behaviour in terms of how people interact with each other. It is a theory that proposes that human beings are best understood in their interactive relation to others and their environment.

Folk devils: A term used to describe how the media construct a narrative that features a clear villain when creating a moral panic.

Moral panic: Is when a condition, an episode, person or group of persons becomes defined as a threat to societal values and interests. Usually driven by the media.

The media can play a central role in representing youth crime as a problem. One of the most significant contributions to debates on the role of the media in moral panics emerged through the work of the British sociologist, Stanley Cohen, and his 1960s study of mods and rockers, *Folk Devils and Moral Panics* (1972a, 1972b). Cohen sought to illustrate the role of **social interactionism** in the creation of **'folk devils'** and **'moral panics'**. Cohen pointed out that:

> ... societies appear to be subject, every now and then, to periods of moral panic. A condition, episode, person or group of persons emerges to become defined as a threat to societal values and interests. (p. 9)

He focussed on how a working class tradition of young working class people visiting coastal resorts in the summer escalated into a nation-wide 'moral panic' about the conduct and propriety of the nation's youth. He showed how the creation of 'moral panics' was largely the result of the reactions of certain sections of society to specific events. For Cohen, this was intimately linked to the nature and organization of power in society that allowed adults, in particular, to label the young and powerless as threats to the social order. This came about because of the actions of the media and a range of significant others. Through their reporting techniques using exaggeration and over-reporting (sensational headlines and reporting), prediction ('it had to happen', 'it was the inevitable result of') and symbolisation (the use of words and styles, such as the mod's scooter, to symbolize a negative phenomenon), a sense of unease and outrage was manufactured, which played on the fears and anxieties of a large section of the British population. The media, by spelling out in vivid detail the actions of what were portrayed as warring factions of youth, running amok and fighting running battles on the beaches, supported the idea that youth had become morally degenerate and particularly delinquent. Rather than working to address the problem, this actually served to confound the situation through a process of 'deviancy amplification' (Cohen, 1972a, 1972b, p.18).

This concern with law and order was nevertheless a crucial aspect of 'moral panics' because they had coercive implications. Not only did the system of beliefs and actions generated by the reaction to the mods and rockers serve to demonize those groups of young people identified as the 'problem', but it did so in ways that used the 'societal control culture' (Cohen, 1972a, 1972b, p. 74). That is, the 'moral panic' surrounding the mods and rockers drew upon widespread parental anxieties about the need to maintain correct standards of behaviour and adhere to the principles of law and order, while also advocating arguments and policies aimed at punishing, controlling and rehabilitating the 'delinquents' involved. Thus a 'moral panic' was also a panic about standards of conduct and how best to regulate and control those who failed to comply, which in turn generated more intensive forms of policing and stiffer court sentences. Cohen's own preferred explanation for the 'moral panic' surrounding the phenomenon of the mods and rockers, outlined in the last chapter of *Folk Devils and Moral Panics*, suggested that it reflected adult attempts to come to terms with the changes in British society after the Second World War.

A second and other important work was Pearson's (1983) highly compelling and influential study, *Hooligans*. Pearson was interested in the history of hooliganism and how this is theorized and acted upon by the state. He argued that much of the discourse surrounding hooligans in the 1970s was linked to a backwards reflection and comparison with a 'golden era' when communities were safe and crime was non-existent. Pearson explored historical documentation to find this elusive time of social harmony in previous 'golden ages' that was constantly referred to. During WWII he found alarm over 'cosh gangs' and 'Blitz kids' rather than the shoulder-to-shoulder picture he expected. Before WWI, he found examples of 'football madness' and 'cycle madness', as well as more familiar concerns about the lawlessness and delinquency of the nation's youth. Indeed, Pearson failed in his endeavours to find this lost period of social peace and instead constantly revealed the same labelling of youth as a social problem in each historical epoch.

Pearson therefore identified the labelling of youth as a phenomenon of every generation. His point was not so much the idea that history merely repeats itself and that nothing really changes. Rather, he was concerned to demonstrate that the history of *hooligans* is also a history of 'formidable stability ... which repetitiously identifies some aspect of 'social change' as the cause of the loosening of tradition, but which is itself paradoxically immune to change' (Pearson, 1983, p. 208). That is, the nature of the complaints and the social response to it provide a normative and consensual language for understanding the turbulence of social change. In doing so, attention is distracted from the past, which points to juvenile crime and delinquency as a *continual* feature of British life and which, for him, reflects persistent middle class anxieties about the impact of social change on the young working class. It is these specific concerns that make *Hooligan*, at least for Pearson, a *history of respectable fears*.

The limits of moral panics

Since these two classic studies, debates over what a moral panic is, and how it operates, have generated a large number of studies and critiques. One such criticism suggests that to see youth crime simply as something that operates to control the young fails to recognize how and why the media behave as they do towards 'youth crime'. As an institution, its intentions are not simply about controlling the young (although its outcomes may still be that). Media organizations have their own interests and values. Attention therefore has to be given to the political economy of the media. It is important for us to recognize that media images are not a reality, but a construction that is culturally determined and shaped in many cases by the industry itself. News is not inherently 'objective' and 'balanced'; state-run media organizations (such as the Australian and British Broadcasting Corporations, ABC and BBC) must work hard to achieve neutrality and non-bias as this is a pre-requisite of their government funding. However, for many other commercial outlets, news is about selling stories and making money. Stories and news are not self-selecting. Stories have to be selected and produced, and they are constructed as a result of a wide range of processes and practices. This includes the use of official and accredited experts or official sources that give weight to a story, the placing of reporters at law courts to find interesting stories and the need to produce stories in a narrow timeframe (i.e. for the 10 pm news or breakfast show). It is therefore also important to recognize the *ideological* position of journalists, editors and newspaper owners – they have a 'position' and an audience that expects them to hold to that 'position'.

A second issue over the usefulness of moral panics was raised by Angela McRobbie (1995). For her, the speed and proliferation of media, especially of 'new' media such as social networking sites and the internet, can be problematic in defining what a moral panic is. Alongside this, the fragmentation of class politics and the proliferation of interest groups who are sophisticated media users requires a more nuanced appreciation of 'moral panics'. For her, the fully fledged, national outburst moral panic as described by Cohen is increasingly being overtaken by an intensification of moral concerns more generally.

So while concerns over morality have become more acute, single 'moral panics' come and go much more rapidly and fail to have the impact of their predecessors. This is not just a feature of a more rapid turnover of moral issues, but a condition intimately linked to the emergence of a post-modern society in which the boundaries between reality and representations are becoming increasingly blurred. In this context it is no longer appropriate to talk about the media 'out there' providing a worldview. Rather, it is important to stress how representations now constitute 'reality' because we no longer have any way of understanding ourselves and the society we live in without reference to these representational forms. Given the massive development of new media, especially new platforms such as Twitter, Facebook, Instagram and blogging, we see that the outlets for different perspectives to emerge and evolve have expanded significantly. They are not controlled by media moguls or the print industry. New media have provided new tools and ways of putting out 'alternative' perspectives or creating legitimacy for other positions. To talk about media as a single entity fails to recognize the current diversity.

Thinking point

Clearly the growth of social media has created opportunities for a diversity of alternative views to be heard. Do you think that the concept of moral panic is still useful in explaining why young people and their behaviour are continually seen as a social problem?

The 'othering' of youth in popular media

The concept of '**othering**' is also important in understanding how young people are represented in popular media. This idea is usually associated with the work of Said (1978). In his development of **post-colonial theory**, he identifies how certain social groups can be excluded and defined as inferior through a set of social and political processes. These act to create a 'world view' across a range of media outlets that differentiates and creates a demarcation between 'us' and 'them'. Usually it is between the powerful and the powerless, establishing and maintaining a social distance between groups. Othering usually operates not only to define the existence of an inferior group but also to define and justify the dominant group. In this context it is not unusual for a powerless group, such as young people, to be defined and stereotyped as morally and intellectually inferior, suggesting that the powerful are superior and morally defendable. The powerless are usually 'dehumanized' and said to be lacking in moral worth. This approach has had significant and recent relevance in youth sociology. One contemporary example is the othering of 'chavs'.

> **Othering:** Creates a view across a range of media outlets that creates 'us' and 'them'. It usually operates not only to define the existence of an inferior group but also to define and justify the dominant group.

Imogen Tyler (2013) draws our attention to how, in contemporary Britain, there has been a focus and an attack, in neoliberal times, on the poor, especially the young. She identifies how, through the figure of the 'chav', working class young people are being stigmatized, blamed and subjected to representations characterizing them as 'revolting'. This group is then subjected to greater attention from the state through legislation and policing, leading to increased exclusion and social injustice for young people from poor communities. What is interesting in this analysis is that she is able to show how, even in the multi-mediated world, youth are portrayed as what Cohen (1972a, 1972b) called 'folk devils'.

> **Post-colonial theory:** Explores the broader interactions between European nations and the societies they colonized, focussing on the impact of these relationships on identity (including gender, race and class), language, representation and history.

'Chavs' were constructed in both political discourses and media representations and used to signify 'broken Britain'. The chav is presented as uncouth, with poor fashion sense (using 'bling' and cheap sportswear). The 'chav' stereotype became highly popularized as a symbol of hate and fear. Built into this was a form of 'territorial stigma' where the 'council estate' was also symbolic of being the 'breeding ground' of the chav and could be 'blamed' for allowing such a negative force to be unleashed.

This imagery of 'bad places' and 'bad people' became a powerful source for the media. For example, while the UK comedy show *Little Britain* was being broadcast on national prime TV, the national media (print and social) continually used such imagery to portray a feckless and violent underclass, 'out there' in council estates. So while the figure of the 'chav' was used in popular culture to 'get laughs', it was used in the media and across political debates as symbolic of what was wrong with the UK. Owen Jones (2012) takes this argument a step further by suggesting that the process of demonizing is not simply snobbery and elitism but an attack on the young working class. As the working class has been defeated (through the downfall of trade unions) and its members have lost work and jobs, the middle class not only ridicule the working class but also take pleasure in their defeat. How far we accept this argument is up for debate, but there is historical evidence that the middle classes have always used social 'put downs' that degrade and de-value working class culture and social life.

Theorizing youth crime: criminological and sociological positivism

Criminological positivism

The discipline of criminology provides a number of ways of theorizing youth crime, including drawing some approaches from sociology. Psychological approaches are also dominant in criminological theories. For example, psychologists such as G. Stanley Hall (1904), who was introduced to us in Chapter 1, were very influential. In Hall's early work he claimed that young people are more likely to be criminal because of the dysfunction of 'normal' biological and cognitive processes that evolve in adolescence. From this point onwards, psychology has had a central role in trying to 'discover' the causal relationship between adolescence and criminal behaviour. In other words, what was it in the biological or psychological stages of adolescence that that made young people more prone to offend? As a result, criminal psychology remains strongly influenced by what Muncie calls '**criminological positivism**'. This is an approach that searches for '... cause-effect relations that can be measured in a way similar to [that in] which natural scientists observe and analyse relations between objects in the physical world.' (Muncie, 2015, p. 86). The key attributes of positive criminology are:

> **Criminological positivism:** Searches for cause–effect relationships that can be measured in ways similar to those used by the natural sciences.

- The use of scientific methodologies that are dominated by quantifiable data, which produce 'facts' that can be tested and replicated.

- The desire to identify 'cause–effect' relationships that can predict criminality.

- Its emphasis on the study of criminal behaviour. This suggests that it is different from 'normality'.

- Criminals and their behaviour to go against the primary values of mainstream society are seen as 'abnormal'.

Thinking point

- When people in your community talk about youth crime, what do they claim are the main reasons why young people are involved in crime?
- What do they see as the causes of youth crime?

What we then tend to see within this criminological positivism is a range of theories that focus on the central cause being located in the individual. For instance, the role of physiology (physical features), genetics, the pathological family and the problem of cognitive development in the adolescent personality have all had an influence (Muncie, 2015). An example of a contemporary approach can be found in the area of developmental criminology and early intervention that we discussed in Chapter 8.

The early sociological gaze and sociological positivism

The sociology of crime and deviance also provides theories on the causes of youth offending. Early sociological theorizing on this subject has focussed on the relationship between young people's social ecology and their offending (Muncie, 2015). However, it tends to be a form of **'sociological positivism'** that understands youth participation in crime as strongly influenced by the idea of social pathology, which locates the problem in dysfunctional families/peers and/or communities, which are:

> Sociological positivism: Gives a focus to young people's social ecology in their offending, although still strongly influenced by the beliefs of social pathology, which locates the problem in dysfunctional families/peers and/or communities.

- a by-product of dysfunctions in broader social and economic conditions such as poverty; and

- differences between regions, neighbourhoods and communities depending on the economic and political context.

Three traditional sociological approaches have been particularly influential:

- *Social ecology and criminal neighbourhoods.* Human geographers and biologists at the University of Chicago in the 1920s (Park and Burgess, 1925) claimed that the development of Chicago City was not random but patterned around different zones. The zone with the most juvenile delinquency was the 'zone of transition' which had poor housing stock, poverty, pawn shops and cheap restaurants. It also had casual workers and was attractive to new migrants. High levels of social disorganization were concentrated in this zone and meant that crime flourished amongst the young.

- *Differential association (learning theory).* Developed by Sutherland and Cressey (1970). This approach proposed that crime was not caused by personality or environment but was learned. It is not just through association with criminals that crime is learnt, but through interactions between people who do not consistently support or adhere to legal codes. This is more likely in areas with high crime and increases the risk of young people learning criminal behaviour.

- *Anomie, strain and subculture theory.* Influenced by the work of Durkheim and Merton (1938). This theory suggested that the failure of American society to provide pathways to the 'American dream' creates a 'strain'. As a result, those whose aspirations are blocked look to other means to achieve and improve their lives. These alternative pathways may be delinquent.

More recently, the role of the offender has been re-emphasized, suggesting that the social ecology model ignores the role of the offender in the decision-making process. In *rational choice theory* (RCT) or *routine activity theory* (RAT), criminality is seen to rest on 'choice' that is usually mediated by 'costs and benefits' and levels of 'self-control' (Gottfredson and Hirschi, 1990). This was developed further by 'realist' criminologists (Clarke, 1992), who suggest that criminal action is both rational and reasoned and requires people to make choices. RCT proposes that, for a crime to be committed, two events most coincide: the opportunity must exist, and the individual must decide that the gains to be made outweigh the risks of getting caught. Similarly,

RCT argues that, when three elements are present, viz. me – a motivated offender, an attractive target and a lack of guardianship – it is highly likely that a crime will be committed (Cohen and Felson, 1979).

Labelling, governance and the criminalization of youth

Thinking points

- How do you think young people can be labelled? Give some examples.
- Do you think they can resist or reject labels?

Crime and labelling theory

As we see by the discussion above, early theorizing about youth crime had a tendency to start from the premise that crime is a 'social fact' (there are criminals and non-criminals) and it exists as a consequence of personal failings or 'bad choices' by individuals. Contemporary sociological approaches, however, emphasize that crime is socially constructed, as can be seen in how 'crimes' are defined and change over time, and are particular to social and cultural contexts. American sociologist Howard Becker (1963) in his book *Outsiders* rejected positivist criminological and sociological accounts of delinquency. For him, delinquency was more the outcome of complex chains of social interaction (i.e. interaction between different social groups) than anything in a young person's individual or environmental conditions that predisposed them towards rule breaking. Becker rejected the idea that there were moral absolutes and values that were 'natural' and unproblematic and that delinquency was a result of rule breaking. Rather, he stressed that 'deviancy' had to be understood as the outcome of a process of social interaction, whereby somebody could become labelled as a transgressor or rule breaker. He suggested that all societies were organized along certain sets of rules and regulations and these rules more or less reflected the organization of power in society. In this sense, one group had the power to say what was right or wrong, and attempts to enforce these rules determine what is illegal or legal. There are no predetermined codes of conduct or unequivocal morality, only interaction between these groups, and it was this, according to Becker, which determined what was and what was not considered delinquent behaviour. As we saw in the discussion on moral panics, these ideas had a significant impact on sociological analyses of youth crime. The idea that crime is something that is 'socially defined' and in some cases constructed outside the control of the individual is central. Labelling theory has been much critiqued (see Muncie, 2015) in that it fails to recognize that people do commit crimes and do have motivations. It is also seen as focussing on 'victimless crimes' such as drug-taking and homosexuality, while ignoring the more serious crimes of domestic violence, murder and rape. However, it has been useful as a 'sensitizing concept', especially in understanding how systems and processes within institutions such as youth justice and the police can label young people (Muncie, 2015).

Theories of social control

Thinking points

- How and why might the state enforce social control on its citizens?
- What types of policies and practice have the potential to criminalize the young? Give some examples.

Labelling theory also set in motion a significant debate about the role of the state in criminalizing young people. In criminological positivism, the concept of 'social control' is seen as embedded in social relationships or the individual; i.e. people must control themselves and their actions. But within sociological discussions on crime, the concept of social control developed in relation to the identification and construction of the 'deviant' or 'criminal' and was seen fundamentally as a 'political' process where the powerful defined such behaviour (Garland, 2001). For example, early work identified how professional practices in areas such as youth training, social work, law, schooling, psychiatry and others were coercive, and involved surveillance, monitoring and regulation that increased the criminalization of the young (Marcuse, 1964).

The work of French post-structural theorist Foucault (1975) has influence here. He proposed that a new technology of power was emerging, embedded in institutional settings such as schools, the military and prisons. This was increasing forms of discipline, social control and regulation. He proposed that punitive techniques of supervision and surveillance have now penetrated the whole of society. He contended that this is aimed not just at the body but at the soul and goes beyond a simple focus on offenders. Social control operates not only through the state but through what Foucault called 'power-knowledge strategies'. What he meant by this is that power is constituted through accepted forms of knowledge, scientific understanding and 'truth', and can be embedded in the discourses of science, the media and academic writing.

These ideas were further developed by Stanley Cohen (1985). He showed that there has been a blurring of the boundaries between the deviant and non-deviant and the public and the private. New techniques of social control have been developed as a result, and what we see is a price being paid where '… ordinary people become either active participants or passive receivers in the business of social control.' (Cohen, 1985, p. 233). One of the major impacts according to Cohen is the expansion of the law and order agenda into a wide range of youth social policy that is increasing the criminalization of the young. Writers such as Rose (1999) argue that children and young people are the 'most intensively governed sector of personal existence.' (Rose, 1999, p. 121). The continual need by the state to provide support or control has seen almost every aspect of young lives become subject to surveillance and regulation. This is then instrumental in increasing the chances they will be criminalized.

The law, social policy and 'creeping criminalization'

This 'creeping criminalization' within social policy has been justified by governments as a way to tackle the 'dangerous', 'the immoral' and the 'dysfunctional underclass'.

A clear example of this was the introduction of anti-social behaviour orders (ASBOs) in the UK. These were established under the Crime and Disorder Act 1998, the Police Reform Act 2002 and the Anti-Social Behaviour Act in 2003. While it was claimed that they would not target the young, it was fundamentally young people who bore the brunt of these new policies and laws. Such interventions are seen to be 'boundary blurring' (Rodger, 2008, p. 129) between civil and criminal law, as governments extend powers to civil agencies and practitioners. For example, the ASBOs gave powers of regulation and control of 'problem behaviours' and populations to a range of agencies and practitioners outside of the police, including housing officers and schools.

In effect, these policies and new laws displaced holistic social policy goals with those focussed specifically on crime control and social order. As a result, housing staff in local authorities have seen their role shift from managing housing stock to managing bad tenants and disruptive children (Rodgers, 2008). ASBO measures became rapidly and increasingly focussed, above all else, on the question of governing "troublesome" youth (Crawford, 2009, p. 753). The Labour Party in the UK also created 'dispersal zones' and local curfew orders. Dispersal zones gave the police powers to remove persons or groups of persons under the age of 16 for a specified period of time within a geographically designated area. Being removed did not itself constitute a criminal offence, but if a person refused to comply, they were committing an offence that was punishable by three months' imprisonment or a fine.

Similar practices have emerged in the area of employment policy. National governments worldwide have been hardening their approach towards those not participating in paid employment, training or education (France, 2016). Those who 'drop out' or become disengaged are usually pathologized and problematized. Alongside this, governments in a wide range of countries have been withdrawing welfare benefits. Quasi-criminalization and criminal sanctions have also been applied to welfare schemes, in which non-compliance can lead to a withdrawal of benefits. This not only increases stigma but also constructs them as 'failed citizens', which further marginalizes them and pushes them towards criminal activities as a form of survival (Fergusson, 2014).

Youth culture and crime

Thinking point

What do you think is meant by the term 'youth crime is cultural'? Think about what this might mean in practice.

Cultural criminology

One of the major problems with labelling theory and those approaches that focus on criminalizing processes is the failure to address the role and response of the young person. This issue has been raised by the work of cultural criminology. As we saw in Chapter 5, early forms of subcultural theory developed by the CCCS had much to say about young people's relationship with crime. These theories claimed that much deviant or criminal behaviour of the young was a form of cultural 'resistance'. While this work was criticized for over-romanticizing these activities, it did highlight how culture could be both criminalized and criminal, giving a stronger acknowledgement of the role of the individual. Cultural criminology (Farrell, 1999) has a similar interest and focusses on exploring a multitude of interactions. These are seen as happening at both the level of the individual and in the discourses that are reproduced in places such as the media and those agencies responsible for controlling and managing crime. These are responsible for creating an image and discourses of crime as cultural. For example, processes of crime control are believed to be shaped by the meanings assigned by culture, wider media and political discourses. Crime is constructed and given both recognition and value. At the same time, culture can also be defined as 'crime'. Certain cultural activities in art, music, dance and sex are increasingly sites of criminalization, as we saw in Chapter 5 on rave culture. It is this interplay between the cultural meanings of crime embedded in political and media discourses and the cultural practices of being criminal that are of interest to cultural criminology.

> The study of crime necessitates not simply the examination of individual criminals and criminal events, not even the straightforward examination of media coverage of criminals and criminal events, but rather a journey into the spectacle and carnival of crime, a walk down an infinite hall of mirrors where images created and consumed by criminals, criminal subcultures, control agents, media institutions and audiences bounce endlessly one off the other. (Ferrell, 1999, p. 397)

Cultural criminologists therefore want to emphasize the importance of pleasure, excitement and fun as a part of the process of 'being criminal'. Crime, especially amongst the young, is in many ways a 'carnival' underpinned by pleasure and risk. Presdee (2000) for example argues that young people transgress rules and regulations because they are there. In this sense, risk is a challenge, not a deterrent. While the state tries to impose greater regulation on behaviour, it creates higher levels of emotional desire to resist. Activities such as joyriding, hacking and raves are expressions of what Presdee calls 'the carnival spirit', but these are not a part of the rationality of the state, which then renders them 'criminal'. In this sense '... everyday life is subjected to a creeping criminalisation process where the carnival of crime becomes a necessity in our lives' (Presdee, 2000, p. 160).

While this approach has gained much interest in youth sociology, it does tend to be selective in what is defined as 'crime'. It also continues the tradition of romanticizing a wide range of problem behaviours, and focussing on the 'spectacular' and on crimes that have few victims. O'Brian (2005) has also criticized its methods, suggesting that it tends to use ethnography and replicates the idea of academics as 'zookeepers of deviance' (p. 603), viewing subjects as interesting objects of study while ignoring the problems and questions of power. In this sense, crimes such as joyriding and graffiti are created as a means of resolving material deprivations and tensions, while structured inequalities remain unexplored in the background.

Territoriality, culture and gangs

A second approach that brings in a more cultural understanding of youth crime is that of territoriality. This brings into the discussion on youth crime the relationship between place and spaces and local culture. Territoriality is defined as '… a situation in which a group claims an identifiable geographical area as their own and seek to defend it against others' (Pickering et al., 2012, p. 945). It is in local neighbourhood spaces where young people, and young men in particular, try to gain some control over their lives. This can create conflict with other young people, adults and especially the police. Bannister et al. (2013) showed how such territorial practices were socially structured by local opportunities and context. They showed that poor and disadvantaged neighbourhoods provide few opportunities to get work and that the cultural practices of previous generations can operate to create cultural meanings of territory. It is not unusual for a culture of violence, especially among young men, to exist as a part of managing themselves in the places and spaces of local neighbourhoods and communities. The use of violence is also important to self-identity, by giving young people on the streets not only self-esteem and recognition amongst their peers, but substantial cultural capital (France et al., 2013). Fraser (2013) talks about '*street habitus*', which refers to embodied dispositions such as language and dress that help young people understand their place in the social order and how they navigate and operate on the streets. Such actions can be both violent and criminal, but they can bring significant rewards.

Thinking points

- How important do you think territory is to young people, and what impact might it have on activities that can be seen as criminal?
- Do you think youth gangs are a problem in your country?

The link between youth culture and criminality in neighbourhoods has also been a central feature of debates about youth gangs. Historically, criminology and sociology have seen the youth gang as a major feature of youth crime. A large number of studies have focussed on how criminal youth gangs operate in highly deprived neighbourhoods. More recently, discussions on youth gangs have been a central concern of governments in Europe (Fraser et al., 2018) and the Antipodes (White, 2016). That said, it is recognized that youth gangs, especially outside of the US context, are difficult to define or identify. In fact, Fraser and Hagedorn (2018) suggest that attempts to measure and categorize youth gangs, '… privilege a static view of gang membership that neglects the localized meanings, historical antecedents and cultural contexts of gangs' (p. 43). Attempts to measure gangs give a narrow view of the role and value of 'gang-type' activity in young people's lives. They go on to suggest that to understand gangs we need to know how social structure intersects with young people's lives and how individual biographies and the cultural context of place play important roles in explaining why young people get involved in gangs. White (2016) has a similar approach, arguing that historical understandings of 'youth gangs' in Australia were driven more by 'moral panics' than evidence. These moral panics consistently demonize young gang members as 'dangerous, deviant and destructive' (p. 84)' or 'immoral' and 'threatening'. Yet in many cases, White's (2016) work shows how youth gangs can operate as important sources of protection and support for many disadvantaged young people. Gangs can provide family-type support, especially for Indigenous young people and those facing racism.

Theorizing difference

Crime and inequality

As we can see from the previous discussions, much work in criminology and sociology has concentrated on the crimes of the poor and disenfranchised. From the early studies of the Chicago studies to more contemporary work of cultural criminologists, the focus has tended to be on the criminal activity of the working class. Interestingly we have very little research on the criminal activity of the middle class or children from wealthy families. In many cases this is not surprising as most crime is seen to happen in some of the most deprived communities and neighbourhoods.

💭 Thinking points

- Do you think there is a causal relationship between youth crime and a person's class?
- Why do you think higher rates of youth crime exist amongst ethnic or Indigenous groups?

It is also the case, as we saw in the introduction to this chapter, that most crime is committed by young men (80 per cent). Young women do commit crimes, but they are in the minority and tend to commit less serious crimes. We also need to recognize that, when it comes to the data, those from ethnic minorities are more likely to be offenders in dominant White societies such as Australia and New Zealand. So the question is why might this be the case? How can we explain some of these differences?

Our starting point is to interrogate the evidence. While it is popularly understood that more crimes are committed by working or underclass youth, young people from middle class backgrounds are just as likely to commit crimes as those from poorer backgrounds (Anderson et al., 1994; Graham and Bowling, 1995). What is different is that many are unlikely to get caught; and if they are caught they are unlikely to be prosecuted. Classic sociological works such as Howard Parker's (1974) *View from the Boys* found that, while petty theft was not unusual, crime was not a major part of young working class boys' lifestyles. Rather, they were more concerned with having fun, adventure and taking risks. One thing we need to recognize is that how a community is policed and managed by the state affects the level of crime (Goldson and Muncie, 2015). Evidence continues to show how communities and neighbourhoods are policed and how the law is biased against the young working class (Goldson and Muncie, 2015). This of course returns to the discussion above about how the state is a critical player in criminalizing certain groups of young people.

When it comes to the over-representation of young people from various ethnic groups, there is a growing body of research that shows this is related to how the state views particular groups. This has been described as a form of institutional racism. May et al. (2010) conducted a large national study of policing and youth justice practices in the UK. They found that a wide range of practices, including stop and search by police, proactive and strategic policing practices, and the administration of justice in the youth justice courts created a disproportionate over-representation of young people from ethnic minority groups. What is being suggested here is that there is no real evidence that racial differences exist in the committing of crime. The difference emerges because of how the institutions of crime control target these groups of young people. As a result, they are more likely to end up in the youth or criminal justice system, creating the view that they are more criminal than other groups.

Young men, masculinity and crime

As we have seen, most youth crime is committed by young men, yet until the 1990s criminology had made little comment on what it was about being male that might be a factor in their offending. In the 2000s, with the growth of masculinity studies, important questions about this relationship were raised. Tony Jefferson (2002), for example, argued that male sexuality and masculinity had historically been seen as reductive within criminology in three senses. Firstly, masculinity was usually conceptualized in the singular. It was man's universal fate to become masculine and by implication to oppress women. Secondly, masculinity was seen, in much criminological theorizing, as the simple outcome of biological or sociological determinism. In other words, it was either biological destiny (in our genes) or sociological fate (socialisation). Thirdly, the continual focus on masculinity as a deterministic concept reduced opportunities for raising questions about agency, choice, desire and responsibility. There was no recognition that 'being male' might be a negotiated process that creates opportunities for other, less oppressive identities to evolve. As we saw in Chapter 2, a solution to this 'reductionism' has been developed by the Australian sociologist, Raewyn Connell (1995) in her writings on *masculinities*. Connell proposes that there are two main types of masculinity, the 'dominant' or what she calls 'hegemonic masculinity' and 'subordinate' masculinities. It is in the latter that 'diversity' and pluralism exist. As a result, there is the possibility for more than one form of masculinity.

Thinking points

- Why do you think young men are more likely to commit crime?
- Why do some young men not commit crime?

These ideas gained traction in studies of youth crime because they suggested that crime is a space and place where young men 'do masculinity' (Messerschmidt, 1993). Crime takes different forms according to how different classes and ethnic groups define masculinity. For White working class young men, crime is constructed around physical aggression. Crimes such as violence and robbery are based on toughness and physical strength. Alternatively, middle class young people are more likely to be involved in vandalism, minor theft and alcohol consumption requiring forms of mental 'labour' rather than physical strength. In this sense, these unique forms of masculinity are situated and accomplished through engagement with different types of crime. Across criminology there has been a growing interest in how masculinity is important to the practice of young men 'doing crime'.

Masculine trajectories of gang violence in Medellín, Colombia

Baird (2017) interviewed gang members in Medellín, Colombia, showing that many young men join gangs to emulate and reproduce 'successful' local male identities. This requires the accumulation by the gang of 'masculine capital', an important material and symbolic signifier of manhood. Youths are involved in stylistic and timely displays of this capital, helping them to a form of male success. This in effect drives the social reproduction of the gang. Once in the gang, young people become increasingly 'bad', using violence to defend the gang's interests in exchange for more masculine capital. Gang leaders, colloquially known as *duros* or 'hard men', tend to be the *más malos*, the 'baddest'. The 'ganging process' is a practical logic as a site of identity formation for aspirational young men who are coming of age when conditions of structural exclusion conspire against them.

Young women and crime

Up until the 1960s, most criminological theorizing on youth crime either ignored girls' involvement or attempted to explain girl delinquency as being based on genetic factors. For example, in the late 19th century, Lombroso (1898) argued that women were locked into a lower state of evolutionary development than men and were, in effect, no more than 'big children'. The driving force of female offending could be found either in unnatural feminine urges or as a result of their more primitive instincts leading them to become engaged in sexual degeneracy. As we saw in Chapter 2, Carol Smart (1976), in her classic critique of how gender was used in criminology, showed that most studies of girls and delinquency have tended to assume a strong link to biological explanations where it was seen that the constitution of 'good' women disposes them to motherhood and home making. Deviations from this are then seen as 'unnatural' and usually linked to some form of sexual misconduct, which then sexualizes the causes of their delinquency. These two assumptions about gender continued to influence both how the criminal justice system responded to girls, and how girls were understood in the academic literature. In response, feminism started to theorize gender using newly emerging theories that challenged the 'malestream' way of looking at this question. This resulted in new ways of exploring girl's relationship to crime. These studies include:

- Ann Campbell's (1984) work on girls in American gangs showed how their sexuality was important in the types of roles and relationships they had with gang

↲ with males. This brought into play concepts such as patriarchy, ᵥay girls were positioned in gangs.

. (1985) showed how social control mechanisms and regulations in ᵢn particular regulated the lives of girls. Parents' perspectives of girls' sexual ᵤrity influenced the type of social control they enforced, showing that when such controls were 'loose' they were more likely to offend.

- Chesney Lind (1984) highlighted the ways in which disproportionate numbers of custodial decisions for girls and young women in the USA were based upon the need to protect young women from compromising their own morality i.e. becoming sexually active. Girls are therefore seen within the system as needing protection from themselves in ways not replicated for boys and young men.

Thinking points

- Why do young women commit less crime than young men?
- Why might some young women commit crimes? How can we explain female offending?

Since this early work, feminist criminologists have had a growing influence on turning the lens on young women's relationship with crime. Not only has this work focussed on how young women are treated unfairly by the criminal justice system, or over-regulated by the state and families, but also how they are more likely to be victims of domestic violence and sexual abuse (Chesney Lind, 2006). Others have also challenged the 'myths' of girls' crimes portrayed by the media and others. For example, girls' involvement in gangs and their growing use of violence has been a dominant theme of the 'youth girl crime problem', and feminist criminologists have had a major role in challenging the misrepresentation of the problem (Batchelor et al., 2001; Chesney-Lind and Irwin, 2004; Carrington, 2013).

Summary

- Youth crime rates are declining, though it is important to understand the patterns in which young people are disproportionately *victims* of crime.

- Media have played a crucial role in how young people are positioned through 'moral panics', although more recent changes suggest that the term is unable to capture the complexity of media representations.

- Theorizing youth crime has been dominated by criminology and forms of positivist approaches. In this, youth crime is seen as a 'social fact', with limited acknowledgement of the social context of youth offending.

- More recently, studies giving attention to labelling, criminalizing, culture, place and spaces have been able to show how youth crime has a relationship to its social, cultural and economic context.

- Crime figures show that certain ethnic groups are more likely to be criminalized because of institutional racism.

- Feminist theorists have challenged 'malestream' forms of analysis in criminology that portray young women's involvement in crime as 'unnatural', leading to them being problematized unfairly.

- The expansion of masculinity studies has produced new ways of thinking about why young men become involved in certain forms of criminal behaviour.

Exercise: The sociological imagination

Think about how crime in your local area is 'constructed'. What are the characteristics of those deemed 'the problem' – e.g. by class, gender, age, and ethnicity? Use your 'sociological imagination' to think through the cultural, social and historical dimensions impacting how 'criminals' are framed. Can you see 'creeping criminalization' at work in your example?

Key readings

Bannister, J., Kintrea, K. & Pickering, J. (2013) 'Young people and violent territorial conflict: exclusion, culture and the search for identity', *Journal of Youth Studies*, vol. 16, no. 4, pp. 474–490.

Chesney-Lind, Meda & Lisa Pasko. (2004) *The Female Offender: Girls, Women and Crime*, 2nd ed. (Thousand Oaks: Sage Publications).

France, A., Bottrell, D. & Armstrong, D. (2012) *A Political Ecology of Youth and Crime* (London: Palgrave Macmillan).

Fraser, A. & Hagedorn, J. M. (2018) 'Gangs and a global sociological imagination', *Theoretical Criminology*, vol. 22, no. 1, pp. 42–62.

Goldson, B. & Muncie, J. (2015) *Youth Crime and Justice* (London: Sage).

Jefferson, T. (2002) 'Subordinating hegemonic masculinity', *Theoretical Criminology*, vol. 6, no. 1, pp. 63–88.

Pickering, J., Kintrea, K., & Bannister, J. (2012) 'Invisible walls and visible youth: territoriality among young people in British cities', *Urban Studies*, vol. 49, no. 5 pp. 945–960.

White, R. (2016) *Youth Gangs, Violence and Social Respect: Exploring the Nature of Provocations and Punch-ups* (London: Palgrave Macmillan).

10 YOUTH, HEALTH AND WELLBEING

In this chapter you will learn about:

- How health and wellbeing need to be understood in their social context
- Different 'models' for theorizing and explaining health, including biomedical, social and relational perspectives
- Key health challenges for young people today
- The growth of youth mental health problems and how they can be sociologically explained.

Youth, health and wellbeing in the global context

Thinking point

- Do you think young people today are healthier than previous generations?
- What do you think are the main health issues for young people today?

Youth health and wellbeing has become a key issue globally in the past decade. Prior to this, it was assumed that youth and health went hand-in-hand: in other words, to be young was to be healthy, at least in relation to older population groups. This was largely due to the definition of health being used (health as absence of disease), as young people are indeed the population group least likely to suffer from disease (Cahill, 2015). Until recently, there was little research and information about the health conditions impacting young people as a different demographic from children and older adults. Many of the primary health and wellbeing issues for young people originate not from disease but from societal factors, related to place and location, social class, gender, sexuality and ethnicity. For example, the most significant wellbeing challenges for youth in wealthier countries such as Australia, New Zealand and the UK relate to mental health conditions, **body image**, drinking and drug use, and sexual health (West, 2017; White and Wyn, 2013). Simple definitions that focus on 'absence of disease' alone do not capture the complex issues and environments shaping young people's health.

> **Body image:** The image, perception, thoughts and emotions a person has regarding their own body in terms of its size and attractiveness.

The World Health Organization's (WHO) definition of health does reflect contemporary understandings that health is about more than merely the absence of disease, to encompass physical and mental health, and general social 'wellbeing'. This more holistic definition and approach to health has led to significant attention from governments, institutions, schools and communities, aimed at improving children's and young people's health globally across all levels of society. The WHO recognizes that the key health issues for young people differ across locales and align with broader themes of social inequality. However, many of these discussions of youth (and health) tend to be dominated by Western approaches to youth in the 'more developed' countries of Australia, North America, Europe, Japan and New Zealand, which account for only around 10 per cent of the global youth population (Population Reference Bureau, 2017). Further compounding these issues are the difficulties in assessing global youth health trends and patterns, as there is a lack of internationally consistent measures and data across countries and regions (Patton et al., 2009). Before we continue our discussions, it is important to identify these challenges since the conditions vary so drastically for young people around the world. We must be careful, when we speak about 'youth', not to merely address the 10 per cent who live in the world's most developed countries; we need to pay attention to the significantly different challenges associated with different contexts:

> In the developed world, concerns about the well-being of young people are often framed around the period of their 'adolescence' and include concerns about mental and social health, risky behaviour in relation to sex or drugs, and successful transition to employment and adulthood. In the developing world, where the vast proportion of young people live, well-being concerns are expressed around nutrition, hygiene, maternal mortality, HIV vulnerability, and survival. (Cahill, 2015, p. 99)

Many of these issues also have a strong gender dimension. For example, young women who endure child marriage have links with increased maternal mortality rates, which are a public health challenge in some areas of South-East Asia such as Northern India, Pakistan and Bangladesh (Raj et al., 2010; UNICEF, 2011a). It is also the case that rates of gender-based violence against women are extremely high in areas such as the Pacific Islands, Kiribati and Papua New Guinea, and some South-East Asian regions, which pose significant health and wellbeing issues for young women (Brunson, 2010; UNICEF, 2011b). Leading causes of mortality globally differ by region, and by gender:

- One of every three deaths among adolescent males in the Americas is due to interpersonal violence.

- One of every five deaths among adolescents in high income countries is due to road traffic injuries.

- One of every five deaths among adolescent males in the Eastern Mediterranean Region is due to war and conflicts.

- One of every six deaths among adolescent females in the South-East Asia region is due to suicide.

- One of every six deaths among adolescents in the African region is due to HIV. (http://apps.who.int/adolescent/second-decade/section3/page2/mortality.html)

HIV and young affected populations in the Asia–Pacific region

While HIV prevalence is low in most countries in the Asia–Pacific region, it tends to be much more prevalent in certain pockets of the population. This is termed a 'concentrated' epidemic. This contrasts with the situation in most countries in Africa, for example (which are experiencing a 'generalized' epidemic), where HIV is spread mainly through sexual intercourse and is prevalent in the general population. Concentrated epidemics require a very different and targeted response compared with generalized epidemics. The Independent Commission on AIDS in Asia 2008 found that young people from 'key populations' in the Asia–Pacific carry a disproportionate burden of new infections: 95 per cent of new HIV infections occur in these groups. Key populations are referred to as such because they are both key to the epidemic's dynamics and key to the response. Key populations vary across countries and region's but they usually include:

- people who buy and sell sex
- people who inject drugs
- men who have sex with men
- transgender people

Young people from these key populations tend to be understood within segregating and individualizing storylines, which position them either as victims (of a disease), as deviants (who brought contagion on themselves through immoral sexual or drug-related behaviour) or as threats (who may pass the contagious disease on to unsuspecting others). The ways in which the HIV virus is transmitted, via sexual exchange and drug use, are key areas of 'risk' typically discussed in relation to young people worldwide (Cahill and Coffey, 2016).

While the patterns and key challenges of youth health look different in each region, some of these issues also impact on the health of young people in wealthier, post-industrial societies such as Australia, the UK and Europe. For example, in Australia, suicide is the leading cause of death for people aged 18–44 (Australian Bureau of Statistics, 2017). The rate of suicide is particularly high for those aged 20–24 in Australia, accounting for around a third of all deaths in both young men and young women (38 per cent and 32.5 per cent, respectively) (Australian Bureau of Statistics, 2017). We shall return to this later in the chapter.

How do young people experience health?

Public policy has become increasingly concerned about the health of young people. It has been suggested that in 'new times' of rapid social change, young people's health is deteriorating, and young people today face greater wellbeing challenges than their parents' generation. West (2017) suggests that concern about the state of youth health has all the makings of a moral panic. There are no longitudinal studies of health across different ages and time periods, so we cannot scientifically compare the experiences of different generations and their health. When trying to understand the health of the young, Patrick West (2017) draws our attention to three sets of data to show what we do know about young people's health. Firstly, using a 'disease/impairment' set of indicators in a UK study, he suggests that approximately 20 per cent of all young people report that they have an impairment that 'limits their activities'. This figure increases with age. These illnesses include respiratory, musculo-skeletal and mental health problems. Secondly, when young people have been asked to rate their health, 14 per cent of young men and 21 per cent of young women aged 11 to 13 see it as 'fair' to 'poor'. This increases by age; by the time they are 15 years old, they increase to 16 per cent for young men and 27 per cent for young women. This means that around 80 per cent of 11 and 13 year olds rate their health as 'good' to 'excellent', but this figure drops slightly for young men and more substantially for young women by the time they reach the age of 15. Why would young people's experience of health deteriorate between these ages? Rates of anxiety and stress may contribute, along with the onset of body image concerns during teenage years. We will explore these dimensions of youth poor health later in the chapter.

Finally, it is also important to remember that health is not a level playing field, as the WHO reminds us:

> There is ample evidence that social factors, including education, employment status, income level, gender and ethnicity have a marked influence on how healthy a person is. In all countries – whether low-, middle- or high-income – there are wide disparities in the health status of different social groups. The lower an individual's socio-economic position, the higher their risk of poor health. (WHO, 2017)

The social determinants of health for young people

Attempts to understand how inequality affects young people have concentrated on looking at the social determinants of health. Anne Hagell et al. (2018) undertook an international review of evidence that examined what social and economic factors influenced the health and wellbeing of youth (aged 12–24). They found compelling evidence that showed how different aspects of inequality affected their health and wellbeing. Examples of these cut across income, education, unemployment and work:

- Low income is associated with poor health, and given that young people are more likely than any other group to be low paid, their health is most likely to be poor.
- Young people living in highly deprived areas are twice as likely to be obese and more likely to be admitted to hospital. They are also 3.7 times more likely to be killed or seriously injured in a road accident.
- Young homeless people and those who have lived in rental accommodation all their lives are more likely to have poor health.
- Education is one of the strongest determinants of good health – if you had an elite education (private school) or went to the best public schools you are likely to have better health. If you have been in education at the highest level (i.e. university) your health will be better than that of those going into vocational training.
- The long-term unemployed have a lower life expectancy and will have worse health over the life course. While young people may not yet have lived long enough to have poor health, continued unemployment will increase the risk.

- While evidence on the impact of precarious work is limited, there is a body of research that shows that young people working on zero hours contracts are more at risk of mental and physical health problems.
- The impact of inequality on a person's health is compounded for those who are working in low-paid industries that are insecure and precarious, and who also come from highly deprived areas and have had a poor education.

Theorizing youth health and wellbeing

The biomedical approach

There are differing and contested approaches to understanding issues of youth health and wellbeing. The most dominant and influential is what has been called the 'biomedical approach'. This tends to view health as a property of the individual, or something that young people 'possess'. This perspective focusses on either the causes of illness as a result of dysfunctions of the body, or the contracting of diseases. As Hankivsky et al. (2017) remind us, '…the model gives primacy to biological explanations of health outcomes, focusing on the body as an island unto itself, and defining illness as primarily internal'. The **biomedical model** has four dimensions:

> **Biomedical model:** The conventional approach to health in Western societies which focusses on illness as a malfunction of an individual body, rather than focussing on social patterns causing illness.

- Disease is seen as a consequence of certain malfunctions of the human body.
- All human dysfunctions may be traced to specific causal mechanisms within an organism.
- The biomedical model is exclusionary in that alternatives and 'non-scientific' approaches are usually seen as invalid and to be ignored.
- It sees a clear distinction between mind and body, where the ultimate cause of illness is located in the body.

Thinking points

- Do individual behaviours or socio-cultural contexts cause health issues?
- What impact does the lens or framework we use have on how health issues are understood and addressed?

Biomedical approaches are dominant in informing the health intervention strategies of governments and medical professions, especially towards issues such as obesity, drinking and substance use. The biomedical approach is also very influential in the field of health prevention. It uses a wide range of 'risk factors' to predict future ill health so that medical professionals can identify patterns of behaviour associated with negative health outcomes and intervene accordingly. This is a problem, since a range of health issues are known to be patterned by social dimensions that are out of an individual's control, such as socio-economic status.

Victim-blaming:
The process whereby marginalized social groups are blamed for the conditions of their marginalization, rather than seeing the structural inequalities that pattern the conditions of people's lives.

Addressing disease prevention as if it is solely within an individual's control can create a situation in which individuals with poor health are blamed for not doing enough to change it. Sociologists refer to this as '**victim blaming**'. Biomedical approaches that suggest there is a simple causal relationship between risk factors and health outcomes fail to understand that health cannot be understood outside of its historical, social and cultural contexts. Sociologists are critical of such an approach as it does not take into account the social patterns of health and illness and therefore tends to unfairly blame people who suffer from chronic health conditions, rather than understanding the factors that are out of an individual's control as central to their experience of health.

Youth sociologists are critical of the ways young people's health tends to be framed in relation to risk discourses. As White and Wyn (2013) explain, many health professionals, particularly in policy and population health settings, use 'risk factors' to try to predict patterns of behaviour that they hypothesize will cause further harm (such as smoking cigarettes leading to an increased likelihood of using marijuana). However, these models of risk can be highly simplistic, 'washing out local contextual factors and interrelationships between different problems' (White and Wyn, 2013, p. 201), such as that rates of smoking tend to be higher in socio-economically disadvantaged groups than the general youth population to begin with. The biomedical model is also recognized to have numerous other limitations, including defining health primarily in terms of ill health, rather than providing ways to understand positive or holistic experiences of bodily health (Blaxter, 2003).

🗨 Thinking point

- What youth health issues do you typically see represented from a 'biomedical perspective'? What other factors might be important influences on the health of young people?

The social model of health

Social model of health: Social factors at personal, family, community and national levels which influence a person's health.

The **social model of health** (also referred to as the social determinants of health model) is an alternative lens for understanding how health and illness occur through interactions between individuals and their socio-cultural environments (Viner et al., 2012). This perspective highlights the idea that poor health tends to stem from structural factors such as wealth inequality and poverty in particular, which are not within an individual's power to change on their own. Health is shown to be socially produced through the interactions a person has with their environment at every level:

The strongest determinants of adolescent health are structural factors such as national wealth, income inequality, and access to education. Furthermore, safe and supportive families, safe and supportive schools, together with positive and supportive peers, are crucial to helping young people develop to their full potential and attain the best health in the transition to adulthood. (Viner et al., 2012, p. 1641)

This perspective addresses youth health by exploring the social determinants that pattern individual experiences of health through a range of structural, institutional and social factors. It is also referred to as a **relational approach** (Wexler and Eglinton, 2015), in which wellbeing is experienced individually but is a reflection of social relationships, including institutional practices (such as 'health-promoting schools') and personal relationships (for example, positive relations within families and at work) (Wyn, 2009). Within this approach, wellbeing is the term most commonly used to understand young people's health. Wellbeing is connected to the WHO's efforts to provide a more holistic definition of health as 'a total state of physical, mental, and social wellbeing'. The addition of 'social wellbeing' to the equation is particularly significant as it disrupts the biomedical perspective that health is confined to an individual's body. This definition specifically locates social forces as being important in shaping, if not determining, the quality of a person's health. Further, wellbeing as an interplay of social and relational factors is therefore useful in pointing out the vastly complex interplay of social, environmental, cultural and historical factors that all play a role in a young person's experience of health, rather than approaching health as solely within an individual's control.

> **Relational approach:** Understanding youth as a social category in relation to constructs of 'childhood' and 'adulthood', as well as in relation to social contexts.

Of course the term 'wellbeing' has itself been contested in youth sociological literature, mainly because it can be so broadly defined that it 'seems to mean everything and nothing' (McLeod and Wright, 2015), making it hard to 'pin down' and compare between contexts. Further, despite the academic focus on the social dimensions informing wellbeing, the term tends to be understood in more individualistic ways by young people as meaning 'happiness' and 'health' rather than focussing on the significance of structural conditions such as poverty and access to education, housing, employment and health services (Bourke and Geldens, 2007). Youth sociologists emphasize the importance of using wellbeing as a critical concept to interrogate the social and relational dimensions that comprise 'health', in order to disrupt the dominant individualizing narratives of biomedical perspectives, which wrongly suggest that we all start from the same level playing field, and can all achieve good health if only we try hard enough. This obscures the systems of power that privilege some groups and disadvantage others from the outset.

A good example of how we might better understand the causes of illness can be found in research on Indigenous youth. For example, the health and wellbeing outcomes of Indigenous peoples in North America, Canada, New Zealand and Australia are significantly poorer than non-Indigenous populations in these countries. In Australia, for example, the life expectancy of an Indigenous person is 17 years shorter than that of the non-Indigenous population. Indigenous adolescents have higher rates of injuries and mental disorders and poorer sexual and reproductive health than non-Indigenous youth (Azzopardi et al., 2018). Almost a third of Indigenous adolescents aged 18–24 years report high levels of psychological distress (twice the non-Indigenous rate) (Azzopardi et al., 2018). These significant health inequalities are caused by a combination of social inequalities related to socio-economic status, as well as the specific context of Indigenous peoples' suffering due to colonization, including loss of language and culture, and disconnection from the land (King et al., 2009). Research into Indigenous health has been largely based on non-Indigenous notions of health, centring on treating and preventing disease following the biomedical model. Indigenous peoples define wellbeing far more broadly than merely physical health or the absence of disease, including physical, emotional, mental and spiritual dimensions contributing to balance in a person's life (King et al., 2009). Despite the acknowledgment (and general in-principle acceptance) that Indigenous concepts of health need to be incorporated into efforts to address Indigenous health inequalities, Indigenous perspectives have been poorly understood (Priest et al., 2012). Efforts to better define and integrate holistic Aboriginal understandings of health in Australia are ongoing.

Youth and the 'imperative of health'

Individualization: Describes the broad social changes over the past century through which the 'state' has less control or responsibility for labour markets and employment, and people are required to individually manage their life trajectories through making 'good choices'.

As we have seen in the previous chapters, broad social and economic shifts over the past century mean that the contexts in which young people are now living are vastly different from those of their parents and grandparents. In Chapters 4 and 8 we have seen that changes from collective ways of life have led to a context of **individualization**, in which the 'state' has less control or responsibility for labour markets and employment (Wyn, 2009, p. 3). Individual young people and their families are being repositioned from individuals as citizens to individuals as consumers – particularly in relation to education and health (Wyn, 2009). In Chapter 8 we saw that social risks, including those related to health issues, have also become individualized. This means that individuals are required to take increased responsibility for managing risks as social welfare programs and services are reduced (Coffey, 2017). This has the effect of obscuring the patterns of disadvantage and inequality which significantly shape people's lives and health. The issue of youth homelessness is a key example of individualized social inequality or how structural inequalities are recast as individual failures (Farrugia, 2011). Those who are already in less advantaged social categories in terms of socio-economic or Indigenous status, for example, become further disadvantaged as they are less likely to have access to the various resources (like money or other networks of support) that are needed to navigate increased risks successfully.

This context of individualization has a particular impact on how health is understood and valorized in contemporary Western societies. In this context, the increased focus on health and wellbeing is analyzed by sociologists as the **imperative of health** (Lupton, 1995). This term draws on the work of philosopher Michel Foucault to highlight that public health initiatives are historically rather new, and are connected to modern efforts to regulate society on moral grounds by focussing on the ethical and moral practices of the self (Lupton, 1995, p. 4). The body and 'self' become a project to be worked on: those who do are

Imperative of health: A term coined by Michel Foucault to refer to the social and moralized status associated with maintaining 'good health' in modern, Western societies.

rewarded as 'good citizens'; those who transgress the narrow physically idealized categories are demonized as 'moral failures'. For example, Deborah Lupton argues:

> While the rise of public health and health promotion in western countries has been associated with improvements in health status at the population level, the discourses and practices of these institutions have also worked to produce certain limited kinds of subjects and bodies, drawing upon binary oppositions associated with discriminatory moral judgments...[we must] critically interrogate the ways the practices and policies of public health and health promotion valorise some groups and individuals and marginalise others. (Lupton, 1995, p. 5)

In Australia, like other Western societies, body ideals are strongly gendered, and emphasize slenderness for women and muscularity for men. Appearance ideals also designate 'health' as an image: one that usually takes the appearance of a youthful, fit and toned, smiling person. The rise of celebrity culture and new technological developments such as interactive social media have placed more emphasis on images of perfection, which now circulate more rapidly than ever before. As a result, body and appearance pressures are a key health concern for contemporary youth related to these societal contexts. This issue is discussed in the next section as a key health challenge for contemporary youth, alongside mental health.

Young people, health and the body

Lupton (1995) and others (see Turner, 1995 for example) have identified that the body and its relationship to health has become a central focus, not only in the public health discourses and practices but also in sociology. Managing the body's appearance is also a major concern for young people. In Australia, body image has consistently ranked in the top three issues of concern for young Australians since 2012 (Cave et al., 2015). Almost one-third of young people (30.6 per cent) – young women and young men – name body image as one of the biggest concerns in their life (Mission Australia, 2016). Young people's 'body ideals' tell us a great deal about the cultural and social norms of a society. Practices aimed at regulating body shape and physical control are understood as central aspects of youth identity (Featherstone 2010; Gill et al., 2005).

Body work and gender ideals

'Body work' is defined as the ways in which people deliberately 'work on' their bodies to align with socio-cultural ideals (Coffey, 2016). Body work practices are an important way young people seek to shape and express identities through bodily presentation and performance (Coffey, 2016). However, health and gender ideals are often very narrowly defined and virtually impossible to live up to. This is a key reason why young people feel concerned about body image (Coffey, 2013). Studies of young people's body work found that gender plays a key role in the range of practices performed by young women and men in an effort to align with 'body ideals' and desired identities (Coffey, 2013, 2016). Gym work and lifting weights, for example, are performed by many young men in an effort to appear more muscular. Some young men, who played professional sport such as AFL (Australian Football League better known as Australian rules football) and baseball, also described feeling pressure to 'keep up' their training even when they no longer played the sport because they wanted to keep the 'identity' of a sportsman. This included being defined as muscular and heterosexual so they could appeal to women (Coffey, 2015b). The desire to appear muscular and live up to physical ideals of masculinity including strength and dominance is a major reason for the increase in steroid use among young men (Ravn and Coffey, 2016). Alternatively, young women in Coffey's study (2016) engaged in 'slimming' practices, through diet and exercise such as jogging or hot yoga. Many said they would be 'happier' if they were able to lose weight and appear more 'toned'; however, some young women who spent many hours working on their bodies to maintain slenderness described feeling 'trapped' in a cycle in which their happiness depended on their body weight, a situation which they felt was unsustainable (Coffey, 2015a). These types of practices of young men and women were central to participants 'feeling good' about themselves and 'who they saw themselves as'. The study found that the current norms and ideals of both health and gender contributed to young people feeling significant pressure about their bodily appearance. Despite there being clear social patterns such as gendered pressures and unrealistic bodily ideals for both women and men, many in the study individualized their experiences and described feeling alone and isolated in being unhappy with their bodies.

Thinking point

- Do you go the gym or 'work out'? If so why do you do it? To keep healthy, to look good? Is it important to your self-identity?

Young urban American Indian women's negotiation of identity, health and the body

A study by Jette and Roberts (2016) shows the intersection between gender and Indigenous culture. It focussed on how a group of young Indigenous women drew on their culture (and that of others) in seeing their health and negotiating access to services and education. The study found that these young women had a more holistic view of health, often framed by their culture, which saw health as being spiritual, physical (through the body) and mental. The also acknowledged the importance of the environment in which they lived in shaping their experience of being healthy. While they held similar views to others about the problems of body size and shape, they were also strongly influenced by Indigenous culture that recognized the importance of personal relationships' inner beauty. The research found that these young women would negotiate their identities and '...the ability of the youths to pass as white, Hispanic, a 'mixed girl' and American Indian suggest that for them identity is complex and brings different types of responses. For example, being seen as 'White' could bring them 'privileges' while alternatively, being seen as the 'marginalized other' was used to distance themselves from being seen as part of the dominant oppressive group in America.

Individualized bodies: body image and obesity

Body image concerns are usually linked to eating disorders, anxiety and depression as well as excessive exercise, steroid use and cosmetic surgery (AIHW, 2011). Eating disorders are an area of major concern for the young. These tend to include the psychiatrically defined conditions of anorexia nervosa, bulimia nervosa, binge eating disorder and related syndromes. The onset of these conditions peaks in the youth phase between 15 and 25 years of age. Young women also tend to make up the majority of people with anorexia and bulimia nervosa, although binge eating disorders are nearly equally common in both young men and women (Schmidt et al., 2016). Alongside this is a major concern about the prevalence of eating disorders, especially in high-income countries. Questions are being asked: is this linked to the broad socio-cultural factors that are framing the body and health, which tend to reward highly individualized approaches to controlling the body's appearance?

Issues of poor body image and its impact on young people's identities can also be seen in discussions about obesity. Obesity is a generalized health concern across populations in Western societies. Sociologists highlight numerous contextual factors related to the 'obesity epidemic', namely the historical, cultural and social dimensions framing the issue. For example, in the UK, USA and Australia, rates of obesity are patterned not simply by individual behaviours but by broader socio-economic factors, with those most socio-economically disadvantaged having the highest rates (Bissell et al., 2016). The broader social changes that have affected living and working conditions and food production over the past century are also important contextual issues framing the issue of obesity beyond individualizing and stigmatizing understandings of obesity as a 'choice' and thus a moral failing. As Deborah Lupton has argued, 'in contemporary Western societies, the fat body has become a focus of stigmatizing discourses and practices aimed at disciplining, normalising and containing it' (Lupton, 2013, p. 13). In the current emphasis on health, fat bodies are often demonized and subjected to discrimination and shaming. Lupton's analysis shows that fat people are viewed as 'objects of pity and contempt'. However, social epidemiological studies have shown that fatness is patterned by socio-economic inequalities, rather than resting solely on individual characteristics such as appetite. Poor urban planning and design, such as housing developments that require inhabitants to drive rather than walk to shops and services, and lack of footpaths, are two significant social and structural contributing factors. In addition, the lowest income postcodes in Australia have 2.5 times more fast food restaurants per person than the highest income postcodes (Thornton et al., 2016, p. 2).

These structural factors affecting body mass index are not the dominant focus in interventions to address the 'obesity epidemic'. Instead, popular discourse focusses on the need for individuals to make better 'choices' in their food and exercise habits. The key strand connecting issues of poor body image and obesity is the significance of the body's appearance as a marker of worth or value and an object of control in advanced consumer societies such as the UK, the USA, Australia and New Zealand.

It is also thought that obesity is connected to the dramatic changes over the past century in consumption practices, such as the growth of fast food and the changing working and living conditions for those who are most socio-economically disadvantaged.

Youth mental health and suicide

Mental health is recognized as a major health issue for young people. It has now become one of the most significant concerns globally (Landstedt and Coffey, 2017), regardless of differences in countries' wealth and level of 'development'. There is growing awareness of the need to address youth mental health in order to reduce the rates of suicide. Additional knowledge and investment in youth mental health is critical because suicide is the leading cause of mortality for young people across the world (Patton et al., 2009). Although it is difficult to compare young people's wellbeing outcomes across countries because of the lack of age-disaggregated data, some studies have shown that mental health conditions of depression and anxiety have a high prevalence in both wealthy, developed countries such as Australia and in those classified as 'less developed' and 'least developed' (Vikram Patel et al., 2007).

Thinking points

- Why do you think young people have the highest levels of mental illness and suicide?
- What social factors might be causing this?

In Australia, suicide is the leading cause of death for young people aged 15–24 (Australian Bureau of Statistics, 2017). In 2015, suicide accounted for one-third of deaths (33.9 per cent) among people 15–24 years of age. While it is the leading cause of death for all young people in Australia, the rates are higher among young men than young women. In 2015, suicide accounted for 13.9 per 100,000 young men aged 15–19 compared with 6.9 for young women. In the 20–24 age bracket, this number increased dramatically for young men (to 22.2 per 100,000), while staying almost the same for young women (6.3). These figures represent a ten-year high in the rate of youth suicide in Australia.

Indigenous Australians experience persistently poorer health outcomes for their entire lives in comparison with non-Indigenous Australians. One of the most stark examples of Indigenous health inequality is in the rates of intentional self-harm and suicide among Indigenous children and young people (Australian Bureau of Statistics, 2017). For example, self-harm among young Indigenous people aged 15–24 years is 5.2 times the rate of non-Indigenous young people (Dudgeon et al., 2014). The rate of suicide for Indigenous youth aged 15–24 is almost four times higher than non-Indigenous youth (Australian Bureau of Statistics, 2017). Youth mental health advocates and Indigenous leaders have called for the need to increase efforts to support young people with mental health issues in light of these tragic statistics. Recent 'Closing the Gap' reports are scathing of recent cuts to Indigenous youth services, arguing 'The provision of mental health services for Indigenous people is both inadequate and inappropriate, and changes need to be implemented immediately' (Dudgeon et al., 2014, p. 2). Structural inequalities therefore cause youth in marginalized social categories, including Indigenous status, low socio-economic status, gender, ethnicity, race and sexuality, to be more likely to suffer poor mental health (Landstedt and Coffey, 2017). This is because marginalized social categories are associated with greater social stress (Aneshensel, 2009). In other words, social inequalities can be understood to cause an individual greater stress, contributing to poor mental health.

Poor mental health is also patterned by gender, with girls and young women reporting higher levels of poor mental health (particularly anxiety and depressive symptoms) than boys/young men (Bremberg, 2015; Fergusson et al., 2007). However, rates of suicide are higher amongst young men. These patterns persist over time, and into adulthood (Patton et al., 2014). This can be understood in relation to the structural and cultural circumstances stemming from gender norms of masculinity (Landstedt et al., 2009), such as the expectation that men are 'strong and silent' when it comes to emotions and showing vulnerability. This dimension of masculinity can be particularly harmful in relation to young men's mental health and wellbeing as it can severely impact the likelihood of seeking help. Further, in relation to sexuality, young people who identify as lesbian, gay, bisexual, transgender, queer or intersex (LGBTQI+) are also shown to suffer poorer mental health outcomes due to discrimination and harassment (Grossman and D'augelli, 2006). In relation to socio-economic status, mental health generally follows the same social gradient pattern as physical health; that is, the poor and disadvantaged suffer disproportionately from mental health problems (Allen et al., 2014). A study of young Australians combining study with work found that financial hardship was a key factor contributing to significant stress and poor mental health (Landstedt et al., 2016).

Peer and family relationships can be both 'stressors' causing stress and poor mental health, and potential 'protective factors' in providing support, which contributes to positive mental health (Woodman, 2012). Exposure to harassment (including bullying and sexual harassment) is also a key contributor to poor mental health (Landstedt et al., 2009). Exposure to bullying and harassment can have long-term consequences in youth and early adulthood, and impacts the mental wellbeing of young people whether they suffer it themselves or witness it (Landstedt and Gillander Gådin, 2011). It is also important to acknowledge that perpetration of harassment and other types of violence are connected to unequal gendered power relations. Sexualized components of bullying, such as sexual harassment and abuse, are common (Nielsen and Einarsen, 2012). This is particularly relevant in the 'social media age' where young women continue to be positioned as the gate-keepers of male sexual advances in relation to moral panics surrounding '**sexting**' (Albury and Crawford, 2012).

> **Sexting:** The exchange of sexual images or messages on social media.

Mental health, cyberbullying and sexting in the digital age

'Cyberbullying' and online harassment have become an important dimension of understanding contemporary youth mental health issues. As we showed in Chapters 6 and 9, it is difficult to know how prevalent it is. Cyberbullying has been analyzed as both an extension and intensification of traditional bullying (offline) (Angus, 2016). That is, the same bully can harass a person at school, and then continue beyond the school grounds in an online environment. This aspect means that the negative impacts of cyberbullying are also magnified, causing severe mental harm. A number of cases have documented a connection between experiencing severe cyberbullying and suicide. Cyberbullying can also have gendered and sexualized dimensions related to coercive sexting. Ringrose et al. (2012) found that young women were pressured into sending pictures, then punished socially through unequal sexual double standards. **Sexualization** is a double-edged sword for young women in a context where overt sexual display is encouraged yet rigidly policed, and quickly stigma- tizes, shames and punishes young women deemed 'too sexual' (see Laverty, 2017).

> **Sexualization:** Social and cultural gender norms which frame young people as particular negative sexual objects.

How can we understand the increase in poor mental health?

Youth sociology literature points to two contemporary structural conditions that have impacted the lives and wellbeing of the contemporary generation of young people in the UK, USA and Australia: changes to education systems and the labour market. It is now an expectation that young people gain a post-secondary qualification in order to be competitive in increasingly globalized labour markets. At the same time, there is increasingly less employment security for the current generation of youth than ever before (Andres and Wyn, 2010; Furlong and Cartmel, 2007; Woodman, 2012). This has led to new categories of marginalized youth being created, including the underem- ployed and overeducated (ILO, 2013).

These changes are highly likely to contribute to increased levels of stress in young people. It has been found that worries about academic achievements have increased in teenagers, especially among girls (West and Sweeting, 2003). In general, studies of young people's transitions through education and into work reveal that they frequently experi- ence the stress of economic hardship (Furstenberg et al., 2004). In addition, insecure employment such as casual work or short-term contracts, which is common in young adults, is associated with elevated levels of psychological distress (Woodman, 2012; Wyn et al., 2015). Youth unemployment is another crucial dimension impacting mental health. Unemployment in young adulthood can have a scarring effect and shows persis- tent association with poor mental health across the life course (Brydsten et al., 2015). Rising levels of unemployment and the increased expectations of gaining a tertiary degree also create highly stressful conditions for the contemporary generation of youth (Landstedt et al., 2009). Academic pressure is a risk factor for mental health problems, especially in girls and young women (Landstedt and Gillander Gådin, 2012). The double burden of economic hardship for many university students has been shown to be par- ticularly stressful and negative for the mental health of young adults (Wyn et al., 2015).

In general, studies of young people's transitions through education and into work reveal that they frequently experience the stress of economic hardship (Furstenberg et al., 2004). In addition, insecure employment such as casual work or short-term contracts, which is common in young adults, is associated with elevated levels of psychological distress (Wyn et al., 2015). Unemployment in young adulthood can have a scarring effect and shows persistent association with poor mental and psychosomatic health across the life course (Brydsten et al., 2015). For example, MacDonald and Shildrick (2012) explored the impact of young people's experiencing bereavement on their wellbeing and transitions. Drawing on a longitudinal study in the North of England, it showed that one of

the major impacts of bereavement, especially when exp
tion area, was depression. Such 'critical moments' a'
lems for young people, delaying or restricting the'
They were able to show that events such as these h
They were not simply fate, or young people being a
the context in which they were living (of poverty and inte.
impact on their wellbeing and abilities to manage their lives. .
further increased by the '… spatially concentrated, class-based ineq
are lived by young people' (p. 157)

Mental health and help-seeking

'**Help-seeking**' for mental health issues is identified as one of the primary ways of alleviating mental health concerns for young people. Though most mental health issues arise between the ages of 12 and 25, unfortunately, this age group is the least likely to access mental health services. It is critical that young people are able to access treatment and assistance at this time when it is most needed (Rickwood, 2015). Australian studies of high school and university students have shown that those

> **Help-seeking:**
> Seeking professional assistance for mental health concerns; usually from a doctor, who then makes a mental health plan and refers to a psychologist or psychiatrist.

who suffer more severe symptoms of mental illness are the least likely to seek assistance (Ciarrochi et al., 2002). Those who do not seek assistance are also the most at risk of developing lifelong mental health problems (Rickwood et al., 2005). Many young people say they would prefer not to seek help at all for personal, emotional and suicide-related problems (Wilson et al., 2005).

Being willing to reach out to a friend or family member, teacher, or even a sports coach, can be a crucial first step in getting the professional services many young people need (Rickwood et al., 2005). The important next step is to visit a doctor, who can then refer to specialist mental health services and counsellors. A study of secondary school students in Australia found that mental health was viewed as the 'most personal' health issue; one that can be extremely difficult to seek help for from anyone, including doctors. As one year-ten student in the study said, 'It is the most personal thing – more difficult to talk about with a doctor than sex' (Cahill and Coffey, 2013). The study highlighted 'the importance of addressing the social discourses that confine help-seeking, the most significant being fear of negative judgement and consequent social stigma' (Cahill and Coffey, 2013, p. 12). Reducing the social stigma associated with mental health is widely viewed as pivotal in improving the capacity for young people to seek help. This is important because seeking help is understood as a critical element, which can reduce the prevalence of poor mental health, and in turn, the rate of suicide that accompanies it.

Gender, sexuality and mental health help-seeking

Help-seeking has a gendered profile, with young women seeking help more readily than young men (Rickwood et al., 2005). The dominant discourse of masculinity stresses the importance of self-reliance, independence, stoicism and emotional strength. Men who emulate a traditionally masculine ideology are less likely to be willing to seek help for physical or mental health problems (Gorski, 2010), as help-seeking viewed as threatening to one's self-esteem and independence (Raviv et al., . There are additional barriers to help-seeking for young people in regional and areas, which include difficulties accessing services due to geography, cost and nsport (Crockett, 2012) as well as sociocultural barriers, such as a heightened fear of loss of anonymity and a stronger ethos of self-reliance (Rughani et al., 2011). In remote and rural Australian communities, reluctance to acknowledge mental health problems, social stigma and a view that equates mental illness with 'insanity' are additional factors that can deter help-seeking (Boyd et al., 2007).

Many LGBTIQ+ young people also experience poorer mental health outcomes than their peers. This is due to suffering from stigma, prejudice, discrimination and abuse from others on the basis of being LGBTI. LGBTI youth also experience additional barriers in accessing health services. A study by Byron et al. (2017) found barriers included fears of homophobia, transphobia and other discriminations, judgemental responses to one's situation or identity, gendered assumptions, concerns around confidentiality, and difficulties with trusting health professionals. There is increasing recognition of the need for progressive gender and sexuality policy in health and education to address the causes of homophobia and discrimination. A key recommendation from Byron et al.'s (2017) study was that health and mental health services should be visibly welcoming and accepting of young people who are LGBTIQ. They suggest services can signal their commitment to LGBTIQ diversity, and open, respectful communication through a number of ways, including service intake forms, websites and administration systems.

💬 Summary

- We must be careful not to assume that we see the health of young people simply through the lens of the Global North. This represents only 10 per cent of the world's youth population.

- Theorizing health and wellbeing has been dominated by a biomedical model of health that locates health problems as individual. This can create a discourse of blame.

- A social model of health recognizes the structural and social inequalities that impact on a person's health.

- One of the major areas of research on young people's health has been on the body. This has shown how bodies are central to young people's health and wellbeing.

- Young people's mental health and suicide have also become major issues across a wide range of countries.

- As young people struggle to cope in a demanding world, where transitions are not simple, linear or secure, and failure is not seen as acceptable, young people's mental health is consistently under pressure.

- Getting support is critical for young people who are struggling with their mental health. Historically many services have not been available or appropriate.

Exercise: The sociological imagination

What do you think is the most important health issue for the current generation of young people? What challenges do young people face that could be affecting their health? Use the sociological imagination to think about the social, cultural and structural aspects framing it.

Key readings

Bourke, L. & Geldens, P. (2007) 'What does wellbeing mean?: perspectives of wellbeing among young people & youth workers in rural Victoria', *Youth Studies Australia*, vol. 26, no. 1, p. 41.

Cahill, H. (2015) 'Approaches to understanding youth wellbeing' in Wyn, J. & Cahill, H. (eds.) *Handbook of Youth and Childhood Studies* (New York: Springer).

Coffey, J. (2016) *Body Work: Youth, Gender and Health* (London: Routledge).

Hagell, A., Shah, R., Viner, R., Hargreaves, D., Varnes, L. & Heys, M. (2018) *The Social Determinants of Young People's Health: Identifying the Key Issues and Assessing How Young People Are Doing in the 2010s*. Health Foundation Working Paper (London: Health Foundation).

Kelly, P. & Pike, J. (2017) *Neo-Liberalism, Austerity and the Moral Economies of Young People's Health and Well-Being* (London: Palgrave Macmillan).

Landstedt, E. & Gillander Gådin, K. (2012) 'Seventeen and stressed – do gender and class matter?', *Health Sociology Review*, vol. 21, no. 1, pp. 82–98.

11 YOUTH, CITIZENSHIP, BELONGING AND MOBILITIES

In this chapter you will learn about:

- The growing influence of citizenship studies on youth sociology
- How 'belonging' is used as a concept for understanding how young people mediate the circumstances of their lives
- Patterns of migration and mobility, which are becoming central to understanding young people's lives
- How mobilities are shaping education and employment patterns
- The significance of mobilities and migration in young people's identities
- The contested nature of the concept of citizenship as it applies to young people and its relationship with belonging and migration.

Youth and citizenship

💭 Thinking points

- What does it mean to you to be 'a citizen', and what are the things that make you feel that you belong?

In the late 1980s, the question of citizenship became a major subject of discussion within sociology (Turner, 1986; Barbalet, 1988). This raised significant questions over what citizenship meant for young people (Jones and Wallace, 1992; France, 1998). Jones and Wallace (1992) argued that the normative discussions on citizenship focussed on adult rights and responsibilities in relation to the state but questions remained as to how this related to young people due to their lack of rights and status. Early youth sociology, like mainstream sociology, engaged in a process of critique and reflection about the usefulness of the concept to understand young people's lives. There has also been a growing interest in citizenship education and how young people can become 'good citizens', undertaking their civic responsibilities and duties (Welsh and Black, 2018). We explore some of the critiques and debates about the usefulness of citizenship as a concept in the next section.

What is citizenship?

The conventional understanding of citizenship is that it 'is a status bestowed on all those who are full members of a community' (Marshall, 1950, p. 28). Emphasizing a social rights-based approach, Marshall (1950) held that all citizens should have 'the right to a modicum of economic welfare and security [and] the right to share to the full in the social heritage and to live the life of a civilized being according to the standards prevailing in the society.' This 'status' emphasized that citizens not only have rights, but that they are also active participants bound by responsibilities and obligations. Increasingly, attention has been paid to an expanded conceptualization of citizenship that includes 'civic engagement, identity, belonging, place, and well-being' (Smith, 2014, p. 358). However, the exact nature of citizenship varies across time and place, and is complicated further by the transformation and increased diversification of communities in times of globalization and heightened migration.

🗨 Thinking points

- What do you think is meant by 'the lived experience' of citizenship?
- How do you think young people might 'negotiate' citizenship and with whom?

Crucially, these definitions have conventionally linked citizenship with adulthood status and thus left young people under the age of majority seen as 'citizens in the making' (Jones and Wallace, 1992; Thomson et al., 2004). This is complicated further by the variety of rights and responsibilities that are bestowed at an array of ages, not just across nation states, but also within them. Young people in Australia and the UK, for example, might have the right to vote at 18, but they can be held (at least partly) responsible for criminality from age 10; they are obliged to be in some form of education until age 18, have no right to full adult minimum wages until they are over 21, and no right to full welfare benefits until at least the age of 25 (see Chapter 1).

Nonetheless, and as we have made clear in this book, the notion of adulthood is now very different compared with previous generations. As Wood (2017, p. 1186) helpfully comments,

> changing patterns of young people's life trajectories have meant that the period of youth is extended beyond that of previous generations with clear implications for the status, recognition, participation and sense of belonging in society.

A major issue here is that, despite these changes, citizenship is all too often discussed as something that is in 'the future' of young people's lives, perhaps related to reaching the voting age and achieving economic independence (Wood, 2017). As Hart (2009) suggests, '... Indeed, in defining young people as not yet-citizens they are, in effect, excluded not just from the formal rights of citizenship, but also from being treated with equality in terms of membership in society' (p. 642). Understanding and indeed encouraging young people's relationship with citizenship also demands a focus on the present (Lister, 2007; Thomson et al., 2004). Youth scholars argue that attention to what young people can already do to participate as citizens in contemporary democratic societies is critical. Even very young children are active meaning makers who actively engage in their world, and can therefore be seen as citizens already. In this sense we have to recognize that citizenship is a 'lived experience' (Smith, 2005), and understand the dynamic and temporal nature of what being a citizen might mean (Wood, 2017). As Isin (2008, p. 7) reminds us, 'critical studies of citizenship over the last two decades have taught us that what is important is not only that citizenship is a legal status but that it also involves practices of making citizens – social, political, cultural and symbolic'.

While a growing body of work has emerged that focusses attention on the lived experience of citizenship, the concept as a way of analyzing the lives of young people has been critiqued for its inability to capture the diversity of experience of young people (Wood, 2017). It has also been seen as problematic in that, in a changing society, it struggles to understand or explain the diversity of ways young people participate and the different spaces they are active in, such as digital spaces and places (see Buckingham et al., 2014).

Bronwyn Wood (2017) also suggested that the concept of citizenship has similar problems to transitions studies:

> a key message that integrates both bodies of literature is that narrow, linear notions of citizenship and transition fixed on age, or markers of 'adulthood' inadequately capture the complexity and heterogeneity of what it means to be young today. (Wood, 2017, p. 1181)

As a result, she suggested a focus on a more flexible notion of youth citizenship that recognizes the way young people negotiate with their families, their peers and the institutions of wider society. Such an approach needs to be more dynamic and embedded in a temporal understanding of citizenship.

Dominant discourses of youth citizenship

Historically, there are two dominant discourses surrounding young people's citizenship that have been central to public and political narratives. These situate young people as either **'civically deficit** and disengaged citizens' or 'the creators of new democratic modes and approaches' (Walsh et al., 2018, p. 218). The notion of 'civically deficit and disengaged citizens' has had two major responses. Firstly, a number of governments, particularly in Western countries, have developed policies and practices that draw upon this discourse to shape social policy. What we see is that it operates to shift the balance in debates about youth, policy and citizenship towards responsibilities and obligations, away from rights, suggesting that a clear linkage needs to exist between 'rights and benefits'. Part of the deficit in young people's social practice arises because of their passive, dependent belief in entitlements in their relationship as citizens. This approach took significant hold in the policies of 'New' Labour in the UK and can be seen most clearly in the work of the Tony Blair government from 1998.

Civically deficit: the opposite to civically active or engaged. A state in which young people are seen as not undertaking their civic duties.

As Hart explains (2009), the notion of citizenship was built upon concerns that rights had overshadowed obligations, that there needed to be understandings of a common set of values, and that the idea of 'active citizenship' in the shape of volunteering needed to be reinvigorated. This was claimed to be a 'new' contract between the state and its citizens, yet in reality it was a form of citizenship that was conditional on behaviour:

> For too long the demand for rights from the state was separated from the duties of citizenship and the imperative for mutual responsibility [...] Strong communities depend on shared values and a recognition of the rights and duties of citizenship – not just the duty to pay taxes and obey the law, but the obligation to bring up children as competent, responsible citizens. (Blair, 1998, quoted in Morrisson, 2004, p. 173)

In this process, parenting and those young people seen as a 'problem' became a central focus in policies. For example, paid work and good parenting became an obligation, and failure to do either (or both) brought sanctions such as the removal of rights. In this context, policies shifted towards removing young people's benefits for not taking paid work and parents being fined for failing to control their children (Hart, 2009). As this set of policies unfolded, Blair's government also introduced the 'respect agenda' (Respect Task Force, 2006) that targeted anti-social behaviour amongst the young, resulting in increased criminalization for minor offences (France, 2017).

A second strand of the deficit discourse was the expansion of 'citizenship education'. The exact composition and delivery of this varies from country to country and sometimes from state to state, but there has been a significant evolution in the content of the delivery of citizenship education. Curricula now often supplement attention to formal civic responsibilities (such as the importance of voting in national-level elections) with a focus on respecting cultural diversity, value differences and issues such as social inclusion, sustainability, migration and the prospect of being a global citizen. Nonetheless, a common critique of the 'citizenship education' agenda is that it operates from a position of understanding young people as being in deficit, although some point out how curricula can start from the position of seeing young people as legitimate social actors who contribute to society both now and in the future (see Smith, 2014). However, the origins and motivations for recent turns to teaching citizenship from around the late 1990s stem from an unmistakable concern with anti-social behaviour and young people's disengagement from education, employment and, ultimately, formal democratic processes (Pontes et al., 2019).

For example, young people's perceived lack of civic engagement has been fundamentally challenged by many academic studies, leading Harris and Wyn (2010, p. 4) to lament that 'the deficit lies in the imaginations and perspectives of researchers and policymakers and in the failure to adjust governance processes to changing times'. One of the major challenges comes from findings that suggest young people are measured against an adult-centric conception of citizenship, which is problematically narrowly defined (Wood, 2017). There is a lack of attention to the ways that young people participate in society in different spaces, such as online (Vromen et al., 2015) or in their everyday lives (Harris et al., 2010), which led Wood (2017, p. 1180) to suggest that 'more expansive, inclusive and youth centred definitions of what it means to be a young citizen are required'.

Young people and 'everyday' political engagement

Anita Harris and her colleagues' (2010) study of more than 900 Australian young people helps us to better understand the narrow nature of the adult-centric conception of citizenship. Studying young people described as neither politically apathetic nor spectacularly 'anti state' protesters, the researchers argued that these young people were not lacking knowledge or in civic deficit, but instead were 'disenchanted with traditional politics that is unresponsive to their needs and interests' (2010, p. 10). Beyond this, issues pertaining to civic engagement loomed large in their everyday behaviours. The researchers found young people commonly sought to participate, shape or reflect on their social and political worlds through recycling, donating money to a cause, signing petitions, discussing social and political issues, making statements through art, music and writing, and listening to political music. These are not spectacular forms of political engagement but all represent 'simple, personal and everyday ways to express political views without requiring funds, collective or party engagement or a relationship with formal political apparatus' (Harris et al., 2010, p. 24). An interesting issue that emerged in this research was that young women were far more likely than men to have engaged in all these modes of political engagement.

The second key discourse on young people and civic life is one that stems from academic research. Walsh et al. (2018, p. 219) explain that a body of work has 'suggested for some years that many young people are seeking new modes and approaches to citizenship in ways that circumvent or challenge conventional political institutions, organisations and ideologies'. This formulation of young people taking on the old guard and 'winning' by reconfiguring conventional politics is somewhat overly optimistic. Several researchers have raised caution about how the 'young people can do anything' motif that runs through these accounts risks leaving young people unsupported and further alienated (Wierenga et al., 2003). Such accounts also overlook, as noted in the box above on young people and 'everyday' political engagement, the ordinary everyday ways that young people engage in acts to shape their worlds, but which fall far short of transforming the political realm as constructed by adults. Relatedly, Walsh et al. (2018) have shown how, for example, young people are at once motivated to act but simultaneously aware of their relative powerlessness to produce genuine change. Their research points to how people become social entrepreneurs or volunteers to challenge the status quo, but feel that '… simply being a young person limited their potential influence because expectations of their ability to contribute to society were as low as the opportunities to do so' (Walsh et al., 2018, p. 229).

Where citizenship approaches to youth tend to be adult-centric, other concepts have been developed in youth sociology in an effort to understand the specific, lived dimensions of young people's everyday lives. 'Belonging' has become a central concept in youth sociology and is explored in the section below.

Belonging

💭 Thinking points

- What do we mean by 'belonging' – what makes you feel you 'belong' in your environment?
- How might youth 'transitions' be re-imagined through a framework of 'belonging'?

Belonging has become an important concept used for understanding the complex dynamics between young people's lives and the broad, generational social changes explored throughout this book, which influence contemporary youth: education and 'transitions', and cultural practices. It has, as we shall see later, also been important in studies of migration. Wyn (2015) defines 'belonging' as a 'relational concept', meaning it is always produced in relation to other people and places, and its meaning must be examined in that context. Belonging 'is a product of the relationships between people, place and mobility' (Wyn, 2015). Belonging is seen as a way of understanding the significance of young people's social attachments and interpersonal, spatial and geographical connections in the ongoing formation of identities, and the (constrained) 'choices' they make throughout their lives. Belonging is a conceptual framework, which aims to make clearer the ways that young people attempt to remain connected to people, places and issues that matter to them, as well as their relationship to the times in which they live.

Bridging 'transitions' and 'cultures' perspectives

This turn to the concept of 'belonging' in youth sociology cuts across theoretical debates about whether 'transitions' or 'cultures' or 'citizenship' perspectives provide the best tools for understanding young people's lives and the conditions they live in. For example, this framework is suggested as an alternative to traditional approaches for understanding young people's trajectories between education and employment. This is seen as important, given how messy and unpredictable these patterns have become in young people's lives, and given the increasing trend in young people's global mobility across countries and contexts (see below). As a concept it aims to disrupt the simplistic and linear notion of youth as a phase of life that can be 'transitioned' out of, instead shifting to focus on 'the nature and quality of connections between young people and their worlds' as significant for understanding the dynamics and constraints of young people's lives (Cuervo and Wyn, 2014, p. 905). Because belonging is fundamentally about understanding young people's connections and affinities, it adds an important tool for explaining how young people negotiate and experience the conditions of education and the labour market. Approaching 'transitions' using this lens adds detail about how the structural factors of economic systems and institutions mediate young people's decisions in these contexts, and how inequalities shape these 'decisions' in the first place.

The concept of belonging is therefore seen as a particularly useful way of understanding those who have been positioned outside of traditional 'transition' narratives, such as Indigenous Australian youth. It has been shown that inter-generational patterns of disadvantage can act as barriers to educational opportunity and achievement for Indigenous youth, and transition approaches are not able to adequately respond to the significance of these forces shaping many Indigenous young people's experiences. (Cuervo et al., 2015). A focus on belonging can instead make the connections and constraints visible in young Indigenous peoples' engagements with education (Cuervo et al., 2015). It recognizes connections and relationships and how these operate in marginalized social groups' access to, and experience of, education and employment. This lens prioritizes the importance of Indigenous people's histories and cultures and their connection to the land and people. Its focus on connections, cultures and history 'challenges normative policy assumptions of what a transition to adulthood means and/or should look like' (Cuervo et al., 2015, p. 28). Other specific recommendations regarding young Indigenous people's engagements with education and employment need to be reframed to include:

> The need to be attentive to Clan specificity when looking at Indigenous youth, the need for institutional and community consultation and collaboration, the need for affirmation of the validity of other ways of lives beyond what policies prescribe, the need for teachers trained to be pedagogically culturally attentive and responsive, and the need for greater institutional cultural awareness and education in training and employment programs. (Cuervo et al., 2015, p. 28)

In this way, the concept of belonging can be seen to offer a way of theorizing youth 'in context', aligning with Connell's (2007) call for theorizing 'from below', rather than importing concepts from the Global North, which may be inadequate for addressing the issue at hand.

Harris (2016) also suggests that 'belonging' is a key dimension of discussions on youth cultures and subcultures research. The strength of attachment to particular subcultural groups is theorized as a key element in considering whether or not subcultures remain the most relevant way of understanding young people's non-mainstream cultural engagements. For example, the concept of neo-tribes that we encountered in Chapter 5 suggests that young people's sense of affinity or 'belonging' to particular groups is now more transient than in previous times; that it no longer 'hardens' into strict categories of identification as in the original CCCS studies of youth subcultures.

The notion of belonging is also being used in young people's usage of social media and the emergence of online cultures. Online spaces can be understood as 'newly mediated forms of belonging' in which on- and offline spaces intersect and overlap (Robards, 2014, p. 27). The concept also tends to resist conceptual binaries in making sense of young people's lives and the entangled contexts of global and local or on- and offline. Young people actively negotiate and shape identities through their connections, affinities and belongings online. For example, Fu's (2018) study of Chinese young people's performance of identities through Weibo and WeChat shows how identity and belonging is actively demonstrated through sharing life moments, posting or forwarding content aligned with their interests and performing their values through commenting on social and political issues. Contemporary studies of young people's cultures use belonging as a way to study the performance and process of identity construction. It can be seen as performative and is about 'doing', or it is something felt, and done, through the body in much the same way as we described in Chapter 2, through Butler's theory of gender performativity (see Bell, 1999). Belonging can be enacted to be felt. It is deeply personal yet emphatically social because the options for belonging are always a product of the socio-cultural context we find ourselves in.

MyTribe: post-subcultural manifestations of belonging on social network sites

This study explored young people's sociality occurring on social network sites such as Facebook, and how young people use these sites to produce reflexive identities and navigate 'belonging'. The authors found young people's engagements online can be read as aligned with 'partial' forms of belonging and more fluid forms of identity, similar to those found in the concept of neo-tribes. Forms of 'belonging' articulated online by young people in this study were shifting and multiple, rather than 'belonging' to one particular 'identity' group. Robards and Bennett write 'Rather than organizing their system(s) of belonging around a particular taste or style (exemplified by the goths in Hodkinson's work) the participants in this study from a general sample of young people on the Gold Coast, Australia, appear to conceptualize their own sense of belonging in a much more multiplicitous (yet, interestingly, simultaneously persistent), interconnected, fluid and individual-centred way' (p. 313). They argue that identity and belonging are performed in online spaces in ways that exceed the terms and concepts provided by the subculture/post-subculture debate. Young people here showed a 'partial' sense of belonging, or belonging to multiple categories, rather than strict or enduring identification with particular identity groupings. At the same time, however, the networks of sociality for young people endure beyond online spaces to engage with the same people and identifications in offline networks and spaces.

A new agenda of research for youth sociology

As we can see, the concept of belonging has a wide range of applications and areas of focus in youth sociology. Its attention to the quality and context of young people's connections means it is being used as a lens for studying almost any dimension of their lives, particularly family and peer relationships; place and space attachments; affinity with identity categories; and consumption and youth cultural practices. It has also been used in trying to understand the experience of multicultural Australian youth and ties between community, place and national identity (Harris, 2013). As a framework it aims to 'expand the youth agenda from the policy emphasis on education and employment participation into issues of social relationships, health, wellbeing, place, culture, and inter-generational relations' (Cuervo et al., 2015, p. 25). In the process, it enables a focus on the dynamics of constraints and opportunities that shape young people's lives, rather than the narrow focus and interest in youth as 'conforming' or 'non-conforming' as related to educational and employment outcomes only, which tend to dominate youth policy. It can therefore be a useful as an analytical tool when paired with a focus on inequalities and power relations. It can perhaps be seen as a way of studying the mechanics of these relations as they play out in young people's specific contexts. Class theorist Pierre Bourdieu's body of work can be seen as studying how individuals 'belong' to families and communities and how deeply ingrained class affinities are in the body through habitus.

While belonging has been gaining substantial interest as an analytical tool in youth sociology, its usefulness as a 'replacement' for youth transitions, and its ability to shift the lens is still being debated. What is evident and critical in these debates is that, when focussing on young people's relationships with belonging, we also give attention to how it is produced within the social, institutional and economic dynamics that operate to create and reproduce inequalities. Recognizing that belonging is a social construct that has a part to play in both producing and reproducing inequalities in young people's lives is essential if it is to make a growing contribution to our understanding of young people's lives.

Youth on the move

Mobilities – the new norm?

In simple terms, mobility refers to movement, or 'to be mobile'. It is a common-sense word that is used to describe many different phenomena in everyday lives, such that researchers think about mobility as being 'the systematic movements of people for work and family life, for leisure and pleasure, and for politics and protest' (Sheller and Urry, 2006, p. 208). The '**new mobilities paradigm**', outlined by Sheller and Urry in 2006, is a well-cited call to social scientists to privilege contemporary conditions of movement and the impacts these have on how we understand, describe and theorize modern society. They provide a framework to help make sense of the multiple, large-scale and growing movements, including not just people, but also information and materials. 'Mobilities' refers to movement in all forms, for instance walking and driving, as well as transnational movement. They claim different forms of mobilities are in 'fluid interdependence' (Sheller and Urry, 2006, p. 212) and cannot be arbitrarily divided. It is claimed that previous social science work is 'a-mobile' and has ignored the wide-scale movement that we see today. Sheller and Urry (2006) challenge theory based on 'sedentarism (that) treats as normal stability, meaning, and place, and treats as abnormal distance, change, and placelessness.' They are critical of what they see as the deep-seated assumption that to be rooted in place, or to be stationary, is the launching point of most research (Sheller and Urry, 2006).

> **New mobilities paradigm:** Introduced in the 1990s, this paradigm argued that the issue of mobility was a significant feature of modern society and therefore social science should be giving more attention to it when examining people's lives.

🗨 Thinking point

What factors can you think of that might have led youth to be more 'mobile' than ever before?

In their work on youthful migration, Laoire et al. (2010) agree that movement across borders or territories is implicitly understood as non-normative, or as that which deviates from the normal state. By such a reckoning, staying in one place, generally the place that you were born, or that you are 'from' (culturally, ethnically, nationally, where your family are from) is the norm. Anything that deviates from this is necessarily conceived as 'other'. Sheller and Urry do not claim that we live in a world without static borders, but instead propose to go 'beyond the imagery of "terrains" as spatially fixed geographical containers for social processes' (Sheller and Urry, 2006, p. 211). Indeed, for many, migration is not a deviation from the norm, but is a part of everyday realities (Laoire et al., 2010), and there has been a much needed shift 'to a recognition that mobility/movement is not a rupture but part of normal/everyday life' (Skelton, 2013).

Youth and transnational mobility

When applied to talk about young people, mobility can help us understand some key changes that have taken place around how people move. Indeed, the question of youth mobility (or mobilities) has become a central area for youth sociologists who are seeking to understand the dynamic patterns of movement shaping young people's identities in contemporary times. Traditionally, transnational mobilities have been seen as a major form of transition for many young people, yet in this global age, where mobility is becoming a central feature of young people's lives, such a model is seen as problematic:

> Mobile transitions' represents a break from traditional ideas of transition. We argue that the increased mobility and aspiration to mobility amongst diverse groups of youth globally problematizes both teleological and sedentarist notions of transition. (Robertson et al., 2018, p. 207)

🗨 Thinking point

How do patterns of migration and mobility between contexts shape young people's education, employment and cultural lives.

As Robertson et al. (2018) go on to argue, the youth studies literature around mobilities tends to focus on mobility as a short-term fix or as a linear model. It fails to grasp the complexity and does not recognize the 'non-linear, reversible, and multi-direction'

(p. 207) nature of transnational mobility. The assumption that transitions are smooth and linear does not account for the contemporary realities of what it is to be young, or an adult, or to be independent in the context of mobility changes across cultural and social contexts. In short, Sheller and Urry's (2006) new mobilities paradigm calls for a greater recognition of mobilities as the norm, rather than a deviation. Cairns (2015) agrees that mobility discussions often intersect theoretically with youth studies approaches that talk about transitions such as leaving full time education, getting a job in the labour market and forming an independent home, family, and relationship, which often result in, or even require, mobilities of some form. Yet transitions studies in youth sociology are seen as not capturing the complex 'mobility requirement' that can now be associated with young people moving into some form of adulthood. While much of the discussion that follows focusses on what is traditionally known as 'migration studies', Robertson et al.'s (2018) use of transnational mobility is a more useful term for thinking about youth mobility. They suggest that a focus on transnational mobility helps capture some of this complexity. As a result, they introduce the idea of 'mobility transitions', which focusses on transitions rather than a transition, seeing them

> ... as a variety of continuous and overlapping processes of transformation and change to identity, opportunity and relationships, enacted through the mundane practices of making a life .... (p. 209)

Such a view is in line with the critique of transitions that we encountered in Chapter 1.

While much of the discussion that follows is focussed on transnational mobility, we also want to bring into focus the issues of internal movements or forms of mobility that exist *within nation states*, for example, from rural to urban, or from one city to another. As we saw in Chapter 7, different policies, laws and structures within nation states can shape and frame people's lives and their movements. Such movements have a bearing on young people's experience of their transition through education and employment and their journey through youth more broadly. Mobility also has implications for young people's citizenship, their sense of belonging and their social, interpersonal, spatial and geographical connections, which in turn are bound up with the way young identities are formed and lived.

Dismantling the home–host dualism

A key discussion about mobility studies concerns how the starting point and the end point are conceptualized. Migration studies have traditionally understood this as a smooth and linear movement from site A to site B, yet the ways in which we think about these 'sites' has changed over time. Understandably, movement across borders and territories necessarily elicits discussion about home and host. While simplistic approaches to understandings of home and host as a binary have been heavily criticized (see for example Robertson et al., 2018), such thinking endures as a common way to conceptualize migration pathways. Discussion about migration tends to differentiate between 'countries of origin' and 'countries of destination', even if it is rarely so straightforward (Triandafyllidou, 2015).

In the case of young people and children, the ways in which a sense of home is conceptualized, and, in particular, the capacity of place to become an idealized, unchanging container for nostalgia, are important to understand. The nature of 'home' is invariably in flux, and this is especially evident in the case of migration. Thinking about what 'home' means is important in discussions about leaving, arriving and belonging. There is therefore a need to 'question the binaries of home/not-at-home and rootedness/rootlessness' (Laoire et al., 2010, p. 160) and for us to focus on:

> ... the situated and contextualized nature of migrant children's negotiations of home and belonging. In other words, while 'home' is not simply viewed as a private domestic space, or a national space, neither is it simply an abstract or deterritorialized site of interaction. (Laoire et al., 2010, p. 159)

Home can be a concrete set of familial relations, and practices across boundaries and territories. As we learnt in Chapter 7 on space and place, place is necessarily more than a material environment; it is also about relationships. In the context of migration what matters is how migrants, especially young people, negotiate their relationship to the idea of 'home' in the 'host' country (Laoire et al., 2010).

Youth and transnational mobility

One major trend that has emerged in relation to transnational mobility has been the international movement of young people across borders as they migrate from one country to another. As we have identified, this is not a simple process and can involve a wide range of movements that are not always captured by large data sets. There has been a massive increase over the last 30 years of people migrating to other parts of the world. For example, the number of international migrants worldwide grew from 154 million in 1990 to 175 million in 2000, 232 million in 2013 and 257 million in 2017. Within this, young people are more likely to migrate than older people, with those aged 15 to 24 increasing from 22.4 million in 1990 to 27.9 million in 2017. Young migrants therefore accounted for 10.8 per cent of the total migrant population. There are significant gender differences, in that young men are more likely to migrate than young women (Cortina et al., 2014). Worldwide, 53.5 per cent of 15- to 24-year-olds who migrate are young men. The main countries that receive migrants are the developed nations, who received approximately 59 per cent of all international migrants, almost half of whom were aged between 15 and 24 (49 per cent) (UN, 2013). The largest numbers of migrants are now living in Asia (10.3 million – 36 per cent), Europe (7.3 million – 26 per cent) and North America (5.4 million – 19 per cent) (United Nations, 2013). However, youth migration is not simply a movement from developing to developed nations. Evidence shows that movement is also taking place across developing nations and between developing and least developed nations (United Nations, 2013). Much migration is also regional. For example, in Japan most migrants are from the South Asian region (China and Korea); in the UK and Norway, they are mainly from Europe; and Australia and New Zealand share migrants, in that many New Zealanders and Australians work across the national borders of the two countries (OECD, 2013b).

Inequality and transnational mobility

Bauman suggested 'mobility has become the most powerful and most coveted stratifying factor' in the world today (Bauman, 1998, p. 9). The tendency is for those who are most mobile to freely move around the globe, gaining substantial privilege and advantage; those with less resources tend to be the 'losers', relegated to poverty and insecurity (Bauman, 1998). These patterns remain amongst the young today, with the economically wealthy having on average more successful migratory experiences relative to those less wealthy. Indeed, the latter may move only to find themselves in situations worse than those they left. That is to say, migration for young people does not always pay the dividends many hope to gain (UN, 2013). For example, in the UK in 2017, approximately 2.25 million 'foreign-born' workers were in low-skilled occupations (personal services, sales, processing or elementary roles). The recent Great Financial Crisis (GFC) increased the risk of unemployment for migrants who arrive with low levels of skills. The unemployment rate amongst migrant populations increased by 5 per cent between 2008 and 2010, compared with 3 per cent for domestic citizens. In this, young people were hit the hardest, especially those with low education and poor language skills (UN, 2013). While this is not simply a result of the GFC, it does show that migration poses a high risk to those without the social and economic resources to manage it.

Alternatively, those migrants who are from an affluent middle class and have wealth to spend and invest do far better. Not only are they more likely to be successful, but also the receiving state is far more supportive and encouraging. For example, in countries such as New Zealand, Australia and Canada, highly skilled migrants are sought after to overcome skill shortages, with receiving countries creating 'special' or 'high skill' visas (OECD, 2019). These categories tend to be met and filled by the more educated and affluent middle class or those with high levels of cultural capital. A wide range of countries such as the UK, Japan, Canada and Australia have, at different points in time, extended their visa categories that encourage wealth migrants and those with high skills. Japan, for example, has created a preferential channel for highly skilled foreigners. This gives special treatment to those with high skills, such as academics, researchers, doctors and corporate executives. Some countries have also created business categories that allow people bringing large sums of money to invest in the new host country to get special treatment. Clearly, if you have the economic resources or have managed to accrue high levels of cultural capital, you can gain easier entry into a range of different countries.

Youth and internal mobility

When it comes to internal migration between, for example, rural and urban areas, it is harder to capture the extent and details of movement. This is because the definition of an 'internal migrant' is '… fraught with conceptual differences between countries – for example, how large is the place of residence? Is it a province, or a municipality? The data on internal migration, therefore, has to be considered with caution.' (World Economic Forum, 2017, p. 22). It is generally thought that internal migration sees flows from rural to urban centres, and at one level this is correct. For example, over the last 30 years in China we have seen the urban population increase from 22.9 per cent of the population to 56.8 per cent. It is now estimated that, by the year 2030, over 75 per cent of China's population will live in urban centres (World Economic Forum, 2017). Similarly, on the

African continent the urban growth rate is 11 times higher than that in Europe and Latin America, with over 83 per cent of Africa's population living in cities.

Thinking point

- What can explain why some countries can have high levels of internal migration? What might be the key drivers?

Of course, young people are significant movers. They migrate throughout the country, moving from place to place, city to country, or rural town to urban neighbourhood. A range of motivations impels such migrations, and similarly spurs them to move on to other places, or return to others. Migration is rarely a linear journey starting at one point and ending at another. **Push and pull factors** are diverse as well. In terms of rural–urban migrations, changes to the youth labour market mean that jobs tend to be increasingly concentrated in urban areas (Farrugia, 2014). This has resulted in age-based migrations whereby young people relocate from across the country to metropolitan localities. Others (e.g. Alston, 2004) link the losses of young people from rural towns to employment restructuring and changes in the agricultural sector. Young people also move in search of tertiary education opportunities, yet the implications of social forces loom large here, too. For instance, Evans (2009) showed how, for highly qualified working-class school girls from south London, gender-specific family ties and obligations constrained mobility, meaning they could not move to take up a university place at Oxford, and all the possibilities for social mobility that may have offered.

> **Push/pull factors:** Represent a way to look at what it is that impels people to leave their homes, while identifying the dynamics that shape decisions on where to go.

Gender and rural–urban internal migration in China

China is a country characterized by large-scale internal migration pathways, particularly from rural to urban places. Different types of motivations impelling young people to migrate are outlined by Chiang et al. (2015). They list individual economic reasons, supporting family and personal development as key reasons to migrate. The permanent and non-permanent migrant status of Chinese internal migrants is referred to as the hukou, or the household registration system, and this government policy has historically had a significant role in shaping internal migration pathways. Under the system, residents are assigned places of residence classified as either rural or urban, and their ability to access social security or welfare is tied to their hukou status. If a migrant is not granted hukou status, they are classified as temporary migrants with limited ability to access such services (Du, 2017). While this system has been relaxed since the 2000s, it continues to affect migration experiences and pathways in the country. However, while internal migrations characterize youthful pathways, mobility plays a crucial role in place-attachment and sense of belonging. Place attachment has been found to change over time, and circular migrations, with young people choosing to return to their rural homes, demonstrate the relational and complex nature of internal migrations in China, irrespective of temporary or permanent status (Du, 2017).

While much of the discussion about mobilities and young peoples' migration pathways describes international or inter-city migrations, movement across relatively smaller geographies constitutes a key dimension in the discussion. Skelton (2013) applied a rationality lens to investigate young peoples' im/mobilities in the city. Skelton focussed on daily forms of movement around the city rather than the usual focus on global mobilities. Based in Auckland, New Zealand, experiences of the city from a youth perspective were necessarily different and unique. Skelton's study found that young people took advantage of opportunities to be mobile in the city. This was a part of growing up, and a transition that required resources, while supporting sociality and identity formation. In order to get around, young people tended to rely on accessible – that is, safe and affordable – public transport. They were also able to rely on their own vehicles, including bikes, motorbikes and cars. Being able to walk with safety was another form of mobility. Independent means of movement, which minimized the need to be reliant on others, were preferred.

Of course, any form of migration is rarely a linear movement in that young people can move from place to place, return home or move permanently to another part of a country or across borders. However, previous academic work on migration has made assumptions that people will move to one country, for a short or long period of time, and maintain links and communication with just one other place, generally their home of origin. Rejecting this, Gold and Nawyn (2013, p. 3) explain:

> ... migration is not a single, discrete event involving movement from one geographically and socially bounded locality to another. Instead, transnational communities embody and exchange concerns, relationships, resources, needs and often people immersed in multiple settings.

Relational mobilities

Understanding why and how young people engage with being mobile needs an approach that identifies the relational nature of mobilities. A greater emphasis on more relational approaches requires us to try to understand the *context of migration* rather than the traditional focus on the individual as the launching point of investigation. While young people may migrate from one place to another on their own, the decision to move, and the manner in which they do so, rarely concerns only the individual. Rather, family context and broader socio-political structures emerge as the major shaping mechanisms in young peoples' migration pathways. King and Raghuram (2013) suggest that homing in on the 'student' in the discussion of student migration obscures the relational aspects of migration, such as students' identities as family members, workers or refugees/asylum seekers.

It is evident that relationships with various family members and other acquaintances together can help to create a broader form of community, which stretches beyond borders, and this can be valuable for the success of the movement (Geisen, 2010). In fact, migration itself needs to be recognized within a life course analysis, which shows how it connects to the life planning and biography-building that may lead to a permanent move over a longer period of time (Geisen, 2010). Brooks and Waters (2010) for example suggest that we need to highlight the means by which 'mobility is often socially-embedded, grounded in networks of both family and friends.' Indeed, for these writers, a key difference between research on the mobilities of the middle/upper class and research on other forms of migrations is that the former tends to focus on the individual level, and often does not sufficiently account for family networks or capital. Alternatively, research on working class migrants tends to emphasize the role of family and social networks in the migration process (Brooks and Waters, 2010). A lens that accounts for a more relational, socially embedded approach to youthful mobilities is one in which intersectional dynamics that affect migration experiences, for instance power, gender and race, can be accounted for.

Middling migration: contradictory mobility experiences of Indian youth in London

Rutten and Verstappen (2014) investigated young people from middle class families from Gujarat, India who migrated to London, UK. Having conducted research with young participants and their families both in London and in India, Rutten and Verstappen found that their participants' motivations were shaped by a desire to improve educational and employment opportunities, alongside more personal reasons based on self-exploration. The researchers found that, for the young people, migration characterized 'contradictory class experiences' that resulted in an 'ambivalence' in terms of economic gain, and a renewed emphasis on opportunities to relieve family pressure, as well as to gain cosmopolitan experiences. In a way, the young Indian respondents had similar desires to other 'gap year' travellers, but also felt pressure to save money, support themselves financially and send money back home. Like other researchers, Rutten and Verstappen are critical of migration literature that focusses on the individual, or homes in on purely economic motivations. Rather, the process is more complex, relational and embedded in social and familial relations. Migration is rarely motivated by a single factor, but related to a complex range of dynamics.

Mobility imperatives

Mobility imperatives usually describe the factors and dynamics impelling young people to move from one place to another. As Wyn (2015) explains, '... mobility is now central to contemporary transition regimes', and many young people understand mobilities as an obligatory process that they must go through if they are to be successful. So why do young people

> **Mobility imperatives:** A term used to explain the dominant explanations of why young people might be mobile.

migrate? Decisions to become 'mobile' are not simply related to 'pull and push' factors, although they do make a significant contribution. Deciding to migrate is a process that involves consideration of where they are in the different points of the life course; whether the person is young, middle aged, or has a family. It is clear that life stage often informs the motivations and expectations, as well as outcomes of migration (Triandafyllidou, 2015).

🗨 Thinking points

- What are the major reasons why young people migrate?
- How might class and gender be a factor in who migrates?

Decisions to migrate are not taken lightly, and as we saw above, relationships with others such as family members and friends are important in the choices that are made. But decisions are also strongly related to the young making major life transitions, especially around getting an education, a job with some form of security, or getting married/formally partnering and building a family. Such decisions are also shaped by the young making comparisons between the opportunities they perceive in their own countries and those in the countries they move to:

> Often, the main driving force behind youth migration (particularly international migration) is the magnitude of perceived inequalities in labour market opportunities, income, human rights and living standards between the countries of origin and destination. (Cortina et al., 2014, p. 22)

The structures, programs and policies in place that support youth migrations are usually complex and multiple. For many who are undertaking educational mobilities as a form of transition, there need to be significant cultural and material resources in place. Migrating with other family members, or having family in the place they are migrating to, or having access to financial support from their parents or other family members can all aid the process. Of course, such opportunities are not always available to all, and are mostly confined to those from middle class backgrounds. The backgrounds and material resources available throughout the migration process necessarily shape and inform experiences and motivations. Indeed, the role of class in student mobilities represents an important way to think about youthful mobilities, and the constraints and opportunities that different groups face. The work of Bourdieu, Brooks and Waters explains that student mobilities lead to the development of 'mobility capital'. This can be defined as '… a sub-component of human capital, enabling individuals to enhance their skills because of the richness of the international experience gained by living abroad' (Murphy-Lejeune, 2002, p. 51). Mobility capital emerges as an additional resource that young people can draw on to propel educational or employment transitions, but is ultimately socially reproduced, and tightly wound in with other forms of capital, including economic and social capital. We also saw in Chapter 3 that many young people, especially those with resources or parental support, now realize that international travel, either for further education or to have an OE (overseas experience), is invaluable to CV building.

Transnational mobilities for education

Of course, as has been suggested above, when we are thinking about mobility we need to recognize the massive movement of young people as students. An extensive body of literature investigates the contours and dynamics of student migration. Recent years have seen a general increase in people studying, including in their countries of origin.

However, there have been significant increases in international student flows, which have been characterized as a global phenomenon. Taking into account only those who undertake degrees in a host country (and not those who undertake single-term or single-year study abroad options), the number of international students grew from 2.8 million to 4.1 million between 2005 and 2013 (UNESCO, 2015a, 2015b), and by 2016 had, according to the UNESCO Institute of Statistics open data source [http://data.uis.unesco.org/], already grown to just over 4.8 million. Such trends have seen increased study of the particular form of educational mobility characterized as 'international student mobility' (Cairns, 2015). Previously this form of student mobility was uncommon and restricted to a privileged few; however, as the numbers attest, now it is much more commonplace (though still a small fraction of overall global student numbers). In particular, China and India have emerged as dominant source countries for English-speaking destinations such as the USA, the UK, and Australia and New Zealand.

🗨 Thinking points

- Which countries do you think have the most international students and why?
- Where do you think most students come from and why?

In research on international student mobility, discussion about how best to characterize migration pathways is underscored by the length of stay, and plans to remain in the country after completing educational commitments. Some of these movements can be characterized as 'institutionally mediated student exchange', such as programs that encourage students to study abroad for a short proportion of their overall degree, which is still awarded by their 'home' institution. These usually do not fall under the category of international migration due to the relatively short duration of stay; however, this is still an area of research interest (see Lesjak et al., 2015). Those migrating for an entire course of study are most typically described as internationally mobile students, especially if they remain after their course of study finishes and become permanent migrants. These distinctions are clear; for example in the work of King and Raghuram (2013), who differentiate between 'credit mobility', in which moving aboard is part of a study program and is generally less than a year before returning to home institution, and 'degree mobility', when a student stays for an entire degree over a period of several years.

🗨 Thinking point

How appealing is international student mobility for you and why? What might be the barriers and challenges for you to undertaking such migration?

Researchers have also highlighted the tensions between competing understandings of student migrants. In some instances, they are characterized as 'desired' migrants insofar as they provide student fees that help institutions and contribute to the scholarly communities in which they study. Conversely, they have also been cast as 'unwanted' in the context of the broader politics around migration that focus on security and reflect broader public pressure and discourses seeking to reduce migration (King and Raghuram, 2013). Students are obliged to navigate these contradictions. King and Raghuram (2013) explain that there is a 'slipperiness' in the concept of 'international student' invariably used to describe this group of young migrants. This relates to the simultaneous acceptance and exclusion that they experience. Related to such work, the risks that international students face are considered in detail by Forbes-Mewett (2018). Looking at the case of international students who have travelled to study in Australia, Forbes-Mewett critically engages with previous discourses pertaining to international students and 'security', focussing instead on the trials and tribulations that such students face in their everyday lives in their host country. Forbes-Mewett challenges researchers to think about the everyday threats to the security of international students with regard to housing, employment, food, personal security and campus settings and to contemplate the (variable) meanings of what it is to feel secure as an international student in a foreign land.

'Educational mobilities' also encompass those migrating for educational opportunities in the secondary school sector. Obviously, this relates to a younger cohort of students, but can also involve young people migrating with their families, or with a parent. Waters (2015) describes 'Kirogi' families; those originating from South Korea who migrate, usually to the USA, for their young children to go to school. Invariably the motivation to migrate was to build social capital and to bolster educational and career opportunities. Indeed, mobility and transnational education has been described as ultimately beneficial, and collectively understood as a worthwhile pathway for young people. However, such mobilities are rarely without significant sacrifice on the part of families, particularly mothers, who sacrifice relationships and careers, and are often difficult transitions for the young members of such families (Waters, 2015).

Mobilities and identity questions

Youth sociologists understand that identity is an important factor relating to patterns of mobility and migration. For young people moving from one socio-cultural context to another, the question emerges of identity development in light of competing domains and sources. With regard to identity, and the ways in which discussions about identity arise during migration experiences, migration scholars have drawn on the work of Barth (1998) to make sense of the process of constructing boundaries between ethnic groups and the ways in which this has shaped identities. According to Barth (1998), the ways in which such boundaries are made and maintained allow shifting relations to be made clear. Crucially, ethnic identities can become more meaningful when the boundaries separating them are highlighted, as occurs often during migration experiences.

Ultimately, identity is a process rather than an outcome (see Chapter 5), and it is something that emerges in transnational spaces occupied by young people migrating to and living in **diaspora** communities. Migration is a process that disrupts the mechanisms through which young people normally form identities. They can be hybrid and reflect a range of domains not tied to geographies, for instance home nation, religious identity, or host nation. Youthful identities of those migrating can then 'reject national/ethnic boundaries and instead develop a more global sense of identity.' (Laoire et al., 2012, p. 132). According to Laoire et al. (2012), in

> **Diaspora:** Refers to communities or groups of migrants with a collective sense of connection to one and other, based on shared cultural, ethnic or religious identities, living in a 'host' country.

many ways, young people can be seen to be at the forefront of complex and intense processes of negotiating belonging (see below for more detail), identity formation and forming a sense of place in host societies. This is because of their close and intense inter-actions mediated via educational institutions, as well as at the neighbourhood level (Laoire et al., 2012). Further, young people play a key role in shaping and negotiating transnational networks with friends, relatives left behind at home, or in other countries, often using social technologies in a way that suits their lives (Laoire et al., 2012).

Issues of mobilities also constitute a part of what is called the 'project of the self'. Examples might include the increased use of leisure travel, working holidays, volunteer tourism or gap year travel. Involvement in these sees young people travelling abroad for an adventure, with a desire to experience another context that creates 'self-exploration'. Such narratives are perhaps more common in developed liberal democratic countries, where being 'free' and independent, as well as enacting individual choice, is a key rite of passage (Haverig, 2011). Yoon's (2014) research on South Koreans on working holi-days in Canada highlights some of these themes. Yoon described participants' travel experiences as something that helped them in seeking their 'true self', an opportunity to build social mobility and develop the self. Yoon argues that narratives around work-ing holidays and self-development make specific forms of neoliberal subjectivities nor-mal and standard insofar as such 'global experience' is increasingly seen as typical (Yoon, 2014). However, it is difficult to disentangle mobilities motivated by a search for 'global experience' from those focussed more closely on education or employment, in that they act as vivid processes of class distinction and capital accumulation (Snee, 2014). Rather than being typical among young people, Haverig and Roberts' (2011) study of New Zealanders' post-degree overseas experience (OE) shows that it is open mostly to middle class students with the requisite banks of economic and social capital. Interestingly, they also demonstrate that the OE is so embedded in middle class culture that it represents an 'obligatory' activity for many middle class people, being positioned not as a choice, but somehow as a mandatory regulated necessity.

Transnational belonging among second-generation youth: identity in a globalized world

Kara Somerville's (2008) study brings together many of the themes we have discussed so far in this chapter concerning young people's increased mobilities, and the impact of migration on how young people create and negotiate identities. She shows how **transnationalism** is experienced by young people who are second-generation migrants from India to Canada, and shows how their identities are negotiated and constructed between and across national boundaries in three ways, at the level of:

> **Transnationalism:**
> Refers to interactions of people, communi-ties and businesses, across and beyond traditional boundaries in new and emerging global spaces that transcend traditional nation-state boundaries.

- emotions: in that they felt Indian, yet also Canadian;
- appearance: they expressed their transnational belonging through fashion styles and clothing;
- allegiance: where they felt a sense of loyalty to India at the same time that they felt a sense of loyalty to Canada.

Her study is useful in showing how young people navigate transnational attachments in their everyday lives, and how crucial transnational elements are in their expressions of identity. These themes of identity and attachment are explored further in the next section on 'belonging'.

Mobility, migration and citizenship

Questions of citizenship for young migrants are, of course, shaped by their legal status in their host nation states. For example, refugees who have resettled because of insecurity and risk find the rights and benefits that are provided to be a form of privileged mobility that grants them secure status and insurance against further uncertainty (Nunn et al., 2015). As a result, '… formal state citizenship can support integration among people with refugee backgrounds by contributing to a sense of ontological security' (Nunn et al., 2015). Research in this area therefore explores the diverse ways that migrants as 'legal citizens' practise their citizenship in their day-to-day lives. In other words, it investigates how citizenship is lived (Lister, 2007).

What we tend to find is that being both a migrant and a citizen is significantly influenced by the interaction between migrants' cultural identity and heritage in the local places they inhabit. Mansouri and Kirpitchenko (2016) showed how a diverse group of young first- and second-generation migrants' active citizenship was practised through their own cultural norms and heritage. 'Being 'active citizens' in their own neighbourhood '… tended to have a variety of ethno-cultural specific motivations for being involved in a range of formal and informal volunteering activities within and outside their communities' (p. 319). This position is supported by the work of Harris and Roose (2014), who suggested young migrants in Australia are:

> … creating forms of solidarity, community and belonging and generating new kinds of social capital and civic involvement, particularly through youth cultural production and consumption, civic networks in everyday spaces, and work on the self. (Harris and Roose, 2014, p. 795)

Normative readings of their social practice fail to identify the types of strategies young migrants are using to undertake civic responsibilities. This form of 'do-it-your-self' practice uses social media outlets, alongside other creative cultural sites on- and offline that create spaces for them to express their perspectives on a wide range of issues related to their cultural and religious identities. These practices can include using music such as hip hop, or fashion blogs or poems that can be used to promote positive images of their culture, such as 'hijab fashions'. While many of these forms of practice could be relevant to other groups of young people, migrant youth also '… interlinked broader civic values with Islamic practice, especially 'giving, service and respect for the community' (p. 808). Seeing their religion as a 'way of life' allows them to position themselves as ethical citizens in civic practices.

Mobility, migration and belonging

Notions of belonging have also been seen as important to the migrant experience. Clearly, in leaving their 'home' and relocating to new countries, young people try to belong. Anita Harris (2015) explored the importance of belonging amongst a group of migrant youth in an urban area of Australia, showing how it contributed to their social identity. Harris found that young people's methods of belonging were negotiated in a wide range of ways in different contexts. Firstly, 'difference' was seen and well represented in the national culture, and as a result these young people could position themselves as 'belonging' at a national level because they were different and this reflected the national identity:

> This is consistent with a dominant story about Australian national identity as embracing the project of multiculturalism. By representing themselves as having the intercultural and cosmopolitan capacities required to be effective citizens of a modern multicultural nation, they could enhance their sense of national belonging. (Harris, 2015, p. 365)

A second area where they could create a sense of belonging was at the local or neighbourhood level. It was here that they felt they could be a part of everyday life, where they could normalize their difference and show it as being enhancing to the community while also reinforcing the positive aspects of being different. Simultaneously, they were able to show they belonged and were not operating significantly outside a community norm, '…local, taken for granted conditions of considerable diversity enabled them to construct difference as unremarkable and dynamic' (Harris, 2015, p. 365). Finally, when it came to local youth culture, the notion of belonging could create tensions and re-enforce existing gender norms endemic in mainstream Australian society. While difference can be a creative force in youth culture as a way of securing inclusion and recognition, it required young people to '… police one another's work with difference reveal[ing] how deeply belonging is structured by hegemonic rules about gender and sexuality (Harris, 2015, p. 372).

As the examples in this chapter have shown, belonging is becoming a central way of understanding the dynamic, mobile conditions of young people's contemporary lives, and of re-framing some of the problems associated with approaches that have dominated traditional youth research, such as 'transitions'.

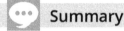 ## Summary

- Citizenship constructs young people as non-citizens or 'citizens in the making'.

- To capture the complexity of young people's citizenship, youth sociologists argue we need to understand the 'lived experience of citizenship.

- The concept of 'belonging' is used to understand the quality of young people's connections to people, institutions, places and spaces, and how these are affected by socio-cultural forces.

- The notion of 'belonging' offers an alternative way of thinking about young people's lives that moves beyond simple binaries i.e. transitions versus youth culture or structure versus agency.

- Youth mobility has increased significantly over the last 20 years, although its meaning is complex and not also simply linear and simple.

- Migration is a relational experience that is embedded in familial, social and cultural structures that shape pathways across the country and/or the world.

- Young people are 'mobile' for a number of reasons, including education and employment opportunities as well as to engage in the project of the self.

- For migrants moving to new countries, their identity development is complex and for many involves negotiating hybrid identities across 'home' and 'host' countries.

- For young migrants, being a citizen or feeling they belong usually involves a complex interaction between their cultural heritage and the locality where they are located.

✏️ Exercise: The sociological imagination

Think about what role 'belonging' has in your life. How do your connections with people and place influence how you engage with work, study, and how you identify yourself? Would you move to another country for work or study for a long period of time? Think about how your attachments to people and places are shaped by your 'position' in the world, e.g. class, gender, sexuality or ethnicity.

📖 Key readings

Cuervo, H. & Wyn, J. (2017) 'A longitudinal analysis of belonging: temporal, performative and relational practices by young people in rural Australia', *Young*, vol. 25, no. 3, pp. 219–234.

Harris, A. & Roose, J. (2014) 'DIY citizenship amongst young Muslims: experiences of the "ordinary"', *Journal of Youth Studies*, vol. 17, no. 6, pp. 794–813.

Robertson, S., Harris, A. & Baldassar, L. (2018) 'Mobile transitions: a conceptual framework for researching a generation on the move', *Journal of Youth Studies*, vol. 21, no. 2, pp. 203–217.

Smith, N. Lister, R., Middleton, S. & Cox, L. (2005) 'Young people as real citizens: towards an inclusionary understanding of citizenship', *Journal of Youth Studies*, vol. 8, no. 4, pp. 425–443.

Walsh, L., Black, R. & Prosser, H. (2018) 'Young people's perceptions of power and influence as a basis for understanding contemporary citizenship', *Journal of Youth Studies*, vol. 21, no. 2, pp. 218–234.

Wood, B. E. (2017) 'Youth studies, citizenship and transitions: towards a new research agenda', *Journal of Youth Studies*, vol. 20, no. 9, pp. 1176–1190.

Wyn, J. (2015) 'Young people and belonging in perspective' in Lange, A., Steiner, C., Reiter, H., et al. (eds.) *Handbook of Child and Youth Sociology*, pp. 1–14 (Dordrecht: Springer).

Yoon, K. (2014) 'Transnational youth mobility in the neoliberal economy of experience', *Journal of Youth Studies,* vol. 17, no. 8, pp. 1014–1028.

POSTSCRIPT

We write this final word as a way of providing some concluding thoughts about the future direction for youth sociology. Of course, it is not an easy task to predict future trends and developments that will drive or shape the research agendas of those working in the field. We believe there are three major changes taking place that are creating a particular 'moment' globally, which will have profound implications for the future and for young people. All three can be seen as situated in and amplified by the emergence of what has become known as the 'post truth' era. This era is characterized by the absence of agreement on what might constitute 'objectivity' and a climate of hostility and suspicion towards expert knowledge. Instead of a reliance on evidence, politics and decision-making has increasingly become aligned with appeals to emotion or the deployment of so-called alternative facts, alongside technological development such as the capacity to relatively easily create a 'deep fake'. Examples of this can include realistic images and videos that depict deliberate falsehoods, such as a politician saying things that they never actually uttered, or (most often) a woman's face being non-consensually superimposed onto a body of someone engaging in a pornographic act. These activities can serve to separate images from truth – what is seen cannot always be believed. This blurring of truth from reality can create uncertainty and mistrust, making 'everything' open to question and up for debate. This can be particularly problematic when trying to hold unethical and harmful behaviours or actions of the powerful to account.

The return and rise of populist ideologies

Far from being a thing of the past, populist and conservative ideologies have mobilized in recent years across the globe, concentrating on winding back the gains made through progressive politics around the rights of women, refugees and minorities. This is embodied in a figure like Donald Trump, whose rebuttal of any attempts by the press or others to hold him to account for political or personal indiscretion has been the cry of 'fake news' – perhaps the key slogan of the post truth era. In Australia, Pauline Hanson's right-wing One Nation party has risen from the dead and virtual obscurity, to become a not insignificant 'player' in Australian politics. Her capacity to win votes on conservative issues (such as calling to 'ban the burqa') has relied in distortion of evidence and appeals to emotion and has had the effect of pulling the major parties away from progressive stances on asylum seeker policy, for example. Europe and the UK grapple with Brexit and its implications for trade, movement across borders and English identities. The resurgence of right-wing and populist ideals is also having a major impact on policy, and in turn has huge repercussions for young people in the future, particularly those who are minorities in relation to sexuality and gender, ethnicity and religion. These challenges are unlikely to diminish. The rise of the White supremacist movement, nationalist politics and 'protectionist' policy making is growing and is an orientation that gets substantial political support. Its impact on the values, beliefs and experiences of this and future generations of young people remains unknown, therefore youth sociology has a critical role in researching and commenting on such developments over the coming decades, bringing to light the ways these ideas impact on the lives of young people.

Climate change

A second characteristic of the current 'moment' which will have huge implications for future generations of young people is rising concern about the impacts of climate change. Climate strikes have seen millions of young people across the globe protest a lack of action on climate change policy. Greta Thunberg, a 16-year-old Swedish girl, began the movement on her own in 2018 when she sat outside the Swedish parliament holding a placard calling for greater action. One year later, she addressed the UN's Climate Change Summit in 2019, stating 'the eyes of future generations are upon you'. Greta has become the 'poster girl' for climate change action, and has attracted fierce criticism, mostly from middle aged White men, who are incensed by her confidence and audacity in speaking so fiercely – some of whom have written columns in tabloids telling her to 'be a good girl and shut up' (Clarkson in The Sun https://www.buzz.ie/celebs/jeremy-clarkson-greta-thunberg-shut-up-spoilt-brat-338829). As well as the public face of such movements, the climate change scientists also find themselves under attack. In the place of actual scientific scrutiny, there is an abundance of disbelief and very often an utter rejection of the suggested changes needed to avert the coming crisis that will be caused by, as is now predicted, global temperatures rising by 3 degrees by the end of the century. If this happens, future generations will face unimaginable hardship caused by living on a planet which is fast becoming uninhabitable. It seems as though the current generation of young people, led by Greta Thunberg and other young climate activists such as Alexandria Villaseñor, Isra Hirsi and Xiye Bastida, will play a pivotal role in raising awareness of climate change through continuing to call for tangible action through global and local policy change. As Greta says, it will be up to the current global leaders to make these changes, if it is not already too late. Again, this suggests an important role for youth sociology. Capturing and reflecting not only the developments of such policies and practices but also engaging and giving voice to this coming generation, helping to ensure their concerns are heard in the post truth era.

The future of work: a fourth industrial age?

A third dimension of the current 'moment' is the debate about the future of work, what jobs will be available for young people in relation to technological advances and the character of changing economies. As we have seen in the previous discussion within the book, work and young people's relationship to it have been changing dramatically. Some have suggested that we have entered a fourth industrial age where a 'revolution' is taking place that will fundamentally change our lives. As the digital world becomes more ubiquitous and core to our everyday lived experiences, new technology such as artificial intelligence (AI) or 'machine learning' is seen to be reconfiguring not only our relationships with machines but also work and employment. More 'things' are being created through automated practices such as the 3D printer, and more 'decisions' are being now made by machines independent of humans. Alongside this, 'driverless cars', 'drones' and a wide range of automated production practices are replacing the need for 'people' in a wide range of industries. Such developments are not simply changing manufacturing but also service and professional practice, and also creating needs for new types of skills and possibly new types of education. In this 'new order', the collection and analysis of data is also seen as helping increase profitability of big business. There is a significant paradox here, and it is somewhat ironic that the post truth era rejects evidence, while at the same time data is being seen as 'the new oil' through which businesses and industries are increasing income by using data analyzed by machines. For example, organisations such as Google, Facebook and Amazon are creating targeted advertising through the use of algorithms which is then increasing revenue for big co-operations, not by charging its customers but its advertisers. This has implications for work but also for democracy, as observed in the 2019 Cambridge Analytica scandal.

As we saw in Chapter 4, there are indications that we live in times where the experience of work is changing. Not only are there questions about how much work will be available in the future for the young but also what will it mean to them? For example, while we need to be cautious about claims by some that we are moving towards a 'gig economy', we do need to recognize that 'gig work' is expanding in a wide range of settings and configurations, and for many jobs it is reshaping the employer–employee relationship and how people work. While such changes cannot necessarily be seen as a 'new age', we do need to recognize that work is going through some form of transformation and this is likely to impact on future generations. In other words, rather than creating a 'revolution', such changes do amount to a reconfiguration of work and the continuation of capitalism in Western, post-industrial economies. Such changes will not be felt equally. This is made very clear by the stark comparison between the earnings of Jeff Bezos, CEO of the digital giant *Amazon* and the many low-level workers the company employs. In the USA, Amazon's minimum wage was set to $15 USD per hour in November 2018, while it is estimated that he 'earns' nearly $2500 USD *every second*. These are only rough calculations, so for further context consider that if someone earned $5000 a day for *547 years*, they would still not have amassed a billion dollars; meanwhile Bezos' own net worth is around $135 billion USD.

Despite aspirations for digital technologies to make work – and life more generally – better for all, a core role for youth sociology is to map, track, analyze and comment on such changes so we are able to understand what impact it is having on what it means to be young, and how this is differentially experienced in this changing landscape.

BIBLIOGRAPHY

Aapola, S., Gonick, M. & Harris, A. (2005) *Young Femininity: Girlhood, Power and Social Change* (New York: Macmillan).

Abidin, C. (2016) 'Visibility labour: engaging with influencers' fashion brands and #OOTD advertorial campaigns on Instagram', *Media International Australia*, vol. 161, no. 1, pp. 86–100.

Abrahams, J. & Ingram, N. (2013) 'The chameleon habitus: exploring local students' negotiations of multiple fields', *Sociological Research Online*, vol. 18, no. 4, pp. 1–14.

ABS. (2017) https://www.abs.gov.au/AUSSTATS/abs@.nsf/mediareleasesbytitle/1533F E5A8541D66CCA2581BF00362D1D?OpenDocument.

ABS. (2018) Labour Force, Australia, September 2018, https://www.abs.gov.au/aus-stats/abs@.nsf/Lookup/6202.0main+features10September%202018.

Accessibility/Remoteness Index of Australia (ARIA). (2014) Map of Australia illustrating the 2006 remoteness structure, the Australian Bureau of Statistics, Canberra, Australia, accessed 5th December 2016, http://www.abs.gov.au/websitedbs/ D3310114.nsf/home/remoteness+structure.

Adams, J. (1995) *Risk* (London: University College).

Adler, F. (1975) *Sisters in Crime; The Rise of the New Female Criminal* (New York: McGraw Hill).

Adnett, N. (2010) 'The growth of international students and economic development: friends or foes?', *Journal of Education Policy*, vol. 25, no. 5, pp. 625–637.

Ai Group. (2016) Workforce Development and the Emergence of the Gig Economy.

AIHW. (2011) Young Australians: their health and wellbeing, date accessed 19th July 2019, https://www.aihw.gov.au/reports/children-youth/young-australians-their-health-and-wellbeing-2011/contents/summary.

Albury, K. & Crawford, K. (2012) 'Sexting, consent and young people's ethics: beyond Megan's story', *Continuum*, vol. 26, no. 3, pp. 463–473.

Allaste, A. & Tilidenberg, K. (2016) 'Sexy selfies of the transitioning self' in Woodman, D. & Bennett, A. (eds.) *Youth Cultures, Transitions, and Generations: Bridging the Gap in Youth Research* (London: Springer).

Allen, S. (1968) 'Some theoretical problems in the study of youth', *Sociological Review*, vol. 16, no. 3, pp. 319–331.

Allen, K. (2014) 'Blair's children': young women as "aspirational subjects" in the psychic landscape of class', *The Sociological Review*, vol. 62, no. 4, pp. 760–779.

Allen, M. & Ainley, P. (2010) *Lost Generation?: New Strategies for Youth and Education* (Sydney: Bloomsbury Publishing).

Allen, K. & Hollingworth, S. (2013) '"Sticky subjects" or "cosmopolitan creatives"? Social class, place and urban young people's aspirations for work in the knowledge economy', *Urban Studies*, vol. 50, no. 3, pp. 499–517.

Allen, J., Balfour, R., Bell, R. & Marmot, M. (2014) 'Social determinants of mental health', *International Review of Psychiatry*, vol. 26, no. 4, pp. 392–407.

Alston, M. (2004) '"You don't want to be a check-out chick all your life': the out-migration of young people from Australia's small rural towns', *Australian Journal of Social Issues*, vol. 39, no. 3, pp. 299–313.

Amin, A. & Thrift, N. (2002) *Cities: Reimagining the Urban* (Cambridge: Polity Press).

Anderson, A. & Jiang, J. (2018) 'Teens, social media and technology', *Pew Research Centre*, viewed 10th August 2018, http://www.pewinternet.org/2018/05/31/teens-social-media-technology-2018/.

Anderson, S., Kinsey, R., Loader, I. & Smith, G. (1994) *Cautionary Tales: Young People and Policing in Edinburgh* (Aldershot: Avebury Press).

Andrejevic, M. (2014) 'The big data divide', *International Journal of Communication*, vol. 8, pp. 1673–1689.

Andres, L. & Wyn, J. (2010) *The Making of a Generation: The Children of the 1970's in Adulthood* (Toronto: University of Toronto Press).

Aneshensel, C. S. (2009) 'Toward explaining mental health disparities', *Journal of Health and Social Behavior*, vol. 50, no. 4, pp. 377–394.

Anglicare. (2017) Jobs Availability Snapshot 2017, https://www.anglicare.asn.au/docs/default-source/default-document-library/jobs-availability-snapshot-2017.pdf.

Angus, C. (2016) Cyberbullying of children, NSW Parliamentary Research Service March 2016 e-brief 2/2016, https://www.parliament.nsw.gov.au/researchpapers/Documents/cyberbullying-of-children/Cyberbullying%20of%20Children.pdf.

Appadurai, A. (1996) *Modernity at Large: Cultural Dimensions of Globalization,* vol. 1. (Minnesota: University of Minnesota Press).

Archer, L., Pratt, S., D & Phillips, D. (2001) 'Working-class men's constructions of masculinity and negotiations of (non) participation in higher education', *Gender and Education*, vol. 13, no. 4, pp. 431–449.

Archer, L., DeWitt, J., Osborne, J., Dillon, J., Willis, B. & Wong, B. (2013) '"Not girly, not sexy, not glamorous: primary school girls' and parents' constructions of science aspirations', *Pedagogy, Culture & Society*, vol. 21, no. 1, pp. 171–194.

Archer, L., Moote, J., Francis, B., DeWitt, J. & Yeomans, L. (2017) 'The "exceptional" physics girl: a sociological analysis of multimethod data from young women aged 10–16 to explore gendered patterns of post-16 participation', *American Educational Research Journal*, vol. 54, no. 1, pp. 88–126.

Armstrong, C., Hill, M. & Secker, J. (2000) 'Young people's perceptions of mental health', *Children and Society*, vol. 14, no. 1, pp. 60–72.

Ashley, M. (2009) 'Time to confront Willis's lads with a ballet class? A case study of educational orthodoxy and white working-class boys', *British Journal of Sociology of Education*, vol. 30, no. 2, pp. 179–191.

Ashton, D. & Field, D. (1976) *Young Workers* (Hutchinson: London).

Atkins, L. (2010) 'Opportunity and aspiration, or the great deception? The case of 14–19 vocational education', *Power and Education*, vol. 2, no. 3, pp. 253–265.

Australian Bureau of Statistics (ABS). (2014–15) 'Household use of information technology, Australia', accessed 22nd May 2017, http://www.abs.gov.au/ausstats/abs@.nsf/mf/8146.0.

Australian Bureau of Statistics (ABS). (2016–7) Household use of information technology, Australia, accessed 10th August 2018, http://www.abs.gov.au/Ausstats/abs%40.nsf/mf/8146.0.

Australian Bureau of Statistics. (2017) 3303.0 – Causes of Death, Australia, 2016. Retrieved from, http://www.abs.gov.au/AUSSTATS/abs@.nsf/allprimarymainfeatures/47E19CA15036B04BCA2577570014668B?opendocument.

Australian Bureau of Statistics (ABS). (2018) Remoteness Structure, accessed 1st February 2019, http://www.abs.gov.au/websitedbs/d3310114.nsf/home/remoteness+structure.

Australian Government. (2018) Shaping a nation: population growth and immigration over time, The Australian Government the Treasury and the Department of Home Affairs (online), https://cdn.tspace.gov.au/uploads/sites/107/2018/04/Shaping-a-Nation-1.pdf.

Australian Institute of Criminology (AIC). (2007) Perceptions of crime. Crime Facts Information no. 143 (Canberra: AIC), http://www.aic.gov.au/publications/current series/cfi/141-160/cfi143.aspx.

Australian Institute of Health and Welfare (AIHW). (2004) Rural, regional and remote health: A guide to remoteness classifications, Canberra, Australia, accessed 4th December 2016, http://www.aihw.gov.au/WorkArea/DownloadAsset.aspx?id=6442459567.

Australian Institute of Health and Welfare. (2018) Australia's Health (Canberra: Australian Institute of Health and Welfare).

Azzopardi, P., Sawyer, S. M., Carlin, J., Degenhardt, L., Brown, N., Brown, A. & Patton, G. (2018) 'Health and wellbeing of Indigenous adolescents in Australia: a systematic synthesis of population data', The Lancet, vol. 391, no. 10122, pp. 766–782.

Back, L. (1996) New Ethnicities and Urban Culture (London: UCL Press).

Back. (2016) 'Moving sounds, controlled borders: asylum and the politics of culture', Young, vol. 24, no. 3, pp. 185–203.

Baird, A. (2017) 'Becoming the "baddest": masculine trajectories of gang violence in Medellín', Journal of Latin American Studies, vol. 50, no. 1, pp. 183–219.

Baker, A. & Pickerill, J. (2019) 'Doings with the land and sea: decolonising geographies, indigeneity and enacting place-agency', Progress in Human Geography, early online view, pp. 1–24.

Ball, S., Reay, D. & David, M. (2002) '"Ethnic choosing": minority ethnic students, social class and higher education choice', Race Ethnicity and Education, vol. 5, no. 4, pp. 333–357.

Bannister, J., Kintrea, K. & Pickering, J. (2013) 'Young people and violent territorial conflict: exclusion, culture and the search for identity', Journal of Youth Studies, vol. 16, no. 4, pp. 474–490.

Barbalet, J. (1988) Citizenship, Milton Keynes (Open University Press).

Barone, C. (2011) 'Some things never change: gender segregation in higher education across eight nations and three decades', Sociology of Education, vol. 84, no. 2, pp. 157–176.

Barth, F. (1998) Ethnic Groups and Boundaries: The Social Organization of Culture Difference (Illinois: Waveland Press).

Batchelor, S., Burman, M. & Brown, J. (2001) 'Discussing violence: let's hear it from the girls', Probation Journal, vol. 48, no. 2, pp. 125–134.

Bates, I. (1993) 'When I have my own studio' in Bates, I. & Riseborough, G. (eds.) Youth and Inequality (Milton Keynes: Open University Press).

Bathmaker, A. M., Ingram, N. & Waller, R. (2013) 'Higher education, social class and the mobilisation of capitals: recognising and playing the game', *British Journal of Sociology of Education*, vol. 34, no. 5–6, pp. 723–743.

Baudinette, T. (2015) 'Negotiating the fetishisation of youth in the gay male media of Japan', TASA Youth Blog, posted 11th January 2015, https://tasayouth.wordpress.com/2015/01/12/negotiating-the-fetishisation-of-youth-in-the-gay-male-media-of-japan/.

Baudinette, T. (2016) 'Ethnosexual frontiers in queer Tokyo: the production of racialised desire in Japan', *Japan Forum*, vol. 28, no. 4, pp. 465–485.

Bauman, Z. (1998) *Globalization: The Human Consequences* (New York, Columbia University Press).

Beck, U. (1992) *Risk Society: Towards a New Modernity* (London: Sage Publications).

Beck, U. & Beck-Gernsheim, E. (2002) *Individualisation: Institutional Individualism and Its Social and Political Consequences* (London: Sage).

Becker, H. (1963) *Outsiders: Studies in the Sociology of Deviance* (New York: Macmillan).

Becker, G. S. (2009) *Human Capital: A Theoretical and Empirical Analysis, with Special Reference to Education* (Chicago: University of Chicago press).

Beck-Gernsheim, E. (1998) 'On the way to a post-familial family: from a community of need to elective affinities', *Theory, Culture & Society*, vol. 15, no. 3–4, pp. 53–70.

Beer, D. & Burrows, R. (2010) 'Consumption, prosumption and participatory web cultures: an introduction', *Journal of Consumer Culture*, vol. 10, no. 1, pp. 3–12.

Bell, V. (1999) 'Performativity and belonging: an introduction', *Theory Culture and Society*, vol. 16, no. 2, pp. 1–10.

Bennett, A. (1999a) 'Rappin' on the Tyne: White hip hop culture in Northeast England–an ethnographic study', *The Sociological Review*, vol. 47, no. 1, pp. 1–24.

Bennett, A. (1999b) 'Subcultures or neo-tribes? Rethinking the relationship between youth, style and musical taste', *Sociology*, vol. 33, no. 3, pp. 599–617.

Bennett, A. (2011) 'The post-subcultural turn: some reflections 10 years on', *Journal of Youth Studies*, vol. 14, no. 5, pp. 493–506.

Bennett, A. (2014) 'Youth culture and the internet: a subcultural or post-subcultural phenomena?' in The Subcultures Network (eds.) *Subcultures, Popular Music and Social Change* (Newcastle: Cambridge Scholars Publishing).

Bennett, A. & Rogers, I. (2016) *Popular Music Scenes and Cultural Memory. Pop Music, Culture and Identity* (London: Palgrave Macmillan).

Benson, M. & Jackson, E. (2012) 'Place-making and place maintenance: performativity, place and belonging among the middle classes', *Sociology*, vol. 47, no. 4, pp. 793–809.

Berger, G. (2016) Will This Year's College Grads Job-Hop More Than Previous Grads? LinkedIn Official Blog (online), https://blog.linkedin.com/2016/04/12/will-this-year_s-college-grads-job-hop-more-than-previous-grads.

Berrington, A., Roberts, S. & Tammes, P. (2016) 'Educational aspirations among UK young teenagers: exploring the role of gender, class and ethnicity', *British Educational Research Journal*, vol. 42, no. 5, pp. 729–755.

Bertrand, M. & Mullainathan, S. (2004) 'Are Emily and Greg more employable than Lakisha and Jamal? A field experiment on labor market discrimination', *American Economic Review*, vol. 94, no. 4, pp. 991–1013.

Bessant, J. (2001) 'From sociology of deviance to sociology of risk: youth homelessness and the problem of empiricism', *Journal of Criminal Justice*, vol. 29, no. 1, pp. 31–43.

Bessant, J. (2008) 'Hard wired for risk neurological science and the adolescent brain and development theory', *Journal of Youth Studies*, vol. 11, no. 3, pp. 347–360.

Bessant, J. (2018) 'Young precariat and a new work order? A case for historical sociology', *Journal of Youth Studies*, vol. 21, no. 6, pp. 780–798.

Best, A. L. & Lynn, R. (2016) 'Youth and consumer markets' in Furlong, A. (ed.) *Handbook of Youth and Young Adulthood* (London: Routledge).

Betts, L. R. & Spenser, K. A. (2017) '"People think it's a harmless joke": young people's understanding of the impact of technology, digital vulnerability and cyberbullying in the United Kingdom', *Journal of Children and Media*, vol. 11, no. 1, pp. 20–35.

Binder, A. J., Davis, D, B. & Bloom, N. (2016) 'Career funnelling: how elite students learn to define and desire "prestigious" jobs', *Sociology of Education*, vol. 89, no. 1, pp. 20–39.

Bissell, P., Peacock, M., Blackburn, J. & Smith, C. (2016) 'The discordant pleasures of everyday eating: reflections on the social gradient in obesity under neo-liberalism', *Social Science & Medicine*, vol. 159, pp. 14–21.

Black, R. & Walsh, L. (2019) *Imagining Youth Futures: University Students in Post-Truth Times* (Singapore: Springer).

Blackman, S. (1995) *Youth: Positions and Oppositions—Style, Sexuality and Schooling* (Aldershot: Avebury).

Blackman, S. (2004) *Chilling Out: The Cultural Politics of Substance Consumption, Youth and Drug Policy* (Maidenhead: Open University Press).

Blair, T. 1998. *The Third Way: New Politics for the New Century* (London: Fabian Society).

Blanchflower, D. G., Bell, D. N., Montagnoli, A. & Moro, M, (2014) 'The happiness trade-off between unemployment and inflation', *Journal of Money, Credit and Banking*, vol. 46, no. S2, pp. 117–141.

Blaxter, M. (2003) *Health and Lifestyles* (London: Routledge).

BLS. (2018a) Accessed 11th January 2019, https://www.bls.gov/news.release/youth.nr0.htm.

BLS. (2018b) Economic News Release: Contingent and Alternative Employment Arrangements Summary, https://www.bls.gov/news.release/conemp.nr0.htm.

Bolton, P. (2019) 'Student Loan Statistics, House of Commons Briefing paper', Number 1079, 6 February 2019.

Bondi, L. & Rose, D. (2003) 'Constructing gender, constructing the urban: a review of Anglo-American feminist urban geography', *Gender, Place and Culture*, vol. 10, no. 3, pp. 229–245.

Bossart, J. & Bharti, N. (2017) 'Women in engineering: insight into why some engineering departments have more success in recruiting and graduating women', *American Journal of Engineering Education*, vol. 8, no. 2, pp. 127–140.

Bourdieu, P. (2000) *La Sociologie est un sport de combat* [trans. Sociology is a Martial Art] Icarus Films.

Bourke, L. & Geldens, P. (2007) 'What does wellbeing mean?: perspectives of wellbeing among young people & youth workers in rural Victoria', *Youth Studies Australia*, vol. 26, no. 1, p. 41.

Bourke, L., Humphreys, J., S, Wakerman, J. & Taylor, J. (2010) 'From 'problem-describing' to 'problem-solving': challenging the 'deficit' view of remote and rural health', *Australian Journal of Rural Health*, vol. 18, no. 5, pp. 205–209.

Boyd, d. (2007) 'Why youth (heart) social network sites: the role of networked publics in teenage social life', *MacArthur Foundation Series on Digital Learning Youth, Identity and Digital Media*, vol. 119, p.142.

Boyd, d. (2008) 'Why youth (heart) social network sites: the role of networked publics in teenage social life' in Buckingham, D. (ed.) *Youth, Identity and Digital Media* (Massachusetts: The MIT Press).

Boyd, d. (2014) *It's Complicated: The Social Lives of Networked Teens* (New Haven: Yale University Press).

Bradley, H. & Ingram, N. (2013) 'Banking on the future: choices, aspirations and economic hardship in working-class student experience' in *Class Inequality in Austerity Britain* (London: Palgrave Macmillan).

Brake, M. (1985) *Comparative Youth Culture: The Sociology of Youth Culture and Youth Subcultures in America, Britain, and Canada* (London: Routledge).

Branch, K, Hilinski-Rosick, C. M., Johnson, E. & Solano, G. (2017) 'Revenge porn victimization of college students in the United States: an exploratory analysis', *International Journal of Cyber Criminology*, vol. 11, no. 1, pp. 128–142.

Bremberg, S. (2015) 'Mental health problems are rising more in Swedish adolescents than in other Nordic countries and the Netherlands', *Acta Paediatrica*, vol. 104, no. 10, pp. 997–1004.

Britton, J., Dearden, L., Shephard, N. & Vignoles, A. (2016) *How English Domiciled Graduate Earnings Vary with Gender, Institution Attended, Subject and Socio-Economic Background* (London: Institute for Financial Studies).

Brolin Låftman, S. & Östberg, V. (2006) 'The pros and cons of social relations: an analysis of adolescents' health complaints', *Social Science and Medicine*, vol. 63, no. 3, pp. 611–623.

Brooks, R. (2016) 'Young people and higher education' in Furlong, A. (ed.) *Handbook of Youth and Young Adulthood* (London: Routledge).

Brooks, R. & Waters, J. (2010) 'Social networks and educational mobility: the experiences of UK students', *Globalisation, Societies and Education*, vol. 8, no. 1, pp. 143–157.

Brotherhood St Laurence. (2018a) *Part-Time Purgatory: Young and Underemployed in Australia* (Melbourne: Brotherhood St. Lawrence).

Brotherhood St Laurence. (2018b) *An Unfair Australia? Mapping Youth Unemployment Hotspots* (Melbourne: Brotherhood St Laurence).

Brown, P., Lauder, H. & Ashton, D. (2011) *The Global Auction: The Broken Promises of Education, Jobs, and Incomes* (Oxford: Oxford University Press).

Brunson, J. (2010) 'Confronting maternal mortality, controlling birth in Nepal: the gendered politics of receiving biomedical care at birth', *Social Science & Medicine*, vol. 71, no. 10, pp. 1719–1727.

Brydsten, A., Hammarstrom, A., Strandh, M. & Johansson, K. (2015) 'Youth unemployment and functional somatic symptoms in adulthood: results from the Northern Swedish cohort', *European Journal of Public Health*, vol. 25, no. 5, pp. 796–800.

Büchi, M., Just, N. & Latzer, M. (2016) 'Modelling the second-level digital divide: a five-country study of social differences in Internet use', *New Media & Society*, vol. 18, no. 11, pp. 2703–2722.

Buckingham, D. (2008) *Youth, Identity and Digital Media* (Cambridge, MA: MIT Press).

Buckingham, D., Bragg, S. & Kehily, M. J. (2014) *Youth Cultures in the Age of Global Media* (London: Palgrave Macmillan).

Butler, J. (1990) *Gender Trouble: Feminism and the Subversion of Gender* (London: Routledge).

Butler, J. (1993) *Bodies That Matter: On the Discursive Limits of Sex* (London: Routledge).

Butler, R. & Muir, K. (2017) 'Young people's education biographies: family relationships, social capital and belonging', *Journal of Youth Studies*, vol. 20, no. 3, pp. 316–331.

Byrne, D. G., Davenport, S. C. & Mazanov, J. (2007) 'Profiles of adolescent stress: the development of the adolescent stress questionnaire (ASQ)', *Journal of Adolescence*, vol. 30, no. 3, pp. 393–416.

Byron, P., Rasmussen, S., Wright Toussaint, D., Lobo, R., Robinson, K. H. & Paradise, B. (2017) "You learn from each other": LGBTIQ young people's mental health help-seeking and the RAD Australia Online Directory'. https://doi.org/10.4225/35/58ae2 dea65d12.

Cahill, H. (2015) 'Approaches to Understanding Youth Wellbeing' in Wyn J. & Cahill H. (eds.) *Handbook of Youth and Childhood Studies* (New York: Springer).

Cahill, H. & Coffey, J. (2013) *Learning Partnerships*, Research Report 38 (Melbourne: University of Melbourne).

Cahill, H. & Coffey, J. (2016) 'Positioning, participation, and possibility: using post-structural concepts for social change in Asia-Pacific youth HIV prevention', *Journal of Youth Studies*, vol. 19, no. 4, pp. 533–551.

Cahill, H., Beadle, S. & Coffey, J. (2013) NewGen Asia: building capacity in emerging young leaders in the HIV response. Research Report 40, Melbourne: University of Melbourne.

Cairns, D. C. (2015) 'Mapping the Youth Mobility Field.' in Lange, A., Steiner, C., Schutter, S. & Reiter, H. (eds.) *Handbook of Child and Youth Sociology* (Wiesbaden: Springer).

Callimachi, R. (2015) 'ISIS and the lonely young American', *The New York Times*, June 27, accessed 10th August 2018, https://www.nytimes.com/2015/06/28/world/ameri-cas/isis-online-recruiting-american.html.

Campbell, A. (1984) *The Girls in the Gang* (Cambridge: Blackwell).

Carleton, C. & Kelly, M. T. (2016) Alternative Work Arrangements and Job Satisfaction, Working Paper No 32. Villanova School of Business Department of Economics and Statistics, https://ideas.repec.org/p/vil/papers/32.html.

Caroll, D., Heaton, C. & Tani, M. (2018) Does It Pay to Graduate from an 'Elite' University in Australia? IZA: Institute of Labor Economics, Discussion Paper No. 11477. Bonn, IZA.

Carrington, K. (2013) 'Girls, crime and violence: toward a feminist theory of female violence', *International Journal for Crime, Justice and Social Democracy*, vol. 2, no. 2, pp. 63–79.

Carrington, B. & Wilson, B. (2004) 'Dance nations: rethinking youth subcultural theory' in Bennett, A. & Kahn-Harris, K. (eds.) *After Subculture: Critical Studies in Contemporary Youth Culture* (London: Palgrave Macmillan).

Castells, M. (2000) 'Materials for an exploratory theory of the network society', *The British Journal of Sociology*, vol. 51, no. 1, pp. 5–24.

Castells, M. (2011) *The Rise of the Network Society* (Vol. 12) (Oxford: John Wiley & Sons).

Cave, L., Fildes, J., Luckett, G. & Wearring, A. (2015) *Mission Australia's 2015 Youth Survey Report* (Melbourne: Mission Australia).

Chatterton, P. & Hollands, R. (2002) 'Theorising urban playscapes: producing, regu-lating and consuming youthful nightlife city spaces', *Urban Studies*, vol. 39, no. 1, pp. 95–116.

Chatterton, P. & Hollands, R. (2003) *Urban Nightscapes: Youth Cultures, Pleasure Spaces and Corporate Power* (Routledge: London).

Chesney-Lind, M. (1984) 'Girls' crime and woman's place: toward a feminist model of female delinquency', *Crime & Delinquency*, vol. 35, no. 1, pp. 5–29.

Chesney-Lind, M. & Irwin, K. (2004) 'From badness to meanness: popular construc-tions of contemporary girlhood' in Harris A. (ed.) *All About the Girl: Culture, Power, and Identity* (New York: Routledge).

Chesney–Lind, M. (2006) 'Patriarchy, crime, and justice: feminist criminology in an era of backlash', *Feminist Criminology*, vol. 1, no. 1, pp. 6–26.

Chesters, J. & Watson, L. (2013) 'Understanding the persistence of inequality in higher education: evidence from Australia', *Journal of Education Policy*, vol. 28, no. 2, pp. 198–215.

Chiang, Y. L., Hannum, E. & Kao, G. (2015) 'It's not just about the money: gender and youth migration from rural China', *Chinese Sociological Review*, vol. 47, no. 2, pp. 177–201.

China Internet Network Information Centre (CNNIC). (2017) Statistical report on internet development in China, January 2017, https://cnnic.com.cn/IDR/ReportDownloads/201706/P020170608523740585924.pdf.

Choudhury, S. (2010) 'Culturing the adolescent brain: what can neuroscience learn from anthropology?' *Social Cognitive and Affective Neuroscience*, vol. 5, no. 2–3, pp. 159–167.

Chowdhury, S., Ooi, E. & Slonim, R. (2017) *Racial discrimination and white first name adoption: a field experiment in the Australian labour market*, University of Sydney Economic Working paper series, paper 15, http://econ-wpseries.com/2017/201715.pdf.

Ciarrochi, J., Deane, F. P., Wilson, C. J. & Rickwood, D. (2002) 'Adolescents who need help the most are the least likely to seek it: the relationship between low emotional competence and low intention to seek help'. *British Journal of Guidance and Counselling*, vol. 30, no. 2, pp. 173–188.

Cieslik, M. (2003) 'Introduction' in Bennett, A., Cieslik, M. & Miles, S. (eds.) *Researching Youth* (London: Palgrave Macmillan).

Cieslik, M. & Simpson, D. (2013) *Key Concepts in Youth Studies* (London: Sage).

Clarke, G. (1982) 'Defending ski-jumpers: a critique of theories of youth sub-cultures,' *CCCS Sub and Popular Culture Series*, SP 71, Birmingham, University of Birmingham.

Clarke, R. V. (1992) *Situational Crime Prevention: Successful Case Studies* (Guilderland: Harrow & Heston).

Clarke, R. V. & Cornish, D. (1985) 'Modelling offenders' decisions: a framework for research and policy', *Crime and Justice: A Review of Research*, vol. 6, pp. 147–185.

Clarke, J., Hall, S., Jefferson, T. & Roberts, B. (1976) 'Subcultures, cultures and class: a theoretical overview' in Hall, S. & Jefferson, T. (eds.) *Resistance Through Rituals* (Birmingham: The Centre for Contemporary Cultural Studies, University of Birmingham).

Clayton, J. (2009) 'Thinking spatially: towards an everyday understanding of inter-ethnic relations', *Social & Cultural Geography*, vol. 10, no. 4, pp. 481–498.

Cobb-Clark, D. A. & Gørgens, T. (2014) '"Parents" economic support of young-adult children: do socioeconomic circumstances matter?', *Journal of Population Economics*, vol. 27, no. 2, pp. 447–471.

Cockx, B. & Picchio, M. (2013) 'Scarring effects of remaining unemployed for long-term unemployed school-leavers', *Journal of the Royal Statistical Society*, vol. 176, no. 4, pp. 951–980.

Coffey, J. (2013) ' "Body pressure": negotiating gender through body work practices', *Youth Studies Australia*, vol. 32, no. 2, pp. 39–48.

Coffey, J. (2015a) 'As long as I'm fit and a healthy weight, I don't feel bad': exploring body work and health through the concept of "affect"', *Journal of Sociology*, vol. 51, no. 3, pp. 613–627.

Coffey, J. (2015b) '"I put pressure on myself to keep that body": "health"-related body work, masculinities and embodied identity', *Social Theory and Health,* vol. 14, no. 2, pp. 169–188.

Coffey, J. (2016) *Body Work: Youth, Gender and Health* (London: Routledge).

Coffey, J. (2017) 'Youth, health and morality: body work and health assemblages' in Kelly, P. & Pike J. (eds.) *Neo-Liberalism, Austerity and the Moral Economies of Young People's Health and Well-Being* (London: Palgrave Macmillan).

Coffey, J. & Farrugia, D. (2014) 'Unpacking the black box: the problem of agency in the sociology of youth'. *Journal of Youth Studies*, vol. 17, no. 4, pp. 461–474.

Coffey, J., Budgeon, S. & Cahill, H. (eds.) (2016) *Learning Bodies: The Body in Youth and Childhood Studies* (New York: Springer).

Cohen, A. K. (1955) *Delinquent Boys: The Culture of the Gang* (New York: Free Press).

Cohen, P. (1972a) *Sub-cultural Conflict and Working Class Community. Working Papers in Cultural Studies. No. 2* (Birmingham: University of Birmingham).

Cohen, S. (1972b) *Folk Devils and Moral Panics* (St Albans: Paladin).

Cohen, S. (1985) *Visions of Social Control* (Cambridge: Polity Press).

Cohen, L. & Felson, M. (1979) 'Social change and crime rate trends: a routine activity approach', *American Sociological Review*, vol. 44, pp. 588–608.

Coles, B. (2014) Small drop in NEETs, but who counts the cost of the missing? *The Conversation,* 28 February 2014, accessed 12th October 2018, https://theconversation.com/small-drop-in-neets-but-who-counts-the-cost-of-the-missing-23746.

Colombo, E. (2015) 'Multiculturalism's: an overview of multicultural debates in western societies', *Current Sociology*, vol. 63, no. 6, pp. 800–824.

Condry, I. (2001) 'A history of Japanese hip-hop: street dance, club scene, pop market' in Mitchell, T. (ed.) *Global Noise* (Middletown: Wesleyan University Press).

Connell, R. W. (1995) *Masculinities* (St Leonards: Allen & Unwin).

Connell, R. W. (2007) *Southern Theory* (Crows Nest, Australia: Unwin and Allen).

Corrigan, P. (1979) *Schooling the Smash Street Kids* (London: Red Globe Publishing).

Cortina, J., Taran, P. & Raphael, A. (2014) *Migration and Youth: Challenges and Opportunities* (Paris, UNICEF).

Craig, S. L. & McInroy, L. (2014) 'You can form a part of yourself online: the influence of new media on identity development and coming out for LGBTQ youth', *Journal of Gay & Lesbian Mental Health*, vol. 18, no. 1, pp. 95–109.

Crawford, A. (2009) 'Governing through anti-social behaviour: regulatory challenges to criminal justice', *British Journal of Criminology*, vol. 49, no. 6, pp. 810–831.

Crawford, M. (2018) Universities 2017, New South Wales: Audit Office, https://www.audit.nsw.gov.au/our-work/reports/universities-2017.

Crawford, C. & Greaves, E. (2015) *Socio-economic, ethnic and gender differences in HE participation.* Research Paper 186, London, Department of Business and Innovation.

Crawford, C. & Vignoles, A. (2014) *Heterogeneity in graduate earnings by socio-economic background.* Unpublished paper: Institute of Fiscal Studies.

Crawshaw, P. & Bunton, R. (2009) 'Logics of practice in the "risk environment"', *Health, Risk & Society*, vol. 11, no. 3, pp. 269–282.

Crenshaw, K. W. (1991) 'Mapping the margins: intersectionality, identity politics and violence against women of color', *Stanford Law Review*, vol. 43, no. 6, pp. 1241–1299.

Cresswell, T. (2015) *Place: An Introduction* (Oxford: John Wiley).

Critcher, C. (2008) 'Making waves: historical aspects of public debates about children and mass media' in *The International Handbook of Children, Media and Culture.*

Crockett, J. (2012) "There's nothing the *@#! wrong with me": youth mental health and substance use in rural and remote Australia and the potential role of school-based interventions', *Youth Studies Australia*, vol. 31, no. 1, pp. 53–59.

Cuervo, H. & Miranda, A. (eds.) (2019) *Youth, Inequality and Social Change in the Global South, Perspectives on Children and Young People* (London: Springer).

Cuervo, H. & Wyn, J. (2012) *Young People Making It Work: Continuity and Change in Rural Places* (Melbourne: Melbourne University Publishing).

Cuervo, H. & Wyn, J. (2014) 'Reflections on the use of spatial and relational metaphors in youth studies', *Journal of Youth Studies*, vol. 17, no. 7, pp. 901–915.

Cuervo, H. & Wyn, J. (2017) 'A longitudinal analysis of belonging: temporal, performative and relational practices by young people in rural Australia', *Young*, vol. 25, no. 3, pp. 219–234.

Cuervo, H., Barakat, N. & Turnbull, M. (2015) Youth, belonging and transitions: identifying opportunities and barriers for Indigenous young people in remote communities, research report no.44, Melbourne, Melbourne Youth Research Centre.

Cuzzocrea, V. & Collins, R. (2015) 'Collaborative individualization? Peer-to-peer action in youth transitions', *Young: Nordic Journal of Youth Research*, vol. 23, no. 2, pp. 136–153.

Davis, K. (2008) 'Intersectionality as buzzword: a sociology of science perspective on what makes a feminist theory successful', *Feminist Theory*, vol. 9, no. 1, pp. 67–85.

Davis, K. (2012) 'Tensions of identity in a networked era: young people's perspectives on the risks and rewards of online self-expression', *New Media & Society*, vol. 14, no. 4, pp. 634–651.

Dawes, M. (1998) '"Theories" in everyday situations', *ETC: A Review of General Semantics*, vol. 55, no. 3, pp. 329–334.

de Beauvior, S. (1972) *The Second Sex* (Harmondsworth: Penguin).

De Ridder, S. & Van Bauwel, S. (2013) 'Commenting on pictures: teens negotiating gender and sexualities on social networking sites', *Sexualities*, vol. 16, no. 5–6, pp. 565–586.

De Stefano, V. (2016) 'The rise of the just-in-time workforce: on-demand work, crowdwork, and labor protection in the gig-economy', *Comparative Labor Law & Policy Journal*, vol. 37, p. 471.

Dean, H. (2006) Activation policies and the changing ethical foundations of welfare, in: ASPEN/ETUI conference: activation policies in the EU, 20–21 Oct 2006, Brussels. Available at: http://eprints.lse.ac.uk/3784/.

Department for Education and Training. (2018) International student enrolments in Australia 1994–2018, https://internationaleducation.gov.au/research/International-Student-Data/Pages/InternationalStudentData2018.aspx#Pivot_Table.

Dillabough, J. & Kennelly, J. (2010) *Lost Youth in the Global City* (London: Routledge).

Dimitriadis, G. (2009) *Performing Identity/Performing Culture: Hip Hop as Text, Pedagogy, and Lived Practice* (New York: Peter Lang).

Donath, J. & Boyd, D. (2004) 'Public displays of connection', *BT Technology Journal*, vol. 22, no. 4, pp. 71–82.

Douglas, T. (1966) *Purity and Danger: An Analysis of Concepts of Pollution and Taboo* (London: Routledge Kegan Paul).

Douglas, M. (1992) *Risk and Blame: Essays in Cultural Theory* (Routledge: London).

Downs, Y. (2016) 'The gap between rich and poor students going to university has reached record levels', *The Conversation*, 21 December 2016, https://theconversation.com/the-gap-between-rich-and-poor-students-going-to-university-has-reached-record-levels-63967.

Drine, I. (2017) 'Education and Entrepreneurship to address Youth Unemployment in MENA Region', Expert Group Meeting on "Strategies for Eradicating Poverty to Achieve Sustainable Development for All" United Nations, New York, 10–11 May 2017.

Driver, S. (ed.) (2008) *Queer Youth Cultures* (New York: SUNY Press).

Driver, C. (2011) 'Embodying hard-core: rethinking 'subcultural' authenticities', *Journal of Youth Studies,* vol. 14, no. 8, pp. 975–990.

Du, H. (2017) 'Place attachment and belonging among educated young migrants and returnees: the case of Chaohu, China', *Population, Space and Place*, vol. 23, no. 1, p. e1967.

Du Bois-Reymond, M. (1998) '"I don't want to commit myself yet": young people's life concepts', *Journal of Youth Studies*, vol. 1, no. 1, pp. 63–79.

Du Bois-Reymond, M. (1999) 'I don't want to commit myself just yet: young people's life concepts', *Journal of Youth Studies*, vol. 1, no. 1, pp. 63–79.

Ducheneaut, N., Wen, M. H., Yee, N. & Wadley, G. (2009) 'April. Body and mind: a study of avatar personalization in three virtual worlds' in *Proceedings of the SIGCHI Conference on Human Factors in Computing Systems*, ACM. pp. 1151–1160.

Dudgeon, P., Walker, R., Scrine, C., Shepherd, C., Calma, T. & Ring, I. (2014) 'Effective strategies to strengthen the mental health and wellbeing of Aboriginal and Torres Strait Islander people', Canberra, Australian Institute of Health and Welfare.

Duffy, B. E. & Chan, N. K. (2019) '"You never really know who's looking": imagined surveillance across social media platforms', *New Media and Society*, vol. 21, no. 1, pp. 119–138.

Dunkley, C. M. (2004) 'Risky geographies: teens, gender, and rural landscape in North America', *Gender, Place and Culture*, vol. 11 no. 4, pp. 559–579.

Durkheim, E. (1938) *The Rules of Sociological Method* (New York: Free Press).

Ei Chew, H., LaRose, R., Steinfield, C. & Velasquez, A. (2011) 'The use of online social networking by rural youth and its effects on community attachment', *Information, Communication & Society*, vol. 14, no. 5, pp. 726–747.

Eisenstadt, S. (1956) *From Generation to Generation* (New York: Free Press).

Elias, N. (1990) *What Is Sociology?* (Columbia: Columbia University Press).

Elias, P. & Purcell, K. (2012) 'Higher education and social background' in *Understanding Society Findings 2012 Link, http://research.understandingsociety.org.uk/files/research/findings/Understanding-Society-Findings-2012.pdf,* pp. 23–24, Institute for Social and Economic Research.

Eurostat. (2018) How common – and how voluntary – is part-time employment? [online] accessed 1st February 2019, https://ec.europa.eu/eurostat/web/products-eurostat-news/-/DDN-20180608-1.

Evans, S. (2009) 'In a different place: working-class girls and higher education', *Sociology*, vol. 43, no. 2, pp. 340–355.

Evans, K. & Furlong, A. (1997) 'Metaphors of youth transitions: niches, pathways, trajectories of navigations' in Bynner, J., Chisholm, L. & Furlong, A. (eds.) *Youth, Citizenship and Social Change in Europe* (Aldershot: Ashgate).

Everatt, D. (2015) 'The politics of non-belonging in the developing world' in Wyn, J. & Cahill, H. (eds.) *Handbook of Youth and Childhood Studies* (New York: Springer).

Fafo. (2001) 'Workfare in Six European Nations: Findings and Evaluation Recommendations for Future Development'. Prepared for the Conference Welfare to Work in Europe and the US Fafo, October 5.

Farrington, D. (1996) *Understanding and Preventing Youth Crime* (York: Joseph Rowntree Foundation).

Farrington, D. (2005) 'Introduction to integrated developmental and life-course theories of offending integrated' in Farrington, D. (ed.) *Integrated Developmental and Life-course Theories of Offending* (New Brunswick: Transaction Publishers).

Farrugia, D. (2011) 'Youth homelessness and individualised subjectivity', *Journal of Youth Studies*, vol. 14, no. 7, pp. 761–775.

Farrugia, D. (2014) 'Towards a spatialised youth sociology: the rural and the urban in times of change', *Journal of Youth Studies*, vol. 17, no. 3, pp. 293–307.

Farrugia, D. (2016) 'The mobility imperative for rural youth: the structural, symbolic and non-representational dimensions rural youth mobilities', *Journal of Youth Studies*, vol. 19, no. 6, pp. 836–851.

Farrugia, D. (2019) 'The formation of young workers: the cultivation of the self as a subject of value to the contemporary labour force', *Current Sociology*, vol. 67, no. 1, pp. 47–63.

Farrugia, D., Smyth, J. & Harrison, T. (2014) 'Emplacing young people in an Australian rural community: an extraverted sense of place in times of change'. *Journal of Youth Studies*, vol. 17, no. 9, pp. 1152–1167.

Farrugia, D., Threadgold, S. & Coffey, J. (2018) 'Young subjectivities and affective labour in the service economy', *Journal of Youth Studies*, vol. 21, no. 3, pp. 272–287.

Featherstone, M. (2010) 'Body, image and affect in consumer culture', *Body and Society*, vol. 16, no. 1, pp. 193–221.

Feixa, C., & Nofre, J. (2012) 'Youth cultures', *Sociopedia. ISA*, vol. 2012, pp. 1–16.

Ferguson, H. (2018) *Updated Higher Education Loan Program (HELP) Debt Statistics* (Canberra: Parliament of Australia). https://www.aph.gov.au/About_Parliament/Parliamentary_Departments/Parliamentary_Library/FlagPost/2018/May/HELP-debt-statistics.

Fergusson, R. (2014) *Young people, Welfare and Crime: Governing Non-Participation* (Bristol: Policy Press).

Fergusson, D. M., Boden, J. M. & Horwood, L. J. (2007) 'Recurrence of major depression in adolescence and early adulthood, and later mental health, educational and economic outcomes', *British Journal of Psychiatry*, vol. 191, no. 4, pp. 335–342.

Fergusson, D., McLeod, G. & Horwood, L. J. (2014) 'Unemployment and psychosocial outcomes to age 30: a fixed-effects regression analyses', *Australian, New Zealand Journal of Psychiatry*, vol. 48, no. 8, pp. 735–742.

Ferrell, J. (1999) 'Cultural criminology', *Annual Review of Sociology*, vol. 25, no. 1, pp. 395–418.

Ferrell, D. & Greig, F. (2016) *Paychecks, paydays, and the online platform economy: Big data on income volatility*, JP Morgan Chase Institute, https://www.jpmorganchase.com/corporate/institute/document/jpmc-institute-volatility-2-report.pdf.

Firth, S. (1986) *The Sociology of Youth* (Ormskirk: Causeway Press).

Foley, P. (2007) *The Socio-Economic Status of Vocational Education and Training Students in Australia*, National Centre for Vocational Education Research Ltd, Adelaide, Australia.

Forbes. (2019) https://www.forbes.com/sites/quora/2019/01/08/what-are-the-pros-and-cons-of-the-gig-economy/#66de94921388.

Forbes, J. & Maxwell, C. (2018) 'Bourdieu plus: understanding the creation of agentic, aspirational girl subjects in elite schools' in Stahl, G., Wallace, D., Threadgold, S. & Burke, C. (eds.) *International Perspectives on Theorizing Aspirations: Applying Bourdieu's Tools. Social Theory and Methodology in Education Research* (London: Bloomsbury).

Forbes-Mewett, H. M. (2018) *The New Security: Individual, Community and Cultural Experiences (Crime Prevention and Security Management)* (London: Palgrave Macmillan).

Foucault, M. (1975) *Discipline and Punish: The Birth of the Prison* (New York: Random House).

Foundation for Young Australians. (2017) *The New Work Smarts: Thriving in the New Work Order*, https://www.fya.org.au/wp-content/uploads/2017/07/FYA_TheNewWorkSmarts_July2017.pdf.

France, A. (1998) "Why should we care?' Young people, citizenship and social responsibility', *Journal of Youth Studies*, vol. 1, pp. 97–111.

France, A. (2007) *Understanding Youth in Late Modernity* (Maidenhead, Open University Press).

France, A. (2012) 'It's all in the brain' Science and the 'new' construction of the youth problem in New Zealand', *New Zealand Journal of Sociology*, vol. 27, no. 2, pp. 75–94.

France, A. (2016) *Understanding Youth in the Global Economic Crisis* (Bristol: Policy Press).

France, A. (2017) *Anti-social Behaviour in Furlong, A. Handbook of Young and Adulthood*, 2nd ed. (London, Routledge).

France, A. & Roberts, S. (2016) 'The problem of social generations: a critique of the new emerging orthodoxy in youth studies', *Journal of Youth Studies*, vol. 18, no. 2, pp. 215–230.

France, A. & Roberts, S. (2017) *Youth and Social Class: Enduring Inequality in the United Kingdom, Australia and New Zealand* (London: Palgrave Macmillan).

France, A., Bottrell, D. & Armstrong, D. (2012) *A Political Ecology of Youth and Crime* (London: Palgrave Macmillan).

France, A., Bottrell, D. & Haddon, E. (2013) 'Managing everyday life: The conceptualisation and value of cultural capital in navigating everyday life for working class youth', *Journal of Youth Studies*, vol. 16, no. 5, pp. 597–611.

Fraser, A. (2013) 'Street habitus: gangs, territorialism and social change in Glasgow', *Journal of Youth Studies*, vol. 16, no. 8, pp. 970–985.

Fraser, A. & Hagedorn, J. M. (2018) 'Gangs and a global sociological imagination', *Theoretical Criminology*, vol. 22, no. 1, pp. 42–62.

Fraser, A., Ralphs, R. & Smithson, H. (2018) 'European youth gang policy in comparative context', *Children and Society*, vol. 32, no. 2, pp. 156–165.

Friedman, G. (2014) 'Workers without employers: shadow corporations and the rise of the gig economy', *Review of Keynesian Economics*, vol. 2, no. 2, pp. 171–188.

Friedman, Z. (2018) Student Loan Debt Statistics In 2018: A $1.5 Trillion Crisis, https://www.forbes.com/sites/zackfriedman/2018/06/13/student-loan-debt-statistics-2018/#4d7b046f7310.

Friedman, S. & Laurinson, L. (2019) *The Class Ceiling: Why It Pays to Be Privileged* (Bristol: Bristol University Press).

Frith, S. (1983) *Sound Effects: Youth, Leisure and the Politics of Rock* (London: Constable).

Frosh, S., Phoenix, A. & Pattman, R. (2001) *Young Masculinities* (London: Palgrave Macmillan).

Fu, J. (2018) 'Chinese youth performing identities and navigating belonging online', *Journal of Youth Studies*, vol. 21, no. 2, pp. 129–143.

Fuchs, C. (2017) *Social Media: A Critical Introduction* (London: Sage).

Fuller, A. & Unwin, L. (2013) *Apprenticeship and the Concept of Occupation* (London: The Gatsby Charitable Foundation).

Funston, A. (2012) Non-traditional students making their way in higher education: An Australian case study, research report 35, Youth Research Centre, University of Melbourne, http://web.education.unimelb.edu.au/yrc/linked_documents/RR35.pdf.

Furlong, A. (2006) 'The zone of precarity and discourses of vulnerability: NEET in the UK', *The Journal of Social Sciences and Humanities*, no. 381, pp. 101–121.

Furlong, A. & Cartmel, F. (1997) *Young People and Social Change* (Buckingham: Open University Press).

Furlong, A. & Cartmel, F. (2007) *Young People and Social Change: New Perspectives*, 2nd ed. (Buckingham: Open University Press).

Furlong, A. & Evans, K. (1997) 'Metaphors of youth transitions: niches, pathways, trajectories or navigations' in Bynner, J., Chisholm, L. & Furlong, A. (eds.) *Youth, Citizenship and Social Change in a European Context* (Aldershot: Ashgate).

Furlong, A., Cartmel, F., Biggart, A., Sweeting, H., & West, P. (2003) *Youth Transitions: Patterns of Vulnerability and Processes of Social Inclusion* (Edinburgh: Scottish Executive Social Research).

Furlong, A., Goodwin, J., O'Connor, H., Hadfield, S., Hall, S., Lowden, K. & Plugor, R. (2017) *Young People in the Labour Market: Past, Present, and Future* (London: Routledge).

Furstenberg, F. F., Kennedy, S., McLoyd, V. C., Rumbaut, R. G. & Settersten, R. A. (2004) 'Growing up is harder to do', *Contexts,* vol. 3, no. 3, pp. 33–41.

Gabriel, M. (2006) 'Youth migration and social advancement: how young people manage emerging differences between themselves and their hometown', *Journal of Youth Studies*, vol. 9, no. 1, pp. 33–46.

Gale, T. & Tranter, D. (2011) 'Social justice in Australian higher education policy: an historical and conceptual account of student participation'. *Critical Studies in Education*, vol. 52, no. 1, pp. 29–46.

Gallie, D. & Paugam, S. (2002) *Social Precarity and Social Integration* (Luxembourg: Office for Official Publications of the European Communities).

Garland, D. (2001) *The Culture of Control: Crime and Social Order in Contemporary Society* (Chicago: University of Chicago Press).

Geisen, T. (2010) 'New perspectives on youth and migration belonging, cultural repositioning and social mobility' in Cairns, D. (eds.) *Youth on the Move: European Youth and Geographical Mobility* (Morlenberg: Springer).

Giddens, A. (1991) *Modernity and Self-Identity: Self and Society in the Late Modern Age* (Redwood City: Stanford University Press).

Gidley, S. (2007) 'Youth culture and ethnicity: emerging youth intercultural in South London' in Hodkinson, P. & Deicke, W. (eds.) *Youth Cultures: Scenes, Subcultures and Tribes* (London: Routledge).

Gieryn, T. (2000) 'A space for place in sociology', *Annual Review of Sociology*, vol. 26, pp. 436–496.

Gill, R. (2008) 'Empowerment/sexism: figuring female sexual agency in contemporary advertising', *Feminism and Psychology*, vol. 18, no. 35, pp. 35–60.

Gill, R., Henwood, K. & McLean, C. (2005) 'Body projects and the regulation of normative masculinity', *Body and Society*, vol. 11, no. 1, pp. 37–62.

Gillander Gådin, K. & Hammarström, A. (2005) 'A possible contributor to the higher degree of girls reporting psychological symptoms compared with boys in grade nine?' *European Journal of Public Health*, vol. 15, no. 4, pp. 380–385.

Goffman, E. (1959) *The Presentation of Self in Everyday Life* (New York: Doubleday and Company).

Gold, S. J. & Nawyn, S. (eds.) (2013) *Routledge International Handbook of Migration Studies* (London: Routledge).

Goldson, B. & Muncie, J. (2015) *Youth Crime and Justice* (London: Sage).

Golpushnezhad, E. (2018) 'Untold stories of DIY/underground Iranian rap culture: the legitimization of Iranian hip-hop and the loss of radical potential', *Cultural Sociology*, vol. 12, no. 2, pp. 260–275.

Goodwin, J. & O'Connor, H. (2005) 'Exploring complex transitions: looking back at the 'golden age' of from school to work', *Sociology,* vol. 39, no. 2, pp. 201–220.

Goodwin-Hawkins, B. (2014) 'Mobilities and the English village: moving beyond fixity in rural West Yorkshire', *Sociologia Ruralis*, vol. 55, no. 2, pp. 167–181.

Goos, M. & Manning, A. (2007) 'Lousy and lovely jobs: the rising polarization of work in Britain'. *The Review of Economics and Statistics*, vol. 89, no. 1, pp. 118–133.

Gore, J., Holmes, K., Smith, M., Southgate, E. & Albright, J. (2015) 'Socioeconomic status and the career aspirations of Australian school students: testing enduring assumptions', *The Australian Educational Researcher*, vol. 42, no. 2, pp. 155–177.

Gorski, E. (2010) 'Stoic, stubborn, or sensitive: how masculinity affects men's help-seeking and help-referring behaviors', *UW-L Journal of Undergraduate Research,* vol. XIII, pp. 1–6.

Gottfredson, M. & Hirschi, T. (1990) *A General Theory of Crime* (Stanford: Stanford University Press).

Gough, K. V. & Franch, M. (2005) 'Spaces of the street: socio-spatial mobility and exclusion of youth in Recife', *Children's Geographies*, vol. 3, no. 2, pp. 149–166.

Graham, J. & Bowling, B. (1995) *Young People and Crime Research Study No. 145* (London: Home Office).

Gray, M. L. (2007) 'From websites to Wal-Mart: youth, identity work, and the queering of boundary publics in Small Town, USA', *American Studies*, vol. 48, no. 2, pp. 49–59.

Gray, M. L. (2009) 'Negotiating identities/queering desires: coming out online and the remediation of the coming-out story', *Journal of Computer-Mediated Communication*, vol. 14, pp. 1162–1189.

Green, E. (2007) 'Outwardly mobile: young people and mobile technologies' in Katz, J. K. (ed.) *Machines That Become Us: The Social Context of Personal Communication Technology* (New Brunswick: Transaction Publishers).

Green, A. (2017) *The Crisis for Young People* (London: Palgrave Macmillan).

Green, F. & Henseke, G. (2016) 'Should governments of OECD countries worry about graduate underemployment?' *Oxford Review of Economic Policy*, vol. 32, no. 4, pp. 514–537.

Green, E. & Singleton, C. (2006) 'Risky bodies at leisure: young women negotiating space and place', *Sociology*, vol. 40, no. 5, pp. 853–871.

Greve, B. (2016) 'Denmark: still a Nordic welfare state after the changes of recent years?' in Schubert, K., de Villota, P. & Kuhlmann, J. (eds.) *Challenges to European Welfare Systems* (Switzerland: Springer).

Griffin, C. (1985) *Typical Girls? Young Women from School to the Job Market* (London: Routledge).

Griffin, C., Bengry-Howell, A., Hackley, C., Mistral, W. & Szmigin, I. (2009) '"Every time I do it I absolutely annihilate myself": loss of (self-) consciousness and loss of memory in young people's drinking narratives', *Sociology*, vol. 43, no. 3, pp. 457–476.

Gross, L. (2007) 'Gideon who will be 25 in the year 2012: growing up gay today', *International Journal of Communication*, vol. 1, no. 1, pp. 121–138.

Grossman, A. H. & D'augelli, A. R. (2006) 'Transgender youth: invisible and vulnerable', *Journal of Homosexuality,* vol. 51, no. 1, pp. 111–128.

Grugulis, I. & Stoyanova, D. (2012) 'Social capital and networks in film and TV: jobs for the boys?' *Organization Studies*, vol. 33, no. 10, pp. 1311–1331.

Haenfler, R. (2006) *Straight Edge: Clean-Living Youth, Hardcore Punk, and Social Change* (New Brunswick: Rutgers University Press).

Hagell, A., Shah, R., Viner, R., Hargreaves, D., Varnes, L. & Heys, M. (2018) *The Social Determinants of Young People's Health: Identifying the Key Issues and Assessing How Young People Are Doing in the 2010s, Health Foundation Working Paper* (London: Health Foundation).

Halberstam, J. (2005) *In a Queer Time and Place: Transgender Bodies, Ubcultural Lives* (New York: New York University Press).

Hall, G. S. (1904) *Adolescence: Its Psychology and Its Relations to Physiology, Anthropology, Sociology, Sex, Crime, Religion, and Education,* vols. I & II (New York: D. Appleton & Co).

Hall, S. (1996) 'What is this 'black' in black popular culture?' in Morley, D. & Chen, K. (eds.) *Stuart Hall: Critical Dialogues in Cultural Studies* (New York: Routledge).

Hall, S. & Jefferson, T. (eds). (1976) *Resistance Through rituals: Youth Subcultures in Post-war Britain* (London: Psychology Press).

Hall, S., Critcher, C., Jefferson, T., Clarke, J. & Roberts, B. (1978) *Policing the Crisis: Mugging, the State and Law and Order* (London: Macmillan International Higher Education).

Hankivsky, O., Doyal, L., Einstein, G., Kelly, U., Shim, J., Weber, L. & Repta, R. (2017) 'The odd couple: using biomedical and intersectional approaches to address health inequities', *Global Health Action*, vol. 10, no. sup2, pp. 73–86.

Haraldsson, K., Lindgren, E. C., Hildingh, C. & Marklund, B. (2010) 'What makes the everyday life of Swedish adolescent girls less stressful: a qualitative analysis', *Health Promotion International*, vol. 25, no. 2, pp. 192–199.

Harris, A. (2004) *Future Girl: Young Women in the Twenty-First Century* (London: Routledge).

Harris, A. (2013) *Young People and Everyday Multiculturalism* (London: Routledge).

Harris, A. (2014) 'Conviviality, conflict and distanciation in young people's local multicultures', *Journal of Intercultural Studies*, vol. 35, no. 6, pp. 571–587.

Harris, A. (2015) Belonging and the uses of difference: Young people in Australian urban multiculture. *Social Identities: Journal for the Study of Race, Nation and Culture,* vol. 22, pp. 359–375.

Harris, A. (2016) 'Belonging and the uses of difference: young people in Australian urban multicultures', *Social Identities*, vol. 22, no. 4, pp. 359–375.

Harris, A. & Roose, J. (2014) 'DIY citizenship amongst young Muslims: experiences of the "ordinary"', Journal of Youth Studies, vol. 17, pp. 794–781.

Harris, A. & Wyn, J. (2009) 'Young people's politics and the micro-territories of the local', *Australian Journal of Political Science*, vol. 44, no. 2, pp. 327–344.

Harris, A. & Wyn, J. (2010) 'Emerging forms of youth participation: everyday and local perspectives', *Young*, vol. 18, no. 1, pp. 3–7.

Harris, A., Wyn, J. & Younes, S. (2010) 'Beyond apathetic or activist youth: 'ordinary' young people and contemporary forms of participation', *Young*, vol. 18, no. 1, pp. 9–32.

Hart, S. (2009) 'The 'problem' with youth: young people, citizenship and the community', Citizenship Studies, vol. 13, no. 6, pp. 641–657.

Haverig, A. (2011) 'Constructing global/local subjectivities – the New Zealand OE as governance through freedom', *Mobilities,* vol. 6, no. 1, pp. 103–123.

Haverig, A. & Roberts, S. (2011) 'The New Zealand OE as governance through freedom: rethinking 'the apex of freedom', *Journal of Youth Studies*, vol. 14, no. 5, pp. 587–603.

Healy, M. (1996) *Gay Skins: Class, Masculinity and Queer Appropriation* (London: Bread and Circuses Publishing).

Heath, S. (2007) 'Widening the gap: pre-university gap years and the 'economy of experience", *British Journal of Sociology of Education*, vol. 28, no. 1, pp. 89–103.

Hebdige, D. (1979) *Subculture: The Meaning of Style* (London: Methuen).

HEFCE. (2015) *Differences in Employment Outcomes: Equality and Diversity Characteristics* (London: Higher Education Funding Council for England).

Heidensohn, F. (1985) *Women and Crime* (London: Macmillan).

Heley, J. & Jones, L. (2012) 'Relational rurals: some thoughts on relating things and theory in rural studies', *Journal of Rural Studies*, vol. 28, pp. 208–217.

Heo, J., Oh, J., Subramanian, S. V., Kim, Y. & Kawachi, I. (2014) 'Addictive internet use among Korean adolescents: a national survey', *PLoS One*, vol. 9, no. 2. p. e87819

Hesmondhalgh, D. (2005) 'Subcultures, scenes or tribes? None of the above', *Journal of Youth Studies*, vol. 8, no. 1, pp. 21–40.

Hesmondhalgh, D. J. & Melville, C. (2002) 'Urban breakbeat culture – repercussions of hip-hop in the United Kingdom' in *Global Noise: Rap and Hip Hop Outside the USA* (Middletown: Wesleyan University Press).

Hill, T. D. & Needham, B. L. (2013) 'Rethinking gender and mental health: a critical analysis of three propositions', *Social Science Medicine*, vol. 92, pp. 83–91.

Hockenberry, S. & Puzzanchera, C. (2019) *Juvenile Court Statistics 2017* (Pittsburgh: National Center for Juvenile Justice).

Hodkinson, P. (1998) 'Technicism, teachers and teaching quality in vocational education and training', *Journal of Vocational Education & Training*, vol. 50, no. 2, pp. 193–208.

Hodkinson, P. (2011) 'Ageing in a spectacular 'youth culture': continuity, change and community amongst older goths', *The British Journal of Sociology*, vol. 62, no. 2, pp. 262–282.

Hodkinson, P. (2012) 'Beyond spectacular specifics in the study of youth (sub) cultures', *Journal of Youth Studies*, vol. 15, no. 5, pp. 557–572.

Hodkinson, P. (2017) 'Young people's fashion and style' in Furlong, A. (ed.) *Handbook of Youth and Young Adulthood*, 2nd ed. (London: Routledge).

Hogan, B. (2010) 'The presentation of self in the age of social media: distinguishing performances and exhibitions online,' *Bulletin of Science, Technology & Society*, vol. 30, no. 6, pp. 377–386.

Hollands, R. G. (2002) 'Divisions in the dark?: youth cultures, transitions and segmented consumption spaces in the night-time economy', *Journal of Youth Studies* 2002, vol. 5, no. 2, pp. 153–173.

Horschelmann, K. & Van Blerk, L. (2013) *Children, Youth and the City* (London: Routledge).

Hough, M. & Roberts, J. (2004) *Youth Crime and Youth Justice: Public Opinion in England and Wales* (London: Institute for Criminal Policy Research).

Howard League. (2007) *Childrenas Victims* (London: Howard League), https://www.statista.com/statistics/288100/violent-crime-victims-in-england-and-wales-by-age-group/

Howells, K. (1997) Address by Mr Kim Howells - Minister of lifelong learning, UK, UNESCO Fifth International Conference on Adult Education, Hamburg, 24–28 July 1997. http://www.unesco.org/education/uie/confintea/pdf/finrepeng.pdf.

http://stakeholders.ofcom.org.uk/binaries/research/media-literacy/oct2012/main.pdf.

Hubbard, P., Gorman-Murray, A. & Nash, C. J. (2015) 'Cities and sexualities' in DeLamater, J. & Plante, R. (eds.) *Handbook of the Sociology of Sexualities* (Heidelberg: Springer International Publishing).

Hunt, A. & Samman, E. (2018) *Gender and the Gig Economy* (London: ODI).

Hunt, G. Moloney, M. & Evens, K. (2010) *Youth Drugs and Nightlife* (London: Routledge).

Hutchby, I. (2001) 'Technologies, texts and affordances', *Sociology*, vol. 35, no. 2, pp. 441–456.

Hutton, F. (2006) *Club Cultures and Feminine Identities* (Aldershot: Ashgate).

Ibrahim, Y. (2008) 'The new risk communities: social networking sites and risk', *International Journal of Media & Cultural Politics*, vol. 4, no. 2, pp. 245–253.

Inggs, A. (2017) 'The suit is mine: Skhothane and the Aesthetic of the African Modern', *Critical Arts*, vol. 31, no. 3, pp. 90–105.

Ingram, N. & Allen, K. (2018) '"Talent-spotting" or "social magic"? Inequality, cultural sorting and constructions of the ideal graduate in elite professions', *The Sociological Review*, vol. 67, no. 3, pp. 723–740.

International Labour Organisation (2013) *Global Employment Trends for Youth 2013: A Generation at Risk*. Geneva: ILO (International Labour Office). https://www.ilo.org/wcmsp5/groups/public/%2D%2D-dgreports/%2D%2D-dcomm/documents/publication/wcms_212423.pdf.

Internet World Stats. (2018) Internet usage statistics: world internet users and 2018 populations stats, June 30, accessed 10th August 2018, https://www.internetworldstats.com/stats.htm.

Isin, E. F. (2008) 'Theorizing acts of citizenship' in: Isin, E. F. & Nielsen, G. M. (eds). *Acts of Citizenship* (London, Palgrave Macmillan).

Jayne, M., Valentine, G. & Holloway, S. L. (2010) 'Emotional, embodied and affective geographies of alcohol, drinking and drunkenness', *Transactions of the Institute of British Geographers*, vol. 35, pp. 540–554.

Jefferson, T. (2002) 'Subordinating hegemonic masculinity', *Theoretical Criminology*, vol. 6, no. 1, pp. 63–88.

Jette, S. & Roberts, E. B. (2016) '"We usually just start dancing our Indian dances": urban American Indian female youths' negotiation of identity, health and the body', *Sociology of Health and Illness*, vol. 38, no.3, pp. 396–410.

Jewell, S. (2014) 'The impact of working while studying on educational and labour market outcomes', *Business and Economics Journal*, vol. 5, no. 3, pp. 1–12.

Joelsson, T. (2015) 'Breaking bored – negotiating spatial boredom and masculinity in the Volvo greaser culture', *Gender, Place and Culture*, vol. 22, no. 9, pp. 1252–1268.

Johansson, A., Brunnberg, E. & Eriksson, C. (2007) 'Adolescent girls' and boys' perceptions of mental health', *Journal of Youth Studies*, vol. 10, no. 2, pp. 183–202.

Johnson, S., Sudhinaraset, B. & Blum, R. W. (2010) 'Neuromaturation and adolescent risk taking: why development is not determined', *Journal of Adolescent Research*, vol. 25, no. 1, pp. 4–23

Johnson, J. T., Howitt, R., Cajete, G., Berkes, F., Louis, R. P. & Kliskey, A. (2016) 'Weaving Indigenous and sustainability sciences to diversify our methods', *Sustainability Science*, vol. 11, no. 1, pp. 1–11.

Jones, O. (2012) *Chavs: The Demonization of the Working Class* (London: Verso Press).

Jones, G. & Wallace, C. (1992) *Youth, Family and Citizenship* (Milton Keynes, Open University Press).

Julkunen, I. (2009) 'Youth unemployment and marginalization' in Furlong, A. (ed.) *Handbook of Youth and Young Adulthood* (London: Routledge).

Justman, M. & Méndez, S. J. (2018) 'Gendered choices of STEM subjects for matriculation are not driven by prior differences in mathematical achievement', *Economics of Education Review*, vol. 64, pp. 282–297.

Kahn-Harris, K. (2006) *Extreme Metal: Music and Culture on the Edge* (Berg).

Kalleberg, A. (2009) 'Precarious work, insecure workers: employment relations in transition', *American Sociological Review*, vol. 74, no. 1, pp. 1–22.

Kanai, A. & Dobson, A. (2016) 'Digital media and gender' in Staples, N. (ed.) *The Wiley Blackwell Encyclopaedia of Gender and Sexuality Studies* (Chichester: Wiley-Blackwell).

Kapi, A., Veltsista, A., Kavadias, G,, Lekea, V. & Bakoula, C. (2007) 'Social determinants of self-reported emotional and behavioral problems in Greek adolescents', *Social Psychiatry* and *Psychiatric Epidemiology*, vol. 42, no. 7, pp. 594–598.

Kazyak, E. (2011) 'Disrupting cultural selves: constructing gay and lesbian identities in rural locales', *Qualitative Sociology*, vol. 34, no. 4, pp. 561–581.

Keep, E. (2012) *Youth Transitions, the Labour Market and Entry into Employment: Some Reflections and Questions*, Research Paper No. 108, Cardiff, SKOPE.

Kelly, P. (2001) 'Youth at risk: processes of individualisation and responsibilisation in the risk society', *Discourse: Studies in the Cultural Politics of Education*, vol. 22, no. 1, pp. 23–33.

Kelly, P. (2006) 'The entrepreneurial self and 'youth at-risk': exploring the horizons of identity in the twenty-first century', *Journal of Youth Studies*, vol. 9, no. 1, pp. 17–32.

Kelly, P. (2012) 'The brain in the jar: a critique of discourses of adolescent brain development', *Journal of Youth Studies*, vol. 15, no. 7, pp. 944–959

Kelly, P. (2017) 'Growing up after the GFC: responsibilisation and mortgaged futures.' *Discourse: Studies in the Cultural Politics of Education*, vol. 38, no. 1, pp. 57–69.

Kemshall, H. (2002) *Risk, Social Policy and Welfare* (Buckingham: Open University Press).

Kenway, J., Kraack, A. & Hickey-Moody, A. (2006) *Masculinity beyond the Metropolis* (London: Palgrave Macmillan).

Kerr, J, R. & Davis, L. (2011) 'Benzylpiperazine in New Zealand: brief history and current implications', *Journal of the Royal Society of New Zealand*, vol. 41, no. 1, pp. 155–164.

Kildal, N. (2000) *Workfare Tendencies in Scandinavian Welfare Policies* (Geneva: International Labour Organisation).

King, A. (2011) 'Minding the gap? Young people's accounts of taking a gap year as a form of identity work in higher education', *Journal of Youth Studies*, vol. 14, no. 3, pp. 341–357.

King, R. & Raghuram, P. (2013) 'International student migration: mapping the field and new research agendas', *Population, Space and Place*, vol. 19, no. 2, pp. 127–137.

King, M., Smith, A. & Gracey, M. (2009) 'Indigenous health part 2: the underlying causes of the health gap', *The Lancet*, vol. 374, no. 9683, pp. 76–85.

Kintrea, K., St Clair, R. & Houston, M. (2015) 'Shaped by place? Young people's aspirations in disadvantaged neighbourhoods', *Journal of Youth Studies*, vol. 18, no. 5, pp. 666–684.

Kosciw, J. G., Greytak, E. A., Bartkiewicz, M. J., Boesen, M. J. & Palmer, N. A. (2012) *The 2011 National School Climate Survey: The Experiences of Lesbian, Gay, Bisexual and Transgender Youth in Our Nation's Schools* (New York: GLSEN).

Kraack, A. & Kenway, J. (2002) 'Place, time and stigmatised youthful identities: bad boys in paradise', *Journal of Rural Studies*, vol. 18, pp. 145–155.

Kraut, R., Patterson, M. Lundmark, V., Kiesler, S., Mukophadhyay, T. & Scherlis, W. (1998) 'Internet paradox: a social technology that reduces social involvement and psychological well-being?' *American Psychologist*, vol. 53, no. 9, p. 1017.

Kuper, A. (1988) *The Invention of Primitive Society: Transformations of an Illusion* (London: Routledge).

Landstedt, E. & Coffey, J. (2017) 'The social context of youth mental health' in Furlong, A. (ed.) *Routledge Handbook of Youth and Young Adulthood* (London: Routledge).

Landstedt, E. & Gillander Gådin, K. (2011) 'Experiences of violence among adolescents: gender patterns in types, perpetrators and associated psychological distress', *International Journal of Public Health*, vol. 56, no. 4, pp. 419–427.

Landstedt, E. & Gillander Gådin, K. (2012) 'Seventeen and stressed – do gender and class matter?', *Health Sociology Review*, vol. 21, no. 1, pp. 82–98.

Landstedt, E., Asplund, K. & Gillander Gådin, K. (2009) 'Understanding adolescent mental health: the influence of social processes, doing gender and gendered power relations', *Sociology of Health and Illness*, vol. 31, no. 7, pp. 962–978.

Landstedt, E., Hammarstrom, A. & Winefield, H. (2015) 'How well do parental and peer relationships in adolescence predict health in adulthood?' *Scandinavian Journal of Public Health*, vol. 43, no. 5, pp. 460–468.

Landstedt, E, Coffey, J. et al. (2016) 'The complex relationship between mental health and social conditions in the lives of young Australians mixing work and study', *Young*, vol. 25, no. 4, pp. 1–20.

Laoire, C., Carpena-Méndez, F., Tyrrell, N. & White, A. (2010) 'Introduction: child-hood and migration—mobilities, homes and belongings', *Childhood*, vol. 17, no. 2, pp.155–162.

Laoire, C. N., White, A., Tyrrell, N. & Carpena-Méndez, F. (2012) 'Children and young people on the move: geographies of child and youth migration', *Geography*, vol. 97, p. 129.

Larkins, F. P. (2018) 'Male Students Remain Underrepresented in Australian Universities. Should Australia Be Concerned?' Melbourne, University of Melbourne, accessed 13th October 2019, https://melbourne-cshe.unimelb.edu.au/__data/assets/pdf_file/0012/2894718/Gender-Enrolment-Trends-F-Larkins-Sep-2018.pdf.

Lashua, B. D. & Kelly, J. (2008) 'Rhythms in the concrete: re-imagining relationships between space, race, and mediated urban youth cultures', *Leisure/Loisir*, vol. 32, no. 2, pp. 461–487.

Laverty, L. (2017) 'Shame, disgust and the moral economies of young women's sexual health in the North of England' in Kelly, P. & Pike, J. (eds.) *Neo-Liberalism, Austerity and the Moral Economies of Young People's Health and Well-Being* (London: Palgrave Macmillan).

Leaper, C. (2015) '"Do I belong?": gender, peer groups, and STEM achievement', *International Journal of Gender, Science and Technology*, vol. 7, no. 2, pp. 166–179.

Lees, S. (1986) *Losing Out: Sexuality and Adolescent Girls* (London: Hutchinson).

Lefebvre, H. (1991) *The Production of Space* (Malden: Blackwell).

Lehmann, W. (2012) 'Working-class students, habitus, and the development of student roles: a Canadian case study', *British Journal of Sociology of Education*, vol. 33, no. 4, pp. 527–546.

Leonard, P., Halford, S. & Bruce, K. (2016) 'The new degree? Constructing internships in the third sector', *Sociology*, vol. 50, no. 2, pp. 383–399.

Lepanjuuri, K., Wishart, R. & Cornick, P. (2018) *The Characteristics of Those in the Gig Economy: Final Report* (London: BEIS).

Lesjak, M., Juvan, E., Ineson, E. M., Yap, M. H. & Axelsson, E. P. (2015) Erasmus student motivation: why and where to go? *Higher Education*, vol. 70, no. 5, pp. 845–865.

Lesko, N. (1996) 'Denaturalizing adolescence: the politics of contemporary representations', *Youth & Society*, vol. 28, no. 2, pp. 139–161.

Lichy, J. (2011) 'Internet use behaviour in France and Britain: exploring socio-spatial disparity among adolescents', *International Journal of Consumer Studies*, vol. 35, pp. 470–475.

Liepins, R. (2000) 'New energies for an old idea: reworking approaches to 'community' in contemporary rural studies', *Journal of Rural Studies*, vol. 16, pp. 23–35.

Lilley, C., Ball, R. & Vernon, H. (2014) *The Experiences of 11–16 Year Olds on Social Networking Sites* (London: NSPCC).

Lincoln, S. (2004) 'Teenage girls' bedroom culture: codes versus zones' in Bennett, A. & Kahn-Harris, K. (ed.) *After Subculture* (London: Palgrave Macmillan).

Lincoln, S. (2005) 'Feeling the noise: teenagers, bedrooms and music', *Leisure Studies*, vol. 24, no. 4, pp. 399–414.

Lincoln, S. (2014) '"I've stamped my personality all over it" the meaning of objects in teenage bedroom space', *Space and Culture*, vol. 17, no. 3, pp. 266–279.

Lister, R. (2007) 'Inclusive citizenship: realizing the potential', *Citizenship Studies*, vol. 11, no. 1, pp. 49–61.

Livingstone, S. (2009) *Children and the Internet: Great Expectations, Challenging Realities* (Cambridge: Polity Press).

Livingstone, S. & Görzig, A. (2012) '"Sexting": the exchange of sexual messages online among European youth' in *Children, Risk and Safety on the Internet. Research and Policy Challenges in Comparative Perspective* (Bristol: Policy Press).

Livingstone, S. & Haddon, L. (eds.) (2012) *Children, Risk and Safety on the Internet* (Bristol, UK: Policy Press).

Livingstone, S. & Helsper, E. (2007) 'Taking risks when communicating on the internet: the role of offline social-psychological factors in young people's vulnerability to online risks', *Information, Communication and Society*, vol. 10, no. 5, pp. 619–643.

Livingstone, S., Davidson, J. & Bryce, J. (2017) *Children's Online Activities, Risks and Safety: A Literature Review by the UKCCIS Evidence Group* (London: UKCCIS).

Lock, M. (2007) *Aboriginal Holistic Health: A Critical Review* (Casuarina, NT: Cooperative Research Centre for Aboriginal Health).

Loh, B. (2016) 'Beyond the discourse of sexualization: an inquiry into the adultification of tween girls' dressing in singapore', *Girlhood Studies*, vol. 9, no. 2, pp. 126–143.

Lombroso, C. (1898) *The Female Offender* (New York: Appleton and Company).

Loveday, V. (2015) 'Working-class participation, middle-class aspiration? Value, upward mobility and symbolic indebtedness in higher education', *Sociological Review*, vol. 63, no. 3, pp. 570–588.

Lupton, D. (1995) *The Imperative of Health: Public Health and the Regulated Body* (London: Sage Publications).

Lupton, D. (1999) *Risk* (London: Routledge).

Lupton, D. (2013) *Fat* (London: Routledge).

Lupton, D. (2014) *Digital Sociology* (London: Routledge).

Lyng, S. (1990) 'Edgework: a social psychological analysis of voluntary risk-taking', *American Journal of Sociology*, vol. 95, no. 4, pp. 851–886.

Mac An Ghaill, M. (1994) *The Making of Men: Masculinities, Sexualities and Schooling* (Buckingham: Open University Press).

MacDonald, R. (2011) 'Youth transitions, unemployment and underemployment Plus ça change, plus c'est la même chose?' *Journal of Sociology*, vol. 47, no. 4, pp. 427–444.

MacDonald, R. & Glazitzoglu, A. (2019) 'Youth, enterprise and precarity: or, what is, and what is wrong with, the 'gig economy'?' *Journal of Sociology*, first online July 2019.

MacDonald, R. & Marsh, J. (2005) *Disconnected Youth?: Growing Up in Britain's Poor in Neighbourhoods* (London: Palgrave Macmillan).

MacDonald, R. & Shildrick, T. (2012) 'Youth and wellbeing: experiencing bereavement and ill health in marginalised young people's transitions', *Sociology of Health and Illness*, vol. 35, no. 1, pp. 147–161.

MacDonald, R., Mason, P., Shildrick, T., Webster, C., Johnston, L. & Ridley, L. (2001) 'Snakes & ladders: in defence of studies of youth transition', *Sociological Research Online*, vol. 5, no. 4, pp. 1–13.

Macqueen, S. (2018) 'Family and social capital for the success of non-traditional students in higher education', *International Studies in Widening Participation*, vol. 5, no. 1, pp. 37–50.

Mäkinen, K. & Tyrväinen, L. (2008) 'Teenage experiences of public green spaces in suburban Helsinki', *Urban Forestry & Urban Greening*, vol. 7, no. 4, pp. 277–289.

Malakieh, J. (2017) 'Youth correctional statistics in Canada, 2015/2016', Canadian Centre for Justice Statistics, Canada, https://www150.statcan.gc.ca/n1/pub/85-002-x/2018001/article/54972-eng.htm.

Mansouri, F. & Kirpitchenko, L. (2016) 'Practices of active citizenship among migrant youth: beyond conventionalities', *Social Identities*, vol. 22, no. 3, pp. 307–323.

Marcuse, H. (1964) *One Dimensional Man* (London: Routledge).

Marks, A. (2003) 'Welcome to the new ambivalence: reflections on the historical and current cultural antagonism between the working class male and higher education', *British Journal of Sociology of Education*, vol. 24, no. 1, pp. 83–93.

Marks, G. N. & Fleming, N. (1998) 'Factors Influencing Youth Unemployment in Australia: 1980–1994. Longitudinal Surveys of Australian Youth', Victoria, ACER Customer Service

Marshall, T. H. (1950) *Citizenship and Social Class* (Cambridge: Cambridge University Press).

Martin, J. (2018) 'Live Longer, Work Longer: The Changing Nature of the Labour Market for Older Workers in OECD Countries', Bonn, Institute of Labor Economics.

Martinez, E. (1993) 'Beyond black/white: the racisms of our time', *Social Justice*, vol. 20, no. 1–2, pp. 22–34.

Massey, D. (2005) *For Space* (London: Sage Publications).

Matthews, H., Limb, M. & Percy-Smith, B. (1998) 'Changing worlds: the microgeographies of young teenagers', *Tijschrift voor Economische en Sociale Geografie*, vol. 89, no. 2, pp. 193–202.

Matthews, H., Taylor, M., Percy-Smith, B. & Limb, M. (2000) 'The unacceptable flaneur: the shopping mall as a teenage hangout', *Childhood*, vol. 7, no. 3, pp. 279–294.

May, T., Gyateng, T. & Hough, M. (2010) '*Differential Treatment in the Youth Justice System*' (London: Institute for Criminal Policy Research King's College).

McCreanor, T., Greenaway, A., Moewaka Barnes, H., Borell, S. & Gregory, A. (2005) 'Youth identity formation and contemporary alcohol marketing', *Critical Public Health*, vol. 15, no. 3, pp. 251–262.

McCurry, J. (2010) 'Internet addiction driving South Koreans into realms of fantasy', *The Guardian*, July 14, accessed 10th August 2018, https://www.theguardian.com/world/2010/jul/13/internet-addiction-south-korea.

McGivney, V. (2004) *Men Earn, Women Learn: Bridging the Gender Divide in Adult Education and Training* (Leicester: NIACE Publications).

McGuiness, F. (2018) 'Unemployment by ethnic background', Briefing Paper Number 6385 (London: House of Commons Library).

McGuire, M. & Dowling, S. (2013) *Cyber crime: a review of the evidence,* Home Office Research Report 75 (London: HMSO).

McKay, J. & Devlin, M. (2014) '"Uni has a different language ... to the real world": demystifying academic culture and discourse for students from low socioeconomic backgrounds', *Higher Education Research & Development,* vol. 33, no. 5, pp. 949–861.

McKay, J. & Devlin, M. (2016) '"Low income doesn't mean stupid and destined for failure": challenging the deficit discourse around students from low SES backgrounds in higher education', *International Journal of Inclusive Education*, vol. 20, no. 4, pp. 347–363.

McLeod, J. & Wright, K. (2015) 'Inventing youth wellbeing' in Wright, K. & McLeod, J. (eds.) *Rethinking Youth Wellbeing: Critical Perspectives* (Singapore: Springer Singapore).

McLeod, J. & Yates, L. (2006) *Making Modern Lives: Subjectivity, Schooling and Social Change* (Albany: State University of New York Press).

McQuaid, R. (2015) 'Multiple scarring effects of youth unemployment', *The London School of Economics and Political Science*, accessed 13th October 2019, https://blogs.lse.ac.uk/europpblog/2017/02/18/youth-unemployment-scarring-effects/.

McRobbie, A. (1978) *Working Class Girls and the Culture of Femininity in Women's Studies Group Centre for Contemporary Cultural Studies, Women Take Issue* (London: Hutchinson).

McRobbie, A. (1980) 'Settling accounts with subcultures: a feminist critique', *Screen Education*, vol. 34, pp. 37–49.

McRobbie, A. (1994) *Postmodernism and Popular Culture* (London: Routledge).

McRobbie, A. (2000) *Feminism and Youth Culture* (London: Palgrave Macmillan).

McRobbie, A. (2007) 'Top girls? Young women and the post-feminist sexual contract', *Cultural Studies*, vol. 21, no. 4, pp. 718–741.

McRobbie, A. (2015) 'Notes on the perfect', *Australian Feminist Studies*, vol. 30, no. 83, pp. 3–20.

McRobbie, A. & Garber, J. (1976) 'Girls and subcultures: an exploration', *Youth and Society*, vol. 28, no. 2, pp. 189–214.

McRobbie, A. & Thornton, S. L. (1995) 'Rethinking "moral panic" for multi-mediated social worlds', *British Journal of Sociology*, vol. 46, no. 4, pp. 561–574.

Measham, F. & Brain, K. (2005) 'Binge' drinking, British alcohol policy and the new culture of intoxication', *Crime Media Culture*, vol. 1, pp. 262–283.

Mendick, H., Ahmad, A., Allen, K. & Harvey, L. (2019) *Celebrity, Aspiration and Contemporary Youth: Education and Inequality in an Era of Austerity* (London: Bloomsbury Publishing).

Merrifield, A. (1993) 'Place and space: a Lefebvrian reconciliation', *Transactions of the Institute of British Geographers*, vol. 18, no. 4, pp. 516–531.

Merton, R. (1938) 'Social structure and anomie', *American Sociological Review*, vol. 3, no. 5, pp. 672–682.

Messerschmidt, J. (1993) *Masculinities and Crime: Critique and Reconceptualization of Theory* (Maryland: Rowan & Littlefield Publishers).

Miles, S. (1995) 'Towards an understanding of the relationship between youth identities and consumer culture', *Youth and Policy*, vol. 51, pp. 35–45.

Miles, S. (2000) *Youth Lifestyles in a Changing World* (Buckingham: Open University Press).

Miller, D. (2011) *Tales from Facebook* (Cambridge: Polity Press).

Ministry of Health. (2017) *New Zealand Health Survey* (Wellington: Ministry of Health).

Ministry of Justice. (2018) *Youth Prosecution Statistics* (Wellington: Ministry of Justice).

Mizen, P. (1995) *The State and Youth Training* (Basingstoke: Palgrave Macmillan).

Mizen, P. (2004) *The Changing State of Youth* (Basingstoke: Palgrave Macmillan).

Modin, B., Östberg, V. & Almquist, Y. (2011) 'Childhood peer status and adult susceptibility to anxiety and depression. A 30-year hospital follow-up', *Journal of Abnormal Child Psychology*, vol. 39, no. 2, pp. 187–199.

Moffitt, T. (1993) 'Adolescence-limited and life-course-persistent antisocial behavior: a developmental taxonomy', *Psychological Review*, vol. 100, no. 4, pp. 674–701.

Mooney, K. (2005) 'Identities in the ducktail youth subculture in post-World-War-Two South Africa', *Journal of Youth Studies*, vol. 8, no. 1, pp. 41–57.

Moreton-Robinson, A. (2008) 'Writing off treaties: white possession in the United States critical Whiteness studies literature' in Moreton-Robinson, A., Casey, M. & Nicoll, F. (eds.) *Transnational Whiteness Matters* (Lanham: Lexington Books).

Morgan, G. (2015) 'Gangsta warrior bro: Hip-hop and urban Aboriginal youth' in Baker, S., Robards, B. & Buttigieg, B. (eds.) *Youth Cultures and Subcultures: Australian Perspectives* (Routledge, London).

Morgan, G. & Nelligan, P. (2018) *The Creativity Hoax: Precarious Work in the Gig Economy* (London: Anthem Press).

Morrison, D. (2004) 'New Labour, citizenship and the discourse of the Third Way' in Hale, S. Leggett, W. & Martell, L (eds). *The Third Way and Beyond* (Manchester, Manchester University Press).

Muggleton, D. (2000) *Inside Subculture: The Postmodern Meaning of Style* (Oxford: Berg Publishers).

Mullen, A. L. (2009) 'Elite destinations: pathways to attending an Ivy League university,' *British Journal of Sociology of Education*, vol. 30, no. 1, pp. 15–27.

Muncie, J. (2015) *Youth and Crime* (London: Sage Publications).

Murphy-Lejeune, E. (2002) *Student Mobility and Narrative in Europe. The New Strangers* (London: Routledge).

National Cyber Crime Unit (NCCU). (2017) '*Intelligence Assessment: Pathways into Cybercrime*' (London: NCCU).

National Health Service. (2017) *National Study of Health and Wellbeing/Children and Young People* (London: Office of National Statistics).

Nayak, A. (2006) 'Displaced masculinities: chavs, youth and class in the post-industrial city', *Sociology*, vol. 40, no. 5, pp. 813–831.

Nayak, A. (2009) *Race, Place and Globalization: Youth Cultures in a Changing World* (Oxford: Berg Publishers).

Nayak, A. (2016) *Race, Place and Globalization: Youth Cultures in a Changing World.* (London: Bloomsbury Publishing).

Nayak, A. (2017) 'Young People, race and ethnicity' in Furlong, A. (ed.) *Handbook of Youth and Young Adulthood* (London: Routledge).

Nayak, A. & Kehily, M. J. (2013) *Gender, Youth and Culture: Young Masculinities and Femininities* (London: Macmillan International Higher Education).

NCVER. (2018) 'Historical time series of apprenticeships and traineeships in Australia, from 1963', 12th October 2019, https://www.ncver.edu.au/research-and-statistics/data/all-data/historical-time-series-of-apprenticeships-and-traineeships-in-australia-from-1963-to-2018.

Nichols, A., Mitchell, J. & Lindar, S. (2013) *Consequences of Long-Term Unemployment* (Washington: The Urban Institute), 13th October 2019, https://www.urban.org/sites/default/files/publication/23921/412887-Consequences-of-Long-Term-Unemployment.PDF.

Nielsen, M. B. & Einarsen, S. (2012) 'Prospective relationships between workplace sexual harassment and psychological distress', *Occupational Medicine*, vol. 62, no. 3, pp. 226–228.

Nilan, P. (2011) 'Youth sociology must cross cultures', *Youth Studies Australia*, vol. 30, no. 3, pp. 20–26.

Nilan, P. & Threadgold, S. (2015) 'The moral economy of the mosh pit: straight edge, reflexivity and classification struggles' in Baker, S., Robards, B. & Buttigieg, B. (eds.) *Youth Cultures and Subcultures: Australian Perspectives* (Routledge: London).

Nilan, P., Burgess, H., Hobbs, M., Threadgold, S. & Alexander, W. (2015) 'Youth, social media, and cyberbullying among Australian youth: "sick friends"', *Social Media and Society,* vol. 1, no. 2, pp. 1–12.

Nunn, C., McMichael, C., Gifford, S. M. & Correa-Velez, I. (2015) 'Mobility and security: the perceived benefits of citizenship for resettled young people from refugee backgrounds', *Journal of Ethnic and Migration Studies*, vol. 42, no. 3, pp. 382–399.

O'Brien, M. (2005) 'What is cultural about cultural criminology?' *The British Journal of Criminology*, vol. 45, no. 5, pp. 599–612.

O'Higgins, N. (2016) 'Youth unemployment' in Furlong, A. (ed.) *Handbook of Youth and Young Adulthood* (London: Routledge).

OECD. (1996) *The Knowledge-Based Economy* (Paris: OECD).

OECD. (2013a) *Education at a Glance 2014: OECD Indicators* (Paris: OECD).

OECD (2013b) *International Migration Outlook* (Paris, OECD).

OECD. (2015) *OECD in Figures* (Paris: OECD).

OECD. (2018) *Education at a Glance 2018* (Paris: OECD).

OECD. (2019) *Migration Policy Debates* (Paris: OECD).

Ofcom. (2012) *Children and Parents: Media Use and Attitudes* (Paris: OECD).

Office for National Statistics. (2013) *British Crime Survey* (London: ONS).

Office for National Statistics. (2017) *British Crime Survey* (London: ONS).

Office of National Statistics. (2018) *Crime in England and Wales: Year Ending September 2017* (London: ONS).

Osbaldiston, N. (2010) 'Elementary forms of place in sea change', *Journal of Sociology*, vol. 46, no. 3, pp. 239–256.

Osumare, H. (2007) *The African Aesthetic in Global Hip-Hop: Power Moves* (New York: Palgrave Macmillan).

Pakulski, J. & Waters, M. (1996) *The Death of Class* (London: Sage Publications).

Palfrey, J. & Gasser, U. (2008) *Born Digital: Understanding the First Generation of Digital Natives* (Philadelphia: Basics Books).

Panelli, R., Nairn, K. & McCormack, J. (2002) '"We make our own fun": reading the politics of youth with (in) community', *Sociologia Ruralis*, vol. 42, pp. 106–130.

Park, R. E. & Burgess, E. W. (eds.) (1925) *The City* (Chicago: University of Chicago Press).

Parker, H. (1974) *View from the Boys: A Sociology of Down-Town Adolescents* (Newton Abbot: David and Charles).

Parsons, T. (1942) 'Age and sex in the social structure of the United States', *American Sociological Review*, vol. 7, no. 5, pp. 604–616.

Patel, V., Flisher, A. J., Hetrick, S. & McGorry, P. (2007) 'Mental health of young people: a global public-health challenge', *The Lancet*, vol. 369, no. 9569, pp. 1302–1313.

Pathak-Shelat, M. & DeShano, C. (2014) 'Digital youth cultures in small town and rural Gujarat, India', *New Media & Society*, vol. 16, no. 6, pp. 983–1001.

Patton, G. C., Coffey, C., Sawyer, S. M., Viner, R. M., Haller, D. M., Bose, K. & Mathers, C. D. (2009) 'Global patterns of mortality in young people: a systematic analysis of population health data', *The Lancet*, vol. 374, no. 9693, pp. 881–892.

Patton, G. C., Coffey, C., Romaniuk, H., Mackinnon, A., Carlin, J. B., Degenhardt, L. & Moran, P. (2014) 'The prognosis of common mental disorders in adolescents: a 14-year prospective cohort study', *Lancet*, vol. 383, no. 9926, pp. 1404–1411.

Peacock, D., Sellar, S. & Lingard, B. (2014) 'The activation, appropriation and practices of student equity policy in Australian higher education', *Journal of Education Policy*, vol. 29, no. 3, pp. 377–396.

Pearson, G. (1983) *Hooligan: The History of Respectable Fears* (London: Palgrave Macmillan).

Pew Centre. (2018) 'A majority of teens have experienced some form of bullying', accessed 13th October 2019, https://www.pewinternet.

org/2018/09/27/a-majority-of-teens-have-experienced-some-form-of-cyberbullying/.

Philipps, J. (2018) 'A global generation? Youth studies in a postcolonial world', *Societies*, vol. 8, no. 1, [Online Journal], https://doi.org/10.3390/soc8010014

Pickering, J., Kintrea, K. & Bannister, J. (2011) 'Invisible walls and visible youth: territoriality among young people in British cities', *Urban Studies*, vol. 49, no. 5, pp. 945–960.

Pilkington, H. (2004) 'Youth strategies for glocal living: space, power and communication in everyday cultural practice' in Bennett, A. & Kahn-Harris, K. (eds.) *After Subculture* (Basingstoke: Palgrave Macmillan).

Pilkington, H., Garifzianova, A. B. & Omel'chenko, E. (2010) *Russia's Skinheads: Exploring and Rethinking Subcultural Lives* (London: Routledge).

Pini, M. (2001) *Club Cultures and Female Subjectivity: The Move from Home to House* (London: Palgrave Macmillan).

Polhemus, T. (1997) 'In the supermarket of style' in Redhead, S., O'Connor, J. & Wynne, D. (eds.) *The Club Cultures Reader: Readings in Popular Cultural Studies* (Oxford: Blackwell).

Pontes, A. I., Henn, M. & Griffiths, M. D. (2019) 'Youth political (dis)engagement and the need for citizenship education: encouraging young people's civic and political participation through the curriculum', *Education, Citizenship and Social Justice*, vol. 14, no. 1, pp. 3–21.

Population Reference Bureau. (2017) 'World Population Data Sheet', accessed 13th October 2019 retrieved from Washington, https://www.prb.org/2017-world-population-data-sheet/.

Pough, G. (2004) *Check It While I Wreck It: Black Womanhood Hip-Hop Culture, and the Public Sphere* (Boston: North-western University Press).

Prensky, M. (2001) 'Digital natives, digital immigrants', *On the Horizon*, vol. 9, no. 5, pp. 1–2.

Presdee, M. (2000) *Cultural Criminology and the Carnival of Crime* (New York: Routledge).

Price, R. (ed.) (2011) *Young People and Work* (London: Ashgate Publishing).

Priest, N., Mackean, T., Davis, E., Briggs, L. & Waters, E. (2012) 'Aboriginal perspectives of child health and wellbeing in an urban setting: developing a conceptual framework', *Health Sociology Review*, vol. 21, no. 2, pp. 180–195.

Purdie-Vaughns, V. & Eibach, R. P. (2008) 'Intersectional invisibility: the distinctive advantages and disadvantages of multiple subordinate-group identities', *Sex Roles*, vol. 59, no. 5–6, pp. 377–391.

Qin, B., Strömberg, D. & Wu, Y. (2017) 'Why does China allow freer social media? Protests versus surveillance and propaganda', *Journal of Economic Perspectives*, vol. 31, no. 1, pp. 117–140.

Quayle, E., Jonsson, L. & Loof, L. (2012) *Online Behaviour Related to Child Sexual Abuse: Interviews with Affected Young People* (Stockholm: Council of the Baltic Sea States).

Qureshi, F. (2016) 'A Comparison of the British crime survey and police statistics for a southern English county', *International Journal of Police Science & Management*, vol. 12, no. 2, pp. 220–237.

Ragnedda, M. & Muschert, G. W. (eds.) (2013) *The Digital Divide: The Internet and Social Inequality in International Perspective* (London: Routledge).

Rahn, J. (2002) *Painting Without Permission* (London: Bergin and Garvey).

Raia-Hawrylak, A. (2005) 'Youth Experiences of Space in a Gentrifying Community: A Case Study of Asbury Park, New Jersey' on-line blog, https://www.metropolitiques.eu/The-Future-of-Asbury-Park.html.

Raj, A., Saggurti, N., Lawrence, D., Balaiah, D. & Silverman, J. G. (2010) 'Association between adolescent marriage and marital violence among young adult women in India', *International Journal of Gynecology & Obstetrics*, vol. 110, no. 1, pp. 35–39.

Rashid, S. F. & Michaud, S. (2000) 'Female adolescents and their sexuality: notions of honour, shame, purity and pollution during the floods disasters', *Disasters* vol. 24, no. 1, pp. 54–70.

Raviv, A., Sills, R., Raviv, A. & Wilansky, P. (2000) 'Adolescents' help-seeking behavior: the difference between self- and other-referral', *Journal of Adolescence*, vol. 23, no. 6, pp. 721–740.

Ravn, S., & Coffey, J. (2016) '"Steroids, it's so much an identity thing!" Perceptions of steroid use, risk and masculine body image', *Journal of Youth Studies*, vol. 19, no. 1, pp. 87–102.

RBA. (2018) 'Labour market outcomes for younger people', accessed 13th October 2019, https://www.rba.gov.au/publications/bulletin/2018/jun/pdf/labour-market-outcomes-for-younger-people.pdf.

Reay, D. (2017) *Miseducation* (Bristol: Bristol Policy Press).

Reay, D., Crozier, G. & Clayton, J. (2010) '"Fitting in" or "standing out": working class students in UK higher education', *British Educational Research Journal*, vol. 36, no. 1, pp. 107–124.

Redhead, S. (1990) *The End of the Century Party: Youth and Pop Towards 2000* (Manchester: Manchester University Press).

Redhead, S. (ed.) (1993) *Rave off: Politics and Deviance in Contemporary Youth Culture* (Aldershot: Avebury).

Rees, G., Williamson, H. & Istance, D. (1996) '"Status Zero": a study of jobless school leavers in South Wales', *Research Papers in Education*, vol. 11, no. 2, pp. 219–235.

Relph, E. (1993) 'Modernity and the reclamation of place' in Seamon, D. (ed.) *Dwelling, Seeing, and Designing: Toward a Phenomenological Ecology* (Albany, NY: SUNY Press).

Renold, E. & Ringrose, J. (2011) 'Schizoid subjectivities? Re-theorizing teen girls' sexual cultures in an era of "sexualization"', *Journal of Sociology*, vol. 47, no. 4, pp. 389–409.

Respect Task Force. (2006) *Respect Action Plan* (London: Home Office).

Retallack, H., Ringrose, J. & Lawrence, E. (2016) 'Fuck your body image!' Teen girls, twitter feminism and networked affect in a London school' in Coffey, J., Budgeon, S. & Cahill, H. (eds.) *Learning Bodies: The Body in Youth and Childhood Studies* (New York: Springer).

Rheingold, H. (2000) *The Virtual Community: Homesteading on the Electronic Frontier* (Massachusetts: MIT Press).

Rice, C. & Watson, E. (2016) 'Girls and Secting: The Missing Story of Sexual Subjectivity in a Sexualized and Digitally-Mediated World' in Coffey, J., Budgeon, S. & Cahill, H. (eds.) Learning Bodies: The Body in Youth and Childhood Studies (New York: Springer).

Rickwood, D. (2015) 'Responding effectively to support the mental health and wellbeing of young people' in Wyn, J. & Cahill, H. (eds.) *Handbook of Childhood and Youth Studies* (Singapore: Springer).

Rickwood, D., Deane, F. P., Wilson, C. J. & Ciarrochi, J. (2005) 'Young people's help-seeking for mental health problems', *Australian E-journal for the Advancement of Mental Health*, vol. 4, no. 3, pp. 218–251.

Ringrose, J., Gill, R., Livingstone, S., & Harvey, L. (2012) A qualitative study of children, young people and 'sexting': a report prepared for the National Society for the Prevention of Cruelty to Children, London, UK.

Ritzer, G. (1992) *The McDonaldization of Society* (Thousand Oaks: Pine Forge Press).

Robards, B. (2014) 'Vernacular subculture and multiplicity in everyday experiences of belonging' in Baker, S., Robards, B. & Buttigieg, B (eds.) *Youth Cultures & Subcultures: Australian Perspectives* (London: Routledge).

Robards, B. & Bennett, A. (2011) 'MyTribe: post-subcultural manifestations of belonging on social network sites', *Sociology*, vol. 45, no. 2, pp. 303–317.

Roberts, K. (1968) 'The entry into employment: an approach towards a general theory', *The Sociological Review*, vol. 16, no. 2, pp. 165–184.

Roberts, G. (2007) 'Masculinity, mental health and violence in Papua New Guinea, Vanuatu, Fiji and Kiribati', *Health Promotion in the Pacific*, vol. 14, no. 2, pp. 35–42.

Roberts, K. (2009) *Youth in Transition: In Eastern Europe and the West* (London: Macmillan International Higher Education).

Roberts, D. (2015) 'Modified people: indicators of a body modification subculture in a post-subculture world', *Sociology*, vol. 49, no. 6, pp. 1096–1112.

Roberts, S. (2010) 'Misrepresenting "Choice Biographies"? A reply to Woodman', *Journal of Youth Studies*, vol. 13, no. 1, pp. 243–251.

Roberts, S. (2011) 'Beyond 'NEET' and 'tidy' pathways: considering the 'missing middle' of youth transition studies', *Journal of Youth Studies*, vol. 14, no. 1, pp. 21–39.

Roberts, S. (2014) *Debating Modern Masculinities: Change, Continuity, Crisis?* (London: Palgrave Macmillan).

Roberts, S. (2017) 'Young people and social Class' in Furlong, A. (ed.) *Handbook of Youth and Young Adulthood* (London: Routledge).

Roberts, S. (2018) *Young Working-Class Men in Transition* (London: Routledge).

Roberts, S. & Antonucci, L. (2015) 'Youth transitions, welfare policy and contemporary Europe' in Lange, A., Reiter, H., Schutter, A. & Steiner, C. (eds.) *Handbuch Kindheits- und Jugendsoziologie* (Frankfurt: Springer).

Roberts, S. & Evans, S. (2013) '"Aspirations" and imagined futures: the im/possibilities for Britain's young working class' in Atkinson, W., Roberts, S. & Savage, M. (eds.) *Class Inequality in Austerity Britain: Power, Difference and Suffering* (Basingstoke: Palgrave Macmillan).

Roberts, S. & Li, Z. (2017) 'Capital limits: social class, motivations for term-time job searching and the consequences of joblessness among UK university students', *Journal of Youth Studies*, vol. 20, no. 6, pp. 732–749.

Roberts, S., Ralph, B. L., Elliott, K. B., Robards, B. J., Savic, M., Lindsay, J. M., O'Brien, K. S. & Lubman, D. (2019) *Exploring Men's Risky Drinking Cultures* (Melbourne, VIC: Victorian Health Promotion Foundation).

Robertson, S., Harris, A. & Baldassar, L. (2018) 'Mobile transitions: a conceptual framework for researching a generation on the move', *Journal of Youth Studies*, vol. 21, no. 2, pp. 203–217.

Robinson, C. (2009) '"Nightscapes and leisure spaces": an ethnographic study of young people's use of free space', *Journal of Youth Studies*, vol. 12, no. 5, pp. 501–514.

Robson, B. (2010) 'New housing, old places: young people's perceptions of place in urban fringe areas', *Youth Studies Australia*, vol. 29, no. 3, pp. 43–51.

Rodger, J. (2008) *Criminalising Social Policy: Anti-social Behaviour and Welfare in a De-civilised Society* (Cullompton: Willan).

Roe, S. & Ashe, J. (2008) 'Young people and crime: findings from the 2006 Offending' in *Crime and Justice Survey* (London: HMSO).

Rollock, N., Gillborn, D., Vincent, C. & Ball, S. (2011) 'The public identities of the black middle classes: managing race in public spaces', *Sociology*, vol. 45, no. 6, pp. 1078–1093.

Rose, N. (1996) *Inventing Our Selves: Psychology, Power and Personhood* (Cambridge: Cambridge University Press).

Rose, N. (1999) *Powers of Freedom: Reframing Political Thought* (Cambridge: Cambridge University Press).

Rose, N. (2018) 'To really close the gap we need more Indigenous university graduates', *The Conversation*, 14th February 2018, accessed 13th October 2019, https://theconversation.com/to-really-close-the-gap-we-need-more-indigenous-university-graduates-91493.

Rudolph, K. D. (2002) 'Gender differences in emotional responses to interpersonal stress during adolescence', *Journal of Adolescent Health*, vol. 30, no. 4, pp. 3–13.

Rughani, J., Deane, F. P. & Wilson, C. J. (2011) 'Rural adolescents' help-seeking intentions for emotional problems: the influence of perceived benefits and stoicism', *Australian Journal of Rural Health*, vol. 19, no. 2, pp. 64–69.

Rutten, M. & Verstappen, S. (2014) 'Middling migration: contradictory mobility experiences of Indian youth in London', *Journal of Ethnic and Migration Studies*, vol. 40, no. 8, pp. 1217–1235.

Rychert, M. & Wilkins, C. (2016) 'What products are considered psychoactive under New Zealand's legal market for new psychoactive substances (NPS, 'legal highs')? Implications for law enforcement and penalties', *Drug Test Analysis*, vol. 8, pp. 768–778.

Rye, J. F. (2006) 'Rural youths' images of the rural', *Journal of Rural Studies*, vol. 22, pp. 409–421.

Sá, C. M. & Sabzalieva, E. (2018) 'The politics of the great brain race: public policy and international student recruitment in Australia, Canada, England and the USA', *Higher Education*, vol. 75, no. 2, pp. 231–253.

Said, E. (1978) *Orientalism, London and Henley* (London: Routledge).

Salter, M., Crofts, T. & Lee, M. (2012) 'Beyond criminalisation and responsibilisation: sexting, gender and young people', *Current Issues in Criminology and Justice*, vol. 24, p. 301.

Sande, A. (2002) 'Intoxication and rite of passage to adulthood', *Norway Contemporary Drugs Problems*, vol. 2, no. 2, pp. 277–303.

Savage, M. (2015) *Social Class in the 21st Century* (London: Pelican).

Schmidt, U., Adan, R., Böhm, I., Campbell, I. C., Dingemans, A., Ehrlich, S. & Zipfel, S. (2016) 'Eating disorders: the big issue', *The Lancet Psychiatry*, vol. 3, no. 4, pp. 313–315.

Schroeder, C. G. (2012) 'Making space for queer youth: adolescent and adult interactions in Toledo, Ohio', *Gender, Place & Culture*, vol. 19, no. 5, pp. 635–651.

Schuler, S. R. & Rottach, E. (2010) 'Women's empowerment across generations in Bangladesh', *Journal of Development Studies*, vol. 46, no. 3, pp. 379–396.

Seaman, P. & Ikegwuonu, T. (2011) '"I don't think old people should go to clubs": how universal is the alcohol transition amongst young adults in the United Kingdom?' *Journal of Youth Studies*, vol. 14, no. 7, pp. 745–759.

Seamon, D. (1979) *A Geography of the Lifeworld: Movement, Rest and Encounter* (New York: St Martin's Press).

Seamon, D. (1993) *Dwelling, Seeing, and Designing: Toward a Phenomenological Ecology* (New York: State University).

Selwyn, N. (2009) 'The digital native–myth and reality', *Aslib Proceedings: New Information Perspectives*, vol. 61, no. 4, pp. 364–379.

Shade, L. R. & Jacobson, J. (2015) 'Hungry for the job: gender, unpaid internships, and the creative industries', *The Sociological Review*, vol. 63, pp. 188–205.

Sharland, E. (2006) 'Young people, risk-taking and risk making: some thoughts for social work', *British Journal of Social Work*, vol. 36, pp. 247–265.

Sheller, M. & Urry, J. (2006) 'The new mobilities paradigm', *Environment and Planning*, vol. 38, no. 2, pp. 207–226.

Shildrick, T. & MacDonald, R. (2006) 'In defence of subculture: young people, leisure and social divisions', *Journal of Youth Studies*, vol. 9, no. 2, pp. 125–140.

Shildrick, T. & MacDonald, R. (2012) *Poverty and Insecurity: Life in Low-Pay, No-Pay Britain* (Bristol: Bristol Policy Press).

Shildrick, T., Blackman, S. & MacDonald, R. (2009) 'Young people, class and place', *Journal of Youth Studies*, vol. 12, no. 5, pp. 457–465.

Simmons, J. & Dodds, T. (2003) 'Crime in England and Wales 2002/3', *Home Office Statistical Bulletin London*, London, National Statistics Department.

Skeggs, B. (1999) 'Matter out of place: visibility and sexualities in leisure spaces', *Leisure Studies*, vol. 18, no. 3, pp. 213–232.

Skelton, T. (2013) 'Young people's urban im/mobilities: relationality and identity formation', *Urban Studies*, vol. 50, no. 3, pp. 467–483.

Smart, C. (1976) *Women, Crime and Criminology: A Feminist Critique* (Henley and London: Routledge).

Smith, L. T. (1999) *Decolonising Methodologies* (Otago: University of Otago).

Smith, C. (2005) 'Financial edgework: trading in market currents' in Lyng, S. (ed.) *Edgework: The Sociology of Risk-Taking* (New York: Routledge).

Smith, K. (2014) 'Childhood and youth citizenship' in Wyn, J. & Cahill, H. (eds.) *Handbook of Children and Youth Studies* (Singapore: Springer).

Smith (2016) 15% of American adults have used online dating sites or mobile dating apps, Pew Centre https://www.pewresearch.org/internet/2016/02/11/15-percent-of-american-adults-have-used-online-dating-sites-or-mobile-dating-apps/

Smith, A. & Anderson, M. (2018) 'Social media use in 2018, Pew Research Centre', March 1, accessed 13th October 2019, http://www.pewinternet.org/2018/03/01/social-media-use-in-2018/.

Smith, J., Skrbis, Z. & Western, M. (2013) 'Beneath the digital native myth: understanding young Australians' online time use', *Journal of Sociology*, vol. 49, no. 1, pp. 97–118.

Snee, H. (2013) 'Framing the other: cosmopolitanism and the representation of difference in overseas gap year narratives', *The British Journal of Sociology*, vol. 64, no. 1, pp. 142–162.

Snee, H. (2014) *A Cosmopolitan Journey?: Difference, Distinction and Identity Work in Gap Year Travel* (London: Routledge).

Social Exclusion Unit. (1999) *Bridging the Gap: New Opportunities for 16-18 Year Olds Not in Education, Employment or Training* (London: Cabinet Office).

Social Mobility & Child Poverty Commission. (2013) *Higher Education: The Fair Access Challenge* (London: Social Mobility and Child Poverty Commission).

Somerville, K. (2008) 'Transnational belonging among second generation youth: identity in a globalized world', *Journal of Social Sciences*, vol. 10, no. 1, pp. 23–33.

Standing, Guy (2011) *The Precariat: The New Dangerous Class* (London: Bloomsbury Academic).

Standing, G. (2014) *The Precariat* (London: Bloomsbury).

Stanwick, J., Forrest, C. & Skujins, P. (2017) *Who Are the Persistently NEET Young People?* (Sydney: NCVER).

Stella, F. (2013) 'Queer space, pride, and shame in Moscow', *Slavic Review*, vol. 72, no. 3, pp. 458–480.

Strandh, M., Winefield, A., Nilsson, K. & Hammarstrom, A. (2014), 'Unemployment and mental health scarring during the life course', *European Journal of Public Health*, vol. 24, no. 3, pp. 440–445.

Straw, W. (1991) 'Systems of articulation, logics of change: communities and scenes in popular music', *Cultural Studies*, vol. 5, no. 3, pp. 368–388.

Streeck, W. (2016) *How Will Capitalism End?* (London: Verso).

Sutherland, D. & Cressey, R. (1970) *Criminology* (Philadelphia: Williams and Wilkins).

Swedberg, R. (2016) 'Before theory comes theorizing or how to make social science more interesting', *The British Journal of Sociology*, vol. 67, no. 1, pp. 5–22.

Sweeting, H., West, P., Young, R. & Der, G. (2010) 'Can we explain increases in young people's psychological distress over time?' *Social Science and Medicine*, vol. 71, no. 10, pp. 1819–1830.

Szmigin, I., Griffin, C., Mistral, W., Bengy-Howell, A., Weale, L. & Hackley, C. (2008) 'Re-framing 'binge drinking' as calculated hedonism: empirical evidence from the UK International', *Journal of Drug Policy*, vol. 19, pp. 359–366.

Tapscott, D. (1998) *Growing Up Digital. The Rise of the Net Generation* (New York: McGraw Hill).

Tapscott, B. & Schepis, T. (2013) 'Nonmedical use of prescription medications in young adults', *Adolescent Medical State Art Review*, vol. 24, no. 3, pp. 597–610.

Taylor, Y. (2016) *Making Space for Queer-Identifying Religious Youth* (London: Palgrave Macmillan).

The Welfare Conditionality Project. (2018) *Final Findings Report* (York: University of York), http://www.welfareconditionality.ac.uk/wp-content/uploads/2018/06/40475_Welfare-Conditionality_Report_complete-v3.pdf.

Tholen, G. (2017) 'Symbolic closure: towards a renewed sociological perspective on the relationship between higher education, credentials and the graduate labour market', *Sociology*, vol. 51, no. 5, pp. 1067–1083.

Thompson, P. (2004) *Skating on Thin Ice – The Knowledge Economy Myth* (Glasgow: University of Strathclyde).

Thompson, S. (2015) *The Low-Pay, No-Pay Cycle* (York: Joseph Rowntree Trust).

Thomson, R., Holland, J., McGrellis, S., Henderson, S., & Sharpe, S. (2004) 'Inventing adulthoods: a biographical approach to understanding youth citizenship', *Sociological Review*, vol. 52, no. 2, pp. 218–239.

Thornton, S. (1995) *Club Cultures* (Cambridge: Polity Press).

Thornton, L. E., Lamb, K. E. & Ball, K. (2016) 'Fast food restaurant locations according to socioeconomic disadvantage, urban–regional locality, and schools within Victoria, Australia', *SSM – Population Health*, vol. 2, pp. 1–9.

Threadgold, S. (2017) *Youth, Class and Everyday Struggles* (London: Routledge).

Thrift, N. (2008) *Non-representational Theory: Space, Politics, Affect* (London: Routledge).

Tolonen, T. (2013) 'Youth cultures, lifestyles and social class in Finnish contexts', *Young*, vol. 21, no. 1, pp. 55–75.

Tomlinson, M. (2013) *Education, Work and Identity: Themes and Perspectives* (London: Bloomsbury Academic).

Torbenfeldt Bengtsson, T. & Ravn, S. (2018) *Routines of Risk: A New Perspective on Risk-Taking in Young Lives* (London: Routledge).

Tranter, B. & Grant, R. (2018) 'A class act? Social background and body modifications in Australia', *Journal of Sociology*, vol. 54, no. 3, pp. 412–428.

Triandafyllidou, A. (ed.) (2015) *Routledge Handbook of Immigration and Refugee Studies* (London: Routledge).

Tuan, Y. (1979) *Space and Place: The Perspective of Experience* (Minneapolis: University of Minnesota Press).

Turkle, S. (1996) *Life on the Screen: Identity in the Age of the Internet* (London: Weidenfeld & Nicolson).

Turner, B. (1986) *Citizenship and Capitalism* (London, Allen and Unwin).

Turner, B. (1995) *Regulating Bodies* (London: Routledge).

Tyler, I. (2013) *Revolting Subjects* (London: Zed Books).

Ulusoy, E. & Fırat, F. A. (2018) 'Toward a theory of subcultural mosaic: fragmentation into and within subcultures', *Journal of Consumer Culture*, vol. 18, no. 1, pp. 21–42.

UNESCO. (2015a) *Education for All 2000-2015: Achievements and Challenges* (Paris: UNESCO Publishing), accessed 13th October 2019, https://unesdoc.unesco.org/ark:/48223/pf0000232205.

UNESCO. (2015b) 'Facts and Figures, Mobility in Higher Education', accessed 13th October 2019, https://www.en.unesco.org/node/252278Funesco.

UNFPA. (2017) 'Child Marriage', accessed 13th October 2013, http://www.unfpa.org/child-marriage.

UNICEF. (2005) 'Kiribati: A Situational Analysis of Children, Women and Youth', accessed 13th October 2019, https://www.unicef.org/pacificislands/04_Situation_Analysis_of_Children_Kiribati.pdf.

UNICEF. (2011a) 'Unite for children: Kiribati, statistics', accessed 13th October 2019, http://www.unicef.org/infobycountry/kiribati_statistics.html.

UNICEF. (2011b) 'Child info: monitoring the situation of children and women', accessed 13th October 2019, http://www.childinfo.org/marriage_countrydata.php.

United Nations. (2013) *Youth and Migration* (New York: United Nations).

Universities Australia. (2018a) 'How international students benefit Australia', accessed 13th October 2019, https://www.universitiesaustralia.edu.au/Media-and-Events/media-releases/OPINION%2D%2DHow-international-students-benefit-Australia#.XlYfuOgzY2w.

Universities Australia. (2018b) '2017 Universities Australia Student Finances Survey', accessed 13th October 2019, https://www.universitiesaustralia.edu.au/ArticleDocuments/208/180713%20%202017%20UA%20Student%20Finance%20Survey%20Report.pdf.aspx?Embed=Y.

Utomo, A., Reimondos, A., Utomo, I., McDonald, P. & Hull, T. H. (2013) 'Digital inequalities and young adults in Greater Jakarta: a socio-demographic perspective', *International Journal of Indonesian Studies*, vol. 1, pp. 9–109.

Valentine, G. & Holloway, S. L. (2001) 'A window on the wider world? Rural children's use of information and communication technologies', *Journal of Rural Studies*, vol. 17, pp. 383–394.

Valentine, G., Skelton, T. & Chambers, D. (1998) 'Cool places: an introduction to youth and youth cultures' in Skelton, T. & Valentine, G. (eds.) *Cool Places: Geographies of Youth Cultures* (London: Routledge).

Valentine, G., Holloway S. L. & Jayne, M. (2010) 'Generational patterns of alcohol consumption: continuity and change', *Health Place*, vol. 16, no. 5, pp. 916–925.

Van Deursen, A. J. & Van Dijk, J. A. (2014) 'The digital divide shifts to differences in usage', *New Media & Society*, vol. 16, no. 3, pp. 507–526.

Van Gennep, A. (1908) *The Rites of Passage*, M. B. Vizedom & G. L. Caffee (trans) (London: Routledge & Kegan Paul).

Varjas, K., Meyers, J., Kiperman, S. & Howard, A. (2013) 'Technology hurts? Lesbian, gay, and bisexual youth perspectives of technology and cyberbullying', *Journal of School Violence*, vol. 12, no. 1, pp. 27–44.

Vickerstaff, S. A. (2003) 'Apprenticeship in the Golden Age: were youth transitions really smooth and unproblematic back then?', *Work, Employment and Society*, vol. 17, no. 2, pp. 269–287.

Viner, R. M., Ozer, E. M., Denny, S., Marmot, M., Resnick, M., Fatusi, A. & Currie, C. (2012) 'Adolescence and the social determinants of health', *The Lancet*, vol. 379, no. 9826, pp. 1641–1652.

Vromen, A., Xenos, M. A. & Loader, B. (2015) 'Young people, social media and connective action: from organisational maintenance to everyday political talk', *Journal of Youth Studies,* vol. 18, no. 1, pp. 80–100.

Wacquant, L. (2006) 'Pierre Bourdieu' in Stones, R. (ed.), *Key Sociological Thinkers*, 2nd ed. (London: Red Globe Press).

Waenerlund, A. K., Virtanen, P. & Hammarström, A. (2011) 'Is temporary employment related to health status? Analysis of the Northern Swedish Cohort', *Scandinavian Journal of Public Health*, vol. 39, no. 5, pp. 533–539.

Waite, C. (2018) 'Young people's place-making in a regional Australian town', *Sociologia Ruralis,* vol. 58, no. 2, pp. 276–292.

Waite, C. (2019) 'Making place with mobile media: young people's blurred place-making in regional Australia', forthcoming *Mobile Media and Communication.*

Waite, C. & Bourke, L. (2015a) 'Rural young peoples' perspectives on online sociality: crossing geography and exhibiting self through Facebook', *Rural Society*, vol. 24, no. 2, pp. 200–218.

Waite, C. & Bourke, L. (2015b) 'Using the cyborg to re-think young people's uses of Facebook', *Journal of Sociology*, vol. 51, no. 3, pp. 537–552.

Wajcman, J. (2004) *Techno Feminism* (Cambridge: Polity Press).

Walker, R. (1996) *Ngā Pepa a Ranginui: The Walker Papers* (Auckland: Penguin Press).

Wall, K. (2016) 'Gathering place: urban indigeneity and the production of space in Edmonton, Canada', *Journal of Urban Cultural Studies*, vol. 3, no. 3, pp. 301–325.

Walsh, D. (2012) 'Using mobility to gain stability: rural household strategies and outcomes in long-distance labour mobility', *Journal of Rural and Community Development*, vol. 7, no. 3, pp. 123–143.

Walsh, L., Black, R. & Prosser, H. (2018) 'Young people's perceptions of power and influence as a basis for understanding contemporary citizenship', *Journal of Youth Studies*, vol. 21, no. 2, pp. 218–234.

Walton, T. & Carillo, F. (2017) 'Mechanisms for fulfilling equity targets at the elite Australian university: a review of scholarship and practice', *Widening Participation and Lifelong Learning*, vol. 19, no. 2, pp. 156–162.

Waters, J. L. (2015) 'Dysfunctional mobilities: international education and the chaos of movement' in Wyn, J. & Cahill, H. (eds.) *Handbook of Children and Youth Studies* (Singapore: Springer).

Watson, B. & Ratna, A. (2011) 'Bollywood in the park: thinking intersectionally about public leisure space', *Leisure/Loisir*, vol. 35, no. 1, pp. 71–86.

Wattis, L., Green, E. & Radford, J. (2011) 'Women students' perceptions of crime and safety: negotiating fear and risk in an English post-industrial landscape', *Gender, Place & Culture*, vol. 18, no. 6, pp. 749–767.

Webb, S. (2006) *Social Work in a Risk Society* (Basingstoke: Palgrave Macmillan).

Webb, S., Burke, P. J., Nichols, S., Roberts, S., Stahl, G., Threadgold, S. & Wilkinson, J. (2017) 'Thinking with and beyond Bourdieu in widening higher education participation', *Studies in Continuing Education*, vol. 39, no. 2, pp. 138–160.

Webster, S., Davidson, J., Bifulco, A., Gottschalk, P., Caretti, V., Pham, T. & Grove-Hills, J. (2012) 'European Online Grooming Project Final Report', European Union.

Wellman, B., Boase, J. & Chen, W. (2002) 'The networked nature of community: online and offline', *IT & Society*, vol. 1, no. 1, pp. 151–164.

Welsh, L. & Black, R. (2018) *Rethinking Youth Citizenship After the Age of Entitlement* (Sydney: Bloomsbury) (change Lucas for Welsh in text).

West, P. (2017) 'Health in youth: changing times and changing influences' in Furlong, A. (ed.) *Routledge Handbook of Youth and Young Adulthood* (Oxford: Routledge).

West, P. & Sweeting, H. (2003) 'Fifteen, female and stressed: changing patterns of psychological distress over time', *Journal of Child Psychology and Psychiatry*, vol. 44, no. 3, pp. 399–411.

West, A., Roberts, J., Lewis, J. & Noden, P. (2015) 'Paying for higher education in England: funding policy and families', *British Journal of Educational Studies*, vol. 63, no. 1, pp. 23–45.

Wexler, L. & Eglington A. K. (2015) 'Reconsidering youth well-being as fluid and relational' in Wyn, J. & Cahill, H. (eds.) *Handbook of Youth and Childhood Studies* (Singapore: Springer).

Wheelahan, L. (2010) *Rethinking Equity in Tertiary Education: Why We Need to Think as One Sector Not Two* (Melbourne: University of Melbourne).

White, R. (2016) *Youth Gangs, Violence and Social Respect: Exploring the Nature of Provocations and Punch-Ups* (London: Palgrave Macmillan).

White, R. & Wyn, J. (2013) *Youth and Society*, 3rd ed. (Oxford: Oxford University Press).

Wierenga, A., Wood, A., Trenbath, G., Kelly, J. & Vidakovic, O. (2003) *Sharing a New Story: Young People in Decision-Making* (Melbourne: Australian Youth Research Centre, The University of Melbourne).

Wilkins, C. (2014) 'The interim regulated legal market for NPS ('legal high') products in New Zealand: the impact of new retail restrictions and product licensing', *Drug Testing and Analysis*, vol. 6, pp. 868–875.

Wilkinson, M. (2015) 'Three missing Brit girls "have crossed into Syria"', *The Sun*, February 24', accessed 10th August 2018, https://www.thesun.co.uk/archives/news/82444/three-missing-brit-girls-have-crossed-into-syria/?CMP=spklr-150452610-Editorial-TWITTER-TheSunNewspaper-20150224-News.

Wilks, J. & Wilson, K. (2015) 'A profile of the Aboriginal and Torres Strait Islander higher education student population', accessed 13th October 2019, http://www.nteu.org.au/article/A-profile-of-the-Aboriginal-and-Torres-Strait-Islander-higher-education-student-population-17909.

Williams, R. (1961) *The Long Revolution* (London: Chatto and Windus).

Williams, J. P. (2006) 'Authentic identities: straightedge subculture, music, and the internet', *Journal of Contemporary Ethnography*, vol. 35, no. 2, pp. 173–200.

Willis, P. (1977) *Learning to Labour: How Working Class Kids Get Working Class Jobs* (Farnborough: Saxon House).

Willis, P. E. (1990) *Common Culture* (Milton Keynes: Open University Press).

Wilson, C. J., Deane, F. P., Ciarrochi, J. V. & Rickwood, D. (2005) 'Measuring help seeking intentions: properties of the General Help Seeking Questionnaire', *Canadian Journal of Counselling*, vol. 39, no. 1, pp. 15–28.

Winkler, C. (2010) 'Feminist sociological theory, historical developments and theoretical approaches in sociology' in Crothers, C. (ed.) *Encyclopaedia of Life Support Systems; Social Sciences and Humanities*, vol. 2, no. 2.

Wood, B. E. (2017) 'Youth studies, citizenship and transitions: towards a new research agenda', *Journal of Youth Studies*, vol. 20, no. 9, pp. 1176–1190.

Wood, M., Barter, C., Stanley, N., Aghtaie, N. & Larkins, C. (2015) 'Images across Europe: the sending and receiving of sexual images and associations with interpersonal violence in young people's relationships', *Children & Youth Services Review*, vol. 59, pp. 149–160.

Wood, A. J., Graham, M., Lehdonvirta, V. & Hjorth, I. (2019) 'Good gig, bad gig: autonomy and algorithmic control in the global gig economy', *Work, Employment and Society*, vol. 33, no. 1, pp. 56–75.

Woodman, D. (2009) 'The mysterious case of the pervasive choice biography: Ulrich Beck, structure/agency, and the middling state of theory in the sociology of youth', *Journal of Youth Studies*, vol. 12, no. 3, pp. 243–256.

Woodman, D. (2012) 'Life out of synch: how new patterns of further education and the rise of precarious employment are reshaping young people's relationships', *Sociology*, vol. 46, no. 6, pp. 1074–1090.

Woodman, D. & Bennett, A. (2015) *Youth Culture, Transitions, and Generations: Bridging the Gap in Youth Research* (London: Palgrave Macmillan).

Woodman, D. & Wyn, J. (2015) *Youth and Generation: Rethinking Change and Inequality in the Lives of Young People* (London: Sage Publications).

Woods, M. (2007) 'Engaging the global countryside: globalization, hybridity and the reconstitution of rural place', *Progress in Human Geography*, vol. 31, no. 4, pp. 485–507.

World Economic Forum. (2017) Migration and Its Impact on Cities, World Economic Forum. Accessed on line September 2019 http://www3.weforum.org/docs/Migration_Impact_Cities_report_2017_HR.pdf

World Health Organization. (2017) 10 facts on health inequities and their causes. https://www.who.int/features/factfiles/health_inequities/en/. Updated 17 April 2017, Accessed 12 December 2019.

Wright Mills, C. (1959) *The Sociological Imagination* (Oxford: Oxford University Press).

Wyn, J. (2009) 'Young people's wellbeing: contradiction in managing the healthy self', *ACHPER Australia Healthy Lifestyles Journal*, vol. 56, no. 1, pp. 5–9.

Wyn, J. (2015) 'Young people and belonging in perspective' in Lange, A., Steiner, C., Reiter, H., Schutter, S. & Steiner, C. (eds.) *Handbook of Child and Youth Sociology* (Dordrecht: Springer).

Wyn, J. & Cahill, H. (eds.) (2015) *Handbook of Children and Youth Studies* (Singapore: Springer).

Wyn, J. & Woodman, D. (2006) 'Generation, youth and social change in Australia', *Journal of Youth Studies*, vol. 9, no. 5, pp. 495–514.

Wyn, J., Cuervo, H. & Landstedt, E. (2015) 'The limits of wellbeing' in Wright, K. & McLeod, J. (eds.) *Re-thinking Youth Wellbeing: Critical Perspectives* (Singapore: Springer).

Yang, S., Quan-Haase, A., Nevin, A. & Chen, Y. (2017) 'The role of online reputation management, trolling, and personality traits in the crafting of the virtual self and social media' in Sloan, L. & Quan-Haase, A. (eds.) *The SAGE Handbook of Social Media Research Methods* (London: Sage Publications).

Yoon, K. (2014) 'Transnational youth mobility in the neoliberal economy of experience', *Journal of Youth Studies,* vol. 17, no. 8, pp. 1014–1028.

Youth Justice Board. (2018) *Youth Justice Statistics* (London: Ministry of Justice).

Zarabadi, S. & Ringrose, J. (2018) 'The affective birth of "jihadi bride" as new risky sexualized "other": Muslim schoolgirls and media panic in an age of counterterrorism' in Talburt, S. (ed.) *Youth Sexualities: Public Feelings and Contemporary Cultural Politics*, vol. 2 (Colorado: Praeger).

Zeeman, L., Aranda, K., Sherriff, N. & Cocking, C. (2017) 'Promoting resilience and emotional well-being of transgender young people: research at the intersections of gender and sexuality', *Journal of Youth Studies*, vol. 20, no. 3, pp. 382–397.

Zinn, J. O. (2019) 'The meaning of risk-taking – key concepts and dimensions', *Journal of Risk Research*, vol. 22, no. 1, pp. 1–15.

INDEX

CPSIA information can be obtained
at www.ICGtesting.com
Printed in the USA
LVHW010550211222
735681LV00005B/296